Fourth Edition

Community-Based Strategic
POLICING IN CANADA

Fourth Edition

Community-Based Strategic
POLICING IN CANADA

Brian Whitelaw

City of Calgary, Calgary Transit, Public Safety and Enforcement

Richard B. Parent

Simon Fraser University, School of Criminology, Police Studies

NELSON EDUCATION

NELSON / EDUCATION

Community-Based Strategic Policing in Canada, Fourth Edition

by Brian Whitelaw and Richard B. Parent

Vice President, Editorial Higher Education:
Anne Williams

Executive Editor:
Lenore Taylor-Atkins

Marketing Manager:
Terry Fedorkiw

Developmental Editor:
Caroline Winter / My Editor Inc.

Photo Researcher and Permissions Coordinator:
Daniela Glass

Content Production Manager:
Jennifer Hare

Production Service:
Cenveo Publisher Services

Copy Editor:
Kelli Howey

Proofreader:
Manikandan

Indexer:
BIM Indexing Services

Manufacturing Manager:
Joanne McNeil

Design Director:
Ken Phipps

Managing Designer:
Franca Amore

Interior Design:
ArtPlus Limited

Cover Design:
Carianne Sherriff

Cover Images:
Top: © Anne de Haas; bottom left: © Igor Vidyashev/Alamy; bottom centre: © Michael Matthews—Police Images/Alamy; bottom right: © Mark Spowart/Alamy.

Compositor:
Cenveo Publisher Services

Library and Archives Canada Cataloguing in Publication Data

Whitelaw, Brian
    Community-based strategic policing in Canada / Brian Whitelaw, Richard B. Parent.—4th ed.

First published under title: Community policing in Canada / Curt Taylor Griffiths, Richard B. Parent, Brian Whitelaw.
Includes bibliographical references and index.
ISBN 978-0-17-650941-5

    1. Community policing—Canada—Textbooks. I. Parent, Richard B., 1958– II. Griffiths, Curt T. (Curt Taylor), 1948– . Community policing in Canada. III. Title.

HV7936.C83G74 2013
363.2'30971   C2012-906445-9

ISBN-13: 978-0-17-650941-5
ISBN-10: 0-17-650941-0

In memory of Douglas Whitelaw-educator, visionary and mentor.
—Brian Whitelaw

To Cathy, Jennifer, Janeen and Zeik.
—Richard B. Parent

Brief Contents

Contents

UNIT 4:   THE KEY PLAYERS IN COMMUNITY POLICING 167
CHAPTER 6: THE COMMUNITY POLICING POLICE SERVICE 169

CHAPTER 7: IMPLEMENTING COMMUNITY POLICING 201

CHAPTER 8: THE COMMUNITY POLICE OFFICER 241

Preface

INTRODUCTION TO THE FOURTH EDITION

As we prepared the fourth edition of *Community-Based Strategic Policing in Canada*, the Canadian police community was involved in a national symposium examining the sustainability of police economics. The key question addressed by leaders in Canadian policing was whether the costs associated with the provision of police service could be sustained. For many participants, the answer was a resounding no—that policing was essentially pricing itself out of its own market.

In 2010 the costs of policing in Canada totalled $12.6 billion for the year. There is no doubt that policing has become expensive and that the current model of policing is becoming unsustainable. This has prompted an intensive self-examination of how police service is delivered across the country and whether there are efficiencies that can be implemented by police services to control escalating costs.

With four decades of experience in community-based policing, we believe the solution to controlling costs lies within the model itself. The current model of community policing has matured and, in our view, has become much more strategic in its approach. Full-service models of police service delivery have given way to discussions about what constitutes core and non-core police service or what types of activities fall within the police mandate. Accompanying this inquiry is a new language of policing based on guiding frameworks such as crime prevention through social development, intelligence-led policing, and problem-oriented policing.

We are encouraged by efforts currently underway in Ontario to implement a revised model of community policing called the Mobilization and Engagement Model of Community Policing. This model breaks with the past legacy of community policing, which attempted to provide full-service policing to all communities and where police resources were justified in terms of the number of citizens per police officer. This "pop-to-cop" ratio did not take into account that communities require varying levels of police support depending on their degree of social cohesion and development. Clearly, policing the east side of Vancouver requires a different level and approach to policing than what is required in upper suburbia Canada.

In addition to addressing the rising costs associated with policing, the need also exists to maintain public trust and confidence in Canadian police services. Issues of police misconduct and the need for transparency and accountability continue to raise concerns in policing.

Ethical and professional conduct, based upon organizational core values, must be a standard practice within every police service. While selection, training, and effective leadership are fundamental to professionalism, community-based policing provides the necessary framework to further this process. Public involvement in police service delivery is a key component of community safety, and in securing public confidence and support.

We hope you find this textbook a great learning experience. While it may serve as an introductory textbook on community policing, we have tried to point to leading-edge approaches and research in the practice and study of Canadian policing.

WHAT'S NEW IN THIS EDITION

Chapter 1

- New Box 1.2 discusses women in policing and historic changes that took place within the Toronto Police Service
- New Box 1.3 explores 9-1-1 and the evolution of emergency reporting to the police

Chapter 2

- Chapter trends have been completely updated and challenge students to think critically about the impacts of these trends on policing. This chapter includes discussion of the idea of virtual communities and using social networks for crime detection and reduction, a phenomenon we call "Community Policing 2.0"
- Statistics have been completely updated
- Updated information in relation to aboriginal policing has been included
- Updated information on the role of railway police in Canada has been added
- New Table 2.2 assists students in understanding the various models of police oversight in Canada. Instructors can use this chart to discuss the relationship of civilian oversight to community policing and to examine local practices

Chapter 3

- Various sections within this chapter have been updated.

Chapter 4

- Recent findings related to police bicycle patrols and the general deployment of police personnel have been added

Chapter 5

- The focus remains on the implementation of problem-oriented policing as a key strategy within the community policing philosophy, clearly relating to the Ontario Mobilization and Engagement Model of Community Policing

Chapter 7

- Business and strategic plans have been updated for Guelph Police Service and Vancouver Police Service, serving as contemporary illustrations of community-oriented police services

Chapter 8

- The discussion of the emerging issues related to recruitment of gays, lesbians, bisexual, and transgender individuals within policing has been updated, with a focus on the general promotion of diversity within the rank-and-file of the police organization and the current focus upon hiring and promoting women
- Updated Table 8.1 lists the educational attainment of Ontario Police College recruits during the period form 1996–2011
- New Box 8.2 discusses the Vancouver Police Department's recruitment online in Second Life
- New Box 8.4 explores the Aboriginal Pre-Cadet Training Program (APTP) and how it offers Canadian Aboriginal people aged 19–29 the opportunity to experience daily police work with the RCMP
- New Box 8.8 presents information regarding the Police Sector Council and their recent collaboration with policing executives from across Canada to develop a competency framework and tools that support all aspects of strategic human resource management for the policing industry as a whole. This work involved leveraging existing best practices and knowledge within the policing sector to develop a nationally relevant system

Chapter 9

- New Box 9.2 discussion of Indian Residential Schools highlights the importance of addressing past wrongs, in this case an aggressive assimilation policy of the Canadian government. Acknowledgement of the wrong by both the church and state demonstrates relationship-building efforts

Chapter 10

- **KEY ADDITION: Ontario's Mobilization and Engagement Model of Community Policing.** The development of a model of community policing by the Ontario Association of Chiefs of Police in 2010-2011 is discussed with support of a new figure. This model recognizes that communities require differing levels/degrees of police support to successfully implement community policing initiatives, principles, and practices. The introduction of this model is a significant addition as it reflects police attempts to prioritize and manage the use of scarce resources in a much better way. At the same time it assists a community in understanding that its own efforts are supported by police in a variety of ways and not solely the police alone doing something for communities
- New Box 10.4 outlines the Ontario development of an Aboriginal Justice Strategy that pursues effective ways for communities to work together, reflecting the diverse needs of rural and urban Aboriginal communities with an emphasis on prevention for children and youth and promoting community safety

SUPPLEMENTS

About NETA

The **Nelson Education Teaching Advantage (NETA)** program delivers research-based instructor resources that promote student engagement and higher-order thinking to enable the success of Canadian students and educators.

Instructors today face many challenges. Resources are limited, time is scarce, and a new kind of student has emerged: one who is juggling school with work, has gaps in his or her basic knowledge, and is immersed in technology in a way that has led to a completely new style of learning. In response, Nelson Education has gathered a group of dedicated instructors to advise us on the creation of richer and more flexible ancillaries and online platforms that respond to the needs of today's teaching environments. Whether your course is offered in-class, online, or both, Nelson is pleased to provide pedagogically driven, research-based resources to support you.

In consultation with the editorial advisory board, Nelson Education has completely re-thought the structure, approaches, and formats of our key textbook ancillaries. We've also increased our investment in editorial support for our ancillary authors. The result is the Nelson Education Teaching Advantage and its key components. For *Community-Based Strategic Policing in Canada,* these components include *NETA Assessment, NETA Presentation,* and *NETA Digital.* Each component includes one or more ancillaries prepared according to our best practices, and may also be accompanied by documentation explaining the theory behind the practices.

NETA Assessment relates to testing materials. Under *NETA Assessment,* Nelson's authors create multiple-choice questions that reflect research-based best practices for constructing effective questions and testing not just recall but also higher-order thinking. Our guidelines were developed by David DiBattista, a 3M National Teaching Fellow whose recent research as a professor of psychology at Brock University has focused on multiple-choice testing. All Test Bank authors receive training at workshops conducted by Prof. DiBattista, as do the copyeditors assigned to each Test Bank. A copy of *Multiple Choice Tests: Getting Beyond Remembering,* Prof. DiBattista's guide to writing effective tests, is included with every Nelson Test Bank/Computerized Test Bank package. (Information about the NETA Test Bank prepared for *Community-Based Strategic Policing in Canada* is included in the description of the Instructor Resource Website below.)

NETA Presentation has been developed to help instructors make the best use of PowerPoint® in their classrooms. With a clean and uncluttered design developed by Maureen Stone of StoneSoup Consulting, NETA Presentation features slides with improved readability, more multi-media and graphic materials, activities to use in class, and tips for instructors on the Notes page. A copy of *NETA Guidelines for Classroom Presentations* by Maureen Stone is included with each set of PowerPoint slides. (Information about the NETA PowerPoint® prepared for *Community-Based Strategic Policing in Canada* is included in the description of the Instructor Resource Website below.)

NETA Digital is a framework based on Arthur Chickering and Zelda Gamson's seminal work "Seven Principles of Good Practice In Undergraduate Education" (AAHE Bulletin, 1987) and the follow-up work by Chickering and Stephen C. Ehrmann, "Implementing the Seven Principles: Technology as Lever"(AAHE Bulletin, 1996). This aspect of the NETA program guides the writing and development of our digital products to ensure that they appropriately reflect the core goals of contact, collaboration, multimodal learning, time on task, prompt feedback, active learning, and high expectations. The resulting focus on pedagogical utility, rather than technological wizardry, ensures that all of our technology supports better outcomes for students.

For Instructors

ANSWER KEY (ISBN 13: 978-0-17-665362-0/ISBN 10: 0-17-665362-7): For each chapter in the textbook, answers for the end-of-chapter Questions and Key Ideas (multiple-choice questions) are provided. For the Questions, the page number where the material appears in the textbook is also included. The Answer Key also provides, in point form, suggested responses for the Exercises: Knowledge into Practice section. Suggested answers for select Case Studies are also provided.

INSTRUCTOR RESOURCE WEBSITE: Key instructor ancillaries are provided on the *Instructor Resource Website* (www.communitypolicing4e.Nelson.com):

- **NETA Assessment:** Revised by textbook authors Brian Whitelaw and Rick Parent, the Test Bank includes more than 130 multiple-choice questions written according to NETA guidelines for effective construction and development of higher-order thinking. Also included are 50 true/false, 100 short-answer, and 30 essay-type questions. Test Bank files are provided in Word format for easy editing and in PDF format for convenient printing whatever your system.
- **PowerPoint® Presentation:** A complete PowerPoint® package is available as a lecture presentation aid for instructors, who may share it with their students as a study aid. NETA principles of clear design and engaging content have been incorporated throughout.
- **Instructor's Manual:** Also new to this edition is an Instructor's Manual, which is available to instructors as a downloadable supplement.

ACKNOWLEDGMENTS

In preparing this edition, we have been very fortunate to have had the exceptional support of a very talented and motivating editorial team at Nelson, comprised of Caroline Winter and Katherine Goodes, Developmental Editors; Lenore Taylor-Atkins, Executive

Editor; Terry Fedorkiw, Marketing Manager; Rajachitra, Project Manager; Kelli Howey, Copy Editor; and Jennifer Hare, Content Production Manager. We can't thank these individuals enough for their encouragement and assistance in taking our ideas and presenting them in a very engaging and learner-focused textbook.

We would also like to thank our longtime colleague Dr. Curt Griffiths at Simon Fraser University, who gave us our start in sharing our insights with the Canadian police academic community. Curt has been an important contributor to the study and practice of policing and his keen insights have helped us develop the evolving model of community-based policing in Canada.

Finally, a special thanks to the faculty and students at universities and colleges, as well as the serving police officers across Canada, who continue to utilize this textbook. We appreciate your continuous support and the valuable feedback that you provide as we attempt to continually enhance the concepts and practice associated with community-based strategic policing in Canada.

Brian Whitelaw, Calgary Police Service, retired
Dr. Rick Parent, School of Criminology: Police Studies, Simon Fraser University

1

Policing in Canada

CHAPTER 1

Evolution of Canadian Policing

Sir Robert Peel represents the father of contemporary policing who envisioned policing as it is today.

Source: © The Print Collector/Alamy

Learning Objectives

After completing this chapter, you should be able to:

- Identify the key historical developments in policing,
- Discuss the emergence of police services,
- Discuss how Sir Robert Peel has influenced modern policing, and
- Describe how the role of police in France differed from those in England.

INTRODUCTION

In this chapter, we provide a brief overview of the evolution of policing. The materials in this chapter are designed to provide you with a backdrop against which to study the emergence and practice of community policing and will be useful in understanding both the possibilities and the obstacles confronting the delivery of policing services within a community policing model. A historical overview provides us with valuable insights into the values, beliefs, and traditions of a community. Furthermore, history plays an important role in how communities define their own identities and how they interact with their local police. As a result, important implications for how policing is delivered in communities can be more fully understood.

THE ORIGINS AND EVOLUTION OF POLICING

The development of full-time, state-sanctioned police forces enforcing sets of codified laws is a relatively recent phenomenon. Prior to the emergence of the state and governmental arrangements with centralized authority, order among groups was maintained through a system of self-policing. Personal, group, and tribal retaliation were used against those whose behaviour contravened established folkways and customs. In these rural, agrarian societies, which were primarily concerned with day-to-day subsistence and survival, there were no individuals or organizations charged with the task of law enforcement.

As societies increased in complexity, however, the effectiveness of these self-policing arrangements diminished. Systems of codified laws were enacted, such as the Hammurabi Code in 1200 BC and similar codes of law in the Shang (1500 BC) and Chou (1000 BC) Dynasties. These codes of law, enforced by military authority, outlined prescribed rules of conduct and penalties for noncompliance. The enactment of these codes of law signalled a shift of the enforcement of conduct from the individual and group level to that of centralized authority.

Several centuries later, in the Greek city-states and in the Roman Empire, similar developments occurred. In Greece, a system of self-policing, called *kin-police*, was implemented. In Imperial Rome, the law was codified in the Law of the Twelve Tablets (450 BC), and officials were designated the task of law enforcement. At the height of the Roman Empire, there were distinct police forces. In both Greece and the Roman Empire, the military was charged with policing. The Romans were the first to use non-military units, the *vigiles*, to assist in maintaining order and to fight fires. The *vigiles* in the Roman Empire and the kin-police in the Greek city-states provide early examples of policing; however, it was in England that the institution of policing was to develop and, subsequently, to have a profound effect upon Canadian policing.

The Development of Policing in England

Prior to the Industrial Revolution and the development of capitalism, England was a feudal society made up of villages. Policing was a *community responsibility* (hold this thought until we return to a discussion of community policing in Chapter 2). Order was maintained under the principle of "hue and cry," which invested in every able-bodied man the responsibility to assist in the pursuit and apprehension of law violators. Failure to respond to the **hue and cry** could result in punishment of the derelict citizen, often a punishment equal to that imposed on the law-breaker.

Under the reign of Alfred the Great (871–901), the responsibilities of local communities for peacekeeping and order maintenance were strengthened. Lacking a standing army to maintain order and not having the financial resources to create a force specifically for peacekeeping purposes, Alfred instituted the **frankpledge system** (see Figure 1.1). This

Figure 1.1 Frankpledge System in Feudal England

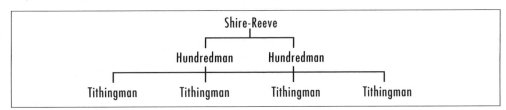

Source: Critchley 1978.

system was based on the principle of the mutual responsibility of each man to his neighbours. Under the frankpledge system, all free men between the ages of 15 and 60 were required to enroll in groupings of ten families, called *tithings*. In each tithing, a tithingman was responsible for keeping order, and citizens were required to report crimes to him and to respond to his hue and cry (commonly heard as "Halt! Who goes there?").

Stenning (1981:17) notes that the tithingman was "an elected community spokesman, responsible for all aspects of local government within his community, and … entirely responsible to the community that elected him as its representative." The tithingman also had the authority to collect fines from those charged with breaching the peace, and to demand surety or bail. Each adult male in the community was required to accept a turn in the position of tithingman.

As the population and size of the villages grew, tithings were formed into *hundreds* (groups of ten tithings), each headed by a hundredman. *Constables,* generally considered to be the first real police officers, were appointed by local noblemen and placed in charge of the equipment and weapons of the hundred. Hundreds were combined to form *shires* (parishes or counties), which were administered by officials known as *shire-reeves* (sheriffs). Shire-reeves were appointed by the king to represent his interests and uphold the authority of the Crown. The shire-reeve was invested with considerable military, civil, and judicial powers and made periodic visits to each hundred to ensure that the system of local policing was operating properly.

This locally based system of crime control evolved from the concept of mutual responsibility by individual residents. Although it invested the tithingman and hundredmen with a certain amount of authority for maintaining order in the communities, an important attribute of the frankpledge system was that it was organized from the ground up. The tithingmen and hundredmen were chosen from within the community, were responsible to that community, and could be removed for dereliction of duties. This system of peacekeeping was in sharp contrast to the policing arrangements that existed at the time in continental Europe, where the police were directly attached to centralized, autocratic rule.

After the Norman invasion of England in 1066, William the Conqueror continued the frankpledge system, despite a movement away from community responsibility for maintaining peace (as established by the tithing system) toward a concept of state responsibility. To assist in the implementation of Norman policing, the shire-reeves were invested with considerable powers, which were often used to collect unjust and oppressive fines and taxes from the community. Military officers were assigned the responsibility for maintaining order in specified areas.

By 1252, under the reign of Henry III, the position of constable had come to be applied to the local law enforcement officers—previously known as tithingmen—and a "watch and ward" system had been introduced in communities to maintain order. Critchley (1978:6) notes that the watch and ward system provided for two watchmen to supplement the duties of the constable: "A watch of up to sixteen men … was to be stationed at every gate of a walled town between sunset and sunrise, and the watchmen were given the power to arrest strangers during the hours of darkness." All able-bodied men in the town were required to serve a term on watch, reinforcing the responsibility of individual citizens to participate in policing.

Between the 13th century and the passage of the Police Act in 1829, two important statutes were enacted that structured both the nature of policing and the role of constables in England. The **Statute of Winchester,** passed in 1285, "sought to rationalize and redefine the police system that had been gradually developed over preceding centuries" (Stenning 1981:23). The statute assigned to each hundred responsibility for all offences committed within it, revived the hue and cry, and reinforced maintenance of the watch and ward system. In 1361, the **Justice of the Peace Act** centralized peacekeeping duties under justices of the peace, who were appointed directly by the king and who were superior in power and authority to the constables. The justice of the peace replaced the shire-reeve as peace officer while also acting in a judicial capacity. This development marked the first instance in which the police had been subordinated to the judiciary—an arrangement that resulted in considerable injustice and corruption.

By the 1500s, the system of community-based policing had begun to deteriorate, due in large measure to the growth of cities such London, the increased mobility of the population, and the beginnings of the shift from a primary agricultural economy to one based on industrialization. As communities were transformed by these events, individuals avoided serving as constables, paying others to assume their duties. This practice had disastrous consequences; often only the unemployed and uneducated were willing to take on the constable's duties. The longstanding system of community-based policing was, therefore, undermined.

As a consequence of the vast changes that were occurring in English society, the increasing corruption of the justices of the peace, and the reluctance of citizens to serve as constables, many towns and cities, including London, were unpoliced by the 1800s. Merchants and industrialists grew more and more fearful of the "dangerous classes" and the threat they posed to law and order. Businesses began to employ private police to protect their establishments and to assist in maintaining order. Against this backdrop—the deterioration of community-based policing and the increasing class distinctions between the propertied business people and industrialists on the one hand and the property-less peasants on the other—modern policing as we know it developed.

Policing Developments in France

The evolution of policing followed a different path in France, and cast the police in a different light among its citizens. During the 17th century, King Louis XIV maintained a small, central police organization consisting of some 40 inspectors who, along with the help of numerous paid informants, supplied the government with details about the conduct of private individuals. The king could then administer a kind of summary justice as he saw fit. This system continued during the reigns of Louis XV and Louis XVI. After the French Revolution (1789–1799), two separate police bodies were set up, one to handle ordinary duties and the other to deal with political crimes. The French Revolution brought about significant reform to French governmental structure but it left lingering fears among the citizenry that the police represented an arm of the absolute monarchy whose primary role was to essentially "spy" on citizens and report back to the king. Based upon the French experience with police, Londoners understandably were fearful and suspicious about the role and intentions of a full-time police force in England.

As the French settled into New France, now Quebec, they brought with them systems of security and policing modelled after those in France. One custom in particular that they continued was the practice of granting wealthy persons large tracts of land. Around 1633, this practice resulted in a wave of immigrants coming to New France as settlers who hoped to obtain land of their own.

The history of early policing in Quebec provides a valuable lesson for contemporary policing in Canada, particularly since September 11, 2001, when the role of the police grew to include what Murphy (2005) calls "security policing." We will examine this in greater detail in the next chapter.

THE DEVELOPMENT OF MODERN POLICING

Modern policing is based on principles first set out in England in the early 1800s. One of the first organized attempts to address the increasing problems of disorder was made in London in 1748 by the novelist and magistrate Henry Fielding. To enforce the decisions of his court, Fielding created the Bow Street Runners, named after the street on which his court was located. The Bow Street Runners were the first organized body of police. However, although Fielding had recruited men of high calibre and paid them well, the efforts of the force were not sufficient to stem the rising tide of social disorder and chaos produced by the emerging Industrial Revolution.

During the late 1700s and early 1800s, London was beset by a series of riots, which were often caused by workers protesting rising prices and by the displacement of workers by increased mechanization. Despite these developments, there continued to be strong resistance to the formation of an organized, 24-hour police force. In 1822, however, Britain's new Home Secretary, **Sir Robert Peel**, set out to establish a full-time police force. Unsurprisingly, his initial efforts met with considerable opposition.

Between 1822 and 1828, no fewer than 17 parliamentary subcommittees studied the need for reform of the system of law enforcement. There was concern about the concentration of power that would accrue to such a police force. Despite the widespread opposition to the formation of a police force, by the late 1820s the fear of crime and disorder had overshadowed the potential threats to liberty inherent in an organized police unit, at least among the propertied classes. In 1829, the ***Metropolitan Police Act*** was enacted and a full-time, unarmed police force of 1,000 men was established in London. Peel's new officers were known popularly as "bobbies" or "peelers," characterizations that were intended as derisive by a largely skeptical public.

Peel sought to legitimize the new police force by arguing that the police would serve the interests of all citizens, would include the prevention of crime as part of their mandate, and would recruit officers from the working class. In a determined effort to create a professional police force and to reduce public suspicion and distrust of the police, Peel instituted high standards of recruitment and training, and selected constables from the community. He also introduced the concept of police stations spread throughout the community.

Peel formulated several principles for law enforcement that have remained the basis for professional police work (see Box 1.1). Although these principles were set out early in the 19th century, they are still very much alive and well today and are reflected in the philosophy and practice of community policing. Although Peel's principles were first set down nearly 200 years ago, they provide the foundation for community policing as it is implemented today. This is fascinating given the immense changes that have occurred in society since the early 1800s.

With this brief historical introduction completed, we can now turn our attention to the development of policing in Canada, a process that was very much influenced by events in England.

A BRIEF HISTORY OF CANADIAN POLICING

Early police work in Canada was characterized by a considerable degree of diversity. Prior to Confederation in 1867, each region of the country had its own policing arrangements that depended on the size of the settlements, the characteristics of the population, and the specific needs of communities. In areas settled by the French, for example,

BOX 1.1

THE PRINCIPLES OF SIR ROBERT PEEL

1. The basic mission of the police is to prevent crime and disorder.

2. The ability of the police to perform their duties depends upon public approval of their actions.

3. Police must secure the co-operation of the public in voluntary observance of the law in order to secure and maintain the respect of the public.

4. The degree of public co-operation with police diminishes proportionately to the necessity of the use of physical force.

5. Police maintain public favour by constantly demonstrating absolutely impartial service, not by catering to public opinion.

6. Police should use physical force only to the extent necessary to ensure compliance with the law or to restore order only after persuasion, advice, and warnings are insufficient.

7. Police should maintain a relationship with the public that is based on the fact that the police are the public and the public are the police.

8. Police should direct their actions toward their functions and not appear to usurp the powers of the judiciary.

9. The test of police efficiency is the absence of crime and disorder, not the visible evidence of the police dealing with them.

Source: The Principles of Sir Robert Peel Oliver and Boyd, (1956) A new study of police history. Reith, Charles.

major town centres were policed under the traditional French system of captains of militias. In Upper Canada, on the other hand, the influence of the English was evident, with the policing system based on the common law and carried out by sheriffs, high constables, constables, and justices of the peace. Historians have made the important observation that communities and settlements created formal police forces only when there was a "felt need" to do so.

Early attempts to establish a formal system of justice, including police, met with failure in Upper Canada and Quebec precisely for this reason (Talbot, Jayewardene, and Juliani 1983:84). This highlights one of the key issues in the emergence of formal policing in Canada: similar to their British counterparts, early Canadians were hesitant to create police forces that had authority and power over the population. Interestingly enough, beginning in the late 20th century and continuing into the early 21st century, a concerted effort is being made to re-involve community residents in preventing and responding to crime and social disorder. The view that professional police forces can, on their own and without the assistance of community residents, prevent and solve problems of crime and disorder is rapidly disappearing. How to re-engage the community in identifying and responding to crime and social disorder is the subject of our discussion in Chapter 10.

Municipal Policing

Prior to the development of organized police forces, community residents performed a sort of informal law enforcement. In Halifax, for example, tavern owners were charged with maintaining order. These arrangements, however, were ultimately insufficient to meet the problems of an increasingly urbanized and industrialized society. It was in the eastern regions of the country that the first appointed police constables appeared, their role most likely being restricted to night watch duties. Eastern port cities such as Halifax and St. John's relied upon militias and the navy, while other, less populated regions of the country remained largely unpoliced. As more settlers moved west, however, the need to control disorder—usually related to drinking, prostitution, and gambling—increased.

The historical record indicates that the first police constables were appointed in Quebec City in the mid-1600s and in Upper Canada (now the province of Ontario) in the early 1800s. In 1835, the City of Toronto replaced its night watch system with six full-time police constables; in 1858, legislation was enacted in Upper Canada that authorized towns and cities to create boards or commissions to oversee the activities of police forces. Given the vast distances and sparse populations, municipal police forces developed much later in the western regions of the country.

In 1845, a bylaw in the newly created town of St. Catharines provided for "pound-keepers and constables," citizen volunteers who provided assistance when it was required and were paid according to a fee schedule. The activities of this "police force" were supervised by a police board, which also served as the town council. The volunteers were paid according to a fee schedule that included a payment of five shillings each for issuing a summons, making an arrest under a warrant, and assisting in an arrest; escorting a prisoner to jail earned 15 shillings. The town hired its first full-time police officers in 1856 (Niagara Regional Police Service 2000).

Police constables were generally assigned other duties as well. In Sudbury, Ontario, for example, the first constable was the jailer, tax collector, sanitary inspector, truant officer, firefighter, bailiff, chimney inspector, and animal pound caretaker (Juliani, Talbot, and Jayewardene 1984:326). In 1826, Kingston appointed its first paid constable, Henry Wilkinson, who also held the position of street surveyor.

The mandate of early municipal police forces covered three primary tasks: (1) policing conflicts that developed between labourers and business owners; (2) attempting to maintain moral standards by enforcing laws against drunkenness, prostitution, and gambling; and (3) apprehending criminals (Juliani, Talbot, and Jayewardene 1984). The historical record indicates that the five-man Kingston police force created in 1841 spent most of its time dealing with drunk and disorderly persons (McCullough 1997).

Provincial Police

All the regions that ultimately became part of Confederation had police forces. These forces were most often created in response to disorder emerging from the opportunities and challenges of exploration and settlement—for example, the disorder that emerged with the discovery of gold in British Columbia and Ontario. The earliest provincial force was established in Quebec in 1870, three years after it entered Confederation. In British Columbia police forces formed in the colonies of Vancouver Island and British Columbia as early as 1858. A large number of these early police officers were Black immigrants from the state of California. In 1866, the two police forces united and, in 1871, became the British Columbia Provincial Police when B.C. entered Confederation.

Provincial police forces created in Alberta, Saskatchewan, and Manitoba experienced a number of difficulties, including poor leadership and a lack of qualified officers; by the late 1920s these provincial forces had been replaced by the RCMP. Provincial policing in Ontario followed a different course. On October 13, 1909, an order-in-council authorized the immediate formation of the Ontario Provincial Police Force. By 1950, the RCMP had assumed provincial policing responsibilities in all provinces except Quebec and Ontario; both provinces continued to operate independent provincial police forces.

BOX 1.2

TORONTO POLICE SERVICE WOMEN—HISTORIC MOMENTS

Use of the Toronto Police Services Images Courtesy of the Toronto Police Services Board

Use of the Toronto Police Services Images Courtesy of the Toronto Police Services Board

1974—Policewomen are first placed on regular patrol duties with men and are expected to do the same work. Thirteen policewomen are transferred to the downtown core to decide whether or not women can perform the same duties as the men.

The decision is also made to arm these 13 women with .38 calibre revolvers.

1975—The title "Policewoman" is changed to Police Constable (Female).

2011—Of the 5,776 police officers in Toronto, 1,063 are female officers (Statistics Canada 2011)

Source: Toronto Police Service (http://www.torontopolice.on.ca/museum/herstory-milestones_in_the_history_of_tps_women.pdf)

Federal Police

While the arrangements for federal policing may not have been a deliberate policy choice of the federal government, it is worth noting the contribution of the Dominion Police to the evolution of Canadian policing. The Dominion Police were created by an act of Parliament in 1868, although there were only two officers at that time. By 1869, their authority and numbers had grown, although mainly in Ontario and Quebec. Over time their duties evolved to include protecting parliamentary buildings, guarding navy yards, and enforcing national interest laws, such as counterfeiting and trafficking in white slaves. The Dominion Police established a national fingerprint bureau and a branch that maintained the records of paroled and reporting prisoners. The Dominion Police existed until 1920, when the Royal Canadian Mounted Police assumed a national presence and absorbed its 150 members.

The Mounties

The RCMP, originally known as the North-West Mounted Police (NWMP), was created in 1873 primarily to maintain law and order and to ensure the orderly settlement of the previously unpoliced and sparsely settled northwest territory. Sir John A. Macdonald, the prime minister of the day, wanted to avoid the experience of settlement in the American West where native tribes clashed in violent uprisings with settlers and miners. The model for the proposed force was the Royal Irish Constabulary, which had been

The RCMP were originally known as the North-West Mounted Police. They were created in 1873 to maintain law and order and to ensure orderly settlement of the unpoliced and sparsely settled northwest territory.

Source: Library and Archives Canada / C-042755

used as a pattern for organizing numerous police forces throughout the British Empire. The NWMP were never intended to become a national police force. Once its original objectives were met in terms of securing peaceful settlement, it was anticipated that the responsibility for policing would shift to local communities as areas became more urbanized. However, this did not generally occur.

In 1916 the Royal North-West Mounted Police (RNWMP) announced that contracts with the Prairie Provinces would be cancelled by the end of that year. As a result, the Prairie Provinces established their own provincial police the following year. For example, the Alberta Provincial Police formed in 1917, following the withdrawal of the RNWMP, and remained the province's police force until 1932. In 1932, the Alberta government reluctantly dissolved the Alberta Provincial Police, primarily due to the economics of the Depression, and by the end of that year the now-national Royal Canadian Mounted Police had assumed policing in the Prairie Provinces and the Maritimes. It is this history, largely forgotten, that serves to establish an important foundation for policing in the province of Alberta. Interestingly, the 2000 *Report on Policing in the Province of Alberta* examines the role of the RCMP in Alberta and takes a serious look at the idea of creating a provincial police service by 2012 (Government of Alberta 2000).

While the evolution of policing in western Canada favoured provincial police over the Royal Canadian Mounted Police, attempts to phase out the force in the 1920s met with resistance in many regions. In fact, the later emergence of the RCMP as a national police force involved in policing provinces and municipalities was more the result of historical accident than any master plan. And, as we will see, this has resulted in the Mounties facing unique challenges in developing and implementing community policing.

The duties and activities of the first police constables were very localized. Officers patrolled on foot and their primary roles were preventive as well as reactive. As night watchmen, the officers were very familiar with the areas to which they were assigned.

Evolution of the Police Role

From the early 1900s through to roughly 1970, reform efforts in policing focused on ensuring police forces functioned free from political influence, operated with strong centralized control, maintained strong discipline, and used both personnel and technology efficiently. This era, described as the **professional era of policing**, sought to increase the control and efficiency of the police (Fleissner and Heinzelmann 1996:2; Goldstein 1990).

During this timeframe, three technological innovations radically altered the delivery of policing services, often in response to the growth of urban centres and communities: (1) the expansion of telephone systems into households, (2) the emergence of police patrol cars, and (3) the introduction of the two-way radio. All three innovations precipitated a fundamental change in how police services were delivered. Police officers became reactive, relying upon complaints telephoned in by community residents. Officers were dispatched to the scene of a crime by two-way radio in patrol cars. Motorized patrol began to emerge as the primary method of police patrol.

Since officers were now more mobile, they could cover a larger area than foot-patrol officers. However, this also meant that officers became more isolated from the communities they policed. The patrol car, rather than the neighbourhood beat, became the "office" of the police officer. This, in turn, resulted in the centralization of police command and control. The introduction of additional technologies, including centralized dispatch systems that prioritized calls for assistance and computer terminals in patrol cars, have further distanced officers from the community. The computer screen, rather than the community residents, has become the primary source of information for officers. This makes it much more difficult for community residents to interact with and communicate their concerns to local police constables. Calls are made to centralized telephone numbers. Dispatchers who are far removed from the neighbourhood and unfamiliar with residents and their concerns prioritize calls for assistance (Reiss 1992).

BOX 1.3

THE HISTORY OF 9-1-1 EMERGENCY REPORTING IN CANADA

Canada adopted 9-1-1 in 1972, and the first city to implement the system was London, Ontario, in 1974. In Quebec, it was Laval that first put 9-1-1 at the disposal of its residents, in 1977.

On April 24, 1981, the Communauté urbaine de Montréal public security commission formed a task force with the mandate to coordinate efforts to create an emergency communications centre (9-1-1).

The Centre officially began operations on December 1, 1985. It received all emergency calls from the CUM territory and directed them to the appropriate emergency services, and also offered telephone information to the public on services offered by the CUM and the transit corporation.

Source: http://www.spvm.qc.ca/en/service/centre-urgence-911-historique.asp

CHAPTER SUMMARY

As we end this chapter, there are some very important observations to consider when thinking about community policing. Historically, Canadian police have assisted with the formation of new communities and their primary role has been to guide the peaceful settlement of new areas, particularly in northern and western Canada. Unlike the history of policing in the United States, where the police were often brought into communities to re-establish order, Canadian policing has evolved in a much more peaceful and orderly fashion. As a result, the local police have, in various degrees, shaped the development of many Canadian communities. Understandably, local residents, who had grown accustomed to their own methods of policing, often resisted the changes introduced by more formalized local policing. A major point that emerges from our brief historical review is that there was considerable public opposition—both in Europe during the early 1800s and in early Canada—to the creation of formal police services. Their necessity was questioned and their role, based on unfavourable experiences in France, was regarded with suspicion. The historical relationship between police and the community serves as an important factor in defining contemporary levels of support, co-operation, and citizen involvement. The blueprint for Canadian policing has been shaped to a large extent by the emergence of the modern police service in London, England. However, the model of Canadian policing has also been influenced by policing practices in the United States, France, and Ireland. Taken together these influences combine to give Canadian policing its distinctive character and positive international reputation.

CHAPTER REVIEW

Key Terms

- frankpledge system, p. 4
- hue and cry, p. 4
- *Justice of the Peace Act* (1361), p. 6
- *Metropolitan Police Act* (1829), p. 7
- professional era of policing, p. 12
- Sir Robert Peel, p. 7
- *Statute of Winchester* (1285), p. 6

Key Points

- Prior to the creation of formal police services, communities policed themselves.
- There was opposition to the creation of formal police services.
- The development of full-time police forces, operating under the authority of the state and enforcing sets of codified laws, is a relatively recent phenomenon.
- The foundations of modern policing are the principles set forth by Sir Robert Peel in England in the early 1800s.
- The role of the police in the history of Canada differs from that of the United States, where police were often brought in to re-establish order.
- Prior to Confederation in 1867, each region of the country had its own policing arrangements, depending on the size of the settlements, the characteristics of the population, and the specific needs of communities.
- The mandate of early municipal police forces covered three primary tasks: (1) policing conflicts that developed between labourers and business owners; (2) attempting to maintain moral standards by enforcing laws against drunkenness, prostitution, and gambling; and (3) apprehending criminals.

- Provincial police forces created in Alberta, Saskatchewan, and Manitoba experienced a number of difficulties; by the late 1920s these provincial forces had been replaced by the RCMP. In British Columbia, the provincial police would be also be replaced by the RCMP in 1950.
- The RCMP, originally known as the North-West Mounted Police, was created in 1873 primarily to maintain law and order and to ensure the orderly settlement of the previously unpoliced and sparsely settled northwest territory.
- From the early 1900s through to roughly 1970, the "professional era of policing" sought to increase the control and efficiency of the police.
- History plays a role in how communities see themselves and how they interact with the police.

Self-Evaluation

QUESTIONS

1. Why is **Sir Robert Peel** an important person in our study of community policing?
2. In what way does the **hue and cry** illustrate the involvement of the community in maintaining order?
3. In what way could the **frankpledge system** be called the first type of community policing?
4. What was the significance of the *Statute of Winchester*, enacted in 1285?
5. Why is the *Justice of the Peace Act* (1321) important in our study of the history of policing?
6. The **mandate of early municipal police forces** covered three primary tasks. Has this changed over the years?
7. What was the significance of the *Metropolitan Police Act* (1829)?
8. What were the initial objectives of the **NWMP** when it was formed?
9. List some of the characteristics of the **professional era of policing**.
10. Discuss the three **technological innovations** that radically altered the delivery of policing services in recent times.

KEY IDEAS

1. Who was Sir Robert Peel?
   a. the first Commissioner of the North-West Mounted Police
   b. the chief constable of the first municipal police force established in Canada
   c. the chief of the first organized police force in London, England
   d. the first provincial police commissioner in Canada

2. According to the historical record, where and when were the first police constables in Canada appointed?
   a. Quebec City in the early 1600s
   b. Halifax in the early 1700s
   c. Upper Canada in the early 1700s
   d. the current province of British Columbia in the 1800s

3. Early Canadians were hesitant to create police forces that had authority and power over the population. What was the result?
   a. police services were developed in a uniform manner with minimal duties
   b. strong support existed for the development of localized municipal police forces
   c. law enforcement functions were performed informally by community residents
   d. the NWMP was created as a national police force to facilitate peaceful settlements

4. In 1829, a full-time, unarmed police force of 1000 men was established in London. What were these new officers popularly known as?
   a. cops or coppers
   b. officers or NCOs
   c. bobbies or peelers
   d. detectives or investigators

5. In the history of policing in France, how were the police considered in general?
   a. as supportive and respectful of human rights
   b. as spies for the king
   c. as focused upon citizen safety
   d. as politically neutral

6. Which police force was the model for the RCMP (originally known as the North-West Mounted Police)?
   a. Victoria Police Department
   b. Royal Irish Constabulary
   c. London Metropolitan Police
   d. New York City Police Department

7. Why did the Alberta government dissolve the Alberta Provincial Police?
   a. a lack of suitable applicants in the province
   b. corruption and scandals within the police department
   c. the economics of the Depression
   d. a political desire for a national police force

8. Which term describes the period from the early 1900s through to roughly 1970?
   a. the professional era of policing
   b. the modern era of policing
   c. the era of reform and restoration
   d. the era of technological change

9. Historically, the neighbourhood beat acted as the "office" of the police officer. Which of the following is considered the police officer's office today?
   a. the community police station
   b. departmental headquarters
   c. local coffee shops and youth centres
   d. the patrol car

10. Which groups made up the earliest police force in British Columbia, created in 1858?
   a. individuals from the logging community
   b. French Canadians from Quebec
   c. Black immigrants from California
   d. former police personnel from Ontario

Canadian Policing: Situations and Strategies

Case Studies

Case Study 1. The Near-Demise of the RCMP

The RCMP is a unique police force. Not only are its officers involved in federal, provincial, and municipal policing across the country, but the force itself is also one of the most widely recognized symbols of Canada. What is not as well known is that during the 1920s, when the RCMP was a small police force involved only in federal policing, there was considerable opposition to its expansion into the various regions of the country, and the force was nearly phased out due to political pressure.

The emergence of the RCMP as the national police force was more the result of historical accident than the product of a master plan. It certainly went against trends in Britain and the United States, where police services were decentralized. In fact, there were attempts to abolish the RCMP in 1922 and 1923. The decision by the federal government to create the Royal Canadian Mounted Police in 1920 by merging the North-West Mounted Police and the Dominion Police (Canada's first federal police force) was met with considerable opposition, particularly among members of Parliament from the Atlantic region. This is reflected in the arguments made by Robert H. Butts, representing Cape Breton South: "I have been a magistrate, sometimes I have been called a judge, of a town of between 9,000 and 10,000 people. We never had need of Mounted Police down there and we have no need of them now.... Do not send hayseed from away across the plains to Nova Scotia.... I say that it is dangerous to send them there. I speak for 73,000 people in Cape Breton, and I can say that they will not appreciate any such intrusion." Another MP from Nova Scotia, J. H. Sinclair, echoed these views, stating: "The Federal Government are assuming a duty that they do not require to assume; that the provinces are not asking them to assume, and that the provinces themselves are well able to take care of" (both cited in Macleod 1994:45–46). Concern on the part of the federal government with increasing labour unrest and "subversives," combined with the ineptitude of provincial police forces, however, provided the Mounties with an opportunity to significantly expand and, ultimately, to become extensively involved in provincial and municipal policing.

Interestingly, much of the opposition to the RCMP arose from concerns that the force was not a local police service, but rather a federal police force that also provided provincial and municipal police services under contract. These issues of local control and accountability continue to be raised today and are particularly relevant within the context of discussions of community policing.

REFERENCES

Critchley, T.A. 1978. *A History of the Police in England and Wales.* London: Constable.

Fleissner, D., and F. Heinzelmann. 1996, August. "Crime Prevention through Environmental Design and Community Policing." *Research in Action, National Institute of Justice.* Washington DC: U.S. Department of Justice.

Goldstein, H. 1990. *Problem-Oriented Policing.* New York: McGraw-Hill.

Government of Alberta. 2000. *Policing Alberta: A Discussion Paper.* Alberta Justice.

Juliani, T.J., C.K. Talbot, and C.H.S. Jayewardene. 1984. "Municipal Policing in Canada: A Developmental Perspective." *Canadian Police College Journal* 8(3):315–85.

Macleod, R.C. 1994. "The RCMP and the Evolution of Provincial Policing." In R.C. Macleod and D. Schneiderman (eds.), *Police Powers in Canada: The Evolution and Practice of Authority.* Toronto: University of Toronto Press.

McCullough, E.C. 1997. "150 Years of Service: The Kingston Police Force, 1841–1991." http://www.police.kingston.on.ca (October 2000).

Murphy, C. 2005. "Securitizing Community Policing: Towards a Canadian Public Policing Model." *Canadian Review of Policing Research 1.* Retrieved http://crpr.icaap .org/index. php/crpr/article/view/41/37.

Niagara Regional Police Service. 2000. "A Brief History of the Niagara Regional Police Service." Retrieved http://www.nrps.com.

Reiss, A.J. 1992. "Police Organization in the Twentieth Century." pp. 51–95 in *Modern Policing: Crime and Justice,* vol. 15, edited by M. Tonry and N. Morris. Chicago: University of Chicago Press.

Statistics Canada. 2011. *Police Resources in Canada.* Cat. No. 85-225-X.

Stenning, P.C. 1981. *Legal Status of the Police.* Ottawa: Law Reform Commission of Canada.

Talbot, C.K., C.H.S. Jayewardene, and T.J. Juliani. 1983. *The Thin Blue Line: A Historical Perspective of Policing in Canada.* Ottawa: Crimcare.

CHAPTER 2

Overview of Canadian Policing

Policing is the largest component of the Canadian criminal justice system. Traditionally, the police mandate has been categorized into crime control (catching criminals), order maintenance (keeping the peace), and service (providing assistance to the public). Increasingly, a large portion of contemporary police work involves gathering and processing information ("knowledge workers") as well as restoring order in conflict situations.

Source: CP PHOTO/London Free Press—Sue Reeve

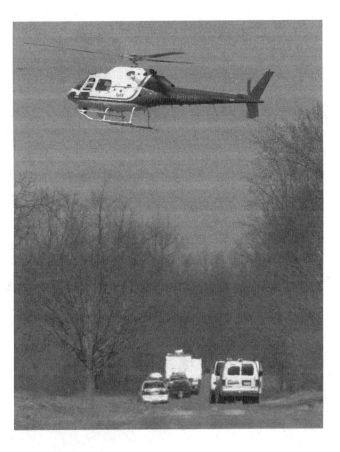

Learning Objectives

After completing this chapter, you should be able to:

- Discuss the structure of policing,
- Describe the contemporary roles of the police,
- Identify and discuss the contexts of police work, and
- Describe trends in police work.

INTRODUCTION

In this chapter we examine the current structure of policing across Canada, including the current arrangements for the delivery of policing services across the country and the contemporary roles of the police. We consider the various contexts within which police work is carried out in Canada and identify a number of key trends and challenges that are having a significant impact on policing. A clear understanding of the limitations facing contemporary police work makes the case for community-based policing much more compelling. It is these challenges and possibilities that require police agencies to be more strategic in their delivery and which we believe represents an evolving model of policing, which we call "community-based strategic policing."

THE STRUCTURE OF CONTEMPORARY CANADIAN POLICING

Policing is the largest component of the Canadian criminal justice system and, accordingly, receives the biggest slice of funding, at $12.6 billion annually in 2010 (Statistics Canada 2011d:6). This works out to $371 per Canadian to cover the costs of policing. There are 238 police services in Canada, and of those 117 services have fewer than 25 staff. Five Canadian police services—the RCMP, the Toronto Police Service, the Ontario Provincial Police (OPP), the Sûreté du Québec (SQ), and the City of Montreal Police Service (Service de police de la Ville de Montréal, or SPVM)—account for just over 60 percent of all police officers in Canada (see Box 2.1). Municipalities across the country, with the exception of those in the Yukon, the Northwest Territories, and Nunavut, have a choice as to whether to create and operate their own independent police service or to contract out to a provincial police service.

Under the **Police Services Act** in Ontario, for example, municipalities have a number of options in terms of the provision of policing services. They may:

- have their own independent municipal police force,
- amalgamate their police service with one or more other services,
- share police services with one or more other municipalities, or
- contract with the OPP to provide police services.

BOX 2.1

QUICK FACTS ABOUT POLICING IN CANADA (2011)

1. Total number of police officers: 69,438

2. Total number of civilian employees: 28,151

3. Total number of private security personnel: 10,200 private investigators and 91,325 security guards (2006)

4. Police strength: 201 officers per 100,000 population (lower than United States [242] and England/Wales [252])

5. Police officers per 100,000 population: Yukon (352), Nunavut (390), Manitoba (207), Quebec (198), Ontario (197), Newfoundland (183), and Saskatchewan (218)

6. Women as a percentage of police officer positions: 19.6 percent or almost one in five police officers

7. Visible minorities as a percentage of police officer positions: 6 percent (2006 data)

8. Aboriginal persons as a percentage of police officer positions: 4 percent (2,440 officers) (2006 data)

Sources: Statistics Canada, Canadian Centre for Justice Statistics, 2007

Table 2.1 Quick Facts about Policing in Canada (2011)

	B.C.	Ontario	Yukon	Quebec	Canada
Total number of police officers	8,966	26,387	122	15,802	69,438
Females as a percentage of total officers	21.2	18.4	12.3	23.7	19.6
Number of police officers per 100 000 population	196	197	352	198	201
Total expenditure on policing ($000)	1,336,248	4,206,322	18,287	2,231,974	12,645,616

Source: Statistics Canada 2011d.

Policing in Canada is carried out at four levels: municipal, provincial, federal, and First Nations. See Table 2.1 for additional information on policing in Canada.

In Quebec, communities with fewer than 5,000 residents may sign service agreements with the provincial Ministère de la Sécurité publique for the SQ to provide police services. Municipalities with more than 5,000 residents may enter into similar arrangements with the authorization of the minister.

In Ontario, the Ministry of Community Safety and Correctional Services is responsible for ensuring that adequate and effective policing services are provided to municipalities. The responsibilities of the Minister of Community Safety and Correctional Services (formerly the Solicitor General), as set out in Section 3(2) of the *Police Services Act,* include developing programs to enhance professional police practices, standards, and training; developing and promoting community policing; and maintaining records and conducting research on police-related issues.

Considerable variation exists among Canadian police services in terms of their size and responsibilities. Most, however, have similar divisions or sections, including:

- *Operational patrol*: patrol division, canine unit, identification squad, traffic, reserve or auxiliary;
- *Investigative*: general investigation (detectives), major crimes, vice offences;
- *Support services*: information technology, communications centre, victim services, community services, and crime prevention;
- *Administrative*: finance and payroll, property office;
- *Human resources*: staff development, recruiting, training; and
- Office of the chief.

Canadian police services, like their counterparts worldwide, have a rank structure that reflects their paramilitary organization. Most police services have a chief constable, deputy chief constable, superintendents, and inspectors (often referred to as "commissioned officers," although they are not actually commissioned), and noncommissioned officers, including staff sergeants, sergeants, corporals, detectives, and constables. In recent years, the move toward community policing has resulted in major changes in the organization and rank structure of many police services. We will consider these changes in greater detail in Chapter 7.

Independent Municipal Police Services

Municipal police forces assume responsibility for enforcing the *Criminal Code,* provincial statutes, and municipal bylaws within the city limits. Across Canada, municipal police services range in size from three members to more than 5,000 officers (the Toronto Police Service has 5,776 plus an additional 2,818 civilian personnel, and the Montreal Police

Service has 4,533 and an additional 1,364 civilian personnel), and have jurisdiction within a city's boundaries. Newfoundland and Labrador, the Yukon, the Northwest Territories, and Nunavut are the only areas in Canada without municipal police services. In addition to enforcing the *Criminal Code,* provincial statutes, municipal bylaws, certain federal statutes such as the *Controlled Drugs and Substances Act* have also come under the jurisdiction of municipal forces. The majority of police "work" is performed by services operating at this level. In recent years, municipal police services have been critical about the lack of resources the Royal Canadian Mounted Police are able to provide to joint-force operations.

Municipalities can select one of three options in providing police services: they can create their own independent police service; they can join with an existing municipal police service, which often means becoming involved with a regional police service; or they can contract with the provincial police service (in Ontario and Quebec) or with the RCMP (in the rest of Canada) to provide police services.

Provincial Police Services

The provincial and territorial governments are responsible for the administration of justice and, to this end, oversee police services, prosecute offences, staff courthouses with judges, operate programs for adult and young offenders, and also operate correctional facilities for offenders who receive sentences totalling less than two years. Police services generally fall under the purview of provincial ministries of justice or attorneys general.

Provincial police forces are charged with enforcing the *Criminal Code* and provincial statutes in areas not covered by municipal police services. These areas generally comprise rural areas and small towns. There are three independent provincial police forces in Canada: the Ontario Provincial Police (OPP), the Sûreté du Québec (SQ), and the Royal Newfoundland Constabulary (RNC). The RNC polices only the communities of Corner Brook, Churchill Falls, Labrador City, and St. John's. The RCMP, under contract, polices the remainder of the province.

In Ontario, the OPP is responsible for policing rural areas and the areas outside municipalities, and enforcing provincial laws as well as the *Criminal Code.* It provides general policing services to more than 2.4 million people (3.7 million during the summer months) throughout Ontario. The OPP deploys 1,845 police officers under contract to Ontario municipalities (Statistics Canada 2011d). The OPP's area of responsibility takes in 993,000 square kilometres of land and 174,000 kilometres of waterways. This wide range of settings presents special challenges, which we will address throughout this text.

A unique component of the OPP is the Aboriginal Policing Bureau, which oversees the delivery of policing services to First Nations communities and provides assistance and training for the transition to self-policing. Aboriginal and non-Aboriginal constables who are posted to First Nations communities are required to complete specialized training to sensitize them to Native culture and communities.

Royal Canadian Mounted Police

The RCMP is a component (along with the Correctional Service of Canada and the National Parole Board) of the Ministry of Public Safety Canada and is divided into 15 divisions, in addition to its National Headquarters in Ottawa and Depot Training in Regina (see Figure 2.1). The headquarters of these divisions are generally located in the provincial and territorial capitals and are under the supervision of a Commanding Officer. These divisions are organized into four regions, each under the direction a deputy commissioner:

- *Pacific Region*: E Division, Vancouver, British Columbia; M Division, Whitehorse, Yukon;
- *Northwest Region*: D Division, Winnipeg, Manitoba; F and Depot Divisions, Regina, Saskatchewan; G Division, Yellowknife, Northwest Territories; V Division, Iqaluit, Nunavut Territory; K Division, Edmonton, Alberta;

Figure 2.1 Organization of the RCMP

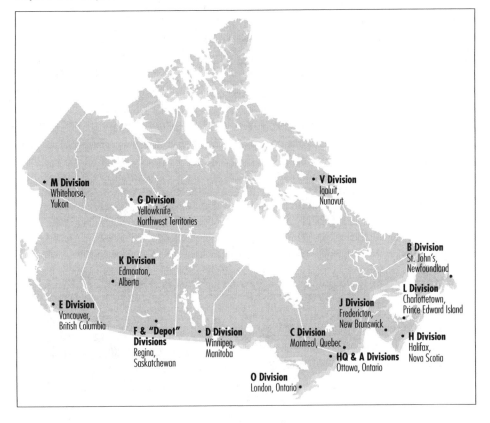

- *Central Region*: O Division, London, Ontario; C Division, Montreal, Quebec; HQ and A Divisions, Ottawa, Ontario;
- *Atlantic Region*: B Division, St. John's, Newfoundland; H Division, Halifax, Nova Scotia; J Division, Fredericton, New Brunswick; L Division, Charlottetown, Prince Edward Island.

There is also a deputy commissioner at the national headquarters in charge of the various directorates located there.

The *Royal Canadian Mounted Police Act* provides the legislative basis for the operations and activities of the RCMP. The RCMP operates as a federal police force in all provinces and territories, enforcing or administering more than 250 federal statutes and agreements including the *Controlled Drugs and Substances Act,* as well as lesser-known statutes such as the *Canada Shipping Act* and the *Canada Student Loans Act.*

Nationwide, approximately 60 percent of RCMP personnel are involved in contract policing—serving in the role of provincial and municipal police officers under agreements that are signed between the RCMP and the provinces/territories. However, there is no RCMP contract policing in Ontario or Quebec.

Regional Police Services

A regional police service generally involves the amalgamation of several independent police departments into one large organization. Regional police services have been a feature of policing for many years, and today there are a number of regional police services, including the Peel Regional Police, the York Regional Police, Niagara Regional Police Service, and the Halifax Regional Police. The regional police services of Peel, York, and

Niagara serve more than 50 percent of Ontario's population. From 1962 to 2002, the number of independent municipal police services in Ontario has steadily declined from nearly 300 to fewer than 100. In 2010, the Ontario Provincial Police provided front-line policing services to over 322 municipalities, 148 of which had entered into formal policing contracts. In Quebec, the Montreal Police Service (formerly the Montreal Urban Community Police Service [MUCPS]) provides policing services to the City of Montreal and several surrounding municipalities. The Montreal Police Service was created as a result of the amalgamation of the urban communities around Montreal in 1971. An important point to keep in mind is the impact upon a community when its local police service is amalgamated into a larger regional organization. We will address this issue later.

The Peel Regional Police was established on January 1, 1974, upon the creation of the Regional Municipality of Peel. It incorporated the former police services of Mississauga, Port Credit, Streetsville, Brampton, and Chinguacousy.

Aboriginal Policing

A unique feature of the policing landscape in Canada is "autonomous" Aboriginal police forces, which have developed across the country over the past three decades. This is occurring within the context of a broader movement leading toward Aboriginal self-government. Under the First Nations Policing Policy (FNPP) the FNPP is implemented across Canada through tripartite agreements negotiated among the federal government, provincial or territorial governments, and First Nations. The agreements are cost-shared 52 percent by the Government of Canada and 48 percent by the province involved. Depending on the resources available, the First Nation may develop and administer its own police service, as is the case in most of Quebec and Ontario, or it may enter into a Community Tripartite Agreement (CTA) negotiated between the federal government, the province or territory in which the First Nation is located, and the governing body of the First Nation. Under such agreements, the First Nation has its own dedicated contingent of officers from an existing police service (usually the RCMP). Every effort is made by these police services to have the department staffed by members of the First Nations community (Statistics Canada 2011d). In Ontario, the Aboriginal Policing Bureau manages First Nations policing in the province.

In 2008 there were 405 Aboriginal communities in Canada with dedicated police services employing 1,217 police officers, most of whom are of Aboriginal descent. There are single-community services, such as at Six Nations where there is a population of 10,000. There are also multi-community agreements, such as Nishnawbe-Aski, which serves 35 communities. These police forces have been established through negotiations and cost-sharing arrangements involving the federal government, the provincial governments, and First Nations communities. The First Nations Policing Policy (FNPP) provides the framework used by the federal government, the provincial and territorial governments, and the First Nations communities to negotiate agreements for policing services that meet the needs of reserve communities. This policy allows First Nations communities to determine the most appropriate type of police services; thus, they can decide either to create their own autonomous, self-administered police service or engage Aboriginal officers from the RCMP, the OPP in Ontario, or the SQ in Quebec.

Among the larger Aboriginal police forces are the Nishnawbe-Aski Police Service and the Six Nations Tribal Police in Ontario and the Amerindian Police Council in Quebec. Officers in Aboriginal police forces generally have full powers to enforce the *Criminal Code* and federal and provincial statutes, as well as band bylaws on reserve lands. The activities of Aboriginal police forces are overseen by reserve-based police commissions or by the local band council. There are also band constables who are appointed under provisions of the *Indian Act* and who are responsible for enforcing band bylaws. Band constables are not fully sworn police officers and their powers are limited.

Railway and Transit Police

Both the Canadian Pacific Railway and Canadian National Railways maintain their own police services which have authority to enforce the federal *Railway Safety Act*. Police in both organizations have the same powers of arrest as police across Canada, although their role is generally restricted to the protection of their property and the safety of people on it. Policing arrangements can be very complex, as both railways run through several U.S. states. This requires a number of legal agreements called Memoranda of Understanding (MOUs) with police in U.S. states.

Across Canada, a variety of transit policing arrangements are in place ranging from the local police agency assuming primary policing responsibility in Montreal and Toronto to dedicated police and security services. Translink BC, responsible for the management of the transit system in the lower mainland British Columbia, employs the South Coast British Columbia Transportation Authority Police Service, which works closely with 21 police jurisdictions that the transit system passes through.

Integrated Policing

Special Constables

In many Canadian provinces a number of law enforcement personnel (special constables, sheriffs, peace officers) exist with limited powers that serve to provide safety and security services at lower costs than police officers with full authorities. Special constables may be found enforcing municipal bylaws and select municipal or federal statutes, performing tasks such as providing transit safety or hospital security, and performing limited duties in relation to other provincial legislation such as traffic enforcement and liquor and gaming legislation. Generally, special constables' authority derives from provincial appointments and are employed by public bodies and employers to provide dedicated "policing" service that jurisdictional police may not be able to provide. Both Alberta and Manitoba, for example, have hired peace officers, sheriffs, and special constables to perform a variety of functions including surveillance, fugitive apprehension, and traffic enforcement on rural highways. These special constables are not counted as part of the overall police resource estimates by Statistics Canada; however, they perform an important role in enhancing public safety. Their overall effectiveness in supplementing the work of the police in Canadian society is thought to be positive, although this is an area for further study.

POLICE ACCOUNTABILITY

In jurisdictions across Canada, police activities are overseen both externally and internally. Police commissions, boards, and agencies established under provisions of the various police acts—or, for RCMP officers, the *RCMP Act*—exist as a measure of external oversight of policing. Boards and commissions ensure accountability at both the municipal and provincial level. For example, the Edmonton Police Commission oversees the Edmonton Police Service, whereas the Law Enforcement Review Board in Alberta hears appeals from citizens and police officers related to the disposition of complaints. In Ontario the Ontario Civilian Committee on Police Services performs this function. In addition, the Office of the Independent Police Review Director (OIPRD), staffed entirely by civilians, serves as an additional independent police oversight role. Similarly, civilian oversight of the Royal Canadian Mounted Police occurs through the Commission for Public Complaints Against the RCMP and through the RCMP External Review Committee, which oversees labour and disciplinary issues. Table 2.2 describes models of police oversight in Canada.

Table 2.2 Models of Canadian Police Oversight

1. Dependent Model		2. Interdependent Model		3. Independent Model
1.1 Police Investigating Police	*1.2 Police Investigating Another Police Force*	*2.1 Civilian Observation*	*2.2 Hybrid Investigation*	*3. Independent Investigation*
Represents police investigating police criminal investigations • Police fully responsible for the investigation and administration of public complaints • No civilian involvement in a *criminal* investigation • Oversight body recognizes complaints regarding service, internal discipline or public trust • Oversight body may be an appellate authority	Represents police investigating *another* police force Involves formal arrangements (memoranda of agreement) in place with another police force to handle investigation of police officers in cases of death or serious bodily harm • Unlegislated process • In place only in select provinces in Canada	Introduces civilian observation to investigation Civilian observer responsible to monitor criminal investigation (not direct or oversee investigation) • Regular reporting on status of investigation required • Police responsible for investigation, adjudication and administration of public complaints	Oversight body may choose from various options which include: a) may supervise/ manage parts of police criminal investigation (beyond monitor/ oversee) conducted by police b) may assume control over police investigation c) may undertake independent criminal investigation • Oversight body can refer investigation to police force • Police can be involved in some form of collaboration, cooperation or coordination of the actual investigation of public complaints with oversight body	Oversight body undertakes independent criminal investigation for cases within its mandate • Police are excluded or removed from process of investigating public complaints • Hallmark of this system is that civilian personnel are fully responsible for investigation • Nil ability to refer investigation to police

Source: Commission for Public Complaints Against the RCMP (http://www.cpc-cpp.gc.ca/prr/rep/rev/chair-pre/pipR/pip_5-eng.aspx)

Within police services, there are units often titled "**Professional Standards**" or "Internal Affairs" that investigate allegations of professional misconduct on the part of officers and, in rare instances, corruption. Police officers may be held liable for violating the policies and procedures of the police service in which they work. They can also be held liable—administratively, civilly, and criminally—for their conduct. Police officers can be held accountable for conduct that occurs both on- and off-duty. Over the last ten years, police officers and police departments have been found civilly liable for negligently supervising employees, conducting deficient investigations, and failing to warn the community about dangerous persons.

Police Boards and Police Commissions

In many jurisdictions, police boards and police commissions play a major role in overseeing or governing the activities of police services. The **governance** function is intended to provide strategic oversight, as opposed to playing a role in day-to-day operational decision making, which falls within the jurisdiction of the chief. Where they exist, provincial and municipal police commissions are involved in developing policing standards, promoting research into police, providing training programs for provincial and municipal officers, and assisting in the preparation of the annual police budget. For example, the duties of a commission in the *Alberta Police Act* include:

- allocating the funds established by council (the police budget),
- establishing policies providing for efficient and effective policing,
- issuing instructions to the chief in relation to the policies established above, and
- ensuring sufficient persons are employed for the police service for the purposes of carrying out the functions of the police service.

As well, they may play a role in police disciplinary matters. In Alberta, for example, both Edmonton and Calgary Police Commissions have appointed a Public Complaints Director who reviews all public complaints and can make recommendations.

There are also municipal police services boards, composed of community members that oversee the activities of municipal police services. However, these boards do not operate in all provinces (they have never existed in Quebec or Newfoundland) or in all municipalities (in Manitoba, only Brandon and Winnipeg have boards). Activities of municipal police services boards may include hiring the chief constable, preparing and overseeing the police budget, and authorizing increases in police personnel.

In Ontario, the police services boards function as the civilian authority over police services. Every Ontario municipality that has a police force is required to have a police services board that assumes overall responsibility for the provision of adequate and effective services. Section 31(1) of the *Police Services Act* identifies the duties of these boards, which include appointing the members of the municipal police force, establishing the priorities and objectives of the police services in consultation with the chief of police, recruiting and hiring the chief of police, and allocating and administering police services budgets.

The size of the board varies: three members for communities with fewer than 25,000 people; five for those with greater than 25,000; and seven for communities with populations greater than 300,000. Each municipality appoints the majority of members, including one community representative who is not an elected official or employee of the municipality; the province retains a minority number of appointments. Under the provisions of the *Police Services Act,* municipalities may also create a joint police services board with one or more other municipalities. Municipalities policed under contract by the OPP may establish a community policing advisory committee to work with the local OPP commander and provide information on community objectives and concerns relating to the delivery of police services.

If this discussion of police boards and commissions seems a little confusing, it is. There is an inconsistency in the work of police boards and commissions across Canada—in some jurisdictions the activities of a commission are similar to a board in another locale. The Canadian Association of Police Boards (CAPB), which oversees approximately 75 police boards and commissions across Canada, who themselves oversee some 33,000 municipal police officers, has as its Mission to work collaboratively and proactively to improve police governance in Canada and to bring about change that will enhance public safety for all Canadians. It is the only national organization existing to improve police governance in Canada.

Police Conduct Review Agencies and Adjudicative Bodies

With the exception of Prince Edward Island, all the provinces have offices that are charged with receiving and reviewing complaints against police officers (excluding RCMP officers policing under contract). These include the Alberta Law Enforcement Review Board, Manitoba's Law Enforcement Review Agency, the Nova Scotia Police Review Board, and the Office of the Police Complaint Commissioner in British Columbia. Oversight of the Royal Canadian Mounted Police occurs through the Commission for Public Complaints Against the RCMP and the External Review Committee (ERC). In Ontario, the Special Investigations Unit (SIU) and the Ontario Civilian Commission on Police Services (OCCPS) perform these tasks. The role of each oversight body varies, ranging from reviewing complaint investigations and making recommendations to conducting the investigation itself.

The SIU is perhaps the best example of external civilian review of police activities. Established under provisions of the *Police Services Act*, it investigates cases involving serious injury, sexual assault, or death that may have been the result of criminal offences committed by police officers. The SIU, which is independent of any police service and operates directly under the provincial attorney general, has the authority to investigate municipal, regional, and provincial police officers. An attempt is made to complete case investigations within 30 days, although in more complex cases this is not often possible. The director of the SIU has the authority to decide whether charges are warranted in a case and he or she reports this decision directly to the attorney general. This model of external civilian review has also been established in Alberta through the creation of the Alberta Serious Incident Response Team (ASIRT). Unlike the SIU, ASIRT has a broader mandate to also investigate sensitive matters. In 2011 the Province of British Columbia created the Independent Investigations Office (IIO), performing a role and function similar to the SIU.

The primary mandate of the OCCPS is to conduct investigations into the conduct of police officers and police services. More specifically, the OCCPS:

- conducts investigations into police services not in compliance with the standards of service prescribed in the *Police Services Act,* including the requirements of community policing, on behalf of the Solicitor General;
- receives appeals from municipalities involving the misconduct of police officers;
- reviews public complaints against police officers that have not been resolved to the satisfaction of the complainant at the local level; and
- conducts inquiries on its own relating to complaints and the disposition of complaints.

Professional Standards Units

All police services have internal policies with which police officers must comply, internal units to investigate alleged misconduct on the part of officers, and a disciplinary process that includes a variety of sanctions that can be imposed on officers

In Ontario, the Special Investigations Unit conducts investigations where serious injury or death has occurred as a result of an interaction between the police and a member of the public.

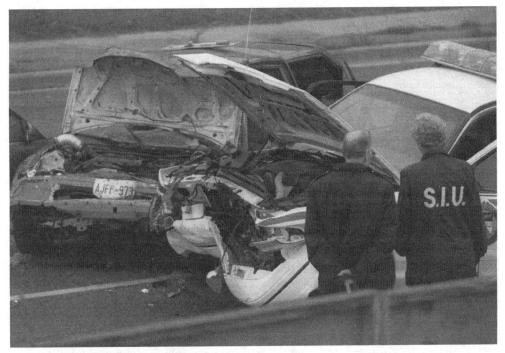

Source: CP PHOTO/Toronto Sun—Juan Fanzio

found guilty of misconduct. Police officers who work in internal investigation units have a difficult and challenging mandate. They must investigate fellow police officers as objectively and neutrally as possible. Critics of this system argue it is virtually impossible for the police to objectively investigate their own personnel, while those who favour this approach argue that investigations are conducted thoroughly by insiders who know policing.

In certain situations, police services will request that officers from another police service conduct the investigation. It is common practice, for example, for the Montreal Police Service to call upon the Quebec provincial police to conduct investigations, particularly in more serious cases. Police legislation in each province governs how police officers from other departments can be requested.

While misconduct in policing has generally been considered an individual officer phenomenon, the investigation of serious misconduct and criminal acts by police officers has required police departments to reorganize their resources to better respond to these emerging problems. The RCMP, for example, has recently established anti-corruption units in major urban centres. The Toronto Police Service has also enhanced their internal investigative capacity following a serious investigation into the misappropriation of money and property in their Drug Unit. To maintain public confidence in policing, investigations must be transparent and open to the public.

THE CONTEMPORARY ROLES OF THE POLICE

Traditionally, the mandate of the police was categorized into crime control (catching criminals), order maintenance (keeping the peace), and service (providing assistance). These distinctions, however, fail to capture the diversity and complexity of the police role in a highly technological, global society. Increasingly, police officers are viewed as "knowledge workers" who spend a considerable amount of time gathering and processing information. Police work also extends far beyond the street level and cuts across jurisdictional and international boundaries.

Section 4.2 of Ontario's *Police Services Act*, for example, states that all police services in Ontario must provide adequate and effective police services including the following:

- crime prevention,
- law enforcement,
- assistance to victims of crime,
- public order maintenance, and
- emergency response.

Note that crime prevention is listed first and that attention to the needs of crime victims is also a stated priority. The Act further states that the OPP will be used in those instances in which a municipality fails to provide these core policing services.

The next step in considering the role of the police is to ask a very simple yet very important question: "What do you want your police to do?" This question requires us to consider the expectations that community residents have of the police, because after all, the police are a public (and often political) agency and are hired to serve the community.

The community policing model is often described as a "full service" model in that it attempts to provide a broad range of comprehensive services to the community. Following the terrorist attacks of September 11, 2001, the role and mandate of the police has broadened to include a significant commitment to controlling terrorism both domestically and abroad. The quick passage of public safety legislation, including the *Proceeds of Crime (Money Laundering) and Terrorist Financing Act*, the *Anti-Terrorism Act*, and the *Immigration and Refugee Protection Act*, has placed even greater demands upon Canadian police to provide for national security. While the mandate of the police has grown to include "security policing," there has been a corresponding need to respond to elevated levels of fear and the management of disorder, which lowers citizens' perception of safety.

Public Perceptions and Expectations of the Police

Most citizens often have unrealistic and conflicting expectations of the police. Police officers catch crooks and make communities safe from crime. Community residents often assign equal importance to crime prevention, crime control, order maintenance, and service functions, and rarely provide any input into how police resources are to be allocated.

Someone who calls the police wants an immediate patrol car response, regardless of the relative seriousness of the situation. The situation could involve dealing with street prostitution, searching for lost children, apprehending criminals, or working with community residents to solve local problems. To put it bluntly, citizens often want the police to be all things to all people, which is an impossible and unachievable goal.

Compounding such expectations is the fact that in many communities, there are differences of opinion among community residents about what the priorities of the police should be. This diversity of opinion may be even more pronounced in urban centres with diverse cultural and ethnic populations. The framework of community policing provides the best opportunity for police services to respond to the needs and concerns of individual communities.

THE CONTEXTS OF POLICE WORK

Police work is complex, and one factor that contributes to this complexity is the fact that police officers carry out their tasks in a number of different contexts. Broadly speaking, these contexts include the frameworks created by:

- the types and levels of criminal activity that confront the police;
- legislation;

- the criminal justice system;
- the police service; and
- the demographics of the community.

Each of these contexts, and their implications for policing, are considered briefly below.

The Crime Context

Examining crime patterns provides insights into the demands that are placed on police services and into the policing policies and practices required to address these demands. Traditionally, police services have been organized to combat "traditional" types of crime, such as robberies, assaults, and various types of property crimes. Often, police services have attempted to increase their budgets and personnel by arguing that crime rates are increasing. However, not only are the overall rates of crime declining, but police services are also being confronted by new types of criminal activity, such as cyber crime, corporate crime, and organized crime, that may require a reconsideration of how police work is carried out. Another factor creating demands on police services is the aging of the population, which is likely to be accompanied by an increasing fear of crime that police services must respond to.

As we will see, community policing is an appropriate model of service delivery for many, though not all, of the challenges confronting police services. Some highlights of Canadian crime are presented in Box 2.2.

The patterns of crime that exist in a neighbourhood, community, or city have significant implications for how community policing strategies are implemented. Every "task environment" within which the police officer works presents unique challenges. These are even greater in remote and northern areas, where cultural barriers between the officers and the community, coupled with geographic isolation and the relatively short period of time that officers are posted to these communities, undermine the best intentions of police officers.

The Legislative Context

Police officers carry out their tasks within several legislative frameworks that define their roles, powers, and responsibilities. When new legislation is enacted, it may result in increased demands on the police. The more significant pieces of legislation are the following:

- The **Canadian Charter of Rights and Freedoms** is part of the **Constitution Act, 1982**. Canada's constitution is the supreme law of the land and guarantees basic rights and freedoms for citizens. The Charter contains specific sections on fundamental freedoms, legal rights, equality rights, and enforcement. Courts may use the constitution to strike down legislation and criminal laws as unconstitutional. In 2012, the Charter turned 30; it has had a significant impact on the powers and activities of the police.
- The *Constitution Act, 1982*, sets out the responsibilities of the federal and provincial governments in the area of criminal justice. The federal government has the sole authority to enact criminal laws and to establish the procedures to be followed in criminal cases (Section 91[14]), and the provinces are assigned the responsibility for the administration of justice (Section 92[14]).
- The *Criminal Code* sets out the criminal laws and the procedures for the administration of justice.
- Other federal statutes include the *Controlled Drugs and Substances Act*, relating to different types of illegal drugs; the *Youth Criminal Justice Act*, relating to the administration of youth justice; the *Canada Evidence Act*, pertaining to evidentiary matters

BOX 2.2

HIGHLIGHTS OF CANADIAN CRIME

1. Police-reported crime, including violent crime, property crime, and sexual assault, has been declining for the last three decades, reaching its lowest point in 2011, down approximately 30 percent since it peaked in 1991. The severity of violent crime was at its lowest since 1999. In 2011, the homicide rate was at its lowest in 44 years.

2. The property crime rate, particularly break-ins, has fallen to its lowest level in over 30 years. Since peaking in 1991, the break-in rate has fallen 50 percent.

3. Motor vehicle thefts have steadily been decreasing since 1991. Drug and impaired driving offences have generally been trending down as well, although both have increased between 2007 and 2011.

4. Drug crime continues to trend upwards, a trend which began in the early 1990s. In 2011, marijuana possession cases accounted for the increase while serious drug offences declined.

5. In 2011, the youth crime rate decreased by 10 percent from the previous year and was 11 percent lower than the previous decade.

6. Since the introduction of the *Youth Criminal Justice Act* (YCJA), more youth have come into contact with the police; however, the proportion of those formally charged declined from 56 percent (pre-YCJA) in 2002 to 42 percent in 2010.

7. Shifts in the age composition of the population are linked to lowered reported crime, as well as changing societal attitudes and police enforcement practices.

8. Large cities generally have lower rates of crime than smaller cities and rural areas, particularly for sexual assault offences, common assault, and weapons offences.

9. Large cities generally have higher crime rates for robbery, break and enter, motor vehicle theft, and prostitution.

10. Violent crime rates in the western provinces and the territories tend to be higher than those in other parts of the country. Violent crime rates in the three territories were double the highest provincial rate in 2010, consistent with previous years.

11. Consistent with the drop in the overall crime rate, the rate of crime incidents per officer has generally been decreasing since 1991. In 2010, there were 30.5 incidents per officer, the lowest in over 35 years.

12. While reported crime is declining, the length of time to thoroughly investigate crimes is increasing.

Sources: Statistics Canada, Canadian Centre for Justice Statistics 2011c; Statistics Canada 2005; Statistics Canada 2011b.

in the courts; and the *Corrections and Conditional Release Act,* which sets out the framework for federal corrections. Recent amendments to the *Criminal Code* establishing criminal liability for organizations that commit criminal offences also have a significant impact on police resources.

- Provincial and municipal acts provide the structure for delivering police services. They set out the process for filing complaints against police officers, establish the procedures for disciplining police officers, and fix the activities of police commissions and municipal police boards.

- The *Royal Canadian Mounted Police Act* provides the legislative framework for the operations of the RCMP. It contains provisions for the operation of the External Review Committee and the Public Complaints Commission, and for handling officer grievances, discipline, discharge, and demotion.

The Legislative and Regulatory Framework for Policing in Ontario

There are two key pieces of legislation that provide the framework for police services in the province of Ontario. These are the *Police Services Act* and the **Adequacy and Effectiveness of Police Services Regulation**, an amendment to the *Police Services Act* introduced in 1999. Similar legislative enactments are underway in other provinces as well, including Alberta, where provincial policing standards have been incorporated into the *Police Act*.

The *Police Services Act* is divided into several parts that set out the responsibility for police services; the role and activities of the Ontario Civilian Commission on Police Services and the municipal police services boards; the mandate and duties of police officers and other police staff; the procedure and process for filing, hearing, and resolving complaints against the police; and the provisions for special investigations into policing. Box 2.3 sets out the principles of policing in Ontario, as defined by the *Police Services Act*.

We will engage in a more in-depth discussion of the *Police Services Act* in Chapter 3. The *Adequacy and Effectiveness of Police Services Regulation* (Ontario Regulation 3/99, also known as the Adequacy Standards) was designed to establish uniform service standards for police services across the province. The regulation sets out standards for police services in seven areas: crime prevention, law enforcement, victim assistance, public order maintenance, emergency response services, administration, and infrastructure. We will also examine the Adequacy Standards in more detail in Chapter 3.

The Criminal Justice System

Police officers operate at the front end of the criminal justice system. Although the general public may be involved in calling the police and participating in various crime prevention and crime response initiatives, the activities and decision making of police officers are what determine which individuals and cases become involved further in the justice system. Officers are vested with considerable discretion in responding to incidents and, therefore, they perform a major screening function.

Despite the fact that the police are a cornerstone of the criminal justice system, historically there has been little contact and co-operation between the police and the criminal justice and social service agencies. Agencies have tended to work in isolation

---

BOX 2.3

PRINCIPLES OF POLICING IN ONTARIO

(1) Police services shall be provided throughout Ontario in accordance with the following principles:

1. The need to ensure the safety and security of all persons and property in Ontario.

2. The importance of safeguarding the fundamental rights guaranteed by the *Canadian Charter of Rights and Freedoms* and the *Human Rights Code*.

3. The need for co-operation between the providers of police services and the communities they serve.

4. The importance of respect for victims of crime and understanding of their needs.

5. The need for sensitivity to the pluralistic, multiracial, and multicultural character of Ontario society.

6. The need to ensure that police forces are representative of the communities they serve.

Source: Police Services Act, Revised Statutes of Ontario, 1990. Copyright © Queen's Printer for Ontario.

from each other. Part of this is due to the fact that criminal justice agencies typically maintain separate computer databases. To address the longstanding problem of poor communication and failure to share useful information among justice agencies (including individual police services), the federal, provincial, and territorial governments realized the need to improve the information sharing practices within Canada's criminal justice information system. To this end they are collaborating on an Integrated Justice Information initiative, the goal of which is to integrate the information systems of all partners in Canada's criminal justice system. The primary means for building this integrated system will be to build the Canada Public Safety Information Network (CPSIN) to serve as the foundation upon which a modern, national network of information sharing will be built. It will be a network of networks and not a mega-database. Another information sharing initiative is the Police Information Portal (PIP), which allows for the sharing of information among police, public safety, and federal agencies across Canada. PIP is a searchable index of all police agency record management systems across the country and is an important means of gathering information during serial predator investigations, organized crime investigations, and investigations where the subject may move from one jurisdiction to another.

Several provinces have embarked on additional projects to foster closer co-operation and information sharing among the different components of the justice system. British Columbia's Justice Information System (JUSTIN) and Ontario's Integrated Justice Project are two examples of the pursuit of integrated justice initiatives at the provincial level. Both provinces are working hard to design cost-effective, efficient, and streamlined systems that will allow police to spend more time policing and less time on paperwork. The courts and corrections staff will have the information required to process cases more quickly and effectively.

The province of Ontario's **Integrated Justice System Initiative** is designed to facilitate a seamless flow of information among justice agencies and throughout the justice system, from policing to the courts to corrections. In addition, with today's emphasis on community policing, police officers now often work closely with their professional counterparts in other disciplines to address problems of crime and disorder in communities. Similar initiatives involving information sharing between police agencies include the Alberta Provincial Information Integration Initiative (API3) and the RCMP Police Records Information Management Environment (PRIME-BC). Throughout this book, we will highlight examples of co-operation and problem solving.

The Police Service

Police officers work in departments and detachments that are diverse in terms of their structure and activities. This fact has a significant impact on how individual police organizations and their officers implement community policing. For example, although an OPP or an RCMP officer may be posted to a small detachment in a remote area, the officer is still accountable to an organizational hierarchy that stretches many kilometres from the detachment to the subdivision to the division headquarters to headquarters. Policies and procedures for the RCMP are formulated in Ottawa and then transmitted on a regular basis to the detachments through the divisional headquarters. The extent of this organizational "reach" is in sharp contrast to the situation faced by a police officer working in a small Aboriginal police service with responsibility for a single First Nation.

Although the provincial police Acts and the *RCMP Act* provide a general framework within which police services establish policies and procedures, set goals and objectives, and assess the performance of officers, each police service has its own unique organizational "climate" and its own ways of fulfilling its mandate. There are also differences among police services in the demands and expectations of the communities, in the numbers of officers in the department, and in the perspectives of police work held by senior police management.

The Social and Demographic Attributes of Communities

Canada has a number of social and demographic attributes that affect the demands that are placed upon police officers. Some of these are discussed below.

• *Demographics.* The majority of Canadians reside in urban centres that are close to the American border. However, police services must also be provided to smaller regional cities, and to rural and remote communities that are often inhabited by First Nations and Inuit peoples. Projections based on census data indicate that Canada's population growth is slowing and that future growth will primarily be due to immigration. In addition, the Canadian population is aging, with the first of the baby boomers reaching the age of 65 in 2010. These factors will result in a multiracial society that is on average older and lives longer.

• *Cultural diversity.* A defining attribute of Canada as a country is multicultural diversity. The primary source of this diversity is immigration. The most recent Census conducted by Statistics Canada in 2006 provides interesting attributes of immigration as follows:

  – In 2006 there were 6,186,950 foreign-born citizens in Canada, representing almost one in five (19.8 percent) of the total population. This was the highest proportion in 75 years and places Canada second only to Australia in the percentage of its foreign-born population (Statistics Canada 2007a; Statistics Canada 2007b).

  – Two-thirds of Canada's population growth was attributable to net international migration, while the U.S. population growth resulted mostly from natural increase, as fertility was higher in the United States than in Canada.

  – In 2006, nearly 25 million people, or more than four-fifths of Canadians, were living in urban areas.

  – Between 2001 and 2006, Canada's foreign-born population increased by 13.6 percent. This was four times higher than the Canadian-born population, which grew by 3.3 percent during the same period.

  – Approximately 1,110,000 recent immigrants came to Canada between January 1, 2001 and May 16, 2006. These newcomers made up 17.9 percent of the total foreign-born population, and 3.6 percent of Canada's 31.2 million total population. The People's Republic of China continued to have the highest percentage of new immigrants to Canada during this timeframe (14 percent of recent immigrants).

  – Recent immigrants born in Asia (including the Middle East) made up the largest proportion of newcomers to Canada in 2006 (58.3 percent).

  – Immigrants tend to settle in urban areas. Toronto, Montreal, and Vancouver were home to 68.9 percent of the recent immigrants in 2006. In contrast, slightly over one-third (34.4 percent) of Canada's total population lived in these three Census Metropolitan Areas.

  – The 2006 Census enumerated 2,320,200 foreign-born people in Toronto, 831,300 in Vancouver, and 740,400 in Montreal. These individuals represented 45.7 percent of Toronto's population, 39.6 percent of Vancouver's, and 20.6 percent of Montreal's. The proportion of foreign-born people in Toronto surpasses cities known for their cultural diversity, including New York, Los Angeles, and Sydney, Australia. By 2031, it is estimated that visible minorities in Toronto will represent 63 percent of the population.

- In 2006, 57.3 percent of immigrants who came to Canada in the last five years were in the prime working age group of 25 to 54. In contrast, only 42.3 percent of the Canadian-born population was in this age group.
- A majority (70.2 percent) of the foreign-born population in 2006 reported a mother tongue other than English or French. Among these individuals, the largest proportion, one in five (18.6 percent), reported Chinese languages. Italian followed (6.6 percent), and then Punjabi (5.9 percent), Spanish (5.8 percent), German (5.4 percent), Tagalog (4.8 percent), and Arabic (4.7 percent).
- Many immigrants come from countries where the police are feared and are to be avoided. This attitude places unique challenges on a police service attempting to implement the principles of community policing (Metropolitan Toronto Police 1996:9; Mitchell 1997:A1; Toronto Police Service 2011).*

The cultural diversity of Canada and its communities presents major challenges to police services, ranging from increasing the number of police recruits from cultural and ethnic minorities, to ensuring that officers receive training that makes them culturally sensitive and aware, to implementing strategies that facilitate the development of police–community partnerships. The philosophy of community policing provides a broad framework within which police services can develop strategic partnerships with communities.

- *Aboriginal peoples.* Aboriginal peoples comprise nearly four percent of the Canadian population. This includes status and nonstatus First Nations peoples, Métis, and Inuit. The numbers of Aboriginal people, however, are unevenly distributed across the country; the highest numbers are found in Ontario and British Columbia. The majority of First Nations peoples reside in rural and remote areas of the country; however, there are significant numbers in the "southern" urban areas of the country, including Toronto, Winnipeg, and Vancouver. In 2006, 1,172,790 people identified themselves as an Aboriginal person; that is, North American Indian (First Nations people), Métis, and/or Inuit. The Aboriginal population is younger than the non-Aboriginal population: almost half (48 percent) of the Aboriginal population consists of children and youth aged 24 and under, compared with 31 percent of the non-Aboriginal population. This makes the Aboriginal population an excellent target group for future recruitment to police services (Statistics Canada 2008a).

The Community Context

The community context plays a significant role in determining the demands that are placed upon police officers, the role that the police assume in the community, and the specific patterns of relationships that exist between the community and the police (which, in turn, will determine the potential for police–community partnerships in preventing and responding to crime).

Communities vary on a number of critical dimensions, including their size; their socioeconomic, ethnic, cultural, and spiritual makeup; the types and levels of crime and disorder; their attitudes toward the police; their expectations of the police; and the levels of citizen interest in becoming involved in police–community partnerships. In Ontario, for example, there is a wide variety of policing environments, ranging from the inner-

*Metropolitan Toronto Police, 1996. 1996 Environmental Scan and 1997–98 Service Goals and Objectives. Toronto: Corporate Planning, Metropolitan Toronto Police, p. 9; Mitchell, A., 1997. "Face of Canada Changes." The Globe and Mail. November 5, A1; Toronto Police Service (2011). Planning for the Future: Scanning the Toronto Environment [Online] accessed 2012 May 18 at http://www.torontopolice.on.ca/publications/files/reports/2011envscan.pdf

city neighbourhoods of Toronto, to suburban communities, to small towns and remote communities.

A key requirement for effective community policing is that police officers have a thorough understanding of the community they are policing. Officers must be able to identify key resource persons in the community who will facilitate the development of police–community partnerships, but also be sensitive to potential sources of resistance in the community that may undermine community policing initiatives.

TRENDS IN POLICING

Up until the mid-1990s, the police and other public-sector institutions had enjoyed continual expansion and a seemingly endless resource base. From the mid-1990s through to 2001, federal, provincial, and municipal governments underwent a period of fiscal restraint with a clear focus on deficit reduction and reduced spending. In recent years, the federal government has reduced transfer payments to the provinces, and provincial governments, including Ontario, have downloaded fiscal responsibilities onto the municipalities. At the same time policing costs are steadily increasing. This has resulted in significant changes to the organization and delivery of police services and has contributed to many of the trends in policing that we see today. Since September 11, 2001, there has been a greater emphasis upon police to ensure community safety. This has caused all levels of government to seriously assess budget requests of police services. While there continue to be fiscal constraints to keep policing costs in check, there is also the fundamental realization that demands for police services have increased. This realization has significantly shaped police services, and will serve to define the role of the police in the future.

Trend 1: As Crime Goes Down, Costs of Policing Go Up

Earlier in this chapter, we observed that crime rates are falling and, despite a temporary spike in crime in 1991, the crime rate has been steadily declining since 1973. In 2010, homicides in Canada were at their lowest in 44 years. This has been accompanied as well by a declining severity of crime. Consequently, the number of criminal investigations per police officer has also been declining. While reported crime rates are down, policing costs have been steadily increasing over the last 14 years. Police services across Canada point out that increasing costs are due to police salaries and benefits and the costs associated with policing large events such as the 2010 G8 and G20 summits in Toronto, the 2010 Stanley Cup playoffs, and the Olympic and Paralympic Games. While reported crime is declining, police services are not necessarily any less busy. Responding to calls for service; investigating organized crime; managing the complexities of the legal process, which lengthens time spent on investigations; addressing complex social issues; and responding to the challenges of increased ethnic diversity all place growing demands on policing. In the study "A 30-Year Analysis of Police Service Delivery and Costing" (2005), the time necessary to handle a case from initial call to acceptance by Crown counsel had increased 58 percent for break-and-enter cases between 1983 and 2003; a driving-under-the-influence case required 250 percent more time; and a domestic assault case required 964 percent more time (Centre for Criminal Justice Research 2005). Recognizing this trend, several police services now base their departmental budgets on how many staff it takes to manage predicted workload (called staffing to workload estimates). Halton, Edmonton, Calgary, and Vancouver are all taking steps to justify increases in personnel based on workload activities. Efforts to reduce costs will require that police services and their boards and commissions conduct in-depth analyses of their current model of police service delivery including an assessment of what constitutes core and non-core service.

Trend 2: Adoption of the Philosophy and Practice of Community Policing

While the philosophy and practice of community policing has been underway for four decades, there remains uncertainty in terms of the role of both the police and the community and their relationship to one another. For police services seeking to enhance community safety there is a fundamental recognition that community involvement is necessary; however, the limits of that involvement have not evolved much past a passive role for the community acting as the "eyes and ears" of the police. At the same time, the police maintain their expert role in "how" police service is delivered to the community. Despite this confusion, the philosophy of community policing is having a significant impact on the structure and delivery of policing services. Although the increasing emphasis on community policing is reflected in numerous federal government documents and in provincial police Acts and legislation, we will see in Chapter 3 that community policing has firm roots in the principles set forth by Sir Robert Peel in 1829.

Community policing represents the continuing evolution of police work and has resulted in an increased emphasis on many of the core principles and activities of early policing: a close relationship between the police and the community, geographic assignment of officers to communities, community involvement in addressing problems of crime and social disorder, and providing officers with the authority to address a wide range of problems at the street level.

Community policing is often described as "full service" policing and, as a result, the demands placed upon contemporary police organizations for service exacts a significant toll on individual police officers. Burnout, frustration, and other stress-related issues require police organizations to re-examine improved strategies for police service delivery. Contemporary Canadian police organizations find themselves trying to incorporate effective practices of policing with tactics and strategies serving to increase community participation and involvement in problem solving. If anything, a greater sophistication has emerged in terms of how police–community relationships are structured. For example, while the police used to be able to attend small Neighbourhood Watch meetings, it is now recognized that the police must prioritize and leverage their resources in more effective ways. The best way of doing this is to provide the knowledge, resources, and leadership to groups and agencies that are capable of fostering crime prevention and community safety initiatives. While this represents a return to the ideals of self-policing it is easier said than done, as we shall see in Chapter 8.

Trend 3: A Growing Crisis in Human Resources

The police sector is currently facing significant human resource challenges created by an aging work force, a smaller youth population with declining interest in policing as a career, and the need for recruitment and retention of police officers who are reflective of Canada's increasingly diverse population.

All police services in Canada are struggling to recruit enough police officers to keep pace with the growing number of retiring baby boomer police officers. By 2013, over 50 percent of police leaders and 40 percent of noncommissioned officers across Canada are eligible to retire, and this will only compound a growing experience gap. While the most pressing challenge over the next decade is to hire enough police officers, simply keeping pace with retirements does not allow police services to increase their capacity to respond to increasing community demands. Surprisingly, there has been very little in the way of a nationally coordinated strategy developed among police services to recruit and retain senior personnel. This has resulted in a dire situation where police services not only compete with one another for new recruits but also actively recruit experienced officers from one another.

The 2007 study "A National Diagnostic on Policing" is very critical of contemporary efforts to adequately staff police organizations, a situation which they fear will result in the collapse of policing, unless police services can act more like a sector and not just individual competitive entities. Despite this dismal prediction, there is some promise of improvement: 2007 saw an increase of 2.9 percent more police officers nationally, which was the largest increase in 30 years. As well, the government of Canada has committed to providing an additional 2,500 more police officers across Canada. Clearly, if community policing is to succeed there must be enough police officers to manage the complexity of demands and to strategically work with communities to foster safe environments. In an effort to address these concerns, the Police Sector Council (PSC) was established in 2004 to identify common human resource challenges among police services and to find innovative solutions to urgent human resource issues in the policing community.

This continuing trend means that police services will need to be more efficient and it has provided the impetus for the use of new approaches, such as best practices and the development of partnerships with the community. The current human resource issues affecting police organizations can be summarized as:

1. recruitment of personnel;
2. retainment of personnel;
3. retirement of senior personnel; and
4. reinvention of personnel.

These topics will be discussed later in the text.

Trend 4: Technology Creates a Borderless World

Globalization and advancements in technology have contributed to increased complexity in policing, increased investigative costs, and increased time necessary to conduct investigations. The expansion of technology not only provides new modes for committing crime but also creates new sources of evidence for police investigations. For example, the 2011 Vancouver Stanley Cup riots were captured on thousands of smartphone cameras, enabling police to identify hundreds of criminal suspects responsible for damaging and looting downtown Vancouver. Many criminal incidents are uploaded to YouTube. While the upside is improved catch rates, the downside is the investigative time and costs associated with evidence retrieval and the disclosure of this evidence when charges are laid. In fact, criminal cases are likely to be withdrawn if police are aware of the existence of video evidence and fail to seize it. Technology also enables criminals to live in one country and commit their crimes in another, such as mass marketing fraud or child exploitation. This imposes significant jurisdictional challenges for police who conduct criminal investigations in which the victims and offenders live in different countries. The mobility of criminals requires that Canada have treaties in place with other countries to facilitate investigations throughout the world.

While technology assists the crime-solving ability of police, by providing stronger analytical tools all of these tools, techniques, and strategies run the risk of gradually eroding the fundamental rights and freedoms of Canadians, including privacy rights. Thus, there are increased demands on police to balance investigative approaches with the constitutional rights and freedoms of all Canadians.

Trend 5: An Increase in the Numbers of Volunteers Involved in Policing

Citizen volunteers play an important role in policing today, and police departments rely upon civilian volunteers to staff community police offices and to assist in crime prevention efforts. Volunteers also play an integral role in victim services and mediation programs, and as police reservists and auxiliaries. Police reserves and auxiliaries also assist in managing the workload of police services. With the aging of the Canadian population, it is anticipated retiring baby boomers will seek meaningful volunteer opportunities in greater numbers, which offers the opportunity for further reductions in crime and disorder and at very low cost. This trend requires police services and police officers to develop skills in recruiting, screening, training, deploying, supervising, and retaining volunteers. It also requires police services to establish the parameters of the work that volunteers are allowed to do, and the information to which volunteers have access, and to ensure that the necessary controls are in place to maintain the privacy of community residents, the confidentiality of files and records, and the security of sensitive information and firearms. We will address this most important component of community policing in Chapter 10.

Trend 6: Increasing Collaboration between Police Services and Other Agencies and Community Organizations

The reduction in fiscal resources available to police services, combined with the emphasis on establishing police–community partnerships within the framework of community policing, has resulted in the increased involvement of the private sector and community organizations in a variety of police activities. In communities across the country, businesses and service clubs sponsor a wide variety of crime prevention programs. To establish effective partnerships with the community, police services and their officers must acquire the skills to work closely with the community, identify areas for collaboration and co-operation, and define the parameters of community involvement.

Police services must often walk a fine line between soliciting and encouraging community support for and assistance with crime prevention activities, and ensuring that the integrity and autonomy of the police are maintained. Considerable controversy, for example, has surrounded the decision of the RCMP to use vehicles donated by local car dealerships for their operational patrol—a practice that has generally been avoided by independent municipal police services and provincial police services. This raises questions about the limits of police–community partnerships, an issue we will examine further in Chapter 10 (see pp. 306–308).

In an attempt to maximize resources, many police services have entered into collaborative arrangements with government ministries and agencies. This includes the use of integrated service teams in which police officers work with their counterparts in other social service and health areas to address problems. For example, a number of municipalities have paired police officers with social workers to respond to children at risk issues. **Integrated service delivery** is part of the evolving model we describe as **community-based strategic policing**, and evidence of these arrangements can be found in every jurisdiction across Canada. In Alberta, for example, a number of integrated police teams are funded under the umbrella of the Alberta Law Enforcement Response Team (ALERT). Nationally integrated proceeds of crime units (IPOCs) targeting money-laundering and criminal organizations, integrated market enforcement units (IMETs) serving to maintain the integrity of Canadian capital markets, and integrated border enforcement units (IBETs) protecting the Canadian–American border all illustrate integrated policing strategies.

Trend 7: Community Policing 2.0—The Virtual Community

Harnessing social media technologies has created new opportunities for both the police and community and may be transforming the way the community reports crime and the way police services respond to it. For police services the strategic advantages of social media include community notifications, crime detection, and crime solving. Almost all police services today make use of social media, whether through Facebook, blogs, Twitter, YouTube, or MySpace. In addition, police services are increasingly using social media to identify criminals and solve crimes. Communicating through social networks can assist in strengthening police–community relations, particularly through police service–endorsed blogs, wikis, and tweets. However, social media can also be used to frustrate law enforcement efforts by identifying the location of speed traps and Check Stop locations. While the use of social media by police services has a number of advantages, there are risks as well. Police services must ensure communication with communities does not violate professional codes of police conduct, and they must be careful that crime reporting through social media does not become a substitute for 9-1-1 emergency calls. Finally, it is important to evaluate the impact of social media in relation to citizen perceptions of crime and personal safety. For example, a tweet reporting social disorder such as an aggressive panhandler can reach thousands of people, which could cause some people to become fearful of their environment. While we identified the need for police to be mindful of Canadians' right to privacy, the same considerations do not apply to private citizens who record the activities of others and themselves and then upload them to social media. It appears millions of Canadians regularly relinquish concerns they may have about privacy in favour of social networking. The use of social media may very well be a game changer as it relates to community policing, which is why we call it "community policing 2.0."

Trend 8: Emerging Crime and a Broadened Police Mandate

Since September 11, 2001, Canadian police have been under additional pressure to add an increasing number of security functions to their traditional crime control/ enforcement mandate. This has contributed to shifts in the mandate, structure, and operations of police organizations. The growing security mandate subtly changes the way in which police services are delivered while also affirming more of a surveillance role for the community, who are now tasked with performing a surveillance role over suspect communities (Murphy 2005). All of this contributes to elevated levels of fear, the very same circumstance that the traditional model of community policing was intended to reduce.

While 9-11 has broadened the mandate of policing to adopt a stronger focus on security, a development Murphy (2005) describes as the "securitization of policing," immigration is resulting in the social isolation of some new Canadians, particularly refugees. Without sufficient resources and supports in place, some individuals may be at increased risk for committing crime. Whether new Canadian or not, social distancing or social isolation also plays a role in the process of radicalization, where individuals plan acts of terrorism domestically. The police must perform a key role in monitoring the activities of these types of individuals.

Emerging forms of crime include mass marketing fraud and a variety of cyber crimes including child exploitation, cyber-stalking, and identity theft. One need only look at the names and titles of new legislation to fully understand emerging crimes and the Canadian response to them. For example, the Parliament of Canada website (www.parl.gc.ca) lists the following new legislative acts: Bill C-2, *An Act to Amend the Criminal Code* (mega-trials); Bill C-49, *Preventing Human Smugglers from Abusing Canada's Immigration System Act*; and Bill C-10, *Safe Streets and Communities Act*. While there are many more, these new legislative acts highlight Canadian efforts to criminalize new types of crime.

Trend 9: Adoption of Business-Like Corporate Models and Best Practices by Police Services

The requirement that police services do more work more efficiently with fewer resources has provided the catalyst for a transformation in the organizational structure and operations of many police services. For example, police services are adopting private-sector principles and establishing administrative and operational structures within a corporate framework. Among the key components of the corporate model of police organization are the creation of mission and vision statements, the identification of organizational values and objectives, and the development of a capacity for short- and long-term strategic planning and evaluation frameworks to assess effectiveness and efficiency of service delivery. Much of this development is due to technology which has significantly enhanced police services business intelligence. Terms such as *efficiency, effectiveness, client service, total quality management (TQM), Six Sigma, balanced scorecard,* and *risk management* are frequently used by police services and reflect the use of a corporate model. We will examine how these approaches have been implemented in police services that have adopted a community policing framework in Chapters 7 and 8.

Trend 10: The Changing Face of Policing

One of Peel's principles was that the public are the police and the police are the public. This includes the requirement that police services reflect the diversity of the communities they police. You will recall that one of the principles of policing in Ontario, as set out by the *Police Services Act,* is that police forces must be representative of the communities they serve. Today's police recruit is older (the average age of recruits in the Ontario Police College is 28); more likely to be a woman or a member of a cultural or ethnic minority, or both; more likely to speak a language other than English (or French); and has a college or university degree. These changes in the composition of police services blend well with a key principle of community policing: police services should reflect the diversity of the communities they serve. The relative merits of this approach will be examined in Chapter 8 in our discussion of the community police officer.

Trend 11: The Rise of Private Security and Collaborative Policing

Private security officers in Canada outnumber public police officers by a ratio of 3 to 2 (Statistics Canada 2008b). This pattern has been unchanged for the last decade: according to the 2006 Canadian Census survey there were 101,525 private security personnel compared with 63,000 police officers. While public police services are facing cutbacks because of the government's attempts to reduce costs, the private security industry is growing rapidly. Between 2001 and 2006, private security grew by 15 percent compared to an overall growth of 3 percent in police officers. The increase in the number of private security officers—sometimes called "rent-a-cops" or "robo-cops"—has been precipitated by a number of factors, including the downsizing of police services, the increase in privately owned public spaces such as shopping malls, and the perception by business and property owners that the public police do not have the resources to serve them effectively. In addition, approximately 30 percent of private investigators and 25 percent of private security guards work for municipal, provincial, and federal governments (Centre of Criminology 1996:12–13).

In some venues, such as sporting events and concerts, private security officers and police officers may work together in a collaborative arrangement. Any community policing strategies developed by a police department must include plans for co-operating with private security firms and must address the suspicion with which private security firms are often viewed by police services.

Police unions across the country have expressed concerns about the entry of private security firms into areas that were traditionally the responsibility of the police. For police unions, private security is viewed largely as an unregulated, unaccountable industry that is guided by the private interests of corporate clients. Some provinces, like Ontario, Alberta, and British Columbia, have addressed these concerns through the development of a legislated regulatory framework for private security. For example, security personnel in Ontario must be licensed under the *Private Security & Investigative Services Act* (2005).

Despite these concerns, private security is quickly establishing itself as a legitimate low-cost alternative to paying for the high costs of police officers. There is a growing recognition among police agencies and governments that private security represents an integral component to ensuring public safety. Private security is now often referred to as "private policing" and one of the emerging issues is to sort out how a model of community-based strategic policing incorporates both public and private policing into an effective service delivery model. We will address this point in greater detail later.

Trend 12: Increasing Accountability of the Police

One of the most important dimensions of community-based policing is the accountability of the police service to the community. The police are responsible for the services they provide to the community as well as for their conduct within the community. The days when police officers were viewed as being beyond reproach, and when community residents were reluctant to complain about the actions of the police that were perceived to be unfair, inappropriate, or unlawful, are over. There are both legislative and administrative frameworks for holding Canadian police officers accountable for their actions. The *Canadian Charter of Rights and Freedoms* has had a significant impact on police work; since its enactment there have been a number of major decisions by the Supreme Court of Canada (so-called Charter cases) that have further defined the role and powers of the police.

Police officers can be held accountable under the *Criminal Code* as well as under civil and administrative law for their actions. For example, the police have been held civilly liable for negligent investigations and both negligent supervision and retention of employees. The various provincial police acts also set out mechanisms and procedures to oversee and review the actions and decisions of police officers. One of the most significant recent developments is the Supreme Court of Canada's decision in *R. v. McNeil* (2009), which requires police services to release a police officer's disciplinary records to defence counsel prior to criminal prosecutions.

Police services and their employees are also held accountable by coroner's inquests or fatality inquiries and by human rights boards and commissions. In addition, freedom of information legislation has also established a heightened level of accountability in relation to police records and their management.

Trend 13: A Focus on Leadership and Professionalism

Historically, police services have given little attention to issues of leadership and professionalism. Promotion and security were a function of longevity rather than of education level attained and specific qualifications and achievements. Today, the rigours of policing require police leaders who possess skills in management, administration, and public relations, as well as a global perspective. As a result, there has been an increased emphasis on the need to train police leaders of all ranks, and this has increased the mobility of police professionals. Police agencies are committed to lifelong continuous learning and educational requirements are being established for senior officers in several Canadian police agencies. The Canadian Association of Chiefs of Police, for example, plays a major role in strengthening the professionalism and leadership skills of senior police personnel by providing research and policy direction on major policing issues as well a commitment to ongoing continuous learning through conferences, information sharing, and advocating legislative reforms.

A number of programs, seminars, and courses are designed to strengthen the leadership skills of police officers. Many of these programs focus on executive development of police leaders and include seminars through the Canadian Police College, the Rotman Police Leadership Program. Outside of Canada, police executives receive leadership training through the FBI National Executive Institute, the Senior Management Institute for Policing sponsored by Police Executive Research Forum (PERF) in Washington, D.C., and the National Policing Improvement Agency in Great Britain.

Also, as part of the move toward increasing professionalism, there has been an increased emphasis on accreditation by the U.S. Commission on Accreditation for Law Enforcement Agencies (CALEA). This process involves evaluating a police service on a number of standardized criteria relating to the management, administration, and delivery of services. Among the police services that have been accredited are the Peel Regional Police and the Winnipeg and Edmonton Police Services.

Trend 14: The Changing Structure of Police Organizations

Community policing is perhaps the most significant development in Canadian policing in the past half-century and has resulted in profound changes in how police services are organized. The traditional police organization was premised on a hierarchical, paramilitary model with very distinct lines of command and control. With the advent of community policing, there has been a "flattening" of police organizations, caused in part by the decentralization of power and the increasing authority and autonomy being given to line officers. We will examine the organizational changes that have occurred (and are occurring) in police services in Chapter 7 and 8.

CHAPTER SUMMARY

This chapter should get you thinking about Canadian policing, the various contexts in which police officers carry out their duties, and some of the more important trends arising in policing today. All these items have significant implications for the development and implementation of community policing strategies and programs. The currently evolving model of policing is more accurately described as community-based strategic policing because the demands on policing require police work to be delivered in strategic ways. Now, two centuries later, things have come full circle: police services are actively soliciting the involvement of communities in preventing and responding to crime and social disorder, and communities are taking steps to ensure that police officers are held accountable for their actions.

CHAPTER REVIEW

Key Terms
- *Adequacy and Effectiveness of Police Services Regulation*, p. 33
- *Canadian Charter of Rights and Freedoms*, p. 31
- community-based strategic policing, p. 40
- *Constitution Act, 1982*, p. 31
- governance, p. 27
- Integrated Justice System Initiative, p. 34

- integrated service delivery, p. 40
- *Police Services Act* (Ontario), p. 20
- Professional Standards, p. 27

Key Points

- There are four levels of policing: federal, provincial and territorial, municipal, and First Nations.
- The various contexts within which police officers carry out their tasks provide both opportunities and challenges for community policing.
- Community-based policing has become the primary framework for the delivery of police services and considerable pressures require police service to be delivered more strategically.
- Trends in police work, including the need to do more with less, the increasing diversity of police services, and the changes that are occurring in police organizations, are related to and affect community policing.
- The police are responsible for the services they provide to the community as well as for their conduct within the community. Accountability of the police service to the community is one of the most important dimensions of community-based policing.

Self-Evaluation

QUESTIONS

1. Why has the ***Canadian Charter of Rights and Freedoms*** had a profound impact on Canadian police work?
2. What is the ***Constitution Act, 1982***, and why is it important in our study of policing?
3. What are the key sections of Ontario's ***Police Services Act***?
4. Discuss the mechanisms that exist in Canada to ensure **police accountability**.
5. What is Canada's **Integrated Justice Information Initiative** and what are its objectives?
6. State the two key pieces of **legislation** that provide the framework for police services in the province of Ontario. Explain the purpose of these pieces of legislation.
7. Explain why is it necessary to continually examine the **contemporary roles of the police**.
8. What is **community-based strategic policing**, and how is it different from earlier community-based policing?
9. Explain how recent changes in the **crime context** have resulted in a change in policing.
10. Reflect upon the **trends in policing**. What developments are occurring in Canadian society that will likely result in new trends in policing?

KEY IDEAS

1. At which level of policing do most Canadian police officers work?
   a. municipal police services
   b. provincial police services
   c. federal police services
   d. police support services, such as information systems

2. Which statement describes Aboriginal police services and their officers?
   a. They operate exclusively under the supervision of the RCMP.
   b. They do not have the same authority and power as municipal police, provincial police, and RCMP.
   c. They are autonomous and have full power and authority to enforce all laws, including the *Criminal Code*, on reserve lands.
   d. They are responsible and accountable to the National Aboriginal Police Commission.

3. What is set out in the *Canadian Charter of Rights and Freedoms*?
   a. the responsibilities of the federal and provincial governments in the area of criminal justice
   b. the criminal laws and procedures for the administration of justice
   c. the jurisdiction of the *Criminal Code* and the *Bill of Rights*
   d. basic rights and freedoms for citizens

4. Which trend is indicated by statistics on Canadian crime?
   a. There is an upward trend in reported crime.
   b. There has been a decline in reported crime.
   c. The rates of violent crime have shown an upward trend.
   d. Property crimes have increased.

5. Why did the government create the *Constitution Act, 1982*?
   a. to establish the responsibilities of the federal and provincial governments in the area of criminal justice
   b. to establish the civil laws of Canada
   c. to establish the criminal laws of Canada
   d. to establish legislation that applies only to the RCMP and other federal agencies

6. What do statistics on visible minorities indicate?
   a. Most new arrivals in Canada settle in rural rather than in urban areas.
   b. Visible minorities, as a percentage of the population, have been declining.
   c. Immigrants to Canada tend to settle in urban areas.
   d. Most visible minorities live in the province of Quebec.

7. Which statement is characteristic of private security officers in Canada?
   a. They outnumber public police officers.
   b. They are permitted to wear side arms.
   c. They have no powers of arrest or detention.
   d. They operate under the supervision of public police services.

8. Which of the following describes community-based strategic policing?
   a. an evolving model of policing in Canada
   b. the community's response to taking over its own policing needs
   c. a new policing initiative run by the federal government
   d. the current model of policing

9. In Ontario, what was the Integrated Justice System Initiative designed to do?
   a. prosecute individuals who have committed crimes throughout the province
   b. coordinate drug trafficking offences and other serious crimes
   c. facilitate a seamless flow of information among justice agencies
   d. provide direction to police services in the area of charge approval

10. Which statement best defines the "growing crisis in human resources"?
    a. the inability for police to attract women and visible minorities into policing
    b. the requirement for police agencies to establish summer police camps and cadet programs
    c. the trend for new police officers to select specialty sections over general duty patrol
    d. the need for recruitment and retention of police officers

11. The SIU in Ontario is perhaps the best example in Canada of which of the following concepts?
    a. how policing has changed since September 11, 2001
    b. external civilian review of police activities
    c. a specialized policing unit
    d. the contemporary role of policing

12. What is a defining characteristic of professional standards units within police agencies?
    a. They ensure adequate dress and deportment levels.
    b. They provide direction to the community on levels of police response.
    c. They investigate alleged misconduct on the part of officers.
    d. They ensure that police applicants can meet recruit entry expectations.

EXERCISES: KNOWLEDGE INTO PRACTICE

Exercise 1. The Images of Policing

Consider the images of the police presented on television shows and in the movies. Make a list using the table below to compare these images with the contemporary roles of the police and with the types of activities in which the police in your home community were/are involved. Why is there a discrepancy between what the police actually do and the image that is presented of them?

Image of Police in Media	Actual Police Activity
1.	
2.	
3.	
4.	
5.	

Why the discrepancy? _____

_____

_____

_____

_____

Do you think the image of policing on TV could have implications for police officers themselves in terms of how they define themselves and their role?

_____

_____

_____

_____

_____

Exercise 2. Regional Police Services

A predominant feature of policing in Eastern Canada is the existence of regional police services. Research suggests that regional police forces are efficient in a number of ways, including reduced per capita policing costs, increased police coverage, higher clearance rates, and increased flexibility in deploying officers. Critics counter that there are often organizational and operational difficulties associated with amalgamating police services and that the size of regional forces makes community policing difficult. What is your view?

_____

_____

_____

_____

Exercise 3: The Relationship between Community Policing and Internal Affairs Investigations

What do you think is the relationship between community policing and the public's trust in the police to investigate complaints against themselves? In parts of Canada where the relationship between police and visible minorities is strained, how essential is it to try to improve this relationship? What can the police and the community both gain by positive and collaborative relationships? Structure your answer using the key terms of *accountability* and *legitimacy*. If you live in a community where the police have resorted to the use of deadly force against a visible minority, use this as an example in your answer.

_____

_____

_____

_____

_____

REFERENCES

Centre for Criminal Justice Research. 2005. *A 30-Year Analysis of Police Service Delivery and Costing: E Division.* British Columbia: Centre for Criminal Justice Research.

Centre of Criminology, University of Toronto. 1996. *A Preliminary Information Review and Gap Analysis of the Public Policing Sector in Canada.* Ottawa: Human Resources Development Canada.

Commission for Public Complaints Against the RCMP. 2009. *Police Investigating Police Final Public Report.* Ottawa: CPC.

Metropolitan Toronto Police. 1996. *1996 Environmental Scan and 1997–98 Service Goals and Objectives.* Toronto: Corporate Planning, Metropolitan Toronto Police.

Mitchell, A. 1997. "Face of Canada Changes." *The Globe and Mail.* November 5:A1.

Murphy, C. 2005. "Securitizing Community Policing: Towards a Canadian Public Policing Model." *The Canadian Review of Policing Research* 1:1–30.

Ontario. 1990. *Police Services Act,* Revised Statutes of Ontario, Chapter P.15.

R. v. McNeil [2009] SCC 3.

Statistics Canada. 2005. "Exploring Crime Patterns in Canada, 2005." *Crime and Justice Research Paper Series.* Cat. No. 85-561-MIE2005005. Ottawa: Statistics Canada, Canadian Centre for Justice Statistics.

Statistics Canada. 2007a. "Immigration in Canada: A Portrait of the Foreign-born Population." *2006 Census.* Cat. No. 97-557-XIE. Ottawa: Statistics Canada.

Statistics Canada. 2007b. "Portrait of the Canadian Population in 2006." *2006 Census.* Cat. No. 97-550-XIE. Ottawa: Statistics Canada.

Statistics Canada. 2008a. "Aboriginal Peoples in Canada in 2006: Inuit, Métis and First Nations." *2006 Census.* Cat. No. 97-558-XIE. Ottawa: Statistics Canada.

Statistics Canada. 2008b. *Private Security and Public Policing, 2006.* Cat. No. 85-002-X, 28(10). Ottawa: Statistics Canada, Canadian Centre for Justice Statistics.

Statistics Canada. 2010. *Projections of the Diversity of the Canadian Population 2006 to 2031.* Cat. No. 91-551-X. Ottawa: Statistics Canada.

Statistics Canada. 2011a. *Annual Demographic Estimates: Canada, Provinces and Territories.* Cat. No. 91-215-X. Ottawa: Statistics Canada.

Statistics Canada. 2011b. "Homicide in Canada." *Juristat.* Cat. No. 85-002-X. Ottawa: Statistics Canada.

Statistics Canada. 2011c. *Police-Reported Crime Statistics in Canada, 2010.* Cat. No. 85-002-X. Ottawa: Statistics Canada, Canadian Centre for Justice Statistics.

Statistics Canada. 2011d. *Police Resources in Canada, 2011.* Cat. No. 85-225-X. Ottawa: Statistics Canada, Canadian Centre for Justice Statistics.

Statistics Canada. 2012. *Police-Reported Crime in Canada, 2011.* Cat. No. 85-002-X. Ottawa: Statistics Canada. Canadian Centre for Justice Statistics.

Toronto Police Service. 2011. "Planning for the Future: Scanning the Toronto Environment." Retrieved May 18, 2012, (http://www.torontopolice.on.ca/publications/files/reports/2011envscan.pdf).

UNIT

2

Understanding Community Policing

What Is Community Policing?

Community policing is a philosophy, an attitude, and an organizational strategy that promotes a partnership between the people in the community and their police service. Together, as equal partners, the police and the community must work toward solving neighbourhood problems related to crime, fear of crime, and social and physical disorder—looking beyond differences and improving the overall quality of life in the community.

Source: Courtesy of Corunna Community Police Committee

Learning Objectives

After completing this chapter, you should be able to:

- Describe the traditional model of police work,

- Discuss measures of police effectiveness,

- Define and identify the principles of community policing,

- Compare the key features of traditional police practice and community policing,

- Describe community-based strategic policing,

- Discuss the evolution of community policing in Ontario,

- Discuss the key sections of Ontario's *Police Services Act* related to community policing, and

- Identify the key players in community policing.

INTRODUCTION

To maintain at all times relationship with the public that gives reality to the historic tradition that the police are the public and the public are the police; the police being only members of the public who are paid to give full-time attention to duties which are incumbent upon every citizen, in the interest of community welfare and existence.
—Sir Robert Peel, First Commissioner of the Metropolitan Police in London, England, 1829

Community policing has become one of the most widely used catchphrases in the criminal justice system and in policing circles. Hundreds of books, articles, and reports have been written on the topic by university scholars and government agencies, and by police services themselves.

A primary objective of this chapter is to sort through the tangle of materials that exist about community policing and to identify what community policing is and, as importantly, what it is not. We will consider the principles of community policing and see how police services implement strategies and programs that increase police–community collaboration while at the same time enhancing traditional approaches. We will also identify the key partners in the community policing model and provide background information on each. This will be important information to keep in mind because we will examine these partners throughout the remainder of the text. Finally, we will conclude the chapter with an explanation of how and why community policing is evolving to a higher stage, which we introduced in Chapter 2, called community-based strategic policing.

At the outset of our discussion, it is helpful to consider the **traditional or professional model of policing**, from which community policing has evolved.

THE TRADITIONAL OR PROFESSIONAL MODEL OF POLICING

The traditional, or professional, model of police work is based on several key principles. These include the following:

- Police officers are the professionals who have sole responsibility for crime control.
- The objectives of police work are legally defined and involve responding to calls that involve criminal incidents.
- The role of the police officer is to control crime, and this role is carried out by way of preventative patrol and rapid response times.
- The police tend not to work in conjunction with community residents or other agencies.
- Police services are centralized.
- Decision making occurs through a hierarchical command and control structure (Kelling and Moore 1988; Murphy 1995).

Traditional Patrol Practice: The Three Rs

Traditional models of patrol practice are premised on the **three Rs**: random patrol, rapid response, and reactive investigation. The central premise of random patrol, also known as the **watch system**, is that the mere presence of patrol cars serves as a deterrent to crime and increases citizens' feeling of safety. Patrol officers spend their shifts responding to calls, and the remaining time is spent patrolling randomly, waiting for the next call for service. This traditional approach to police work is:

- *incident oriented:* the primary focus is on responding to specific incidents, calls, cases, or events;
- *response oriented:* police management and operations are oriented to responding to events as they arise, response capacity and capability are emphasized, and little time and few resources are devoted to proactive intervention or prevention activities;

- *focused on limited analysis*: as rapid response and the availability of resources are top priority, information gathering is limited to specific situations and does not include analysis of the causes of events; and
- *focused on the means rather than the end*: the emphasis on response efficiency means that little significance is placed on the impact of police strategies of preventing, reducing, or eliminating problems (Oppal 1994).

Traditionally, police officers have been deployed in teams, platoons, and watches. This has meant that:

- patrol officers work the same shift rotation;
- patrol operations are based on a hierarchical and centralized "military" model of policing;
- there is an emphasis on command and control principles; and
- there is a narrow range of police response options.

Although this approach provides for better supervision of field patrol officers, it has a number of problems, including:

- insensitivity to community needs: officers deployed to one neighbourhood during a shift rotation are not redeployed to the same neighbourhood on the next rotation;
- creativity is stifled among front-line police officers; and
- policing becomes internally focused rather than having an external community focus.

In the words of retired Edmonton police inspector Chris Braiden, "Traditional police work becomes an unknown police officer patrolling familiar buildings and unfamiliar faces."

Traditional Police Practice: How Effective Is It?

The reactive battle against crime and other community needs has been soundly lost.
—Chief J. Harding, Halton Regional Police Service (Retired)

Within the traditional model of police work, effectiveness is determined by response times and the **clearance rate**. This rate is the percentage of cases in which an offence has been committed and a suspect identified, regardless of whether the suspect is ultimately convicted of the crime.

Another measure often used to assess the effectiveness of the police is the crime rate. However, a rising crime rate can reflect either good or poor police performance: when the official crime rate goes down, the police are generally credited with doing a good job; when the crime rate goes up, the police are seen as doing a poor job. However, an increase in the official crime rate could indicate good police performance, both in terms of more calls being reported by a supportive public and more criminals being apprehended. This is a bit confusing, to say the least, and it's one more reason why police performance should not be based solely on crime-control measures.

Clearance Rates as a Measure of Police Effectiveness

There are a number of reasons why clearance rates should not be used as the only indicator of **police effectiveness**. These include the following:

- *Police officers do not spend most of their time chasing criminals*. Most of their time is spent on non-enforcement situations revolving around maintaining order, providing services, and preventing crime. Today, the movement toward restorative justice approaches, which we will talk about later, places less weight on laying charges.

- *The crime rate should be interpreted carefully to determine the effectiveness of the police.* If there is an increase in the official rate of crime in a community, does that mean that the police are (a) ineffective, which is why the crime rate went up, or (b) effective, with the official crime rate being an indicator that the police are catching more criminals? A number of research studies have found the police have very little impact on the crime rate.
- *Not all police officers serve in the same types of communities.* While some officers are assigned to remote and rural areas, others work in suburban and urban areas. The specific levels and types of crime in these areas vary as well, which means that police officers are confronted with different types of problems and situations.
- *Not all police officers are engaged in the same type of police work.* Some officers work out of community police stations; others work in specialty units such as the gang squad and the auto theft task force. This makes it even more unrealistic to use only one single measure of police effectiveness.

Because the police play a variety of roles in the community and engage in a wide range of activities, we need to consider other ways of measuring their effectiveness. This is particularly important with the adoption of a community policing model, which pays a considerable amount of attention to preventing crimes, rather than merely reacting to them.

The Effectiveness of Random, Reactive Patrol

Research studies over the past decade have continued to cast doubt on the effectiveness of random patrol, which is the cornerstone of traditional models of policing and remains at the core of most police services today. Similarly, questions have been raised about the effectiveness of rapid response and the preventive value of reactive arrests. One critic of random patrol suggested it makes as much sense as firefighters patrolling for fires. Check out Box 3.1 for an assessment of the three Rs of the traditional service delivery model.

It is important that the traditional model of police work not be set up as a "straw man" for the discussion of community policing. The material presented in Unit 4 will reveal that many of the strategies and programs implemented within the community policing framework have either proven to be less effective than originally anticipated or have not been adequately evaluated to determine their effectiveness. This suggests that the challenges facing Canadian police are varied and that no single approach to crime and social disorder is effective.

The Persistence of Traditional Police Attitudes and Practices

Many police officers still carry out their duties within a traditional model of patrol practice. In many respects, this is a product of the calls for service faced by modern police officers, leading some observers to refer to officers as "9-1-1 cops." Officers and senior personnel in many police services complain that they are too busy responding to calls to shift their focus to a problem-solving, community-based approach, despite the fact that random, preventive patrol does not contribute to the reduction of crime and disorder or foster partnerships with the community. Indeed, the persistence of this model of patrol may also be a major contributor to low officer morale and high levels of career dissatisfaction; police officers do not see positive results from their work.

While the deterrent value of random patrol is limited, communities often complain about the lack of visible police presence. This is a difficult issue for police services to resolve.

Later in this chapter, we will see that the implementation of community policing may have a positive effect on officer morale and levels of job satisfaction. However, as noted, we will also see that many community policing strategies have not produced the positive outcomes that had been anticipated and that the shift back to increasing contact with the community is more of an evolution of police work than a separate model of police work.

BOX 3.1

THE EFFECTIVENESS OF TRADITIONAL PATROL PRACTICE

Question: Does an increase in random police patrols have an impact on crime levels?

Answer: Probably not.

- Although the studies that have assessed this dimension of police crime prevention have many methodological problems, research generally has recorded no appreciable impact from an increase in random patrol.

- Directed or targeted patrol is effective.

Question: Is the response time of the police related to reductions in the level of crime?

Answer: Not likely.

- Reduced response time appears to have very little impact on the crime rate, due in large measure to the delays in initial reporting of crimes to the police.

Question: Is there any relationship between the number of arrests that the police make and the crime rate? In other words, do reactive arrests serve as a general deterrent to crime?

Answer: No.

- Reactive police arrests do not serve as a general deterrent to criminal activity. The exception may be in communities of under 10,000 residents, but even here the research findings are inconsistent.

Question: Is there any relationship between the reactive arrest of specific individuals and the crime rate? In other words, do reactive arrests function as a specific deterrent to crime?

Answer: Generally not, with a few possible exceptions.

- For many individuals, arrest increases subsequent reoffending.

- Targeting prolific offenders does prevent them from reoffending if they are held in custody.

- The impact of arrest varies with employment status: unemployed people who are arrested tend to reoffend; however, arrest appears to act as a deterrent for people who are employed.

Source: Sherman, L. et al., 1997. *Preventing Crime: What Works, What Doesn't, What's Promising.* Washington, DC: United States Department of Justice, National Institute of Justice.

OTHER WAYS TO MEASURE POLICE PERFORMANCE AND EFFECTIVENESS

In addition to the clearance rate, there are a number of measures that can be used both to assess the effectiveness of a police service and to more accurately reflect the broad range of activities that officers are involved in when doing police work. These include:

- the extent to which a police service has been successful in developing partnerships with the community;
- the experiences with and attitudes toward the police held by community residents, particularly members of cultural and ethnic minorities;
- the experiences and attitudes toward the police of crime victims;
- the ability of the police service to solve serious crimes that involve violence, have multiple victims, and create fear in the community;
- the extent to which senior police administrators use contemporary management practices, are familiar with the research and current techniques of policy formulation and application, and are able to provide leadership;
- the morale and attitudes of line police officers, who are the core of the police organization;

- the success of particular individual police officers or a particular unit in meeting specific goals and objectives, which in turn are defined by the specific nature of their work; and
- how the police service defines its core values and its ability to achieve organizational goals and objectives.

Can you think of others?

These indicators of performance are far broader and include much more than just a focus on crime levels and "catch" rates. In fact, these are the very types of indicators that are used in community policing. Community policing focuses on the role of the community in identifying, preventing, and responding to crime and disorder, so the extent to which local residents are effective in fulfilling their part of the police–community partnership is equally important (see Chapter 10 for more discussion on this matter). So, although community policing is not the opposite of the traditional model of police practice, it does broaden the role that the police are asked to play. It also expands the measures that are used to assess their effectiveness and efficiency.

WHAT IS COMMUNITY POLICING?

The "new" approach to policing that has recently begun to sweep through North America, Europe, and the major common law countries is community policing. Rather than being a new approach, however, it is more correctly a renewal or re-emergence of the old approach developed in Metropolitan London.*
— *A. Normandeau and B. Leighton (1990)*

Defining community policing is one thing; attempting to determine whether or not a police service is *doing* community policing, whether a policy or program falls within the framework of community policing, and, importantly, whether the participation of the community with the police constitutes a true partnership is often much more difficult. The term "community policing" has been used (and misused) to such an extent that there is a considerable amount of confusion on the part of both the public and the police as to what it actually means.

Over the past decade, the term has come to refer to both a philosophy of police work and an operational practice. So what exactly is it? And how do we know whether a police service is engaged in community policing? How do we know that the involvement of the community is substantive rather than superficial? What are the requirements of a true police–community partnership? One way in which we will address these questions is via a Community Policing Implementation Checklist, which is discussed below.

It is important to view community policing as more than what traditional policing is not. In other words, the definition of community policing must acknowledge the fact that this model of police work incorporates many elements of traditional police practice, while at the same time extending and expanding the role, activities, and objectives of police services and patrol officers.

Let's see if we can get our heads around the philosophy and practice of community policing. Remember, at this point we are identifying some of the key components of community policing—in subsequent chapters we will examine them in more detail. At the risk of sounding repetitive, a number of different explanations of community policing will be presented. Taken together, these should provide a good idea of the principles and practices of community policing. Keep in mind, however, that police services will implement the

*NORMANDEAU, A., & LEIGHTON, B. (1990). *A Vision of the Future of Policing in Canada: Police-Challenge 2000*: background document. [Ottawa], Police and Security Branch, Ministry Secretariat, Solicitor, Library and Archives Canada. Reproduced with the permission of the Minister of Public Works and Government Services, 2012.

The Citizens on Patrol program was initiated in Western Canada. Today there are Citizens on Patrol programs all across Canada, including the one depicted in this photo from the city of Côte Saint-Luc, Quebec.

Source: © City of Côte Saint-Luc

principles of community policing in a variety of ways and that community policing represents an evolution of the police role to address the increasingly complex issues of modern society. Ironically, as we have noted before, the principles set out by Sir Robert Peel in 1829 reflect the principles of community policing that are being set out nearly 200 years later. We are seeing today the re-emergence of community policing.

Community Policing Defined

For purposes of this text, we will use the following definition of **community policing**:

Community policing is a philosophy, management style, and organizational strategy centred on police–community partnerships and problem solving to address problems of crime and social disorder in communities.

Trojanowicz and Bucqueroux (1997:6) have broken the term "community policing" into three interrelated parts:

1. Community policing is a philosophy and an organizational strategy that promotes a new partnership between people and their police. It is based on the premise that both the police and the community must work together as equal partners to identify, prioritize, and solve contemporary problems such as crime, drugs, fear of crime, social and physical disorder, and overall neighbourhood decay with the goal of improving the overall quality of life in the area.
2. Community policing requires a department-wide commitment from everyone—sworn and civilian—to the community policing philosophy. It challenges all personnel to find ways to express this new philosophy in their jobs, thereby balancing the need to maintain an immediate and effective police response to individual crime incidents and emergencies with the goal of exploring new proactive initiatives aimed at solving problems before they occur or escalate.
3. Community policing rests on decentralizing and personalizing police service, so that line officers have the opportunity, freedom, and mandate to focus on community building and community-based problem solving, and so that each and every neighbourhood can become a better place in which to live and work.

These dimensions are reflected in the operational definition of community policing provided by the Halton Regional Police Service:

Community policing in Halton is a philosophy based on the concept that police officers and private citizens work together, in partnership, resulting in creative ways to solve community problems related to crime, fear of crime, social and physical order, and neighbourhood decay.

Let's take a closer look.

The Principles of Community Policing: The Three Ps

Community policing requires patrol officers to take a proactive, interventionist, problem-solving approach. This is captured in the "**three Ps**":

- prevention,
- problem solving, and
- partnership with the community.

We will explore each of these three building blocks of community policing throughout this book. At this point, however, the important point to note is that the three Ps are the building blocks on which community policing is built. Check out the 12 elements of community policing as identified by the Ministry of the Solicitor General in Box 3.2.

The Policy and Practice of Community Policing

In principle, policy, and practice, community policing is reactive, proactive, and coactive. Coactive refers to the police–community partnerships that are developed within the community police framework. More specifically, community policing:

- *Reassesses who is responsible for public safety and redefines the roles and relationships between the police and the community.* The community is identified as both the source of problems of crime and disorder and as having a key role to play in preventing and responding to these problems.
- *Requires shared ownership, decision making, and accountability, as well as a sustained commitment from both the police and the community.* The police must acknowledge they cannot solve community problems on their own, and the community must become empowered to take responsibility for community safety and well-being.
- *Establishes new public expectations of and measurement standards for police effectiveness.* Community policing focuses the attention and efforts of the police on developing partnerships to facilitate collaborative intervention, rather than merely reacting to incidents. Measures of police performance are expanded beyond crime control indices, such as 9-1-1 statistics and arrest/crime statistics, to include quality of service, customer (community) satisfaction, responsiveness to issues identified by the community, and cultural sensitivity.
- *Increases understanding and trust between police and community leaders.* Police services become directed toward community needs and concerns, and officers are assigned to specific geographic zones, which provides them with the opportunity to develop relationships with the business and residential communities.
- *Empowers and strengthens community-based efforts.* Community organizations and residents are provided the opportunity to develop substantive partnerships with the police, centred on solving problems.
- *Requires constant flexibility to respond to all emerging issues.* This includes the expansion of alternatives for prevention and intervention available to the police, including restorative and community justice.
- *Requires an ongoing commitment to developing long-term and proactive strategies and programs to address the underlying conditions that cause community problems.* This

BOX 3.2

THE ELEMENTS OF COMMUNITY POLICING

1. Police officers are **peace** officers rather than just law enforcement officers. Police organizations are a **service** to the community for crime and social disorder problems, rather than a force focused primarily on crime.

2. **Community consultation** is a key strategy designed to identify short-term priorities for addressing crime and social disorder and to secure, in the longer term, a reaffirmation of the police mandate from the public.

3. There is a **proactive approach** to policing, whereby the police can anticipate demands for service by identifying local problems of crime and social disorder. This is accomplished by the use of techniques such as scanning and forecasting (to be discussed in Chapter 5 [see page 123]).

4. A **problem-oriented policing strategy** combines reactive, proactive, and coactive approaches to address the underlying causes of crime and social disorder.

5. Crime prevention initiatives focus on **responding to underlying causes of problems**.

6. **Interagency co-operation** involves the police developing strategic partnerships with social service agencies and community organizations.

7. Police personnel function as **information managers** and engage in interactive policing by routinely exchanging information with community members.

8. Strategies are used to **reduce unfounded fears of victimization**, particularly among children, the elderly, and vulnerable groups in the community.

9. Police officers are permitted to become career **generalists** rather than specialists and are responsible for a broader range of activities than was permitted under the professional model of police work.

10. Front-line police officers are given **greater responsibility and autonomy** to identify and address problems of crime and social disorder.

11. The **changed organizational structure** of a flat structure with front-line officers assuming primary importance replaces the traditional hierarchical, paramilitary organizational model.

12. There is increased **accountability to the community** through ongoing public consultation and structures and through procedures for reviewing police officer conduct.

Source: NORMANDEAU, A., & LEIGHTON, B. (1990). *A Vision of the Future of Policing in Canada: Police-Challenge 2000:* background document. [Ottawa], Police and Security Branch, Ministry Secretariat, Solicitor, pp. 43–46, Library and Archives Canada. Reproduced with the permission of the Minister of Public Works and Government Services, 2012.

commitment, on the part of the police and the community, involves an assessment of community needs, the participation of all sectors of the community in formulating response strategies, and the redirection of available police and community resources to support the problem-solving strategy.

- *Requires knowledge of available community resources and how to access and mobilize them, as well as the ability to develop new resources within the community.* This ensures that there will not be duplication of effort between the police, other agencies, and community organizations and that maximum use will be made of available resources.
- *Requires a commitment from the top management of the police and other local government agencies, as well as a sustained personal commitment from all levels of management and other key personnel.* Skills of police leaders that are important include the ability to maintain a vision and manage through values rather than rules, to focus on teamwork,

to seek widespread input prior to making decisions, and to solicit feedback from offi-cers and the community on how policies and programs can be improved.

- *Decentralizes the operations and management of police services, relaxes the traditional "chain of command," and encourages innovation and creative problem solving.* In con-trast to traditional policing, community policing and problem solving are based on decentralized, community-based services driven from the bottom up, making full use of the knowledge, skills, and expertise found throughout the organization.
- *Shifts the focus of police work from responding to individual incidents to addressing problems identified by the community as well as by the police.* Problems, rather than incidents, are the central focus of community policing, and careful analysis of the problem precedes the development of specific responses.
- *Requires a commitment to developing new skills through training.* This training is pro-vided at all levels of the police organization, from senior police leaders to line officers. Police managers must learn new styles of leadership, based on consensus manage-ment, while line officers must be taught skills in problem analysis and problem solving, facilitation, community organization, communication, mediation and con-flict resolution, and networking, to name a few (Community Oriented Policing and Problem Solving [COPPS] Advisory Committee 1995:4–11).

What Community Policing Is Not

As we have noted, considerable confusion surrounds discussions of community policing. Often, community policing is offered as a polar opposite to traditional police practice. In fact, community policing incorporates many elements of traditional police work considered to be effective. One way to assist in clearing this up is to address what it is *not*. Among other things, community policing is not:

- a panacea for solving all of a community's problems of crime and disorder;
- a replacement for many traditional police services and crime-prevention strategies, including reactive police response and serious crime investigation;
- a single police initiative, although specific programs can be developed within a com-munity policing strategy;
- solely the responsibility of the police—rather, it requires a true (not symbolic) police–community partnership;
- a generic, "one size fits all" policing model that can be applied without adaptation to the specific needs of all individual communities across the country;
- a program or series of initiatives that can be appended or added onto existing police organizational structures; or
- a policing strategy appropriate for addressing all types of criminal activity.

Community policing is best viewed as the most recent phase in the evolution of police work that, ironically, has resulted in police services returning to the original roots of policing as set forth by Sir Robert Peel early in the 19th century. In fact, many police services and their officers, particularly in smaller communities, have always pur-sued a "no call too small" approach to policing. This approach has allowed officers to develop close relations with the community, to collaborate with residents in identifying and responding to problems of crime and social disorder, and to respond to the needs and concerns of residents. Unfortunately, as we shall see later, the "no call too small" full-service model of policing has become increasingly difficult to sustain, and it is now necessary to look for more strategic ways to deliver police service and ensure vital community–police partnerships.

It is important to point out, however, that the increasing sophistication and glo-balization of crime require that the police have access to the latest technologies as well as to officers who are technology-literate. The strategies for combating crimes committed over the Internet, for example, are considerably different from those required to implement community policing at the neighbourhood level. This suggests that over the next decade, urban police services will have to develop tactics and strategies which are responsive to community problems yet effective at responding to sophisticated criminal activity. Community policing is not a substitute for having the capability in a police service to fight the more sophisticated types of criminal activity.

TURNING PRINCIPLES INTO PRACTICE

Now that we have a good understanding of what community policing is (and, as importantly, what it is not), the next step is to examine how the principles of community policing actually play out.

- Within the framework of community policing:
    - citizens are actively responsible for policing their own neighbourhoods and communities;
    - the community is a source of operational information, crime-control knowledge, and strategic operations for the police;
    - the police are more directly accountable to the community;
    - police have a more proactive and preventive role in the community that goes beyond traditional law enforcement;
    - the cultural and gender composition of a police agency reflects the community that it serves; and
    - the organizational structure of the police agency facilitates broad consultation on strategic and policing issues.

- The objectives of community policing are:
    - greater police legitimacy and public acceptance: more responsive, less authoritarian, more inclusive;
    - increased police accountability: more open communication, consultation, and collaboration with the community;
    - more efficient use of police resources: new styles of police management, working relationships with the community, and use of community resources;
    - increased police effectiveness through innovative strategies: problem-oriented policing, intelligence-led policing, and preventive and proactive strategies;
    - decreased fear of crime and enhanced public safety: foot patrols, community police stations, and increased police presence and visibility;
    - increased job satisfaction and improved officer productivity: broadening operational responsibilities, reducing bureaucracy, and increasing autonomy of line officers; and
    - a reduction in the number of public complaints against the police.

- In terms of operations, community policing is:
    - customer oriented;
    - responsive to community needs;
    - open to input from citizens;
    - visible in the community;
    - available on the streets;
    - knowledgeable and interested in the neighbourhoods and their problems;
    - proactive in its approach; and
    - accountable for its actions (Oppal 1994:C-3, C-6, C-8).

Check back to Box 1.1 on page 8. Note the close resemblance between the principles of modern policing first identified by Sir Robert Peel in the early 1800s and the basic principles of community policing. Both are premised on the philosophy advocated by Peel: "The police are the public, the public are the police." Yet it is clear that community-based policing represents an expansion of the role and activities of the police beyond merely focusing on law enforcement.

Although community policing incorporates key elements of traditional police practice, there are points of comparison that can be made between the two. These are set out in Table 3.1.

The concept and principles of community policing are thus perhaps best viewed as constituting a philosophy based on improving the effectiveness and efficiency of police services and establishing partnerships in the communities to address problems of crime and disorder. How to implement the principles of community policing, how to measure whether the objectives have been achieved, and what specific initiatives are required on the part of the police and the community remain to be determined. This determination is best accomplished on a community-by-community basis, depending on the needs and requirements of the community in question and the outcomes of the dialogue between the police and community residents.

Table 3.1 Comparison of Traditional Policing and Community Policing

Question	Traditional	Community Policing
1. Who are the police?	A government agency principally responsible for law enforcement	Police are the public and the public are the police; police officers are those who are paid to give full-time attention to the duties of every citizen
2. What is the relationship between the police and other public service departments?	Priorities often conflict	The police are only one department among many responsible for improving the quality of life
3. What is the role of the police?	To solve crimes	To take a broader problem-solving approach
4. How is police efficiency measured?	By detection and arrest rates and by the absence of crime and disorder	By the absence of crime and disorder
5. What are the highest priorities?	Crimes that are high value, e.g., bank robberies and those involving violence	Whatever problems disturb the community the most
6. What, specifically, do the police deal with?	Incidents	Citizens' problems and concerns
7. What determines the effectiveness of the police?	Response times	Public co-operation
8. What view do police take of service calls?	Deal with them only if there is no real police work to do	Vital function and great opportunity
9. What is police professionalism?	Swift and effective response to serious crime	Keeping close to the community
10. What is the essential nature of police accountability?	Highly centralized; governed by rules, regulations, and policy directives; accountable to law	Emphasis on local accountability to community needs

Source: Comparison of Traditional Policing and Community Policing Implementing Community Policing, 1988 No 9. by Malcolm K. Sparrow (pg. 8–9)

Of course, the particular strategies that a police service develops to implement community policing will vary depending on the specific attributes of the community being policed, the demands made on the police, and the community's interest in and capacity for substantive involvement. As well, the strategies employed by a community to become an equal partner in preventing and responding to crime and disorder will depend on the capacities and fiscal resources that a community can commit to the endeavour, as well as on the levels of interest that exist among different segments of the community—often referred to as "community readiness."

COMMUNITY POLICING: ALL THINGS TO ALL PEOPLE?

Community policing holds considerable promise as a way to increase the effectiveness of the police, to involve the community significantly in the identification of and response to problems of crime and disorder, and to maximize police and community resources in times of fiscal restraint. It is important to acknowledge, however, that police organizations and their officers cannot be all things to all people. Priorities must be set. Police services must decide, ideally in consultation with communities, the private sector, and other governmental agencies, what they can do best and how they can assist governments and the community in developing alternative arrangements to deal with areas that are beyond the sole proprietorship of the police.

Communities must be made aware of the numerous challenges that confront police services and understand that choices must be made about the core role of the police. One fundamental question that must be addressed, for example, is whether the police are the most appropriate agency for resolving problems of disorder in the community or, given what we know about the multifaceted causes of crime, whether that task is best left to other agencies with a mandate to do community development (Findley and Taylor 1990:76). In the words of one chief of police: "It is ludicrous to relegate the police to the role, responsibility, and accountability for urban renewal and social reform" (Fantino 1996:21). This is certainly an issue that must be addressed as we enter a new era in policing.

Criticisms of Community Policing

Beyond the assertion that the police may not be the most appropriate agency to address social problems in the community, there are a number of additional criticisms that have been levelled against community policing. These include the following:

- *Community policing is too soft an approach to the prevention of and response to crime.* This statement reflects the view that community police officers are social workers in uniform, a view that conflicts with the traditional image of police as crime fighters.
- *Police services become beholden to communities.* This is the view that, if communities are provided the opportunity to participate as partners in preventing and responding to crime, the integrity and activities of the police will be compromised.
- *Community policing is not real policing.* This belief represents the clash between the traditional occupational subculture of the police and the new culture of community policing.
- *Community policing is nothing new—we have always done it.* There is considerable diversity in the size and specific organizational arrangements for carrying out police work across Canada. Many police officers—either out of necessity or because of their own personal style of policing—have always had close contacts with the community and have, as a result, solicited community participation. Police officers assigned to inner-city neighbourhoods with high rates of crime and social disorder as well as officers posted to remote areas must rely on both their professional skills and their individual resourcefulness to be effective in their work. These officers, while members of a highly centralized, hierarchical police service that has clear lines of command and control, are

very far removed from their organization. However, community policing represents a systematic approach to crime prevention and response that goes beyond the efforts of individual officers who embrace the ideals of being close to the communities they police.

- *It is too difficult to determine who and what the community is.* The community of the 21st century is different from its counterparts in earlier centuries—more diverse, more mobile, more tech savvy, more focused on accumulating wealth, and less interested in taking time to be part of a police–community partnership.

The successful development and implementation of community policing requires that the police and communities acknowledge and address these criticisms.

STRATEGIC PARTNERSHIPS AND COMMUNITY POLICING

A core component of community policing is the development of strategic partnerships. Transferring community policing from an abstract notion to actual practice requires a concerted effort on the part of a number of key players. Whereas under the traditional model of police practice it was the police who assumed the primary role in the design and delivery of police services, community policing involves a partnership between the police and the community.

A Partnership of the Key Players

The **key players in community policing** include elected officials, social and government agencies, managers, police officers, their unions and associations, and the community at large. Our discussion will focus on the managers and chief constables (Chapters 6 and 7), police officers (Chapter 8), and the community (Chapter 10). See Box 3.3 for a description of the key players.

A Partnership of Public Services

Community policing also provides the opportunity for partnerships between public services that traditionally have not collaborated with one another and that have pursued their own organizational goals and objectives. Public-service partnerships are able to develop a more integrated approach to addressing the underlying causes of crime and social disorder than the police acting alone. This is particularly true in the areas of unemployment, job training, housing, and the strengthening of social cohesion in communities. This approach is most commonly referred to as "crime prevention through social development" (CPSD) and will be considered later in the text.

Figure 3.1 depicts the partnerships that can be developed between public services within the framework of community policing, while Box 3.4 sets out the participants in each public service area.

COMMUNITY POLICING IN ONTARIO

Many police services across the country have struggled with how to alter the organization, administration, and delivery of policing services to incorporate the philosophy and principles of community policing. Individual police services have often been left on their own to develop the capacity for community policing and to develop partnerships with the community. The province of Ontario has established a legislated requirement for community policing, which is the focus of this section.

Ontario can be considered a leader in community policing, providing a supportive environment for municipal and regional police services and the Ontario Provincial Police (OPP) to implement the principles of community policing. Let's take a brief look at how community policing evolved in Ontario and the framework within which police

BOX 3.3

THE KEY PLAYERS IN COMMUNITY POLICING PARTNERSHIPS

I. Community Interest Groups

- Citizen, taxpayer, voter
- Media
- Associations
- Nongovernmental organizations
- Consultative committees
- Colleges, universities
- Volunteers
- Victims of crime
- Families, schools, churches
- Workplace
- Leisure milieux

II. Police Managers

- Police chiefs
- Police managers
- Public safety, private security

III. Police Officers

- Police unions or associations
- Rank-and-file police constables
- Public safety, private security

IV. Elected Officials

A. Municipal–Regional Government

- Mayors, municipal councillors
- Local boards of police commissioners

B. Provincial Government

- Ministers and provincial departments in charter of provincial police acts
- Police directorates in provincial departments (policy, program, research)
- Provincial police commissions

C. Federal Government

- Ministry of Public Safety Canada (formerly the Solicitor General of Canada), which oversees the Canada Border Services Agency (CBSA), Canadian Security Intelligence Service (CSIS), Correctional Service Canada (CSC), National Parole Board (NPB), and the Royal Canadian Mounted Police (RCMP)

- Department of Justice of Canada (minister and ministry) in charge of some dossiers: crime prevention, victims of crime, gun control, etc.

Source: NORMANDEAU, A., & LEIGHTON, B. (1990). *A Vision of the Future of Policing in Canada: Police-Challenge 2000*: background document. [Ottawa], Police and Security Branch, Ministry Secretariat, Solicitor, pp. 81–82, Library and Archives Canada. Reproduced with the permission of the Minister of Public Works and Government Services, 2012.

Figure 3.1 Community Policing: A New Partnership between Public Services

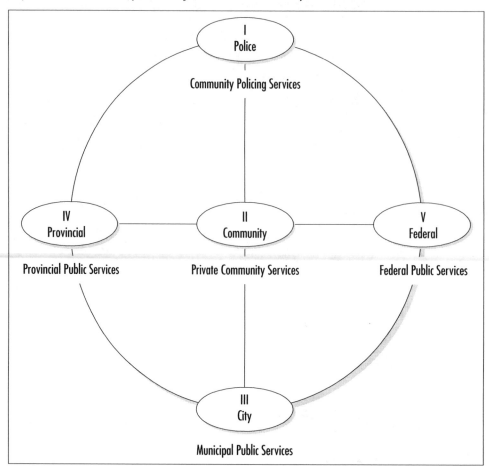

Source: NORMANDEAU, A., & LEIGHTON, B. (1990). *A Vision of the Future of Policing in Canada: Police-Challenge 2000*: background document. [Ottawa], Police and Security Branch, Ministry Secretariat, Solicitor, p.85, Library and Archives Canada. Reproduced with the permission of the Minister of Public Works and Government Services, 2012.

services across the province operate today. This will provide us with a good case study of how community policing has evolved (and continues to evolve) from the traditional or professional model of police work.

The Evolution of Community Policing in Ontario

The commitment to modern-day, community-based policing in Ontario can be traced back more than 30 years. In the early 1970s a task force examined the impact of technology on policing and found that it had tended to widen the gap between the police and the community (Task Force on Policing in Ontario 1974). Police dispatch centres, reliance on radios, and the police patrol vehicle all contributed to reduced contact between the police and the public. For example, although radios allowed officers to be dispatched more quickly to telephone requests for service, officers' attention shifted to cases that required immediate resolution. Traditionally, officers on foot patrol had spent a considerable portion of their time becoming familiar with the citizens and problems in the geographic areas they patrolled (Task Force 1974:25).

The task force also noted that policing in Ontario was heavily influenced by military personalities and military structures. The organization and management of police services was based on a military model, and included centralized command and control, a top-down model of management, and rank structures. Centralized command

BOX 3.4

THE PUBLIC-SERVICE PARTNERS

I. Community Policing Services

- Consultative committees: citizens–police

- Neighbourhood watch

- Business watch

- Victims' services

- Special projects

II. Private Community Services

- Families, schools, churches

- Workplace

- Leisure milieux

- Media

- Associations

- Victims' and community release services

- Special projects

III. Municipal Public Services

- Employment, housing, health

- Social services

- Parks, sports, leisure

- Cultural equipment (libraries, theatres, etc.)

- Environmental design

- Special projects

IV. Provincial Public Services

- Employment, housing, health

- Social services, education

- Justice and Solicitor General

- Courts and corrections

- Special projects

V. Federal Public Services

- Employment, housing, health

- Family allowances, unemployment insurance

- Justice and Ministry of Public Safety and Emergency Preparedness Canada

- Courts and corrections

- Special projects

Source: NORMANDEAU, A., & LEIGHTON, B. (1990). *A Vision of the Future of Policing in Canada: Police-Challenge 2000:* background document. [Ottawa], Police and Security Branch, Ministry Secretariat, Solicitor, pp. 86–87, Library and Archives Canada. Reproduced with the permission of the Minister of Public Works and Government Services, 2012.

and control are effective in emergency situations where clear lines of authority and communication are important; however, this structure is a key obstacle to the implementation of the principles of community policing. Rank structures may set out clear lines of accountability and function and thus increase stability within the organization, but this stability is achieved at the expense of flexibility to adapt to demands from the community.

A number of developments provided the impetus for the move toward community-based policing in Ontario. In the early 1970s, questions were raised about the effectiveness of conventional policing strategies and tactics. Random, motorized patrol appeared to be having little impact on rates of crime and social disorder in communities. This required police services to extend their attention beyond responding to incidents to consider public fear of crime and quality-of-life issues in the community.

A second development was the restructuring of Ontario policing that had begun in 1957, with the consolidation of 13 municipal police forces into the Metropolitan Toronto Police (now the Toronto Police Service). This resulted in nine regional police forces, including the Halton Regional Police and the Peel Regional Police, which were established between 1971 and 1974 in conjunction with the initiative to create regional governments across the province. The OPP began to adapt to incorporate the principles of community policing during the 1980s.

Community Policing Today in Ontario

Two key pieces of legislation relate to Ontario's police forces, both of which focus heavily on community policing. These are the *Police Services Act* (Revised Statutes of Ontario 1990, Chapter P.15) and the *Adequacy and Effectiveness of Police Services Regulation* (Ontario Regulation 3/99, commonly referred to as the **Adequacy Standards**).

The *Police Services Act* contains a number of provisions designed to integrate community policing into all segments of policing. Furthermore, the Act requires that the performance of police services be monitored and allows for intervention to correct any perceived deficiencies in service delivery, if necessary. The key sections of the Act and the provisions relating to community policing are summarized in Box 3.5.

As well, the Adequacy Standards that have been developed in conjunction with the *Police Services Act* set out specific guidelines for police services in relation to community policing. The most relevant sections are listed in Box 3.6.

There are several additional sources of support for Ontario police services in their efforts to develop and implement community policing policies, programs, and strategies. This includes the Program Development Section organized under the Ministry of Community Safety and Correctional Services, Policing Services Division.

The Policing Services Division is responsible for the ongoing development and improvement of policing throughout the province. The Division seeks to ensure a world-class law enforcement network protects Ontario by providing effective training, professional standards and policies, systematic inspections and reviews, and advisory support to police services. The division also supports the development of community safety and crime prevention initiatives, operates Criminal Intelligence Services Ontario, and licenses the private security industry. As of 2007, the *Ontario Private Security and Investigative Services Act* requires all security companies and their personnel be licensed. This represents a significant step forward in regulating and professionalizing the private security industry. Similar regulation of the security industry occurred in the provinces of Alberta and Nova Scotia in 2010.

The Program Development Section works in partnership with police and community agencies to develop and coordinate the planning, implementation, and evaluation of crime prevention and community safety initiatives. The section also provides input into policy and legislative amendments that affect policing, crime prevention, and road

BOX 3.5

ONTARIO'S POLICE SERVICES ACT: KEY PROVISIONS FOR COMMUNITY POLICING

Section 1. Declaration of Principles. Identifies the need for co-operation between the police and communities, the importance of police sensitivity to the multicultural diversity of communities, and the need to ensure that police services are representative of the communities they serve.

Section 3. The Solicitor General. Sets out the duties and powers of the Solicitor General, which include ensuring that adequate and effective police services are provided, that police service boards comply with the prescribed standards of service, and that the development and promotion of community policing programs are pursued.

Section 5(2). Same-Different Methods in One Municipality. Authorizes policing to be delivered differently in communities where two or more communities are widely dispersed or police services have historically been provided to one or more discrete areas of the municipality in a way that is different from the way police services are provided in the rest of the municipality.

Section 5.1(4). Community Policing Advisory Committees. Authorizes municipalities policed by the OPP to establish community policing advisory committees to advise OPP detachment commanders of community priorities and concerns.

Sections 21–26. The Ontario Civilian Commission on Police Services. Sets out duties including investigating police services not in compliance with prescribed standards of service and hearing public complaints against police services and officers.

Sections 27–40. Municipal Police Services Boards. Describes responsibilities including the provision of adequate and effective policing services in the municipality and determining priorities for police services.

Section 41(1). Chiefs of Police. Sets out duties including ensuring that policing services are provided in a manner that reflects the needs of the community; ensuring that the police force provides community-oriented police services.

Section 42(1). Police Officers. Sets out duties including preventing crimes and other offences and providing assistance and encouragement to other persons in their prevention;

Section 135(1). Regulations created by the Lieutenant Governor in Council. Sets out duties including proscribing standards for police service and creating provisions for monitoring the extent to which these standards are met by police services.

Source: Police Services Act, ONTARIO REGULATION 3/99: ADEQUACY AND EFFECTIVENESS OF POLICE SERVICES

safety initiatives. The section liaises with other ministries, participates in the federal/provincial/territorial working group on crime prevention and community safety, and supports other related initiatives.

LEGISLATIVE REQUIREMENTS FOR COMMUNITY POLICING ACROSS CANADA

Ontario was profiled in the last section because it has adopted a strong commitment to community policing. The enactment of legislation has established a statutory framework for community-based policing, which has greatly assisted police organizations to become community-based in their orientation and practices. Most other provinces, while committed to the concept of community policing, have not taken the steps of the Ontario government. The Police Acts of other provinces include the following:

- In British Columbia, Part 6 of the *British Columbia Police Act* authorizes the creation of local police committees to foster positive relationships between the police and local residents and to raise issues concerning the adequacy of policing and law enforcement.
- In Alberta the *Alberta Police Act* (section 38) establishes police officer duties including assisting the community to prevent crime and establishing co-operative relationships

BOX 3.6

THE ADEQUACY AND EFFECTIVENESS OF POLICE SERVICES REGULATION: KEY PROVISIONS FOR COMMUNITY POLICING

Section 1(1). Police forces shall provide community-based crime prevention initiatives.

Section 2(1). A police force may use members of the police force, auxiliary members of the police force, special constables, and volunteers in community-based crime prevention initiatives.

Section 3. Every chief of police shall establish procedures and processes on problem-oriented policing and crime prevention initiatives, whether the police force provides community-based crime prevention initiatives or whether crime prevention initiatives are provided by another police force or on a combined or regional or co-operative basis or by another organization.

Section 13(2). Every police services board shall establish a policy on sharing data on crime, calls, and public disorder and information on crime trends with its municipal council and with the school boards, community organizations and groups, businesses, and members of the public it serves.

Section 30(1). Every police services board shall prepare a business plan for its police force at least once every three years.

Section 30(2). The business plan shall address:

a. the objectives, core business, and functions of the police force, including how it will provide adequate and effective police services;

b. quantitative and qualitative performance objectives and indicators relating to:

– the police force's provision of community-based crime prevention initiatives, community patrol, and criminal investigation services;

– community satisfaction with police services.

Section 35. Every board and chief of police shall implement a quality assurance process relating to the delivery of adequate and effective police services, and compliance with the act and its regulations.

Source: Police Services Act, ONTARIO REGULATION 3/99: ADEQUACY AND EFFECTIVENESS OF POLICE SERVICES

between the police service and the community. Throughout 2007 and 2008, the Alberta Solicitor General and Public Security ministry finalized policing standards for all police services in the province except the Royal Canadian Mounted Police. In addition, the Ministry established a Law Enforcement Framework for the province in 2011, incorporating community peace officers and sheriffs within this framework. In 2011, the Ministry also moved forward with the regulation of the private security industry, requiring mandatory training for in-house and contract security personnel, alarm responders, and loss prevention personnel.

- Nearly all police legislation across Canada establishes duties for the police to assist with crime prevention and to work with the community.
- Some police departments across Canada, such as the Edmonton Police Service and Peel Regional, are also members of the Commission on Accreditation for Law Enforcement Agencies (CALEA), an American organization committed to the improvement of law-enforcement service delivery that offers a body of standards on a wide range of up-to-date policing topics. This organization recognizes policing excellence and requires police agencies to maintain the standards established by CALEA. In jurisdictions that do not have a strong legislative foundation for community policing, voluntary membership to CALEA can help establish community-policing organizations. If you are interested in this initiative, check out CALEA's website at www.calea.org.

THE COMMUNITY POLICING CHECKLIST

Because a primary objective of this text is to provide you with a "how to" for community policing, a **Community Policing Implementation Checklist** is given for each of the major areas covered. This checklist will appear in the sections titled "Situations and Strategies" and will list the types of indicators used to determine the extent to which a community policing strategy and the key players are involved in the activities required by a community policing framework. This is particularly important in view of the fact that many police administrators and police officers "talk the talk" about community policing, but on further inspection do not "walk the walk" (i.e., they do not do it).

COMMUNITY-BASED STRATEGIC POLICING

Modern democratic countries like the United States, Britain and Canada have reached a watershed in the evolution of their systems of crime control and law enforcement. Future generations will look back on our era when one system of policing ended and another took its place.

—*David Bailey and Clifford Shearing (1994)*

So far we have been examining what community policing is. If you recall, we said it is a full-service model of policing, focused not just on law enforcement and crime control but also more broadly on social disorder and community quality-of-life concerns. Beginning in the mid-1990s, and particularly after September 11, 2001, the mandate of the police has grown considerably to include a strong focus aimed at protecting Canada from threats of terrorism and extremism. The problem is that it has become increasingly more difficult for police organizations to sustain current levels of police service to the community. Police officers are feeling overwhelmed with community demands for service, and citizens question the basic ability of their police to fulfill their mandate. As a result, police departments across Canada are looking for better ways to deliver their service.

The factors that are serving to shape the evolving model of police service delivery (refer back to the trends in the previous chapter) require a more strategic approach to policing than has existed in the past. This approach is called **intelligence-led policing** and can be described as follows:

Intelligence-led policing is a collaborative enterprise based on improved intelligence operations and community-oriented policing and problem solving, ... To implement intelligence-led policing, police organizations need to reevaluate their current policies and protocols. Intelligence must be incorporated into the planning process to reflect community problems and issues. Information sharing must become a policy, not an informal practice. Most important, intelligence must be contingent on quality analysis of data. The development of analytical techniques, training, and technical assistance needs to be supported. (Bureau of Justice Assistance [U.S.] 2005)

The evolving model of community-based strategic policing incorporates intelligence-led policing along with the following elements:

- Policing activities must continue to forge strong relationships with all communities, particularly ethnic ones who account for the majority of population growth in Canada.
- Policing people, places, and crime requires a high level of crime data analysis with the goal that crime and disorder are predictable and therefore preventable.

- Policing utilizes technologies to improve crime detection and crime-solving ability.
- Policing is delivered not just by public police but also by a variety of public safety service providers including private security personnel, private investigators, special constables, sheriffs, and auxiliary constables.
- Better use of crime and disorder reduction strategies such as problem solving policing (Chapter 5), crime prevention through environmental design or social development (Chapter 4), and broken windows (Chapter 4) policing produce measurable results.
- Changed organizational structures and strategies including integrated service delivery improve the capacity of the police to respond to the broadened mandate of policing.

As community-based policing continues to evolve, the key challenge and priority is to ensure the community remains an integral partner in the management of crime and disorder within society. To achieve this goal, new strategies and tactics need to be evaluated which enhance the role of the community beyond simply acting as the "eyes and ears" of the police (the watchman role). While a number of technologies are available to assist in the crime-solving abilities of the police, it is essential these technologies do not serve to distance the police from the communities and re-establish the criticisms of the earlier "professional" era of policing.

Table 3.2 summarizes some of the key differences between traditional policing and community-based strategic policing. It is still too early to determine whether community-based strategic policing represents an altogether new model of police service delivery or, rather, a more evolved form of community policing, shaped by the change agents we have described. The critical idea is that a "smarter" model of policing is developing.

Table 3.2 Community-Based Strategic Policing versus Other Policing Models

	Traditional	**Community**	**Strategic**
Administrative Approach (locus of control)	Centralized	Decentralized	Integrated control
Authority	Statute	Community	Community/statute
Community Role	Report violations of the law	Partnered with police to address crime, disorder, and quality of life	Strategic community partnerships, formalized by protocols and agreements, which integrate into police operations
Operational Focus	Crime and disorder	Crime, disorder, quality of life, fear of crime, and disorder	Crime, disorder, security, quality of life, fear of crime, and disorder
Operational Strategies	Random patrol, reactive investigation, rapid response	Targeted patrol partnerships, problem solving, proactive or preventative policing, geographic-based deployment of personnel	Target management focused on "hot spots, hot people and hot crimes," strategic partnerships, resource sharing and integrated service delivery; greater reliance on analysis and technology

Source: Whitelaw 2004.

CHAPTER SUMMARY

This chapter provided a general orientation to the philosophy, principles, and practice of community policing. Community policing was compared to the traditional, professional model of police practice, and it was noted that community policing represents an expansion of the traditional or professional model of police practice, rather than a replacement of it. The emergence of community policing in Ontario was discussed, and the key players in the police–community partnerships were identified.

The discussion also examined the evolution of community policing in the province of Ontario. The move toward community policing began during the 1970s, when questions were raised about the effectiveness of traditional police practices. At that time, the restructuring of Ontario police services also began, with the creation of a number of regional police services.

Today in Ontario, the *Police Services Act* contains a number of provisions designed to ensure that community policing is central to all police services; also, the *Adequacy and Effectiveness of Police Service Regulation* sets out specific guidelines that police services must follow in implementing the core principles of community policing.

In Chapter 7, we will examine the attributes of police services that have built the principles of community policing in the organization and delivery of policing services. You will see that these police services are organized differently from traditional, hierarchical police services and that the delivery of policing services is centred on the development of police–community partnerships. In Chapter 8, we will present a number of case studies to illustrate how several police services across Canada have attempted to alter their organizational structure, service delivery, and planning process to incorporate the principles of community policing. These case studies provide important insights into the significant changes that community policing requires and reaffirm the point that such changes do not occur overnight but can take a decade or longer.

CHAPTER REVIEW

Key Terms

- Adequacy Standards, p. 70
- clearance rate, p. 55
- community policing, p. 59
- Community Policing Implementation Checklist, p. 73
- intelligence-led policing, p. 73
- key players in community policing, p. 66
- police effectiveness, p. 55
- the three Ps—prevention, problem solving, partnership, p. 60
- the three Rs—random patrol, rapid response, reactive investigation, p. 54
- traditional or professional model of policing, p. 54
- watch system, p. 54

Key Points

- The "three Rs" of traditional policing—random patrol, rapid response, and reactive investigation—are not generally effective in preventing or responding to crime.
- Clearance rates alone are not an accurate measure of police effectiveness.
- Community policing is based on the "three Ps": prevention, problem solving, and partnership with the community.
- Community policing is most accurately viewed as an evolution of the police role, rather than as a completely different model from traditional policing.
- Community policing includes law enforcement and reactive response to crime and disorder.

- There are key differences between community policing and traditional policing in terms of the role of the police, how the effectiveness of the police is assessed, the priorities of the police, and accountability of the police.
- The specific needs and demands of a community will determine how community policing is implemented.
- Community policing has been criticized for being soft on crime, as not "real" police work, and as nothing new.
- The move toward community policing began in Ontario during the 1970s, when the effectiveness of traditional police practice began to be questioned and when regionalization of police services began in earnest.
- Ontario can be considered a leading jurisdiction in the implementation of community policing.
- The *Police Services Act* provides the framework within which community policing operates in Ontario.
- The *Adequacy and Effectiveness of Police Services Regulation* (more commonly referred to as the "Adequacy Standards") sets out guidelines for police services in relation to community policing.
- The key players in community policing are the police service, the police officers, criminal justice agencies and organizations, volunteers, and the community.
- A smarter approach to police service delivery is occurring called "community-based strategic policing."

Self-Evaluation

QUESTIONS

1. What do research studies indicate about the effectiveness of **traditional patrol practice**?
2. What is a **clearance rate** and why might it not be a good measure of police effectiveness?
3. Within the framework of community policing, what would be good measures of **police effectiveness**?
4. What are the **three Rs** of traditional policing?
5. Define the term **community policing** and then identify its components.
6. What are the **three Ps** of community policing?
7. What are the key provisions of the Ontario *Police Services Act* that relate to community policing?
8. What are the key provisions in the Ontario **Adequacy Standards** that relate to community policing?
9. Who are the **key players in community policing**?
10. What is **intelligence-led** policing?
11. Explain how **community-based strategic policing** represents an enhanced level of community policing.
12. Contrast and compare **traditional policing** with community policing. What are the key differences?

KEY IDEAS

1. In policing, what are "the three Rs"?
   a. random patrol, rapid response, and reactive investigation
   b. random patrol, reconnaissance, and review of investigation
   c. rapid response, rescue, and reworking investigation
   d. random patrol, reactive call delivery, and response investigation

2. Which of the following best defines clearance rate?
   a. a measure of police effectiveness in a community policing model
   b. a measure of police effectiveness no longer used by police services
   c. the percentage of cases where an offence has been committed and a suspect identified
   d. the percentage of cases where an offence has been committed and a suspect convicted

3. Which of the following has been indicated in studies of police services?
   a. Most police services have implemented community policing.
   b. Although provincial police forces have adopted community policing, municipal police services still rely on traditional police practice.
   c. The majority of police officers in Canada still carry out their duties within a traditional model of patrol practice.
   d. The Royal Canadian Mounted Police have achieved the highest level of community policing implementation due to their federal role.

4. What has been revealed by research studies on traditional patrol practice?
   a. Increasing random patrols has a significant impact on the levels of crime.
   b. The response time of the police is not related to levels of crime.
   c. The number of arrests made by the police reduces the levels of crime.
   d. The number of female police officers in an agency reduces the levels of crime.

5. Which of the following is NOT a characteristic of the traditional model of police work?
   a. patrol officers working the same shift rotation
   b. an emphasis on centralized command and control
   c. partnerships with the community
   d. a highly centralized, hierarchical organizational structure

6. How is community policing best described?
   a. as a series of crime prevention programs
   b. as an approach to policing based on prevention, problem solving, and partnership
   c. as a series of traditional police practices that have been renamed
   d. as an approach to policing largely abandoned by Canadian police services

7. In community policing, what are "the three Ps"?
   a. protection, privacy, and perfection
   b. prevention, problem solving, and partnership
   c. police, pistols, and pretence
   d. politics, perseverance, and protection

8. Which of the following does NOT define community policing?
   a. it incorporates many elements of traditional policing
   b. it is a strategy that involves partnering with the community
   c. it is an appropriate policing strategy for all types of criminal activity
   d. it is the responsibility of the police and community

9. What was found in research studies that assessed the impact of community policing?
   a. People tend to dislike community policing as it is time consuming.
   b. With a few exceptions, community policing reduces the levels of crime.
   c. Officers involved in community policing tend to have higher levels of job satisfaction.
   d. Community policing reduces the fear of crime among residents.

10. Which provincial legislation establishes the framework for police agencies in Ontario?
    a. the *Police Services Act*
    b. the *Criminal Code*
    c. the *Criminal Apprehension Act*
    d. the *Police Enforcement Act*

11. In which decade did the move toward community policing in Ontario begin?
    a. the 1960s
    b. the 1970s
    c. the 1980s
    d. the 1990s

12. In the 1970s a task force report examined policing and technology in Ontario. What did the task force report find?
    a. The increasing use of technology was facilitating the implementation of community policing.
    b. There was need for more up-to-date technology for police services.
    c. Technology was widening the gap between the police and the public.
    d. Most police services made very little use of technology.

13. What provided the impetus for the move toward community policing in Ontario?
    a. increasing concerns about the effectiveness of traditional police practice
    b. increasing demands by community residents that the police change
    c. increasing concerns by the government to hold the police more accountable
    d. increasing demands by civil libertarians for the community to shape the police services that are provided.

14. Ontario's *Police Services Act* contains sections relating to which one of the following?
    a. a declaration of principles for public partnerships
    b. the role of provincial police service boards
    c. the duties of community police practitioners
    d. the Ontario Civilian Commission on Police Services

15. In 2003, which body replaced the Solicitor General of Canada?
    a. Department of Justice
    b. Director of Homeland Security
    c. Public Safety Canada
    d. the Prime Minister's Office

16. What are the organizational characteristics of the traditional police organization?
    a. flexible working conditions
    b. private-sector managerialism
    c. decentralized operations
    d. centralized command, and control operations

17. Which performance measure is NOT a contemporary performance measure?
    a. quality of police work
    b. number of arrests
    c. quality of victim experiences with police
    d. number of community partnerships

Community Policing: Situations and Strategies

Case Studies

Police Reform in Alberta

During the last eight years, the province of Alberta has conducted a complete and thorough review of policing. A number of reports were prepared, including "Policing Alberta—A Discussion Paper" (2000), "Report of the MLA Policing Review Committee" (2004), and, finally, "Keeping Communities Safe: Report and Recommendations" (2007). Each report examined the effectiveness and efficiency of police service delivery in Alberta; taken together, the reports identify a number of deficiencies and make a number of key recommendations.

In response to the uneven distribution of policing resources, the Solicitor General of Alberta created provincial sheriffs and peace officers through the passage of new legislation called the Peace Officer Act (Alberta). Public Safety Peace Officers have limited powers and authorities, and as of 2008 there were over 3,000 PSPOs in Alberta, working for some 284 different agencies, with provincial government offices being the largest employer. The role of sheriffs includes traffic enforcement, investigative support including surveillance, and fugitive apprehension. These new sheriff functions allow police officers to focus on more serious crime in the communities they serve and supplement police efforts when required.

The Government of Alberta also created the *Alberta Policing Secretariat* to implement recommendations of the Crime Reduction and Safe Communities Task Force. In keeping with these recommendations, more Crown prosecutors and support positions had been authorized, file ownership policies were instituted to ensure better prosecutorial file management, a comprehensive bail application process was developed to better respond to repeat offenders, and the province was examining the development of specialized courts designed to tailor better response options (e.g., drug and addiction courts).

Additional initiatives include the establishment of organized crime investigation funding through an arm's-length body headed by a Chief Executive Officer. Further, additional policing oversight was established through the creation of Alberta Serious Incident Response Teams (ASIRT), whose mandate is to investigate incidents or complaints involving serious injury or death of any person and matters of a serious or sensitive nature that may have resulted from the actions of a police officer. Finally, provincial policing standards were instituted.

The steps taken to date strengthen the overall response to crime and community disorder by increasing police visibility and improving overall capacity to investigate, and strengthen overall deterrence by reducing gaps in investigation and enforcement.

Can you think of any other options available to increase visibility without significantly increasing spending? What other options are available? Are any of these options available in your local police service?

EXERCISES: KNOWLEDGE INTO PRACTICE

Exercise 1. Your Hometown

Recalling the community where you spent most of your childhood, complete the following:

Population: _____ Remote rural/Rural/Suburban/Urban			
Ethnic diversity:	High	Medium	Low
Police Service:	Provincial	Regional	City/Municipal Independent
Level of Crime:	High	Medium	Low

The most common types of crime:

_____

_____

_____

The most common social problems:

_____

_____

_____

Your perceptions of the sources of problems in the community:

_____

_____

_____

	Positive				**Negative**
Your perceptions of the police:	1	2	3	4	5
Your contacts with the police:	Positive/Negative				

The major challenges that the police in your community faced:

_____

_____

_____

	Highly Effective				**Not Effective**
Were the police effective in meetings these challenges?	1	2	3	4	5

The Challenge   Effectiveness of Response

1. _____

2. _____

3. _____

4. _____

5. _____

For those challenges you feel the police were effective in addressing, list the reasons why you feel they were effective.

1._____
2._____
3._____
4._____
5._____

For those challenges you feel the police were less effective in addressing, list the reasons why.

1._____
2._____
3._____
4._____
5._____

Compare your responses to those of your classmates.

Exercise 2. Measuring What Counts in Policing

Critical Idea: The performance measures listed earlier in this chapter assess the quality of a police service. Traditional measures of police performance tend to be quantitative—concerned more with measurable data such as number of arrests, calls responded to, response times, and so on. If you were to develop a "report card" for your local police service, what would the advantages and disadvantages of qualitative and quantitative performance measures be? If you were the chief of police, how might you use each of these measures when (a) crime rates are increasing and City Hall is very concerned, and (b) crime rates are decreasing and the police chief wants to hire more personnel?

_____
_____
_____
_____
_____
_____

REFERENCES

Bureau of Justice Assistance. 2005. *Intelligence-led Policing: The New Intelligence Architecture*. Washington, DC: Bureau of Justice Assistance.

Community Oriented Policing and Problem Solving Advisory Committee. 1995. *Community Oriented Policing and Problem Solving*. Sacramento, CA: Attorney General's Office, California Department of Justice.

Fantino, J. 1996. "Community Policing: The Myth and the Reality!" *Blue Line Magazine* 8(5):20–23.

Findley, K.W. and R.W. Taylor. 1990. "Re-Thinking Neighborhood Policing." *Journal of Contemporary Criminal Justice* 6(2):70–78.

Government of Alberta. 2000. "Policing Alberta: A Discussion Paper." Alberta Justice.

Government of Alberta. 2004. "Report of the MLA Policing Review Committee." Alberta Justice.

Government of Alberta. 2007. "Keeping Communities Safe: Report and Recommendations." Alberta's Crime Reduction and Safe Communities Task Force.

Kelling, G.L. and M.L. Moore. 1998. "From Political to Reform to Community: The Evolving Strategy of Police." pp. 3–25 in *Community Policing: Rhetoric or Reality?* edited by J.R. Green and S.D. Mastrofski. New York: Praeger.

Murphy, C. 1995. Community Policing and Police Leadership. Unpublished manuscript. Halifax: Henson College, Dalhousie University.

Normandeau, A. and B. Leighton. 1990. *A Vision of the Future of Policing in Canada: Police-Challenge 2000.* Ottawa: Police and Security Branch, Solicitor General Canada.

Ontario Regulation 3/99—Adequacy and Effectiveness of Police Services (1999).

Ontario. *Police Services Act (2009).*

Oppal, W.T. (Commissioner). 1994. *Closing the Gap: Policing and the Community.* Policing in British Columbia Commission of Inquiry Final Report, vol. 1. Victoria: Attorney General of British Columbia.

Sherman, L. et al. 1997. *Preventing Crime: What Works, What Doesn't, What's Promising.* Washington, DC: National Institute of Justice.

Sparrow, M.K. 1988. *Implementing Community Policing.* Washington, DC: National Institute of Justice, U.S. Department of Justice.

Task Force on Policing in Ontario. 1974. *The Task Force on Policing in Ontario: Report to the Solicitor General.* Toronto: Ministry of Attorney General.

Trojanowicz, R. and B. Bucqueroux. 1997. *Community Policing. How To Get Started,* 2nd ed. Cincinnati, OH: Anderson Publishing.

Whitelaw, B. 2004. *Policing the Modern Community.* Halifax: Henson College/Dalhousie University.

UNIT

3

Crime Prevention and Crime Response within a Community Policing Framework

CHAPTER 4

Responding To and Preventing Crime within a Community Policing Framework

Drug houses and derelict properties can be a major source of criminal activity in a community and they can lower citizen's perceptions of safety.

Source: Courtesy Edmonton Police Services

Learning Objectives

After completing this chapter, you should be able to:

- Define targeting strategies, community service approaches, and crime prevention programs;

- Provide examples of primary prevention programs, secondary prevention programs, and tertiary prevention programs;

- Describe how environmental design can prevent crime;

- Provide examples of the strategies for reducing opportunities for crime and social disorder;

- Discuss the effectiveness of and limits on crime prevention programs; and

- Discuss the mediation and conflict resolution strategies used by patrol officers.

INTRODUCTION

What actions do you believe will be the most effective in reducing the level of crime?
1. *Tougher sentencing*
2. *Increasing social programs, e.g., education, job training, drug treatment, recreation, job creation*
3. *Providing more police and correctional officers*
4. *Increasing crime prevention*
5. *Public/community awareness and neighbours watching out for one another*
      —*Top five responses to an Environics public opinion poll in 1997*

Preventing and reducing the levels of crime is a high priority for community residents and for police services across the country. This is due to the economic, social, and human costs of crime. It has been estimated that reacting to crime—apprehending, sentencing, incarcerating, and rehabilitating offenders—costs Canadian taxpayers approximately $31 billion annually, or about $943 per person. This figure is, in fact, only a small portion of the actual cost of crime. It does not include the costs of property loss, security services, insurance fraud, and crime-related hospitalization. Nor does it include the human costs—the impact of crime on victims and their families; the loss of the sense of personal and community well-being, security, and safety; and the fear of crime. When these impacts are factored in, the cost of crime in Canada is estimated to be as much as $70 billion per year (National Crime Prevention Centre 2008).

In Chapter 3, we noted that community policing involves three types of police work: proactive, reactive, and coactive. Over the past decade, there has been a rapid expansion of community-based programs designed to respond to a variety of problems and issues. Many of these developments are in response to the 1993 Report of the Standing Committee on Justice and the Solicitor General that outlined the Safer Communities Strategy, commonly referred to as the **safer communities approach to crime prevention**. The four principles of the safer communities approach are:

1. The community is the focal point of effective crime prevention.
2. The community must identify and respond to both short- and long-term needs.
3. Crime prevention efforts should bring together individuals from a range of sectors to tackle crime.
4. Strategies for preventing crime should be supported by the entire community.

Another major initiative is the Safer Communities Initiative, which was launched in 1998 as part of the federal government's National Strategy on Community Safety and Crime Prevention. This initiative, which is administered by the National Crime Prevention Centre, promotes integrated action between governmental and nongovernmental partners, and assists communities in developing and implementing community-based solutions to crime with a particular emphasis on children, youth, Aboriginal people, and women. It also provides funding to assist communities in developing partnerships and programs that address the underlying causes of crime. The National Crime Prevention Strategy (NCPS), as it is called today, is administered through Public Safety Canada's National Crime Prevention Centre (NCPC). For further information, check out http://www.publicsafety.gc.ca/index-eng.aspx.

Across Canada, police services are engaged in a wide variety of activities designed to prevent and respond to crime, as well as to increase the likelihood that people involved in criminal activity will be detected and apprehended. Programs include community police stations, police storefronts, and foot patrols. School-based programs include school liaison officers, safety presentations to students in primary grades, the DARE program to fight drug abuse at the middle and high school levels, bullying programs, and various recreational and sports programs that bring police officers together with students in nonconfrontative activities. These programs and strategies depend on the front-line patrol officers who, within the model of community policing, are empowered to work with community residents to identify and resolve problems and issues.

These various programs and activities can be generally grouped into proactive targeted strategies, community service approaches, and crime prevention programs; each category is discussed below. An element common to all of these approaches is the central role played by patrol officers. The implementation of the principles of community policing has resulted in a fundamental shift in the roles and activities of line patrol officers. This was accomplished by decentralizing the traditional command and control hierarchy. Granting officers responsibility for crime and disorder prevention at the neighbourhood level has created opportunities for both a more proactive approach and for broadening the role and activities of police officers beyond merely responding to calls for service. We will explore this in greater detail in our discussion of community police officers in Chapter 8.

PROACTIVE TARGETED STRATEGIES

Proactive targeted strategies rely on the use of patrol for the apprehension, deterrence, and incapacitation of criminal offenders. Among the strategies used are:

- cover patrol,
- repeat offender targeting,
- saturation patrol,
- roadblocks, and
- repeat complaint address policing (Mastrofski 1990:34).

In contrast to traditional patrol, which is random and incident-driven, patrol within a targeted strategy is undertaken for three related reasons:

- *To achieve visibility.* The presence of an officer may eliminate the opportunity for someone to commit a crime, as well as allowing the officer to investigate leads and observe infractions of the law.
- *To pursue proactive policing.* Patrolling allows the officer to be proactive by determining the opportunities for criminal behaviour and initiating appropriate preventive strategies. This maintains contact with the community and encourages co-operation and trust between officers and citizens.
- *To provide for rapid response.* Patrolling provides the officer with an opportunity to respond or react quickly to calls for service.

Addressing Crime: Tactical or Directed Patrol

Tactical or directed patrol involves saturating high-crime areas, called "hot spots," with police officers or targeting individuals involved in specific types of criminal activity. Hot spots are operationally defined as small clusters of addresses with frequent **hard crime calls** (hold-up alarms, shootings, stabbings, auto thefts, thefts from autos, assaults, and sexual assaults) as well as substantial **soft crime calls** for service (audible break-in alarms, disturbances, drunks, noise, unwanted persons, vandalism, prowlers, fights, and physical injuries).

Tactical or directed patrol projects share four common characteristics:

1. Patrol is based on a thorough analysis of crime data.
2. Officers use uncommitted time to engage in purposeful activity.
3. Officers have specific instructions directing their activities.
4. Officers are proactive and, as a result, may seem aggressive.

Directed forms of patrol are usually either location- or person-oriented. Police resources are focused in areas identified as hot spots of crime and disorder or they target offenders. Directed patrol may also be event-oriented, especially at large public gatherings where violence is anticipated. In contrast to random, reactive strategies, tactical or directed patrol strategies give police managers greater control over their most valuable resource—the time and activities of patrol officers. Police services may also make use of citizen volunteer groups to conduct static or mobile surveillance in hot spots.

The Effectiveness of Tactical or Directed Patrol

The proactive approach of tactical or directed patrol to crime prevention and intervention produces positive results (see Box 4.1).

BOX 4.1

THE EFFECTIVENESS OF PROACTIVE STRATEGIES

Question: Does the number of police officers have an impact on the levels of crime?

Answer: In certain situations, yes.

- There is some evidence that crime rates increase during police strikes. During a police strike in Montreal in 1969, for example, the rate of bank robberies increased 50 times and the number of burglaries of commercial establishments was 14 times the average.

- Increases in the numbers of police officers appear to reduce the levels of crime in urban areas and to have a preventive effect as well; this is most likely due to increased police visibility.

Question: Do proactive police arrests that focus on high-risk individuals and offences reduce the levels of serious, violent crime?

Answer: Yes, for certain types of offences.

- Police drug crackdowns appear not to affect the levels of violent crime.

- Police campaigns against impaired driving have an impact and reduce death rates.

- "Zero tolerance" arrest policies directed toward street activity can reduce serious crime, particularly if the needs of those persons arrested are addressed.

Question: Do directed preventive patrols that target hot spots and that are directed at peak times of criminal activity affect levels of crime?

Answer: In many instances, yes.

- Increasing the numbers of uniformed police officers in patrol cars in hot spots and during "hot times" (crime peaks) may significantly reduce levels of criminal activity.

Question: Is there an optimal time that officers should remain at a hot spot in order to be effective?

Answer: Yes.

- Patrol stops must reach a threshold dosage of about 10 minutes in order to generate significantly longer "survival" or time spans without disorder, as opposed to simply driving through a hot spot.

- The optimal length for patrol stops appears to be 11 to 15 minutes, after which continued police presence brings diminishing returns.

- Increasing the number of patrols may not be as important as time spent at a hot spot targeting specific individuals.

Question: Does tactical or directed patrol result in the displacement of criminal activity to other areas?

Answer: Potentially, yes.

- Recent research finds little evidence to support the "belief" that geographic displacement occurs due to location based directed patrol.

Sources: Koper, C.S., 1995. "Just Enough Police Presence: Reducing Crime and Disorderly Behavior by Optimizing Patrol Time in Crime Hot Spots." Justice Quarterly 12(4): 649–72; Sherman, L.W., and D. Weisburd, 1995. "General Deterrent Effects of Police Patrol in Crime 'Hot Spots': A Randomized, Controlled Trial." Justice Quarterly 12(4): 625–48. Sherman, L.W., et al., 1997. *Preventing Crime: What Works, What Doesn't, What's Promising.* Washington, DC: Office of Justice Programs, U.S. Department of Justice.

It is essential, however, that tactical patrol strategies be implemented on the basis of a careful analysis and evaluation of crime data if the objectives of the specific project are to be achieved. Since aggressive patrol may involve car stops, person checks, zero-tolerance enforcement, and other crackdowns, officers must ensure that their actions do not violate the citizens' rights guaranteed in the *Canadian Charter of Rights and Freedoms*. Furthermore, strategies that combine tactical patrol with longer-term problem-solving approaches may be more effective and have more impact in the long run.

The Problems of Tactical or Directed Patrol

While there is conclusive evidence that tactical or directed patrol produces more positive outcomes than does random, reactive patrol, the success of this approach to police work requires that police services resolve a number of issues. These include:

- developing strategies to alter the role and attitude of police officers from reactive to proactive;
- convincing patrol officers that their current call loads do not preclude carrying out tactical or directed patrol projects;
- analyzing crime patterns, trends, and patrol officer workloads and activities (time and tasks); and
- dealing with diminished police resources, which inhibit the ability to implement tactical or directed patrol.

COMMUNITY SERVICE APPROACHES

The shift toward community policing as the model of police service delivery has also resulted in significant changes in the role of community residents: from passive consumers of policing services to active participants in the prevention of and response to crime and disorder. **Community service approaches** "focus on protecting, aiding, and mobilizing members of the community in dealing with crime, disorders and the underlying factors contributing to these problems" (Mastrofski 1990:33). These strategies include foot patrols, community police stations, and organizing the community to become involved in addressing problems of crime and disorder. The objective of these initiatives is to "shift the focus of police-citizen contacts toward the 'good' people, the victims, and the potential victims in the community" (p. 36).

Foot Patrol: Back to the Beat

Foot patrols, or **beats**, are prevalent among many Canadian police departments and predate the use of automobiles in patrol work. Despite the fact that organized foot patrol first appeared in 1829 in London, when Robert Peel hired officers for the Metropolitan Police, foot patrols have been heralded as a breakthrough in the 1990s and as a major component of community policing.

Foot patrols address the major criticism that patrol cars—equipped with computers, cellular phones, video cameras, and police radios—distance officers from the community and, in fact, discourage them from leaving the confines of their "office" to interact with residents. Foot patrols are often found in urban centres where the population density is much higher and concentrated vertically (e.g., high-rise apartments), unlike the horizontal distribution found in suburban communities. In urban areas across North America, foot patrol has produced some interesting results that suggest it holds great potential.

Nonetheless, with a few exceptions (the city of Edmonton being one), there is no evidence that foot patrols directly affect the levels of crime in neighbourhoods. Field research studies do, however, indicate that foot patrols:

- reduce citizens' fear of crime;
- increase feelings of personal safety among community residents;
- reduce calls for service;
- increase officer familiarity with neighbourhoods; and
- increase officers' feelings of safety on the job, which results in greater job satisfaction and a higher level of morale than is experienced by those in patrol cars.

Foot patrols generally receive high marks from community residents, who appreciate the increased visibility and accessibility of police officers. In fact, community residents often equate beat officers with community policing.

Although foot patrols may provide an opportunity for officers to focus on common reoccurring problems that tax police resources, such patrols can be difficult to implement, as many front-line supervisors would prefer to have patrol units available to deal with calls for service, especially during peak service times.

Bicycle Patrols

Officers on mountain bikes are often deployed into areas of high crime and social disorder. On bicycles, officers are able to deploy and manoeuvre where patrol cars are unable to travel. Bicycles have the additional feature of being silent. In addition, the health benefits to officers as well as the environmental aspects of bicycle patrols are significant. The first urban uniformed mountain bike patrol was established by the Seattle Police Department in 1987; since that time, many Canadian police services have implemented year-round bike patrols modelled after the successful Seattle program (see Box 4.2).

An evaluation of the Seattle Police Department bike patrol program identified the following advantages:

- Bicycle patrol officers made more arrests in a shorter period of time over a larger beat area.
- The Seattle bike patrol averaged four times more arrests than foot patrols and were able to extend their patrol area over several square kilometres.
- Bicycle officers arrived sooner than the patrol cars to most of the calls for service in the downtown core. In addition, mountain bikes had greater mobility than patrol cars in serious snowfalls.
- Bicycle patrol units are much less expensive to operate and maintain than patrol cars (Grady 1990).
- The findings of a recent study also noted that bicycle patrols result in over twice as much contact with the public compared with automobile patrols. In addition, the study documented the clear tactical advantages to bicycle patrols over other methods (Menton 2008).

BOX 4.2

CITIZEN BIKE PATROLS IN THE COMMUNITY OF COLLINGWOOD, VANCOUVER

The Collingwood Community Policing Centre in Vancouver runs a volunteer bike patrol with more than 125 volunteers. The volunteers conduct bike patrols, assist in delivering pamphlets for the marijuana Growbusters team, and conduct neighbourhood surveys. The bike patrols, along with citizen foot and "pooch" patrols, have assisted in overall reductions in crime including stolen motor vehicles. The program allows for tracking and monitoring of patterns of criminal activities within the community, and it has fostered a greater sense of community pride, particularly in relation to volunteers' own homes. Finally, the patrols have enhanced feedback from the community. For more information, take a look at their website at http://collingwoodcpc.com/programs/.

Source: Collingwood Community Policing Centre (http://collingwoodcpc.com/programs/2011/12/14/patrol-programs.html)

While we have examined only two dominant modes of patrol, there are several others, including helicopters, snowmobiles, motorcycles, boats, and mounted patrol.

Deployment of Police Personnel

The effective use of police resources requires deployment of personnel in a manner that is responsive to a number of factors including:

- predicted call load and call volumes;
- police collective agreements which specify the length of police shifts or the deployment of one- or two-person patrol units;
- specific crime and disorder problems; and
- community concerns seeking dedicated police personnel.

The goal is to develop deployment models which do not over- or underdeploy police officers, allow police to get to know communities, and are flexible enough to respond to developing crime and disorder trends. We now examine some of these models.

Team Policing

Team policing or platoon/squad policing originated in the late 1940s in Aberdeen, Scotland, and appeared, albeit briefly, in a number of Canadian and U.S. police services during the 1970s. Among the ideal attributes of team policing include:

- the same group of police officers work the same set of shifts on a continuous basis;
- geographic stability of patrol through permanent assignment of teams of police to small neighbourhood areas;
- maximized communication among team members assigned to a specific area around the clock, seven days a week; and
- maximum interaction and communication between team members and the community.

The objectives of team policing include:

- capitalizing on the strengths of individual team members,
- improved police–community relations,
- reduced crime and disorder problems,
- improved police officer morale, and
- improved officer productivity.

A number of Canadian police agencies have implemented team-based deployment models, including the Calgary Police Service (see Box 4.3). Team policing models share the following characteristics:

- Teams of 8 to 12 officers work the same rotating shift schedule, under a decentralized system of policing.
- Officers are assigned to geographic areas or zones, which allows the development and retention of ties with the community.
- Community liaison officers work strategically and tactically with communities, ensuring the exchange of information between communities and teams.
- Teams are supervised by a sergeant, who works alongside team personnel on a rotating shift schedule.

In terms of current leadership theory, the deployment of police personnel as teams makes sense; however, the following implementation problems have been observed:

- Teams develop an inward focus, as opposed to an external community-based focus.
- Community liaison officers work directly with communities, leaving line officers for reactive patrol duties; this inhibits rather than enhances whole-team interaction with the community.

BOX 4.3

ATTRIBUTES OF AN EFFECTIVE POLICE DEPLOYMENT MODEL

Based on sound research and experience, all Canadian police services attempt to incorporate the following elements into their deployment of front-line police officers.

1. Police officers are assigned to specific geographic areas.

2. Police officers are encouraged to work with communities in the identification of problems.

3. Communities have a say in how police services are delivered.

4. Crime analysis combined with community consultation enables a more targeted deployment approach.

5. Officer workload is taken into account in an effort to ensure staffing levels that will allow police officers to work on proactive policing activities.

6. Citizen access to police service is available in a number of formats including telephone-based service delivery, Web-based crime reporting, access to police stations, and police dispatch to calls.

7. Supervision of personnel, often called "span of control," sees 7 to 10 officers assigned to every supervisor. This is essential in police organizations where there is considerable inexperience among police officers having front-line responsibilities (remember our discussion of demographic trends in Chapter 2).

- Workload demands on supervisors create difficulties in supervision.
- Entire teams would respond to incidents of crime and disorder, fostering a "mob" policing mentality.
- Without adequate supervisory/leadership training, team leaders may have difficulty performing their role.

Other service delivery deployment models include the following:

- *Zone or geopolicing,* in which police officers are assigned to geographic-based communities typically for periods of one to two years. Personnel start at different times throughout a 24-hour period and they are all responsible for policing the same area.
- *Problem-based policing,* in which police are deployed according to the zone policing model. However, resources are mobilized to target prioritized problems requiring officers to police outside geographic "zone" assignments. This is a sophisticated deployment model consistent with community-based strategic policing.

COMMUNITY POLICE STATIONS AND STOREFRONTS

Community or storefront police stations have become very popular in Canada and are often staffed by a mixture of uniformed police personnel, civilian staff, and volunteers. There is considerable variation in the activities of these police stations, but there is some evidence to suggest that community police stations may result in more positive evaluations of the police by community residents. However, these facilities appear to have little impact on crime rates.

Among the difficulties experienced by community police stations are staffing concerns, limited hours of operation, a lack of awareness among motorized patrol officers about community police stations and their activities, and a lack of coordination between officers assigned to community police stations and patrol (Graham 1997). To be effective, community police stations must be part of a much larger process of the decentralization of police services and must involve the empowerment of officers to work with community residents to address problems of crime and disorder.

CRIME PREVENTION PROGRAMS

The emphasis on crime prevention is not a recent phenomenon. At the same time Sir Robert Peel proposed his Nine Principles of Policing, Sir Richard Mayne, a London Chief Commissioner, stated "The primary object of an efficient police (service) is the prevention of crime" (1829).

Any discussion of the effectiveness of crime prevention initiatives must be tempered with the following observation: the causes of crime and disorder in any community are varied and complex. It is unrealistic to expect that the police alone, or even the police acting in concert with dedicated community residents, can reduce or eliminate all of society's problems. This is particularly true for those types of crimes that are international in scope and involve large criminal syndicates, and for those offenders who are products or the victims of the emerging technological society. With this caveat in mind, we can proceed.

Canadian police services are involved in a variety of **crime prevention programs**. Many were developed within the general framework of community policing; others were in existence before community policing became fashionable. Today policing efforts fall within the **National Crime Prevention Strategy**, which aims to reduce crime and victimization by tackling crime before it happens. The National Strategy is based on the principle that the surest way to reduce crime is to focus on the factors that put individuals at risk, such as family violence, school problems, and drug abuse (National Crime Prevention Strategy 2004).

The diversity of crime prevention programs can be classified into two broad groups:

1. situational crime prevention strategies, which seek to reduce the availability and attractiveness of opportunities to commit criminal activity; and
2. crime prevention through social development, which focuses on addressing the root causes of crime and disorder.

While there is considerable diversity in the scope and objectives of these programs, the primary objective is to prevent crime and reduce the levels of criminal activity. Underlying crime prevention efforts are a number of theories that serve to guide prevention efforts. Let's briefly look at two dominant theories.

- *Rational choice theory.* This theory focuses on the decision making of potential offenders. Offenders are considered to act rationally and make decisions based on the information they have at hand about costs and benefits, without thinking through alternative courses of action. This theory forms the foundation for a number of situational crime prevention strategies (Cornish and Clarke 1986; Newman et al. 1997).
- *Routine activities theory.* This theory, which is one of the main theories of "environmental criminology," falls under rational choice theory, because offenders are involved in a rational and calculated assessment of criminal opportunities, risks, and potential rewards. The routine activities theory requires three elements to be present for a crime to take place—a suitable target, a motivated offender, and the absence of a safeguard to protect the victim or deter the offender (Cohen and Felson 1979; Felson 1994). To prevent crime, at least one of these elements needs to be altered; this is described in Box 4.4. In Chapter 5, we will examine this idea further when we describe the "problem analysis triangle."

Traditionally, crime prevention initiatives fall into three categories: primary prevention, secondary prevention, and tertiary prevention.

Primary Prevention Programs

Primary prevention programs are the most common type of crime prevention initiative and are most often directed toward property offences. They are designed to identify opportunities for criminal offences and to alter these conditions in an attempt to reduce

BOX 4.4

PREVENTING CRIME USING ROUTINE ACTIVITY AND RATIONAL CHOICE THEORY

Criminologists Lawrence Cohen and Marcus Felson developed "routine activity theory" to assist in developing crime prevention approaches. Their theory suggests that for crime to occur there must be the presence of three conditions:

- a suitable target,

- the lack of a suitable guardian to prevent the crime from happening, and

- the presence of a motivated offender.

Altering any of the above factors would reduce the likelihood of a crime occurring.

A "target" might include a person, location, or object. Suitable guardians are typically people; however, a guardian may also include the use of technology such as CCTV systems. Guardians include:

- police patrols,

- security guards,

- Neighbourhood Watch programs,

- doorstaff,

- vigilant staff and co-workers,

- friends,

- neighbours, and

- closed-circuit television (CCTV) systems.

An offender may be motivated to commit a crime if, based on their situational assessment of risk and reward, the likelihood of gain exceeds the risks of being caught (rational choice theory). For additional information you will find the United Kingdom's Home Office website at www.crimereduction.homeoffice.gov.uk to be very useful.

Source: American Sociological Review by MAXWELL, GERALD; AMERICAN SOCIOLOGICAL ASSOCIATION; AMERICAN SOCIOLOGICAL SOCIETY Copyright 1979 Reproduced with permission of SAGE PUBLICATIONS INC. JOURNALS in the format Republish in a textbook via Copyright Clearance Center.

the likelihood of crimes being committed. Primary prevention programs may include both general approaches to crime prevention and specific crime prevention initiatives.

The more common primary crime prevention programs are discussed below.

Operation Identification

Citizens mark their property with identification numbers for two purposes: (1) to make the disposal of stolen goods more difficult and (2) to assist in the recovery of items by the police. A similar program for businesses is called Operation Provident.

Neighbourhood Watch

Neighbourhood Watch is the oldest and best known of all crime prevention programs. It involves raising residents' awareness of strangers and criminal activities—particularly break and enters—in their neighbourhoods. "This Is a Neighbourhood Watch Community" signs are a common sight across Canada. Variations of this concept appear as Apartment Watch, Block Watch, Rural Crime Watch, and, in rural Ontario, Cottage Watch.

Citizen Patrols

In many communities there are citizens' crime watch programs, which involve foot and vehicle patrols by trained volunteers under the supervision of police officers. The primary function of these patrols is to observe and report. Volunteers do not become involved with suspects or leave their vehicles without explicit instructions from their police supervisors. The primary responsibility of citizen patrols is to observe, not to intervene (Harman 1996). The Edmonton Mill Woods Community Patrol and Halton Regional Police Service, Communities on Phone Patrol (COPPS) are good examples of citizen patrol initiatives. You can check out both of these programs online at http://www.mwcp.ca and http://www.hrps.on.ca (see http://www.hrps.on.ca/CommunityPolicing/PublicSafetyEducation/COPP/Pages/default.aspx).

Media-Based Programs

Media-based programs include those designed to educate the public about crime, and "crime time" programs that solicit the public's assistance in locating known criminals. Perhaps the best known programs of this sort are the television programs *America's Most Wanted* and *Unsolved Mysteries*, which, unfortunately for criminal offenders from the U.S. who slip across the border, are also watched by Canadians. Many police services have also developed "hot tip" lines and televised re-enactment programs such as *Crime Stoppers*, which offer cash rewards for information leading to the arrest and conviction of offenders. In 2012, *Crime Stoppers* turned 30 years old. Remember our discussion of trends in Chapter 2, in which we identified the use of social media as a powerful tool for crime solving—for example, suspect identification and communicating with social networks for preventive purposes. The full development and expansion of social media within community policing merits further study as there are immense opportunities for development.

Preventing Crime at Places: Crime Prevention through Environmental Design

Proper design and effective use of the built environment can lead to a reduction in the incidence and fear of crime and an improvement in the quality of life.
—Timothy D. Crowe,
Crime Prevention through Environmental Design [2nd ed.] 2000

Police services have developed a wide range of initiatives in an attempt to prevent crime in specific types of places, such as in apartment complexes, subway and transit stations, stores, and homes. A common element of these approaches is an attempt to "block" criminal opportunities, making it difficult and risky for potential offenders. One of the better-known approaches is called **crime prevention through environmental design (CPTED)**, which sets out to reduce criminal opportunities by altering the physical environment of structures and places. These changes may include improving lighting and altering access routes for pedestrians and vehicles. Another tactic, target hardening, involves proactive measures such as installing locks and improving property security to reduce break and enters. Property marking and the use of closed-circuit television are also often employed. A number of opportunity-reducing techniques are presented in Table 4.1.

Table 4.1 Sixteen Crime Opportunity-Reducing Techniques

1. Target Hardening
- Install strengthened coin boxes in telephone kiosks
- Use steering column locks on cars
- Install anti-robbery screens in banks

2. Control of Access to Crime Targets in Multiple-Unit Dwellings
- Install fencing around buildings to reduce vandalism
- Install entry phones
- Employ caretakers

(continues)

3. Deflection of Offenders from Targets
- Segregate fans at sporting events
- Pay attention to pub locations
- Alter streets to stop cruising for prostitutes

4. Control of Crime Facilitators
- Include photographs on credit cards
- Use toughened glasses and bottles in pubs
- Require passwords for mobile phones

5. Entrance and Exit Screening
- Install automatic ticket gates at stations
- Screen baggage at airports
- Use merchandise tags in shops

6. Formal Surveillance
- Install speeding and red light cameras
- Install burglar alarms
- Employ guards

7. Surveillance by Employees
- Locate pay phones where employees can see them
- Employ park attendants
- Install closed-circuit television systems

8. Natural Surveillance
- Use "defensible space" environmental design
- Improve street lighting
- Promote Neighbourhood Watch

9. Target Removal
- Install removable car radios
- Open women's refuges
- Install public telephones that require phone cards instead of change

10. Property Identification
- Implement property-marking programs
- Require vehicle licensing

11. Temptation Reduction
- Encourage gender-neutral phone listings
- Create well-lit, attended off-street parking
- Promote rapid repair

12. Crime "Benefits" Removal
- Use ink merchandise tags (that mark shoplifters)
- Clean graffiti promptly
- Disable stolen mobile phones promptly

13. Rule Setting
- Require customs declarations
- Establish harassment codes
- Require hotel registration

14. Conscience Raising
- Install roadside speedometers
- Post "shoplifting is stealing" signs
- Post "Idiots drink and drive" signs

15. Control of Factors That Undermine Constraint
- Pass a law controlling drinking age
- Install V-chip in TVs to block violent programs
- Control alcohol at public events

16. Ease of Compliance
- Make easy library checkouts to discourage book theft
- Install public lavatories
- Install litter bins

Source: Adapted from Glodblatt and Lewis 1998, p. 24

CPTED assumes that many criminal acts are the result of a cost/benefit decision by the offender, and that such offences can be prevented when there is a high risk of apprehension and a corresponding lack of potential gain from committing the act (see Box 4.5). CPTED has been incorporated into local government crime prevention plans (Ottawa, Toronto, and Edmonton), into police mandates (in Peel Region, Ontario), on applications in the design of towns (in Tumbler Ridge, B.C.), and in the encouragement of resident interaction and social cohesion (in Montreal). Today, CPTED principles are incorporated as part of the overall urban planning process, particularly in the development of high-density transit-oriented developments and their accompanying transit stations. A case study conducted for the Ottawa Police Service found that the application of CPTED principles resulted in crime and fear reduction in both planned communities as well as crime-prone locations. In locations where CPTED was not applied, crime and disorder problems either continued or occurred as predicted. You can see the full case study at www.safe-environments.com. If you would like to learn more about CPTED principles and practices, check out www.cptedontario.ca.

Problem-Oriented Policing

Problem-oriented policing (POP) is most often cited as a primary component of community policing and as an alternative to the traditional, reactive model of policing. This strategy focuses on the prevention of criminal activity rather than merely the response to it. It involves the community as a partner in identifying and resolving community problems. There are several clearly defined stages, usually referred to as SARA:

- *Scanning*: identifying the problem;
- *Analysis*: determining the cause, scope, and effect of the problem;
- *Response*: developing a plan to address and solve the problem; and
- *Assessment*: determining whether the response was effective.

The particular problem to be addressed may be community-wide and require a long-term plan of action, or it may involve a single individual and a situation that can be addressed in relatively short order.

Given the central role of problem-oriented policing in the framework of community policing, we will consider POP in greater detail in Chapter 5.

Secondary Prevention Programs

Secondary prevention programs focus on areas that produce crime and other types of disorder and seek to identify high-risk offenders. They are often based on crime-area analysis. Strategies include neighbourhood dispute resolution and the diversion of offenders, as well as various school-based crime prevention initiatives and intervention programs for youth.

Emergency phone services, such as the blue emergency phone shown here at the University of Western Ontario, help create a safe environment. There are 19 emergency phones located strategically on the campus that provide a direct link to the police should a situation arise where assistance is required.

Source: Courtesy, The University of Western Ontario

BOX 4.5

USING CPTED TO REDUCE CRIME AND FEAR OF CRIME

CPTED is an appropriate crime reduction strategy that can reduce crime and fear through:

- **Territoriality:** fostering residents' interaction, vigilance, and control over their neighbourhood
- **Surveillance:** maximizing the ability to spot suspicious people and activities
- **Activity support:** encouraging the intended use of public space by residents
- **Hierarchy of space:** identifying ownership by delineating private space from public space through real or symbolic boundaries
- **Access control/target hardening:** using physical barriers, security devices, and tamper-resistant materials to restrict entrance
- **Environment:** a design or location decision that takes into account the surrounding environment and minimizes the use of space by conflicting groups
- **Image/Maintenance:** ensuring that a building or area is clean, well maintained, and graffiti-free

Source: Crime Prevention through Environmental Design, 1998, Royal Canadian Mounted Police. Reproduced with the permission of the Minister of Public Works and Government Services, 2012.

School Programs

Residential school programs involve police officers assigned to a school and on campus full-time. These school liaison officers, as they are commonly called, participate as fully as possible in all facets of school life. The objectives include developing positive relations with teens, improving youth attitudes toward the police, and providing security for the school and students. Nonresidential school programs most often involve officers periodically making presentations on various topics. At the elementary school level, for example, these presentations tend to focus on safety issues, including "stranger-danger" and bicycle safety.

One of the innovative programs of the Halton Regional Police Service is its Safety Village. Operated with the assistance of the Optimist Clubs of Halton, the village consists of 12 miniature replica buildings in a community setting. Students in kindergarten and grades two to three are taught traffic safety in the village and are exposed to traffic simulations with bicycles and battery-operated cars. At the middle school and high school levels, presentations may focus on such topics as drug and alcohol abuse and gangs.

Tertiary Prevention Programs

Tertiary prevention programs are designed to deter, incapacitate, and rehabilitate offenders. The focus is on intervening with youth and adult offenders in an attempt to reduce the likelihood of further criminal behaviour. The majority of tertiary prevention programs are conducted within the criminal justice system and generally do not involve police.

OTHER APPROACHES TO PREVENTING AND REDUCING CRIME

Crime Prevention through Social Development

Crime prevention through social development (CPSD) attempts to eliminate some of the underlying factors that contribute to crime. These approaches include initiatives to reduce poverty, improve childhood nutrition, and increase the availability of proper housing, employment, educational opportunities, and adequate play and recreational facilities. Some of the factors that place people at risk for criminal activity include:

- child poverty;
- inadequate living conditions;
- inconsistent and uncaring parenting;
- childhood trauma, such as physical and sexual abuse;
- family breakdown;
- racism and other forms of discrimination;
- difficulties in school;
- friends who engage in criminal behaviour; and
- living situations involving alcohol, drugs, and other kinds of substance abuse.

Among the prevention and intervention programs designed to prevent and respond to these underlying conditions are family-based programs, school-based programs, and peer-group-based programs.

Early intervention with children at risk has become a particular focus of attention. Preschool or "head start" programs, aimed at improving the mental and social skills of high-risk children, operate in many parts of the country.

A prominent U.S. study of child development that followed children into adulthood found that children born into poverty who attended a targeted daycare program had fewer arrests, depended less upon welfare, were more likely to complete high school, and had higher earnings than those who did not participate in this type of program. Furthermore, it was found that taxpayers saved $7.16 for each dollar invested in the program. Preschool participants consumed fewer resources because they were less likely to come into conflict with the law (Schweinhart et al. 1993). Patrol officers are increasingly involved in these programs, often in collaboration with other agencies and community groups.

In 2005, the Canadian Association of Chiefs of Police (CACP) received funding from Canada's National Crime Prevention Centre to develop a coalition of national organizations not traditionally involved in community safety, to promote the concept of crime prevention through social development. The Federation of Canadian Municipalities, the Canadian Association of Police Boards, and the Canadian Professional Police Association formally supported this objective.

From 2005 to 2007, the CACP further developed and implemented a public awareness strategy to help build support for community-owned approaches to crime prevention through social development. The CACP website provides important details on strategic crime prevention initiatives across Canada and demonstrates police leadership through the inclusion of strategic partners in strengthening public safety. For more details, take a look at the CACP website at www.cacp.ca.

Increasing Police Legitimacy

One strategy that is generally not included in discussions of crime prevention is called **police legitimacy**. This approach, which holds considerable promise, refers to the collective efforts by a police service to ensure that citizens are treated fairly, and to the initiatives taken by police to explain their role and activities through personal contact.

Two of the more common strategies to increase police legitimacy are police–community meetings and door-to-door visits by police officers. Police–community meetings include community consultative committees that provide a forum for identifying problems and concerns of community residents and strategies for addressing them (see Chapter 10). Police–community meetings also help break down stereotypes and open lines of communication between the police and the community.

Door-to-door visits by police officers provide officers with the opportunity to seek information from residents on specific persons and criminal activities. They also provide an opportunity for police officers to distribute information to residents and to introduce themselves. Such visits are one of many ways that police services and officers try to legitimize their role and activities and create the perception among community residents that the police behave in a fair and impartial manner.

There is some evidence from the U.S. that this strategy to increase police legitimacy produces positive outcomes including reduced fear of the police, a reduced crime rate, lower recidivism among offenders, and increased obedience to the law (Sherman et al. 1997).

The "Broken Windows" Approach

In the early 1980s, two U.S. criminologists, James Q. Wilson and George L. Kelling (1982), wrote an article entitled "Broken Windows: The Police and Neighbourhood Safety." **Broken windows** was a metaphor for neighbourhood deterioration based on the observations of patrol officers that if a window was broken in a building and not repaired, in very short order all the windows would be broken. A broken window that remains unrepaired is a statement that no one cares enough about the quality of life in the neighbourhood to bother fixing the little things that are wrong. While a broken window is a small thing, it triggers further neglect and results in the progressive deterioration of the entire neighbourhood. Wilson and Kelling argued that police services had neglected little things—the law enforcement equivalent of broken windows—and that there was a need to reorient the efforts of police work. "Broken windows" policing addresses minor nuisances and offences, based on the assumption that if these offences are left unchecked they will lead to more serious crime and disorder.

The "broken windows" approach to policing was implemented in New York City during the 1990s, and while it is difficult to isolate the effects of any one particular intervention, one study generally credits the approach with a significant and consistent decline in violent crime. Kelling and Sousa (2001) credit "broken windows" policing with the prevention of more than 60,000 violent crimes in New York City between 1989 to 1998.

High Technology in Crime Prevention: CCTVs—Big Help or Big Brother?

One of the more recent applications of high technology—and one that seems to be gaining favour worldwide—is closed-circuit television (CCTV) systems. These systems, which are extensively used in Europe, use cameras that are monitored by operators; the operators are able to contact the police if an event occurs. Traditionally, CCTVs have been deployed in stores and other businesses such as banks; however, in recent years they have been used to scan streets in several European cities. These street-focused systems target property crimes, such as car theft and break and enters, as well as violent offences, such as muggings.

Research on CCTV systems suggests they may be effective in reducing some types of criminal behaviour. However, the following observations have been made:

- CCTVs assist police to solve crimes after the fact.
- CCTVs do little to deter public disorder offences.
- CCTVs should be utilized as part of an overall crime reduction strategy and tailored to community needs.

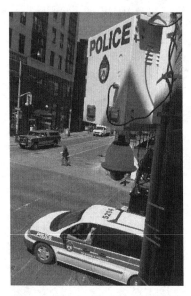

Closed-circuit television (CCTV) systems are monitored by operators who are able to contact the police should an event occur. CCTVs are positioned in "hot spots" to deter crime and to identify the individuals responsible for criminal activity.

Source: © Copyright The Globe and Mail Inc./CP images

BOX 4.6

TECHNOLOGY VERSUS PRIVACY RIGHTS: WALKING A SLIPPERY SLOPE

Proponents of CCTV argue that law-abiding citizens have nothing to fear from being monitored by CCTV cameras. Opponents fear that the technological monitoring of public spaces represents an unjustified intrusion on a citizen's rights to privacy. What do you think about this issue? If technology could prevent all crime or identify all offenders, would it be worth the investment? Now think about other forms of current technology that can track our every movement—from biometric scanning devices such as facial recognition software in Heathrow Airport to gunshot detection systems in Chicago, from so-called black boxes in motor vehicles to global positioning systems (GPS). Another technological system is a photo-radar grid system that calculates the speed and distance travelled by a motor vehicle between several points. If the motor vehicle passes another camera located in the grid earlier than predicted, then a speeding ticket is issued. All these examples of technology are in use around the world. In Canada, provincial and federal privacy bodies (i.e., Ontario Office of the Information and the Privacy Commissioner) recommend all public bodies, including the police, prepare Privacy Impact Assessments in order to achieve a balance between the use of intrusive technology and privacy rights.

- Evaluations conducted in the United States and United Kingdom found CCTVs had a deterrent effect in car parks in terms of theft from and of vehicles.
- CCTVs enhance the perception of personal safety and may assist in reducing citizen fear of crime and disorder.
- Deterrence effects of CCTV are mixed and well-designed evaluations are necessary to ensure they are deployed correctly (Deisman 2003; Gill and Spriggs 2005).

Many Canadian municipalities are currently wrestling with whether or not to add CCTVs to their crime prevention arsenals. Kelowna, British Columbia, Sudbury, Ontario, and Calgary, Alberta have installed CCTV cameras to monitor public spaces. The Toronto Police Service (TPS) has developed a very good CCTV program that uses mobile CCTVs that can be moved into an area and deployed for a short period of time until the problem has been addressed. (The TPS program is profiled as a case study at the end of this chapter.) Concerns have been raised, however, that the dangers of these "electronic spies"—most notably the invasion of citizens' privacy—outweigh any crime prevention benefits (see Box 4.6). Critics have pointed out that the general absence of privacy laws allows anyone to film others secretly without reprisal. With the growing sophistication of technology, it is likely that there will be increased pressure to use CCTVs and other devices in an attempt to prevent crime. A comprehensive evaluation of CCTVs has been done in the United Kingdom, and the report can be found at the Home Office website at www.homeoffice.gov.uk.

THE EFFECTIVENESS OF CRIME PREVENTION PROGRAMS

Assessing the effectiveness of a particular police strategy or program is difficult under the best of circumstances (see Box 4.7). Among the obstacles are the following:

- Research studies vary in their methodologies, in the types of data gathered, and in the outcomes measured.
- How a specific program or strategy is implemented is influenced by the priorities and resources of the police service, the enthusiasm and commitment of the police officers and community residents involved, and the specific attributes of the community itself.
- Most of the research studies have been done in the United States, not Canada.
- The slippery issue of **crime displacement**—the possibility that offenders and their activities have relocated. Canadian criminologist Kim Rossmo (1995:5–6) has identified five forms of crime displacement:

BOX 4.7

THE EFFECTIVENESS OF SELECTED CRIME PREVENTION STRATEGIES

Operation Identification/Operation Provident: Impact on property crimes unclear. Studies on similar programs in the United States found they do not reduce break and enters or property loss. The programs do increase police–citizen interaction and citizen awareness of crime prevention activities. They may function to displace crime to neighbouring areas not participating in the program.

Neighbourhood Watch: Does not prevent crime. Areas of high crime have less involvement, while the strategy is most successful in middle-class communities that have little crime. May increase the fear of crime among community residents. The anonymity of most neighbourhoods and apartment complexes—the fact that people do not get to know their neighbours—is a primary obstacle to the success of Neighbourhood Watch. Typically, most community residents hesitate to become involved with their neighbourhoods, even if such involvement is limited to being watchful for suspicious behaviour.

Community meetings: Have little impact on the crime rate. Exceptions include a program in Chicago where community meetings focus specifically on crime patterns in the neighbourhood and on developing ideas to attack them. Although it is not certain that the crime rates have been reduced, the project has been successful in involving residents in high-crime areas in the meetings and specific projects.

Door-to-door visits: Some evidence that visits may reduce the rates of crime victimization. In addition, visits increase police legitimacy; this may in turn relate to a number of police outcomes (see below).

Citizen patrols: No published evaluations in Canada. Findings from U.S. and European research indicate that such patrols may reduce property crime, levels of violence, and residents' fear of crime.

Problem-oriented policing: No formal evaluations of POP in Canada. Results from studies that have examined the application of POP to specific problems by several U.S. police departments have been mixed: some have indicated reduced levels of certain types of crime, improved police–community relationships, and the acquisition of problem-solving skills by police officers. At other sites, POP initiatives have had no apparent impact.

Crime prevention through environmental design: Target hardening, property marking, improving security (including the installation of CCTV), and altering building design and pedestrian routes have, in some jurisdictions, reduced levels of residential break and enters, robberies, and assaults. Closing or selling properties used for drug abuse has, in certain jurisdictions, reduced calls for service. Some evidence suggests that using CCTV and employing multiple clerks in stores that are open late hours may reduce the rates of robbery and property theft.

Sources: Polowek 1995; Sherman et al. 1997.

- *geographic,* which involves offenders relocating their criminal activity to another area;
- *temporal,* where criminals alter the times they commit offences;
- *tactical,* where offenders develop different strategies to commit crimes;
- *target,* which involves offenders selecting different places to commit crimes or different persons to victimize; and
- *functional,* where changes in technology reduce criminal opportunity in some areas (e.g., bank robberies decline as we move toward a cashless society but new criminal opportunities such as wire fraud are created).

With these caveats in mind, consider the findings presented earlier in Box 4.2.

There is increasing evidence that the police can indeed affect crime levels if police services manage and deploy their resources wisely and address problems systematically and comprehensively. It should also be remembered that reducing the crime rate should not be the only indicator of program success. There are other important considerations, such as the quality of police–community relationships, the fear of crime and related perceptions of personal safety, the experiences of crime victims and their attitudes toward the police, and the extent to which the specific initiative was successful in securing the participation of community residents over the long term. Do not forget that a reactive model of policing has very little impact on the crime rate.

Factors Limiting Program Effectiveness

At the very worst, the findings as to the "noneffectiveness" of many community policing initiatives might lead one into deep depression; at the very least, they suggest that there are a number of obstacles—in police organizations, among line officers, in other community agencies, and in the community itself—that may undermine the objectives of crime prevention programs.

Promoting change among the rank-and-file subculture has been described as being as easy as "bending granite" (Guyot 1979). This is especially evident any time a police organization implements new procedures, as in the case of police response to domestic violence. Because of increasing demands on police organizations and the explosion in information, we require police who are flexible and adaptable and who are excellent information managers. Contemporary police officers must be able to process information quickly (e.g., new laws, new procedures, new case decisions) and incorporate them into policing responses. This requires effective change management strategies both organizationally and individually. In Chapter 8, we will see that even in progressive police services there are obstacles and sources of resistance to the implementation of community policing, including:

- apathy toward and lack of participation in crime prevention programs by residents,
- the frequent absence of a clearly defined role for the community, and
- the fact that communities afflicted by high rates of crime and disorder are often those where it is most difficult to interest community residents.

CRIME PREVENTION IN ABORIGINAL COMMUNITIES

Developing and implementing effective crime prevention programs in Aboriginal communities has proven to be a challenge both for police services (Aboriginal and non-Aboriginal) and for the communities themselves. The crime prevention initiatives that have been developed fall into two categories:

1. Programs that are part of an overall crime prevention strategy developed by senior police administrators and implemented in both Aboriginal and non-Aboriginal communities.
2. Programs developed by police officers at the local community level in collaboration with chiefs, band councils, and community residents. Needless to say, these latter programs have been the most effective.

Crime prevention initiatives that have been established in Aboriginal communities across Canada include the following:

- *Outreach Support Worker Project.* The Winnipeg Native Alliance developed this project to help youths leaving gangs or institutions reintegrate into society.
- *Stl'atl'imx Citizens on Patrol (COPS).* In British Columbia, the Stl'atl'imx Tribal Police received funding to establish a Citizens on Patrol (COPS) network in 10 communities of the Stl'atl'imx Nation. Through the COPS network, volunteer citizens are trained to patrol their communities, recognize suspicious activities, and report them to police. This initiative assisted in building the capacity of the community to prevent crime.

- *Atikamekw Community-Based Training on Suicide Intervention/Recognition.* Funding was provided to the Conseil de la Nation Atikamekw to support the delivery of two training sessions on suicide intervention to 24 Atikamekw community professionals who work with at-risk youth. The program takes a community-based approach to suicide intervention by linking existing national training resources to people and organizations at the community level. The program included the following elements:
  - two days of suicide intervention training,
  - a one-day Healing Circle,
  - a component on Aboriginal spirituality,
  - training in critical incident stress debriefing, and
  - training in community building.

- *Home Repairs Fraud Prevention Program.* This program was developed in response to incidents in which elders on Six Nations Territory had been victimized by home repair fraud. Working with the Ohsweken Branch of the Royal Bank, located on Six Nations Territory, the police developed a plan to warn the elders about different ways they could be victimized by fraudulent contractors. This involved producing and distributing a brochure, and meetings with the territory's elders' clubs (Lewis et al. 1995).

The greatest potential lies in the development of community-focused crime prevention, which ensures that program initiatives are adapted to the specific needs of individual communities and, furthermore, that community residents play an integral part in identifying the problems to be addressed and then participate in the programs.

PUBLIC NOTIFICATION

Within the traditional model of police work, police involvement in the prevention of and response to crime ended when suspects were arrested. Increasingly, police involvement is being extended to the post-sentencing and post-incarceration stages of the justice system. Whenever an offender is released back into the community, either through a decision of a parole board or after having served most or all of the sentence, one critical question is whether the public should be notified. In Ontario, for example, Christopher's Law (Sex Offender Registry), passed in 2000, sets out the statutory framework for the registration of sex offenders in the province. The practice of **public notification** raises a moral dilemma, as offenders who have served their time in jail are deemed to be suitable for return to the community. The debate can be characterized as one between the rights of society and the rights of the individual.

The pressure on politicians and the police to notify the community when certain offenders are released from correctional institutions originated from various victims' groups across the country. Most jurisdictions have passed, or are in the process of passing, legislation that provides for notification. In Ontario, for example, the *Community Safety Act* was designed to increase the amount of information about offenders available to victims and the community and to supplement the *Victim's Bill of Rights*. Under the Act, police and corrections authorities may provide victims and the community at large with personal information about an offender who is being released and may pose a risk to public safety. The Act also includes provisions for tracking name changes by offenders—a first in Canada.

There are programs that target offenders who have been released from confinement. These include the Repeat Offender Program Enforcement Unit (ROPE) of the Toronto Police Service; the High Risk Offender Units in Edmonton and Calgary; and Project SMART (Surveillance and Monitoring of All High-Risk Targets), a partnership between the Ontario Provincial Police, Correctional Service of Canada, and the Kingston Police.

ASSESSING EFFECTIVENESS

Even with a community policing framework, police services continue to assume the primary role in the control of crime in the community. It is critical that crime prevention and crime reduction strategies be evaluated in order to determine their overall effectiveness. This is increasingly becoming a requirement to obtain funding. For example, the National Crime Prevention Centre requires program evaluations for the continued funding. There are a number of standard measures for assessing the effectiveness of the police in controlling crime and social disorder (see Table 4.2).

Table 4.2 Measures of Crime Control Effectiveness

Objective	Quality Characteristic	Specific Measure	Data Collection Procedure
Prevention of crime	Reported crime rates	Number of reported crimes per 100,000 population, total and by type of crime	Incident reports
	Victimization rates	Number of reported plus unreported crimes per 1,000 households (or residents or businesses), by type of crime	Household survey, such as the General Social Survey conducted during each federal census.
	Victimization of households and businesses	Percentage of (a) households, (b) businesses victimized	Household survey, business survey
	Physical casualties	Number and rate of persons (a) physically injured, (b) killed in course of crimes or nontraffic, crime-related police work-including victims and the police	Incident reports
		Percentage of domestic disputes and other disturbance calls with no arrest and no second call within x number of hours	Dispatch records, incident reports
	Peacekeeping in domestic disputes	Number of injuries to (a) citizens (after police arrival), (b) police per 100 domestic quarrel calls	Incident reports
Apprehension of offenders	Crimes "solved" at least in part	Percentage of reported crimes cleared, by type of crime and whether cleared by arrest or by "exception"	Incident reports
	Completeness of apprehension	Percentage of "person-crimes" cleared, by type of crime	Incident reports, arrest reports
	Quality/ effectiveness of arrest	Percentage of arrests that survive preliminary court hearing and percentage dropped for police-related reasons, by type of crime	Arrest and court records

(continues)

Objective	Quality Characteristic	Specific Measure	Data Collection Procedure
		Percentage of arrests resulting in conviction or treatment (a) on at least one charge, (b) on highest initial charge, by type of crime	Arrest and court records
	Stolen property recovery	Percentage of (a) stolen vehicles, (b) other stolen property subsequently recovered	Incident reports, arrest or special property records
Responsiveness of police	Response time	Percentage of emergency or high-priority calls responded to within x minutes and percentage of nonemergency calls responded to within six minutes	Dispatch records
	Perceived	Percentage of (a) citizens, responsiveness (b) businesses that feel police respond fast enough when called	Household survey, business survey, complainant survey
Feeling of security	Perceived safety	Percentage of (a) citizens, (b) business persons who feel safe (or unsafe) walking in their neighbourhoods at night	Household survey, business survey
Fairness, courtesy, helpfulness/ co-operativeness, honesty	Fairness	Percentage of (a) citizens, (b) businesses that feel police are generally fair in dealing with them	Household survey, business survey, complainant survey
	Courtesy	Percentage of (a) citizens, (b) businesses that feel police are generally courteous in dealing with them	Household survey, business survey, complainant survey
	Helpfulness/ co-operativeness	Percentage of (a) citizens, (b) businesses that feel police are generally helpful, co-operative and sensitive to their concerns	Household survey, business survey, complainant survey
		Number of reported incidents or complaints of police misbehaviour, and the number resulting in judgment against the local government or employee (by type of complaint civil charge, criminal charge, other service complaints), per 100 police	Police and mayor's office records
	Honesty	Percentage of citizens who feel police are in general honest and can be trusted	Household survey, complainant survey

Objective	Quality Characteristic	Specific Measure	Data Collection Procedure
	Citizen satisfaction with police handling of miscellaneous incidents	Percentage of persons requesting assistance for other than serious crimes who are satisfied (or dissatisfied) with police handling of their problems, categorized by reason for dissatisfaction and by type of call	Complainant survey
	Citizen satisfaction with overall performance	Percentage of (a) citizens, (b) businesses that rate police performance as excellent or good (or fair or poor), by reason for satisfaction (or dissatisfaction)	Household survey, business survey, complainant survey
	Police safety	Number of injuries to police officers (a) per 100 officers, (b) per 100 calls	Police injury reports

Source: Hatry et al., 1992, pp.72-73. Reprinted with permission of The International City/County Management Association, 777 North Capital Street, NE, Suite 500, Washington, DC 20002. All Rights Reserved.

CHAPTER SUMMARY

This chapter has focused on how police services, often in collaboration with the community, respond to crime and social disorder. Within the framework of community policing, a variety of strategies can be used, including proactive strategies, community service approaches, and crime prevention programs. This variety reflects the key point that community policing involves police work that is reactive, proactive, and coactive (with the community).

In recent years, police services have also adopted additional approaches to crime prevention and response, including preventing crime through social development, creating programs that increase police legitimacy, and supporting the increased deployment of CCTVs. A critical issue that must be addressed in determining the effectiveness of crime prevention initiatives is that of crime displacement—the possibility of offenders and their activities having merely relocated, rather than crime having been eliminated. Among the obstacles that often limit the effectiveness of crime prevention are resistance on the part of police services and disinterest on the part of the community to become involved.

CHAPTER REVIEW

Key Terms

- broken windows approach, p. 100
- community service approaches, p. 89
- crime displacement, p. 101
- crime prevention programs, p. 93
- crime prevention through environmental design (CPTED), p. 95
- crime prevention through social development (CPSD), p. 98
- foot patrols or beats, p. 89
- hard crime calls, p. 87

Key Points

- The strategies used to prevent and respond to crime can be generally grouped into proactive targeting strategies, community service approaches, and crime prevention programs.
- Although foot patrols do not appear to reduce overall levels of crime, they do function to reduce citizen fear of crime and create favourable community perceptions of the police.
- The three categories of crime prevention programs are primary prevention programs, secondary prevention programs, and tertiary prevention programs. Strategies in each of these areas may be situational or focus on social development.
- Crime prevention through environmental design (CPTED) attempts to reduce criminal opportunities by altering the physical environment of structures and places.
- Problem-oriented policing (POP) is a primary component of community policing and focuses on the identification and resolution of community problems.
- Crime displacement—the relocation of offenders and their activities—makes it difficult to determine the effectiveness of many crime prevention programs.
- There are a number of factors that may limit the potential effectiveness of crime prevention strategies.
- Public notification, a strategy to inform communities when certain offenders are released from custody, raises the issue of individual rights versus the rights of society.

Self-Evaluation

QUESTIONS

1. What is the **safer communities approach to crime prevention**?
2. What is meant by **proactive targeted strategies**?
3. What are **community service approaches** to preventing crime?
4. What are **crime prevention programs** and how do they differ from proactive targeted strategies and community service approaches?
5. What is **tactical or directed patrol** and how is it carried out?
6. Compare **hard crime calls** and **soft crime calls**.
7. What is **team policing** and what role does it play in community policing?
8. Compare **primary prevention programs**, **secondary prevention programs**, and **tertiary prevention programs**.
9. Provide an example of a **situational crime prevention** program and one that seeks to prevent crime through **social development**.
10. What is **crime prevention through environmental design (CPTED)**?
11. What is meant by increasing **policing legitimacy**?
12. What is the **broken windows approach** to crime prevention?
13. What is **crime displacement** and what are the various forms it may take?
14. Why is **public notification** the subject of controversy?

KEY IDEAS

1. Which of the following relies on police patrols for the apprehension, deterrence, and incapacitation of criminal offenders?
   a. proactive targeting strategy
   b. community service approach
   c. crime prevention
   d. team policing

2. Which kind of calls are hold-up alarms, shootings, stabbings, auto thefts, and assaults examples of?
   a. community-initiated crime calls
   b. hard crime calls
   c. soft crime calls
   d. victim-precipitated crime calls

3. What is suggested by research studies on crime attack strategies?
   a. The number of police officers does not significantly reduce the levels of crime.
   b. Proactive police arrests, focusing on high-risk persons and offences, may reduce levels of serious violent crime.
   c. Random police patrols may reduce levels of crime.
   d. Non-violent crimes continue to increase but at a modest level.

4. Foot patrols, bicycle patrols, team policing, and community police stations and storefronts are examples of which of the following categories?
   a. crime prevention programs
   b. proactive targeting strategies
   c. community service approaches
   d. crime prevention strategies that do not work

5. According to research studies, which of the following is a result of foot patrols?
   a. decreased fear of crime among citizens
   b. increased calls for service
   c. increased reports of patrol officer misconduct
   d. decreased job satisfaction for patrol officers due to fatigue

6. What type of crime prevention programs identify opportunities for criminal offences and alter these conditions in order to reduce the likelihood of crimes being committed?
   a. tertiary crime prevention programs
   b. secondary crime prevention programs
   c. primary crime prevention programs
   d. ancillary crime prevention programs

7. What is the intended purpose of door-to-door visits by police officers and police–community meetings?
   a. increasing police information and intelligence
   b. increasing community awareness of police programs
   c. increasing crime prevention through environmental design (CPTED)
   d. increasing police legitimacy

8. One approach to crime prevention attempts to alleviate the conditions that contribute to crime, such as poverty, poor housing, unemployment, and lack of educational opportunities. What is this approach called?
   a. crime prevention through opportunity
   b. tertiary crime prevention
   c. the broken windows approach
   d. crime prevention through social development

9. In one type of crime displacement offenders develop different strategies to commit crimes. What is this called?
   a. tertiary crime displacement
   b. temporal crime displacement
   c. target crime displacement
   d. tactical crime displacement

10. Which of the following statements has been suggested by research studies?
    a. Operation Identification significantly reduces the levels of property crime.
    b. Neighbourhood Watch is an effective approach to crime prevention.
    c. Citizen patrols may reduce property crimes and citizens' fear of crime.
    d. Crime prevention through environmental design (CPTED) is generally ineffective in reducing property crimes.

Responding To and Preventing Crime: Situations and Strategies

Case Studies

Case Study 1. Aboriginal Community Involvement in Crime Prevention through Community Development

A successful program in Alberta is the First Nations Crime Prevention Program in association with Alberta Justice. First Nations people have expressed a strong desire to create and deliver crime prevention programs appropriate to their unique culture and local needs. Through funding provided to the First Nations Crime Prevention Program, four crime prevention coordinator positions have been established to serve nine reserves located throughout the province. Coordinators are responsible for developing local initiatives, particularly for youth, in the areas of recreation, employment, social care, and family violence, and for monitoring crime trends on reserves, designing programs to address the needs of the residents, and collaborating with groups such as the local police service, community agencies, elders, and schools in addressing the particular crime-related problems of the reserves.

Case Study 2. Problem-Oriented Policing in Action

In Antigonish, Nova Scotia, the community and local Royal Canadian Mounted Police were concerned with increasing disorder related to alcohol consumption, crowds, violence, traffic congestion, property damage, and noise in relation to an identified "hot spot"—Pipers Pub. The RCMP coordinated an approach with the bar owners, patrons, neighbours, and business community, and developed the following interventions:

- CPTED approaches included adding extra lighting to the street outside the pubs, removing seating that encouraged crowds to gather, adding a crosswalk, landscaping areas for safety, and installing a camera to monitor activity;
- including campus security to control crowds;
- preventing alcohol sales to minors and intoxicated parties;
- moving fast-food stands away from crowd areas to discourage gathering;
- creating a taxi stand for better traffic flow;
- generating town council participation and support;
- attending town meetings that include business owners, students, the university, taxi drivers, town council, and the Detachment; and
- conducting an ongoing evaluation of the impact of each intervention.

As a result of the partnerships and the response, the town saw a 40 percent decrease in assaults, a significant reduction in property damage, fewer crowds and fights, and a safer nightlife environment. Campus security developed a better working relationship with the Detachment. Students offered positive feedback through newspaper articles, citing increased safety in the pub area.

Case Study 3. Crime Prevention through Environmental Design: Planned Design Changes

Design can involve a single building, a single park, a single school, or a large multi-building development. In this case, a police constable used the principles of CPTED to reduce the calls for service and levels of criminal activity around a video arcade in a shopping mall. An assessment was made of all of the problems associated with the arcade, both inside the store and in the area. In addition, other arcades in the municipality and in neighbouring municipalities were studied. The design features associated with low-problem video arcades were noted and incorporated into a plan to address the problem arcade.

Among the recommended changes, which were presented to the municipal council and to the owner of the arcade, were internal alterations that included the placement of the video machines (against the walls only, and not in the centre of the floor, to ensure good sight lines for the on-duty cashier) and ample inside lighting. External changes involved limiting the number of parking spaces to prevent overcrowding in the arcade. In addition, changes were made in the management of the arcade, including restricting the hours of operation to those of other businesses in the mall, enforcing age restrictions, and controlling access to the washrooms. Implementation of these changes resulted in a 150 percent reduction in crime and calls for service during the first year and a further 5 percent reduction the following year. The project provided the basis for developing model bylaws for video arcades that have been adopted by a number of municipalities across Canada and the United States.

Source: Griffiths, Whitelaw, and Parent 1999:214.

Case Study 4. The OPP Cottage Watch Program: A Partnership of the Police and the Community

In 1997, there were approximately 3,510 cottage break-ins across Ontario. The Cottage Watch program is a police–community partnership designed to prevent break and enters, damage, and theft from cottages. It takes a three-pronged approach of property identification, community patrols, and police break-and-enter investigation teams. The three major partners in Cottage Watch are the Ontario Provincial Police through the local detachment, the local cottagers' associations, and the Federation of Ontario Cottagers' Association (FOCA).

Additional support comes from insurance companies and telephone and utility companies. For example, the Rural Crime Prevention Strategy in Ontario established a provincial Cottage Watch crime prevention program in conjunction with FOCA and its corporate sponsors, LMS Prolink Limited and the Royal & Sun Alliance Insurance Company, as well as local cottage associations and OPP detachments. Cottage Watch is similar to Neighbourhood Watch programs in larger communities.

Source: Ontario Provincial Police, 1999. "Cottage Watch: A Community Crime Prevention Program." CPDC News 5 (April).

Case Study 5. Conflict Resolution at 4:00 a.m.: A Case of Unpaid Taxi Fare

In the early morning hours, a two-officer unit in an urban police service is sent to a scene where two young adults, after having been driven by taxi, are unable to pay the fare of approximately $50. One of the passengers had run from the scene, leaving the other passenger in the back seat. Upon arrival, the officers question both the driver and the passenger. Satisfied that the passenger has no money with which to pay, the driver, passenger, and the officers proceed to the passenger's home several blocks away. The officers instruct the passenger to secure the funds to pay the driver or else provide property as collateral.

Source: Griffiths, Whitelaw, and Parent 1999:190

Case Study 6: Public Surveillance: Closed Circuit Television (CCTV) in Cornwall, Ontario

In November of 2009, The Cornwall Community Police Service submitted a grant application through the Civil Remedies Grant Program to secure funding for the purchase and installation of a public surveillance CCTV network in the City of Cornwall. The grant application was approved and the CCPS received over $100,000 in July 2010 from the Ministry of the Attorney General for this initiative.

It is proposed that, in support of the vision statement of the Cornwall Community Police Service, "A Safer Cornwall, reducing crime always" that 6 cameras be purchased and installed within the city on a three-year pilot period. It is further proposed that the effectiveness of the CCTV Public Surveillance Project be measured during this time period to determine the effect on enhancing a sense of safety among the public who use Cornwall's downtown areas, and further to measure its deterrent effect on the commission of crime in the areas under surveillance.

Purpose and Principles of Monitoring

The key purpose of the Cornwall Public Surveillance CCTV Project is to promote public safety in the downtown areas of the City of Cornwall.

The goals of the Cornwall Public Surveillance CCTV Project are:

- to contribute to the safe environment of the downtown areas;
- to assist as one of the components of the downtown areas revitalization efforts; and,
- to improve the ability of the Cornwall Community Police Service and community to respond to crime and anti-social behaviour occurring in Cornwall's downtown areas.

The objectives of the Cornwall Public Surveillance CCTV Project are:

- to deter crime and anti-social behaviour;
- to increase the perception of safety; and,
- to use camera images as evidence to identify suspects involved in criminal activities.

Many business owners support cameras

In Toronto, many business owners have been particularly supportive of the police installing CCTV cameras. Some have even offered to help pay for the pilot program, although it's $2 million cost is being picked up by the province. "If you're not doing anything wrong, you've got nothing to worry about," John Kiru of the Toronto Area Business Improvement Association told the Globe and Mail. "I'm of the view that this (CCTV program) is the right thing to do."

Law enforcement officials say video surveillance can be both a deterrent to crime and a valuable forensic tool. Cameras are highly visible and might stop a mugger or a rapist. If an offense is committed within view of police cameras, investigators can pore over video images to find clues and suspects. (As in the case of the June 2011 Stanley Cup riot that occurred in Vancouver and subsequent police investigation utilizing public CCTV images and those held by private retail stores as well the use of cell phone images provided by members of the public.)

Statistics from U.S. cities that use video surveillance point to reductions in crime in areas where cameras are installed. Civil libertarians have counter-arguments to these and other points made by those in favour of video surveillance but the fact remains that the public in Canada and elsewhere wants crime deterred, and offenders caught. High-profile cases like the London Underground bombings or the Creba slaying in Toronto tend to ramp up support for police CCTV programs. Canadians may not be sleep-walking to British levels of video surveillance, but life in Canadian cities is definitely becoming more camera-friendly.

Source: © Cornwall Community Police. http://www.cornwallpolice.com/en/our-programs/public-surveillance-cctv.html.

EXERCISES: KNOWLEDGE INTO PRACTICE

Exercise 1. Developing and Implementing Crime Prevention Programs

The development and implementation of crime prevention programs in unique environments presents challenges to police officers. Consider each of the following "task environments." Then, for each environment, (1) identify the types of challenges that might confront police officers developing partnerships with the community, and (2) note how each of these challenges might be successfully met and resolved.

Task Environment 1. Inner-City Neighbourhood with a High Population of Recent Immigrants

A community is populated by recent immigrants to Canada who come from countries where the police are feared and avoided. Many of the immigrants speak English as a second language and are still adjusting to life in Canada. There have been several high-profile incidents involving the police and allegations of excessive use of force. Community residents are fearful of being victimized by gangs of youth in the neighbourhood, but are reluctant to involve the police.

Challenge   Meeting the Challenge

_____

_____

_____

_____

Task Environment 2. Suburban Bedroom Community

This upper-middle-class community is adjacent to a large urban centre and is largely residential. During the day, most residents are away from their homes working in the city. Although break-ins have been occurring with increasing frequency, to date residents have been generally unresponsive to police efforts to become involved in crime prevention initiatives. In the words of one resident: "I'd rather play golf during my free time. Let the police and the insurance companies figure it out."

Challenge   Meeting the Challenge

_____

_____

_____

_____

Task Environment 3. Cottage Country

An increase in property vandalism, theft, and break and enters—particularly during the off-season—has accompanied the explosive growth of cottage country. Most cottage owners are residents in the area during the summer months, and there is a small population of residents who live in the region year-round. Cottages on some lakes are accessible during the winter months, while others are not because of snowfall and unploughed roadways.

Challenge	Meeting the Challenge

Task Environment 4. A Remote Community in Northwestern Ontario

This community has a population of 450. It is accessible by air and, during several months of the year, by road. It has one resident police officer, and other services, such as the courts, are provided on a "fly in" basis. There is an active band council. The community follows a traditional way of life, centred on hunting and fishing, although in recent years there have been increasing problems with youth misbehaviour, including solvent and alcohol abuse.

Challenge	Meeting the Challenge

Exercise 2. CCTVs: Effective Crime Prevention or Big Brother?

The municipal council in your community is considering a proposal by the police to install CCTVs to reduce crime and disorder in an area of restaurants and nightclubs. The proposal is supported by local business owners as well as by the police officers assigned to the area. Opposition has come from a citizens' group that feels the CCTVs infringe on rights of privacy and mark the beginning of "Big Brother" society.

Consider the issues related to CCTVs generally and then specifically in this context.

a. Would you support the installation of CCTVs in the area as a member of the municipal council?

b. Would you support the installation of CCTVs in the area as a resident of the community not residing in the area to be placed under CCTVs?

_____

_____

_____

_____

c. Would you support the installation of CCTVs in the area as a resident of the community residing in the area to be placed under CCTVs?

_____

_____

_____

_____

d. Would you support the installation of CCTVs in the area as a patron of the restaurants and nightclubs in the area?

_____

_____

_____

_____

e. Would you support the installation of CCTVs in your neighbourhood?

Yes _____ No _____

f. Why?

_____

_____

_____

_____

Exercise 3. Social Media Task

In Chapter 2 we raised the topic of how social media is serving to change the way communications can assist the police as well as undermine policing efforts, leading to changes in a variety of factors from crime detection and crime solving to mobilizing communities. Using YouTube, Facebook, and Twitter, find examples relating to crime—these may consist of the police or members of social networks seeking assistance from social networks to identify criminals, to find new evidence for a crime, or to alert people to developing issues.

What have you discovered? Should the government be involved in regulating citizen uploads to social networks? What are the crime prevention possibilities through social networks? Are you concerned by the proliferation of this type of information over the

Internet? When you have thought this through, take a look at the Toronto police chief's discussion of the Toronto Police Service Social Media Strategy at http://www.youtube .com/watch?v=LTuKGOuvfVk.

REFERENCES

Cohen, L. and Felson, M. 1979. "Social Change and Crime Rate Trends: A Routine Activity Approach." *American Sociological Review* 44:588–608.

Cornish, D. and R. Clarke, eds. 1986. *The Reasoning Criminal: Rational Choice Perspectives on Offending.* New York: Springer-Verlag.

Crowe, T.D. 2000. *Crime Prevention through Environmental Design*, 2nd ed. Washington, DC: National Crime Prevention Institute.

Deisman, W. 2003. *CCTV: Literature Review and Bibliography,* Royal Canadian Mounted Police, Research and Evaluation Branch. Retrieved April 23, 2008 (http:// www.rcmp-grc.gc.ca/ccaps/cctv_e.htm).

Felson, M. 1994. *Crime and Everyday Life.* Thousand Oaks, CA: Pine Forge Press.

Gill, M. and A. Spriggs. 2005. *Assessing the Impact of CCTV: Home Office Research Study 292.* London, UK: Home Office Research, Development, and Statistics Directorate.

Goldblatt, P. and C. Lewis. 1998. *Reducing Offending: An Assessment of Research Evidence on Ways of Dealing with Offending Behaviour.* London, UK: Home Office Research and Statistics Directorate, Home Office.

Grady, P. 1990. *Policing by Mountain Bike.* Seattle: PDG Enterprises.

Graham, K.L. 1997. *An Evaluation of the Strathcona Neighbourhood Police Office.* Vancouver: Strathcona Neighbourhood Police Office Advisory Committee.

Griffiths, C.T., B. Whitelaw and R. Parent. 1999. *Canadian Police Work.* Toronto: ITP Nelson.

Guyot, D. 1979. "Bending Granite: Attempts to Change the Rank Structure of American Police Departments." *Journal of Police Science and Administration* 7(3):253–84.

Harman, A. 1996. "Citizens' Crime Watch." *Law and Order* 44(12):41–44.

Hatry, H.P. et al. 1992. *How Effective Are Your Community Services? Procedures for Measuring Their Quality*, 2nd ed. Washington, DC: International City/County Management Association (ICMA).

Kelling, G.L. and W.H. Sousa. 2001. "Do Police Matter? An Analysis of the Impact of New York City's Police Reforms." *Civic Report No. 22.* New York, NY: Centre for Civic Innovation.

Koper, C.S. 1995. "Just Enough Police Presence: Reducing Crime and Disorderly Behavior by Optimizing Patrol Time in Crime Hot Spots." *Justice Quarterly* 12(4): 649–72.

Lewis, P., K. Roberts, C.T. Griffiths and D.S. Wood. 1995. *Crime Prevention in Rural Aboriginal Communities.* Ottawa: Aboriginal Policing Directorate, Solicitor General Canada.

Mastrofski, S.D. 1990. "The Prospects of Change in Police Patrol: A Decade in Review." *American Journal of Police* 9(3):1–79.

Menton, Chris. 2008. "Bicycle Patrols: An Underutilized Resource." *Policing: An International Journal of Police Strategies & Management* 31(1):93–108.

National Crime Prevention Centre. 2008. *Safer Communities: A Parliamentarian's Crime Prevention Handbook.* Ottawa: Department of Justice Canada.

National Crime Prevention Strategy. 2004. *Risk Factors and Protective Factors Fact Sheet.* Ottawa: National Crime Prevention Centre. Department of Justice Canada.

Newman, G., R. Clarke and S. Shoham, eds. 1997. *Rational Choice and Situational Crime Prevention.* Aldershot: Dartmouth.

Ontario Provincial Police. 1999. "Cottage Watch: A Community Crime Prevention Program." *CPDC News* 5 (April).

Polowek, K. 1995. *Community Policing: Is It Working and How Do We Know? An Introductory Guide for Police Managers and Police Boards.* Victoria: British Columbia Ministry of the Attorney General.

Rossmo, D.K. 1995. "Strategic Crime Patterning: Problem-Oriented Policing and Displacement." pp. 1–14 in *Crime Analysis Through Computer Mapping,* edited by C. Block, M. Dabdob, and S. Fregly. Washington, DC: Police Executive Research Forum.

Royal Canadian Mounted Police. 1998. *Building Safer Communities: An Introduction to Crime Prevention through Environmental Design for Architects, Planners and Builders.* Retrieved April 24, 2008 (http://www.rcmp-grc.gc.ca/ccaps/safecomm_e.htm).

Schweinhart, L.J., H.V. Barnes and D.P. Weikart. 1993. *Significant Benefits: The High/Scope Perry Preschool Study Through Age 27.* Ypsilanti, MI: High/Scope.

Sherman, L.W. and D. Weisburd. 1995. "General Deterrent Effects of Police Patrol in Crime 'Hot Spots': A Randomized, Controlled Trial." *Justice Quarterly* 12(4):625–48.

Sherman, L.W. et al. 1997. *Preventing Crime: What Works, What Doesn't, What's Promising.* Washington, DC: Office of Justice Programs, U.S. Department of Justice.

Toronto Police Service. 2006. "Closed Circuit Television." Online (http://www.torontopolice.on.ca/media/text/20061214-tps_cctv_project.pdf).

Wilson, J.Q. and G.L. Kelling. 1982. "Broken Windows: The Police and Neighborhood Safety." *Atlantic Monthly* 249:29–38.

Problem-Oriented Policing

Problem-oriented policing (POP) involves the police taking a proactive approach to address the underlying causes of a problem in the community and a formulated response designed to alleviate the problem. For example, a community may be facing a series of property crimes that are linked to illicit drug use—individuals are committing thefts in order to fuel their drug dependency. A POP response would direct police resources towards drug enforcement and harm reduction as well as the overt property crimes.

Source: © Janine Wiedel Photolibrary / Alamy

Learning Objectives

After completing this chapter, you should be able to:

- Define problem-oriented policing and discuss its importance to community policing,
- Explain the steps of problem solving,
- Describe what is meant by the problem analysis triangle,
- Describe and apply the Ontario Provincial Police's PARE problem-solving model,
- Differentiate between the expert model and collaborative model of problem solving, and
- Identify the conditions for successful problem solving.

INTRODUCTION

Police work generally consists of responding to problems. When patrol officers arrive at a call for service, the matter is seldom clear. The officer must listen to the complainant to determine whether an offence has occurred or whether the person is seeking information. In fact, for most officers, enforcing the law composes only about 25 percent of their activities. All incidents require officers to assess the best way to address the situation, but in a reactive model of police work, they would respond to the situation at hand with little thought to the underlying causes of the incident or its long-term solution.

The advent of community policing has had a significant impact on how officers respond to the situations and incidents in which they become involved. One of the primary response strategies within the framework of community policing is problem-oriented policing, or POP. Problem-oriented policing involves the police taking a proactive approach to addressing the underlying causes of a particular problem as well as formulating a response designed to solve or alleviate the problem. It is a more efficient approach to policing than traditional reactive approaches. POP is the focus of our discussion in this chapter.

The Situations and Strategies section of the chapter contains a checklist for carrying out problem-oriented policing, along with case studies that illustrate how POP has been applied. As well, there are a number of exercises that provide you with the opportunity to apply problem-oriented policing to various situations.

WHAT IS PROBLEM SOLVING?

When implemented properly, problem solving represents the very essence of community-based policing. This essence is the collaboration of the police with the community in dealing with issues of concern.

Problem solving attempts to address the underlying or root causes of crime and social disorder. Research studies on crime and the police response to it have revealed the following important facts:

- Simply applying additional resources in response to individual crimes appears to have little real impact.
- Few incidents or crimes are isolated. Most are symptoms of underlying problems, which means that many will recur predictably.
- Since the causes of crime are multifaceted, the most effective responses should be those that coordinate police, government, and private citizens and businesses (Eck and Spelman 1987a).

WHAT IS A PROBLEM AND WHOSE IS IT?

Surprisingly, defining the problem that will be the focus of attention by the police and the community can be the most difficult part of the problem-solving process. A problem can be:

- a cluster of similar, related, or recurring incidents or a single incident;
- a substantive community concern; or
- a unit of police business.

For the purposes of our discussion, a **problem** is defined as a group or pattern of crimes, cases, calls, or incidents that are of concern to the public or police, or both, and that require a solution. This definition is broad enough to allow for a wide variety of situations. In community policing, a "problem" is the basic unit of police work; in contrast, traditional police work focused on single crimes, cases, calls, or incidents.

The second question is "Whose problem is it?" Community residents and the police may have different views about what is and what is not a problem. In the traditional model of police work, the police defined who and what was a problem and assumed full ownership of it.

If the problem is defined only as a police problem, then either there is no role for the community in addressing it or, as important, the community does not see a role to play. For example, the police may be very concerned about a trend in night-time break and enters along a commercial strip. The identification of this as a problem would result in the allocation of police resources through targeted saturation techniques of police patrol. The community, on the other hand, may identify problems such as speeders on residential streets, or constant pedestrian and vehicle traffic around a suspected drug house.

Collaborative Problem Solving

Community policing has altered the process of defining a problem and has extended the responsibility for problems to include the community and other non-police agencies and organizations. This has created a framework for collaborative problem solving, which involves the police and the community agreeing that a problem exists, and what the dimensions of the problem are, and formulating and then implementing a strategy to address it. Problem solving represents a more effective use of community and police resources and it is a good illustration of the evolving model of community policing we have described as "community-based strategic policing" (see Chapter 3 if you need to review this concept).

The number of situations that qualify as problems is limitless. Among those that might be identified by police and communities are:

- house break and enters in rural cottage areas,
- speeding and vehicle collisions,
- youth drag racing,
- groups of youth trespassing on private land or congregating in public places,
- suspected drug activity in private residences,
- vagrants or street people,
- street prostitution and related robberies,
- houses used for prostitution,
- false alarm complaints,
- graffiti, and
- repeat domestic violence calls to certain addresses.

Not All Problems Are Law Enforcement Problems

Television portrays the activity of police as primarily conducting investigations and arresting criminals; however, in reality this work consumes only an estimated 10–25 percent of an officer's time. The rest of the time is spent performing duties that do not invoke the "law enforcement" response of the police. Most police work is characterized by non–law enforcement responses related to maintaining order and providing service. Therefore, clearly, not all community problems involve violations of the law.

In fact, community residents are often more concerned about quality-of-life issues than violations of law. These may include the visible presence of prostitutes in a neighbourhood, discarded hypodermic needles and condoms, noise from stereos, the presence of street people, or people suffering mental disabilities wandering through neighbourhoods. One of the most common problems in urban areas is speeders and dangerous drivers.

PROBLEM-ORIENTED POLICING

Although the two concepts are complementary, **problem-oriented policing (POP)** and community policing are grounded in slightly different principles. The least confusing way to distinguish the two is to view POP as a strategy that puts the community-oriented policing philosophy into practice. It advocates that police examine the underlying or root causes of recurring incidents of crime and disorder. The problem-solving model helps officers identify problems, analyze them completely, develop response strategies, and assess the results.

The principal architect of POP is the criminologist **Herman Goldstein**, who wrote the book *Problem-Oriented Policing* in 1990. Central to his argument is the point that police work is problem-oriented—that is, police officers responding to calls for service are presented with a problem and must find a solution to the problem. The type of analysis the patrol officer uses is much more detailed and in-depth than the assessment of whether a formal law has been broken.

Problem-oriented policing goes beyond assessing whether a law has been violated to examine the underlying causes of crime and disorder in the community and to tailor a solution to the dynamics of the problem. Often, the violation of the law itself is the tip of the iceberg. This is known as the **iceberg or 80/20 rule:** like an iceberg, no matter how large the part above water is, 80 percent of the iceberg—or problem—lies below the surface. To eliminate a problem, therefore, it is necessary to attack the 80 percent that is not visible. These are the underlying causes or conditions that expose the remaining 20 percent. In addressing problems of crime and social disorder, the police and the community must consider not only the crime or incidents (the 20 percent), but also the broader community, social, and economic contexts within which the incidents occur. This approach represents a major shift in police work, from a focus on isolated incidents to a consideration of the factors that contributed to these incidents. POP is consistent with contemporary police management approaches that strive to empower front-line police officers and encourage creativity and risk taking.

Table 5.1 sets out several of the basic principles of problem-oriented policing. As you review them, think about how they differ from the principles of traditional police work.

Table 5.1 Doing Problem-Oriented Policing: A Guide for Police Departments

• Focus on problems of concern to the public	• Avoid using overly broad labels in grouping incidents so separate problems can be identified
• Zero in on effectiveness as the primary concern	
• Be proactive	
• Be committed to systematic inquiry as the first step in solving substantive problems	• Encourage a broad, uninhibited search for solutions
• Encourage the use of rigorous methods in making inquiries	
• Make full use of data in police files and the experience of police personnel	• Acknowledge the limits of the criminal justice system as a response to problems
• Group like incidents together so they can be addressed as a common problem	• Identify multiple interests in any one problem and weigh them when analyzing the value of different responses
• Be committed to taking some risks in responding to problems	

Source: "Doing Problem-Oriented Policing: A Guide for Police Departments." *Problem-Solving: Problem-Oriented Policing in Newport News.* Ecke, J.E. and W. Spelman, 1987.

The Problem-Solving Process

The process of problem solving has four steps, usually referred to as **SARA**:

- **S**canning
- **A**nalysis
- **R**esponse
- **A**ssessment

The SARA model is depicted in Figure 5.1.

Below, we examine components of the basic problem-solving model and then consider the PARE model of problem solving, which has been developed by the Ontario Provincial Police (OPP).

Scanning

The primary purpose of the scanning stage is to conduct a preliminary inquiry to determine whether a problem really exists and whether further analysis is required. Police have a number of resources available to them to assist with this inquiry, including data on calls for service, victim surveys, citizen complaints, census data, data available from other government agencies, media reports of citizens' concerns, officer observations, and community surveys. Each source provides useful information in problem identification.

The police can use other methods in order to determine the existence of problems, including:

- crime analyses;
- letters of complaint;
- input from elected officials, business groups, and neighbourhood organizations;
- data on fluctuations in the market value of property;
- data on cases treated in emergency rooms;
- probation and parole records; and
- the insights of social agencies and other public institutions, such as schools, that have responsibility for problems that are also of concern to the police, such as runaways, the homeless, victims of sexual assault, and the mentally ill (Eck and Spelman 1987b).

Analysis

In the analysis stage, there is an effort to determine the cause, scope, and impact of the problem. This is the most critical stage of the problem-solving process, and it may require considerable time and attention. The results will be used to allocate resources and mobilize the community.

Figure 5.1 The Problem-Solving Process

Source: Hough and Tilley 1998:7.

It is important to identify the following:

- Who is being harmed by the problem? Is the harm inflicted on specific persons or groups, or does the problem detract from the quality of life in an area and increase the fear of crime?
- Can the problem be broken into specific elements or subsets of problems such that progress can be achieved on each subset until a positive result is obtained for the overall problem?

A useful method for understanding the dimensions of a problem involves understanding it in relation to the victim, the accused, and the location. These are represented in a **problem analysis triangle** (see Box 5.1).

Response

The analysis is used to develop an appropriate response tailored to the problem. While arrest is often the primary response option in traditional police work, in problem solving within a community policing framework it is only one of many options. Other possible responses include:

- *Concentrating attention on the individuals responsible for a disproportionate share of the problem.* This approach, often described as "targeting," involves tactical or directed patrol aimed at individuals involved in a specific type of criminal activity and is also known as perpetrator-oriented patrol.

BOX 5.1

THE PROBLEM ANALYSIS TRIANGLE

For a problem to exist, there must be three elements: an offender, a victim, and a location. We can think of it as a "problem analysis triangle" that helps us to understand the relationship among those three elements and that may indicate areas where further information is required.

There may be a potential victim in an area that is prone to crime, but if there is no offender present, then there is no crime. Similarly, if there is an offender in a crime-prone area but no potential victim, then no crime will occur. Furthermore, the location may be an area that is relatively unsafe, but without the presence of both a potential victim and potential offender, no crime will occur. The key point is that if any of the triangle's sides are missing, there is no problem. This is similar to the crime triangle we discussed in Chapter 4, in which there is a target, a lack of a suitable guardian, and a motivated offender.

Source: Hough and Tilley, 1998, p. 23

Applying the problem-solving triangle allows front-line officers to develop appropriate intervention strategies. Patrol strategies, which are the most common form of police-initiated strategy, have proven successful in the short term when directed at a specific problem. Targeted or directed patrol strategies commonly focus on offenders (offender-specific patrol) or locations (location-specific patrol [LSP]). Victim-oriented strategies often require a combination of situational (SCP) and social development (CPSD) strategies to effectively address the problem.

- *Connecting with other government and private agencies.* A thorough analysis often indicates the need for:

  – more effective referrals to existing governmental and private services,
  – improved coordination with agencies that exert control over some of the problems or individuals involved in the incidents, and
  – initiatives that respond to deficiencies identified in existing municipal services or to the fact that services do not exist.

- *Using mediation and negotiation skills* rather than traditional police responses of arrest or aggressive targeted patrol.
- *Conveying information.* Surprisingly, conveying sound and accurate information is one of the least used responses. Open communication can foster the attainment of a number of goals, including:

  – reducing anxiety and fear,
  – enabling citizens to solve their own problems,
  – obtaining conformity with laws and regulations that are not known or well understood,
  – warning potential victims about their vulnerability and advising them how to protect themselves,
  – demonstrating to people how they unwittingly contribute to problems,
  – developing support for addressing a problem, and
  – acquainting the community with the limitations on government agencies and defining what can be realistically expected of those agencies.

- *Mobilizing the community.* This is essential and can result in more sustainable outcomes. Mobilization may occur through various strategies including:

  – establishing neighbourhood watches;
  – identifying abandoned vehicles;
  – promoting community interaction to reduce fear, mistrust, or tension;
  – installing telephone notification systems to alert potential victims;
  – forming citizen patrols; and
  – soliciting information on criminal activity.

- *Making use of existing forms of social control.* This involves solving problems by using specific forms of social control inherent in existing relationships, such as the influence of a parent, teacher, employer, or church.
- *Altering the physical environment to reduce opportunities for problems to recur.* In other words, adapting the principles of crime prevention through environmental design (CPTED) and situational crime prevention (SCP).
- *Using civil law to control public nuisances, offensive behaviour, and conditions contributing to crime.* This means initiating a number of other legal proceedings, including those related to:

  – licensing,
  – zoning,
  – property confiscation,
  – nuisance abatement, and
  – injunctions.

Expert versus Collaborative Approaches to Problem Solving

There are two models of problem solving that can be implemented by the police. These are known as the expert model and the collaborative model. The **expert model of problem solving** involves an outside person—the "expert"—going to the location (community, neighbourhood, school) where the problem is occurring, identifying and analyzing the problem, and developing a solution. In contrast, the **collaborative model of problem solving** emphasizes shared responsibility between an expert and those in the neighbourhood, area, or setting where the problem is being experienced. In this model, the community members use the expert to assist as they participate in problem identification and analysis, brainstorm possible solutions, select a plan they view as appropriate, and implement the plan. The role of the expert is to serve as a facilitator, posing questions and leading the other participants in the development of a solution.

Assessment

In this stage of the problem-solving process, the police and the community examine the outcomes that have occurred as a result of the problem-solving response. The intent is to measure the effectiveness of the response, which can be a very difficult task. Scott (2000), who evaluated 20 years of POP in the United States, found this stage often receives the least attention, although it is critical from the standpoint of resources being utilized effectively.

Degrees of Impact on the Problem

The police and the community may have varying degrees of success in solving the problem, including:

- eliminating the problem,
- reducing the number of incidents created by the problem,
- reducing the seriousness of the incidents created by the problem,
- designing methods for better handling the incidents created by the problem, and
- removing the problem from police consideration (Eck and Spelman 1987a:5–6).

PROBLEM-SOLVING MODELS USED BY THE ROYAL CANADIAN MOUNTED POLICE AND ONTARIO PROVINCIAL POLICE

While the problem-solving process varies among police services, the basic process is fundamentally the same. For example, the Royal Canadian Mounted Police have developed a problem-solving model called CAPRA, which stands for:

- **Clients**
- **Acquire/Analyze** information
- **Partnerships**
- **Response**
- **Assessment**

The CAPRA problem-solving model is taught to new police officers and is applied throughout the RCMP to a number of internal and external problems. The CAPRA model draws attention to important stakeholders, whether the community itself (clients) or agencies that may contribute to problem-solving efforts (partnerships).

An essential component in Ontario is the development of teams. Patrol officers are assigned to Community Policing Teams that are responsible for the communities in a geographically defined area called a zone. The OPP calls its approach **PARE**, which stands for the stages of problem solving (see Figures 5.2a and b):

- **Problem** identification
- **Analysis**
- **Response**
- **Evaluation**

The stages are very similar to those of SARA discussed earlier.

Figure 5.2a The PARE Problem-Solving Model

Figure 5.2b

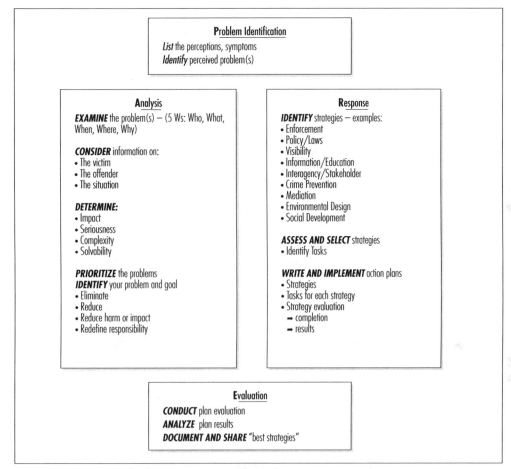

Source: Ontario Provincial Police 1997, pp. 6–7. Copyright © Queen's Printer for Ontario, 1997.

Problem Identification

Identifying the problem is perhaps the most important stage of the entire process, and it involves a number of steps:

1. *List* everyone's perceptions of the problem.
2. *Identify* the perceived problem(s) and ask the question: "Is this the real problem or just a symptom or indication of a bigger or different problem?"
3. *Examine* the problem using the five Ws—Who, What, When, Where, and Why.
4. *Consider* the information available on the victim, offender, and situation to understand what has contributed to the problem.

Analysis

The objective of the analysis stage is to generate information on the underlying causes or conditions of the problem. More specifically, at this stage there is an attempt to answer the five Ws: Who, What, When, Where, and Why. A number of strategies may be used to gather this information, including:

- calls for service,
- community meetings,
- incident analysis,
- direct observation,
- focus groups,
- interviews,
- library research,
- meetings with other agencies, and
- surveys and questionnaires administered to community residents and other stakeholder groups.

Information must be gathered on the victim, the offender, and the situation—the three "sides" of the problem analysis triangle.

To assist patrol officers and communities in screening, prioritizing, and ranking problems, four **problem analysis filters** have been developed. These filters include the following:

- Impact of the problem:
    - How big is it?
    - Who is affected by it?
    - What other problems are affected by the situation?
    - Who are the stakeholders?

- Seriousness of the problem:
    - How much danger or damage would there be if it were left unchecked?
    - How much public concern is there on the issue?
    - What is the police priority or status regarding the issue?

- Complexity of the problem:
    - How complex or deep-rooted is it?
    - Are resources available to handle it (police, community, government, social agencies, etc.)?
    - Who owns it?

- Solvability of the problem:
    - To what degree can individuals or teams affect it?

It is important to remember that considerable time and human resources can be expended on a problem to very little effect. Alternatively, quality-of-life improvements can be obtained with considerably less effort and expense. However, if the information gathered during the analysis stage indicates that there is, in fact, no verifiable problem then the problem-solving process is terminated.

Prioritizing Problems: A Scoring System

During the analysis stage, it is not uncommon to discover related problems, so it may become necessary to prioritize. The PARE problem-solving model provides a mechanism for assigning a numeric value to each of the problem analysis filters to help set priorities. This technique is illustrated in the following example.

• Impact	1 (least) to 5 (most)
• Seriousness	1 (least) to 5 (most)
• Complexity	1 (very) to 5 (little)
• Solvability	1 (difficult) to 5 (easy)

Note: For complexity and solvability, the scale is designed to ensure that the least complex and easiest to solve are the higher priority (OPP 1997:7–11).

By adding total scores and comparing results, the problems with the highest scores may be ranked highest in terms of priority.

Strategic Response

In this stage the police team develops a strategic response in collaboration with the community. The strategies are limited only by the imagination and resourcefulness of the partnership.

Objectives of the Response

The objectives of the problem-solving process may include one or several of the following:

- *Eliminate the problem.* This response often works when the problem is small, relatively simple, and involves few people and policing resources.
- *Reduce the size of the problem.* An effort is made to reduce or eliminate parts of the problem, recognizing that it may be too deep-rooted or persistent to be entirely eliminated (e.g., prostitution).
- *Reduce the harm or impact.* If the problem is too difficult to reduce or eliminate, an attempt is made to reduce the impact on the immediate victim, broader community, or indirect or secondary victims (e.g., children who witness domestic violence). Harm-reduction strategies include victim-assistance initiatives and domestic-violence assistance programs.
- *Improve the response to the problem.* For complex, societal problems, improvements in services to crime victims or to the broader community may be the only realistic goal.
- *Redefine responsibility for the problem.* An important requirement of the problem-solving process is to assess not only which individuals and agencies are affected by a problem but also who should assume the primary role in terms of a strategic response. As we have noted, the police are often called upon to address problems that would be handled better by another organization. Relative to other organizations, they may be limited in their ability to bring about long-term progress. Often, an appropriate strategic response for police is to recognize other agencies with mutually vested interests in a problem and to defer authority to these groups, thereby shedding the "expert" role.

Response Options

Depending on the goals and objectives of the problem-solving process, a number of response options are available:

- *Traditional response strategies and investigation.* Traditional strategies are used, such as targeted saturation techniques and increased patrol, including foot patrol. These approaches often combine investigation and enforcement. Generally, the benefits are limited and the problem returns when traditional strategies are exhausted. For this reason, it is preferable to consider alternative strategies that may be used in combination with traditional strategies, such as the others described here.
- *Interagency strategies.* Collaboration between the police and other agencies that share mutual concerns in relation to a problem are used. Many police services, for example,

have response teams for youth at risk that pair a police officer with a social worker, mental health worker, or youth worker, thus providing a more comprehensive approach. Interagency strategies may be formal or informal depending on the specific problem and the level of response required.

- *Use of noncriminal laws and regulations.* This approach recognizes that the enforcement of private and public laws, regulations, and statutes, such as building codes, noise bylaws, and health regulations, can affect many problems. It may be more effective to enforce these laws and regulations than to apply the criminal law or statutes that would typically require enforcement by the police.
- *More discriminate use of law enforcement.* The police service examines past approaches and determines possible improvements to the problem-solving process. For example, neighbourhood programs to eradicate prostitution may have simply displaced the problem to another community. Future programs would focus on preventing the problem from displacing from one community or neighbourhood to the next.
- *Information, communication, and education strategies.* Information or educational campaigns are directed at educating the community, with the goal of preventing or reducing further victimization.
- *Community mobilization.* This approach involves mobilizing the community residents and any community resources that can be brought to bear on the problem.
- *Focused strategies.* These strategies focus on individuals and locations that are prone to crime. The underlying assumption is that a relatively small number of individuals or locations are responsible for a disproportionate number of problems. Strategies then focus on the individual or location.
- *Crime prevention strategies and programs.* Crime prevention strategies and programs include initiatives such as the Cottage Watch Program, profiled in our discussion of crime prevention programs in Chapter 4. Such strategies and programs are considered only after a careful analysis of the problem is undertaken; once these programs are selected, continuous evaluation and monitoring is required to ensure that they remain effective and meet their stated objectives.
- *Mediation strategies.* Mediating community problems and disputes may be a more effective approach than legal responses when there is a clear dividing line between wrong and right. Police tend not to get involved in formal mediation, although part of an appropriate police response is referral to mediation agencies.
- *Environmental design.* This involves participating in community development, including the planning and design of features such as roadways, parks, parking lots, the placement of shrubs, street lighting, and so on. Such changes can be an immediate response to an identified concern, or can be part of long-range community planning.
- *Social development.* This addresses improvements to quality of life through community and social development initiatives, which may address deep social problems relating to the decaying family structure, child poverty, substance abuse, domestic violence, unemployment, illiteracy, inadequate housing, mental illness, and so on.
- *Community control.* The police must attempt to establish meaningful collaboration with the community so they do not become solely responsible for solving problems. Public safety becomes the responsibility of the community as well as the police (Osborne and Gaebler 1993).

Individual police officers, problem-solving teams, and specific government and social service agencies, as well as community residents, organizations, and groups may participate in these response options. Many of the problems that are identified in communities require a collaborative response that involves police officers and the community. Some can be addressed by individual police officers on their own.

The Intervention Plan

Once response options are selected according to the goals and objectives of the specific problem-solving process, the team develops its intervention plan. The intervention plan should follow **SMART** guidelines; that is, it should involve tasks that are:

- **S**pecific, identifying individual/agency and community responsibilities;
- **M**easurable (quantitatively or qualitatively, or both);
- **A**ttainable, such as reducing the severity or prevalence of a problem,
- **R**ealistic and related to previously established goals and objectives;
- **T**imely (bound to a schedule for implementation)

Gathering Information on the Response

In order to evaluate the effectiveness of the response, it is important to gather information specifically related to the problem. For example, if the objective is to reduce or eliminate a problem, quantifiable measures, such as a decrease in the number of house break and enters over a specified period, are easily obtained. If the objective is to reduce harm or impact or to improve responses to the problem, then qualitative measures are required. This information can be obtained from victim and citizen surveys designed to measure levels of satisfaction and reduced perceptions of fear.

Evaluation

At this stage, the police team assesses whether response options were effective and whether the goals and objectives were achieved. Both process evaluation and impact evaluation should be used.

Process Evaluation

The first step in **process evaluation** is to analyze the implementation of the strategies by asking such questions as:

- Were the strategies easy to implement?
- If the team has to implement the process again, are there any factors that would act as barriers to success?
- Are there steps that would facilitate implementation?
- What should others be aware of if attempting to implement a similar plan?

Impact Evaluation

Impact evaluation involves assessing the qualitative and quantitative outcomes or consequences of problem-solving strategies. Not all outcomes may have been positive. An honest assessment is made to determine whether the strategies worked and what steps could be taken to improve them.

Once the process of evaluation is complete, there should be ongoing maintenance and monitoring of the problem to ensure it does not appear again. Often the immediate symptoms of a problem disappear, only to emerge again.

Furthermore, records of problem-solving plans must be kept. Keeping a history allows the process to be shared with community policing committees, operational planning forums, and other officers facing similar problems.

THE PARE PROBLEM-SOLVING PROCESS IN ACTION

To illustrate how the PARE problem-solving approach works in practice, we have adapted a case example from The *"How Do We Do It" Manual* produced by the OPP Community Policing Development Centre (1997). The information describes the process followed by OPP members and the Community Policing Committee to identify and respond to several problems in their community.

Problem Identification

At a monthly meeting of the Community Policing Committee, the OPP officers and the committee members perceived that the following problems existed in their small town:

- Dump trucks speeding on a residential street that connects the highway with a stone quarry.
- Problems in the town park caused by youths, including vandalism, drinking parties, and fear among older residents who use the park.
- Lack of recreational opportunities for youths.
- Business break and enters.
- A lack of police patrols.

Identify the Perceived Problems

By discussing the perceptions and asking "why," the group identified three problems:

- Speeding dump trucks on 5th Street, a residential area.
- Youths with nothing to do causing problems in the park.
- Business breaks and enters.

Analysis

Examine the Problem (the five Ws)

The problems were assessed (who, what, where, when, and why) by gathering information about the victims, offenders, and situation. This information was applied in considering the impact, seriousness, complexity, and solvability of the problems. The police provided statistical information on all of the perceived problems, including:

- The number of automobile accidents on 5th Street, the number of business break and enters, and the number of offences that occurred in the park in the last year.
- The hours of patrol and radar enforcement in the area, the number of complaints received related to the perceived issues, and the types of charges laid.
- Where and when offences and complaints occurred.
- The ages of the accused.
- Information on the victims and complainants (age, sex, driver, passenger, etc.).
- The number of complaints from senior citizens.

The community provided the following information:

- Demographics on the number of youth and senior citizens in the community.
- The number of organized activities for youth.
- Current physical characteristics and environment of the park, 5th Street, and the downtown.

Consider the Victim, Offender, and Situation

From this information, the following picture emerged of the perceived problems:

- *Speeding dump trucks.* There were no accidents related to speeding dump trucks in the town in the past year. Police radar enforcement in response to calls revealed very few charges and, in fact, most of the trucks were travelling within the speed limit. Several homes on 5th Street were situated very close to the road and this was where most of the complaints originated.

- *Youths causing problems in the park.* The park had poor lighting and people could easily hide from sight. The seniors and youths do not communicate. There was a lack of recreational facilities, and as a consequence the youths congregated in the park, where they committed various offences. The police had investigated a number of vandalism and liquor complaints during the past few months involving youths.
- *Business break and enters.* There had been only three break-ins in the preceding six months. The businesses targeted could benefit from some crime proofing, as they were found to be vulnerable to this type of crime. The break-ins involved minor thefts of no greater than $500.

Prioritize the Problems

Each problem was assigned a numeric classification:

- **Problem 1:**   **Speeding dump trucks on 5th Street**
  Impact   3
  Seriousness   3
  Complexity   3
  Solvability: 2

                              11

- **Problem 2:**   **Youths causing problems in the park**
  Impact   4
  Seriousness   4
  Complexity   3
  Solvability: 4

                              15

- **Problem 3:**   **Business break and enters**
  Impact   1
  Seriousness   1
  Complexity   5
  Solvability: 5

                              12

Outcome: Based on a prioritization of the problems, the first priority was the problem of youth in the park, followed by business break and enters and speeding dump trucks.

Problem Identification

During the past year there had been 80 offences in the park, largely related to youths drinking and damaging park equipment. The youths had nothing to do and congregated in the park on weekends to drink, set campfires, and party. The park's poor lighting concealed the offenders. Older residents felt intimidated when walking in the area.

The Goal

To reduce the number of offences being committed by youths in the town park by 50 percent during the next 12 months as compared to the previous 12-month period.

The Response

- Identify strategies
- Assess and select strategies

After reviewing each available response strategy, the partners decided on strategies to achieve their goals, which are listed in Table 5.2.

Table 5.2 Strategies to Deal with Youth in the Park

Strategy	Strategy Type	Advantage	Disadvantage
• Increase police patrols of park	• Visibility	• Increases enforcement • Deters youth violations • Reduces senior citizens' fear	• Unable to commit police resources consistently
• Improve park environment with additional lighting, and basketball and tennis courts	• Environmental design	• Improves visibility • Encourages youth activities • Encourages adult attendance	• Cost to install facilities and equipment
• Meet with youth to discuss concerns and seek solutions	• Mediation	• Involves youth in the solution • Encourages youth to take ownership of the problem	• Youth perceiving they are the problem • Reluctance of youth to participate
• Alternative youth sentencing to community service in the park	• Interagency/stakeholder	• Encourages youth to take responsibility for their actions	• Needs youth agreement to participate in alternative measures

Source: "Strategies to Deal with Youth in the Park." *Problem-Solving: Problem-Oriented Policing in Newport News.* Ecke, J.E. and W. Spelman, 1987, pg. 3

After an assessment of the strategies, those selected were incorporated into an action plan with assigned tasks.

Write and Implement Action Plans

Let's consider one of the strategies in the action plan.

One of the strategies for the plan was to improve the town park environment through the installation of additional lighting, and basketball and tennis courts by the end of December. The tasks identified to accomplish this strategy were as follows:

1. The Community Policing Committee (CPC) chair is to approach the town's parks maintenance supervisor by the end of June and identify the need for the addition of three light standards in designated areas in the park.
2. A CPC subcommittee is to be formed immediately to develop a proposal by the end of July considering the costs, possible funding sources, and possibility of installing two tennis courts and a basketball court in the park.
3. The CPC subcommittee chair is to present the park environment proposal to council by the end of September, for its consideration and acceptance.
4. The OPP detachment commander is to forward a letter of support to the CPC subcommittee chair for the installation of lighting and sporting facilities.
5. The CPC subcommittee chair is to report to the CPC at each regular meeting on the progress of tasks 1 to 4.

Plan and strategy results were recorded upon completion. The Community Policing team leader was responsible for completing a template, for making sure that the required activities were monitored at the local level, and for forwarding any recommended "best strategies" to the OPP.

Figure 5.3 Plan Overview

Plan #: 97-0001-A	
Detachment: Anywhere	Location Code: 0000
Town/Township: Our Township	OMPPAC Zone: 1111
CP Committee: Whoville	CP Team Leader: Team A — Sgt. Black
Plan Start Date: 01 JUN 97	Plan Completed Date: 31 DEC 97
Problem Description: During the past year there have been 80 offences in the park, largely related to youths drinking and damage to park equipment. The youths have nothing to do and congregate in the park on weekends to drink, set campfires, and party. The park is poorly lit, which helps conceal the offenders. Older residents are intimidated when walking in the area.	
Goal Statement: To reduce the number of offences being committed by youths in the town park by 50% during the next 12 months as compared to the previous 12-month period.	
Identified Strategies: #1 Improve park environment with lighting, basketball and tennis courts #2 Increase police patrols #3 Meet with youth to discuss concerns and solutions #4 Alternative youth sentencing to community service in park	
Plan Results: 	

Source: Ontario Provincial Police 1997, pp. 7-41. Copyright © Queen's Printer for Ontario, 1997.

The Documented Plan

The documented plan for one of the above-noted cases is illustrated in Figure 5.3.

CONDITIONS FOR SUCCESSFUL PROBLEM SOLVING

Police services that have successfully made problem solving a core component of their services within a community policing framework share a number of characteristics. From an organizational perspective, they have recognized the following principles.

- Policing involves addressing a wide range of problems, not just crime.
- These problems are interrelated and the priority given them must be constantly reassessed rather than ranked in traditional ways.
- Each problem requires a unique response rather than a generic "one size fits all" response.
- The criminal law is only one of several response options.
- Police services can be successful by working to prevent problems, rather than simply by responding to incidents that are only symptoms of underlying problems.
- Developing an effective response to a problem requires prior analysis rather than simply invoking traditional police practices.
- Contrary to the traditional image of the police—held by both the police and the public—the capacity of the police to solve problems is extremely limited.

- The role of the police is best viewed as one of facilitating, enabling, and encouraging the community in order to maintain problem-solving capacity, rather than as one that assumes full responsibility for the identification of and response to problems (Goldstein 1990:179).

Herman Goldstein (1990:179) argues that police agencies that have embraced these notions develop a "new honesty" about the role of the police, their relationship with the community, and their capacity and role limitations vis-à-vis problem solving. Ultimately, these police services are better positioned to respond to community problems, and to create organizations that focus on community problem solving rather than simply saying that they are focused on community issues and concerns.

Police Management's Role in Creating a Problem-Solving Police Organization

If problem solving is to succeed organizationally, there must be a significant commitment from police management. This is necessary to provide direction to the effort, communicate vision, and ensure that problem solving assists the organization in achieving its broader goals and purposes.

There are a number of specific practices that police executives must adopt in order to ensure that the entire police service becomes involved in problem solving. These include:

- communicating to all department members why responding to and solving problems is more effective than responding to incidents, and why police services and patrol officers should engage in problem solving;
- providing incentives to those members who engage in problem solving;
- reducing the barriers to officers engaging in the process, such as by making more time available and eliminating administrative practices that hinder initiative and creativity; and
- providing examples of what constitutes good problem solving (Eck and Spelman 1987a:100–101).

Police managers must effectively "walk the talk"; that is, they must lead and manage in ways that are consistent with the vision and values of the organization. This requires principle-centred leadership on the part of front-line supervisors and managers to ensure that an "entrepreneurial" atmosphere exists that encourages officers to experiment, create, develop, and test their intellectual and creative capacities and to take risks without fear of being punished for unintentional mistakes and failures.

BARRIERS TO EFFECTIVE PROBLEM SOLVING

There are a number of potential barriers to effective problem solving, some of which are discussed below.

- *Failing to plan is planning to fail.* One of the most common barriers is simply not examining a problem in sufficient detail. Where only a surface understanding exists, what often results is a superficial response to a problem. This, again, sensitizes us to the fact that the problem identification stage is perhaps the most important phase of the entire problem-solving process.
- *Failure to conduct a thorough analysis of the problem or working on the wrong problem.* Failure to conduct a thorough diagnosis of the problem results in a response that does not address the real issue. The problem-solving process may be ineffective so that valuable resources are wasted.
- *Failure to dedicate resources to the problem, leaving officers feeling ill equipped and undersupported.* A major impediment to success is the incident-driven policing environment. Patrol officers may be too busy responding to calls to engage in problem

solving. Patrol sergeants are often caught between ensuring that dispatched calls are answered promptly and trying to free up resources to deal with the underlying issues that place the demands on police resources in the first instance. This often represents an organizational "Catch-22" for the police service and illustrates the significant tension that often exists between the dispatch function and priorities of a police service and community expectations.

- *Failure to follow up in the assessment stage.* As noted earlier in the discussion, the assessment stage is often the weakest link in the entire problem-solving process. This is due, in part, to the fact that patrol officers may rotate to new assignments before a thorough assessment of the intervention can be carried out. In addition, the resources allocated to the original problem may end after some of the objectives relating to the original problem have been achieved. Little time or attention may be given to issues such as the displacement of the problem to another area of the community.

- *Failure to initiate a process or take ownership of problem.* In this case, neither the police nor the community recognizes that a problem exists, or a problem is acknowledged to exist but neither the community nor the police will take the responsibility for addressing it. This effectively prevents the development of a collaborative effort.

- *Problems in implementing an agency-wide program.* The agency charged with lead responsibility for a problem is unable to establish implementation plans that translate into plans for operational action.

- *The police take an expert role as opposed to a collaborative one.* The police fail to develop an effective collaborative response and end up assuming an expert role in relation to the problem. The expert approach is much more resource intensive and difficult to implement and sustain.

- *Failure to communicate successes and results.* It is essential to establish a level of problem-solving memory of what works and what does not work. This can occur only through effective documentation and sharing of lessons learned about the problem-solving process with other patrol officers and with the communities.

- *Difference in definitions between the community's perception and the police service's perception.* There may be a lack of agreement that a problem exists, or there may be a disagreement between the police and the community about the nature of the problem.

- *Problems in implementation at the organizational, front-line, or community level.* Problems in implementation may relate to lack of buy-in from involved police personnel or stakeholders. It is important that responses be developed through a process of consensus. The assessment stage then evaluates the effectiveness of the problem-solving efforts.

- *Failure of police technology to identify problems beyond the police service.* A balance must be achieved between using technology-based crime analysis for identifying problems and seeking community input. There is a risk that the increasing use of computer technology to analyze patterns of crime will overshadow community participation and undermine community collaboration.

Chapter Summary

This chapter has focused on problem-oriented policing (POP), which is one of the core components of community policing. Our overview began with a discussion of what constitutes a problem and of the importance of the community and the police being involved in defining problems. We then turned our attention to an examination of problem-oriented policing, a term coined by the criminologist Herman Goldstein three decades ago. A key element of POP is the 80/20 rule, which holds that crime and other problems in a community or neighbourhood are only the tip of the iceberg and that the underlying conditions or causes of the problem lie beneath the surface. It is these underlying conditions that are the focus of POP.

The problem-solving process, based on SARA (scanning, analysis, response, and assessment) was outlined, followed by a brief examination of the Royal Canadian Mounted Police CAPRA problem-solving model and discussion of the PARE (problem identification, analysis, strategic response, and evaluation) model used by the Ontario Provincial Police. A case study was presented to illustrate how patrol officers working in collaboration with the community apply the PARE model. Finally, the conditions for the successful implementation of POP, as well as the barriers that hinder problem solving, were discussed.

If you would like to learn more about any of the information described in this Unit, we would highly recommend you visit the websites for the Ontario Provincial Police (www.opp.ca) and for the Royal Canadian Mounted Police (www.rcmp.ca). The RCMP site http://www.rcmp-grc.gc.ca/ccaps-spcca/capra-eng.htm explains how CAPRA is applied to all aspects of the organization.

Chapter Review

Key Terms

- collaborative model of problem solving, p. 126
- expert model of problem solving, p. 125
- Herman Goldstein, p. 122
- iceberg or 80/20 rule, p. 122
- impact evaluation, p. 131
- PARE, p. 126
- problem, p. 120
- problem analysis filters, p. 128
- problem analysis triangle, p. 124
- problem solving, p. 120
- problem-oriented policing (POP), p. 122
- process evaluation, p. 131
- SARA, p. 123
- SMART, p. 131

Key Points

- Problem solving is a key element of community policing and it attempts to address the underlying causes of crime and social disorder.
- It is important that problems be appropriately identified and that the responsibility for the problem be established.
- Collaborative policing involves the police and the community agreeing that a problem exists, identifying the dimensions of the problem, and formulating and then implementing a strategy to address the problem.
- Problem-oriented policing (POP) puts the community-oriented policing strategy into practice.
- The iceberg or 80/20 rule holds that only a small portion of a problem is visible and that in order to eliminate a problem the root causes must be attacked.
- The problem-solving process is captured in the term SARA—scanning, analysis, response, and assessment.
- The problem-solving model of the Ontario Provincial Police is known as PARE—problem identification, analysis, strategic response, and evaluation.
- Problem analysis filters are used by the police and community to prioritize problems.
- A number of conditions must exist in police services for problem solving to be successful.
- A number of barriers in police services may undermine problem-solving efforts.

Self-Evaluation

QUESTIONS

1. What is meant by **problem solving** and what role does it play in community policing?
2. Define what is meant by a **problem**.
3. What is **collaborative problem solving**, and why is it important in any discussion of problem-oriented policing?
4. Who was **Herman Goldstein**, and what was his contribution to the field of problem-oriented policing?
5. Define and discuss the key elements of **problem-oriented policing (POP)**.
6. What is the **iceberg** or **80/20 rule**, and why is it important in our study of community policing and problem-oriented policing?
7. What is **SARA**?
8. Discuss what is meant by the **problem analysis triangle**, and what its role is in problem-oriented policing.
9. Compare the **expert model of problem solving** to the **collaborative model of problem solving**.
10. What is **PARE** and what are its components?
11. What are **problem analysis filters** and what role do they play in problem-oriented policing? Provide an example.
12. Compare **process evaluation** and **impact evaluation**.

KEY IDEAS

1. Problem solving attempts to address the underlying causes of crime and social disorder. How is problem solving best described?
   ✓ a. as one element of community policing
   b. as a new and emerging model of community policing
   c. as a technique that is no longer used in contemporary policing
   d. as a method of policing with minimal community involvement

2. During the strategic response stage, the police team develops a response in collaboration with the community. What is the only limit to the strategies used?
   a. the funding amount allocated to the project
   b. the size of the police agency and community facilities
   c. the tax base and budget of the community
   ✓ d. the imagination and resourcefulness of the partnership

3. What is problem-oriented policing (POP)?
   a. an approach to policing used primarily in the United States
   ✓ b. a strategy that puts community policing into practice
   c. a strategy most often used for identifying high-risk offenders
   d. an approach that has largely been abandoned due to costs

4. Who was Herman Goldstein?
   a. the first police chief in Ontario to implement problem-oriented policing
   b. the author of a book that was critical of problem-oriented policing
   ✓ c. the principal architect of problem-oriented policing
   d. the chief proponent of traditional policing

5. What does the acronym SARA stand for?
   ✓ a. scanning, analysis, response, assessment
   b. safety, alertness, readiness, awareness
   c. security, awareness, review, analysis
   d. sensing, arming, reacting, activating

6. Which statement describes the collaborative model of problem solving?
   a. it involves patrol officers and the community working together
   ✓ b. it emphasizes shared responsibility between the police and the community
   c. it uses experts to assist in the identification and response to problems
   d. it emphasizes multi-police agencies working together on a major crime

7. Which of the following is most often of concern to community residents?
   ✓ a. quality of life issues rather than violations of law
   b. white-collar and corporate crime
   c. police response times as well as dress and deportment
   d. allegations of police misconduct including excessive force

8. What are problem analysis filters?
   a. statistical methods used in calculating the number of crimes in a community
   b. tools used by police services that have not adopted community policing
   ✓ c. tools used in the analysis phase of problem-oriented policing to prioritize problems
   d. methods of preventing the displacement of a problem

9. In the evaluation stage of PARE, the process of asking questions such as "Were the strategies easy to implement?" and "What should others be aware of if attempting to implement a similar plan?" is known by which term?
   a. impact evaluation
   ✓ b. process evaluation
   c. assessment evaluation
   d. inquiry evaluation

10. The RCMP has developed a problem-solving model called CAPRA.   What does the acronym stand for?
   a. customer, agents/ability, people, respond, assess
   b. crime, answers/actions, police, react, allow
   ✓ c. clients, acquire/analyze information, partnerships, response, assessment
   d. capability, allow/answer information, persistence, readiness, action

Problem-Oriented Policing: Situations and Strategies

Problem-Solving Process Checklist

Problem solving is a key component of community policing, and there are specific questions and issues that must be asked and addressed at each of the scanning, analysis, response, and assessment stages of SARA.

Scanning

- Has the problem been described by all affected persons or groups?
- Has the problem been scrutinized for unforeseen elements?
- Has the problem been identified by more than one person or group? How do others describe the problem?
- Does your description contain all of the observed elements or components?
- After reviewing the problem from a variety of viewpoints, what are the common elements that can be used to develop a collective (community) description of the problem?

Analysis

- Who are the people involved or affected by the problem? Who are the victims? Who are the offenders? Who should respond to the problem?

- What is the scope of the problem? How large is it? Why did it develop?
- How did the problem develop? What actions or events constitute the problem?
- What is the sequence of events that produced the problem?
- When and where does the problem occur?
- What is the physical setting in which the problem is taking place? Does the location contribute to the problem?
- Has all of the available information or data on the problem been collected and analyzed?
- What underlying conditions precipitated the problem? Has the problem's causal relationship to agency or government policies, procedures, or practices been examined?
- What is the current community and governmental response to the problem? How do individuals and agencies react to the actions or problem? What have they done about the problem? What results have they had?

Response

- Have those individuals involved or affected by the problem (including residents) participated in a brainstorming session to identify potential responses?
- Has the response been tried before? If so, what were the results?
- What actions does the response include? What agencies need to be involved? Are representatives from those agencies present to discuss feasibility of action?
- What other resources are available for the response?
- What is the time frame for implementing the response?
- What barriers exist to implementing the response?
- What results can the stakeholders realistically expect?
- Can you reach consensus on a response, based on all the information you have gleaned?
- Have you developed an action plan for implementing the process?
- Have you set the response goals and objectives?
- Can you identify the steps necessary to implement the response?
- Can you identify the key stakeholders involved in or affected by each step?
- Have you assigned individual responsibilities for carrying out each step?
- Have you set time lines for completing each step?

Assessment

Process Evaluation

- Was the response implemented as intended? What problems were encountered, and how were they overcome?
- What specific steps were implemented? Were they all implemented? Were they implemented according to the timetable?
- Did these steps lead to the attainment of specific objectives? Were objectives revised? Were any additional objectives added?
- Were the overall goals achieved?
- To what extent were successes or failures a result of factors other than the response?
- What was the level of co-operation and participation among team members? Were the lines of communication between individuals and groups adequate?
- What changes in policies, procedures, or practices occurred or should have occurred during the implementation?

Impact Evaluation

- What were the expected results of the response?
- Were there any unintended effects?
- What will be measured and how? How long should the response remain operational to give a fair opportunity to show results or failure?

- How will data be collected? Did the response include a citizen survey, an examination of police statistics, or some other method?
- How will the data be analyzed? Was the response cost-effective? Did the response make a substantial difference?
- Will the response be replicated in other areas experiencing the same problem?

Case Studies in Problem Solving

The following cases illustrate how police officers have applied a problem-solving approach to address a wide range of problems in the community.

For each case study, list what you consider to be the most important items of information at each stage of the SARA process.

Case Studies

Case Study 1. Robberies at a Major Transit Station

Scanning: Several robberies had taken place at a major transit station. A large amount of pedestrian traffic from the nearby shopping centre was creating a target-rich environment for criminals. The problem had been identified by local police, on-site security personnel, the public, and the transit police.

The most important items of information at this stage are:

1. _____

2. _____

3. _____

Analysis: The transit station had become a gathering place for young people travelling to the city core or suburban areas. The theatres and video arcades catered to youth populations in particular. Gangs and youth at risk in the area were preying on transit patrons in the form of "strong-arm" robberies. The station had become a lucrative turf for groups of youths intent on exploiting the situation. They set up "offices" at this location. The sheer volume of patrons using the transit station (approximately 80,000 per day) made usual surveillance techniques ineffective. Young victims hesitated to contact the police for fear of retribution from "gang types." In addition, the general public was intimidated by the number of young people loitering in and around the station. As a result, the number of incidents increased. The incidence of collateral crimes such as drug use, recruiting of juveniles for prostitution, and assaults also increased at the station.

Crime analysis found that strong-arm robberies occurred almost daily, with three or four incidents reported to the police per week. This pattern had been present for two years. Each robbery lasted approximately five minutes, and gang members had become so confident that they would not be caught that they took their time searching the victims' belongings (clothing, knapsacks, purses, etc.). Upon releasing their victims, the gang members even remained in the immediate area, confident their victims would not call the police.

The immediate impact was that young victims were traumatized. The public avoided the area due to fear. Local retailers lost business. The neighbourhood suffered a reputation of being a "hot spot" of crime activity.

The most important items of information in this stage are:

1. _____

2. _____

3. _____

Response: Police personnel in the specialized youth squad gathered additional information and increased the level of "perceived" police presence in the station area. The Crime Analysis Computer correlated the dates and locations of incidents and suspect information. Staff members also submitted a CPTED (crime prevention through environmental design) report to transit management that recommended removing benches in the area, cutting back shrubbery, and installing sodium lighting and CCTVs. Patrols by security personnel were also increased. Neighbourhood officers worked in tandem with the transit police to photograph and videotape loitering youth known to be involved in the strong-arm robberies. This "in your face" technique had two effects: (1) it helped to identify gang members, and (2) it created a type of "benign intimidation" that had a noticeable effect.

The goal of the response was to reduce the number of robberies and calls for service to the transit station. Vital partnerships were formed to share intelligence and surveillance equipment.

The most important items of information in this stage are:

1 _____

2. _____

3. _____

Evaluation (Assessment): There was a noticeable effect, but no data were provided about qualitative or quantitative results. No ongoing assessment measures were reported.

The most important items of information in this stage are:

1. _____

2. _____

3. _____

Your Views: Using the SARA checklists presented above, assess whether you feel the problem-solving intervention was carried out well.

_____

_____

_____

_____

_____

_____

What were the strengths of the approach?

_____

_____

_____

_____

_____

_____

What improvements would you suggest?

_____

_____

_____

_____

_____

Case Study 2. Trespassing at a High School

Scanning: A member of the regional police service received a letter from a local high school requesting advice on how to make the campus more secure from trespassers. The school had developed a reputation for not being safe. There had been 62 calls for service that year.

The most important items of information at this stage are:

1. _____

2. _____

3. _____

Analysis: There were 2,000 students at the school, and staff did not know every student. This allowed the problem of intruders to escalate. On any given day, the school received 20–25 trespassers, some travelling a distance of up to 25 kilometres to be with friends and acquaintances. Furthermore, by employing a CPTED approach, a number of deficiencies were identified, including: (1) a parking lot that divided the campus physically and psychologically into two halves, (2) a parking lot entrance characterized by an irregular border and multiple access points and escape routes, (3) an open and undifferentiated classroom and gymnasium area, (4) a lack of effective or well-placed signage, (5) a lack of walkways for people to move safely between school buildings, and (6) a complete lack of bus-loading facilities to address the loitering and congestion problems in the parking lot.

The problem had existed for less than a year and was creating a general nuisance and increasing fear, especially in relation to an incident when a handgun was brandished at a basketball game. School officials, students, and police were very concerned.

The most important items of information at this stage are:

1. _____

2. _____

3. _____

Response: A local officer developed a 64-page CPTED study illustrating a series of external changes to accomplish the following objectives:

1. Provide for the anticipated increase in pedestrian traffic between the soon-to-be-amalgamated schools.
2. Introduce regular natural surveillance opportunities into the parking lot and between school buildings.
3. Define the parking lot entrance better and develop clearly marked transitional zones between semipublic and private spaces.
4. Reduce parking-lot entry points from three to two while limiting escape routes by 50 percent.
5. Develop safe, raised concrete walkways and bus-loading areas complete with feeder sidewalks.
6. Establish a fire route.
7. Develop a sense of territoriality by effectively communicating campus rules, bolstering property rights, and reinforcing transitions from public to private space.
8. Slow traffic.
9. Distinguish undifferentiated corridors from more active hallways.
10. Establish out-of-bounds hallways and territorial feelings.
11. Provide the continued surveillance of problem corridors.

The plan also included reorienting the school's parking lot from an east–west bias to a north–south bias and strategically placing signs, speed bumps, and partitions throughout the campus and driveway areas. In addition, the plan recommended installing safety glass in problem corridors in order to increase surveillance. The document was presented to the principal and board of superintendents.

The goal of the plan was to reduce trespassing around the school. A broader objective was to develop an effective and efficient school environment.

The most important items of information at this stage are:

1. _____

2. _____

3. _____

Evaluation (Assessment): Construction began a few months after the presentation of the report. In the three years following the modifications police occurrences at the 2,000-student high school dropped by an average of 87 percent, to between seven and nine occurrences per year. The environment became self-policing, and strong feelings of ownership had developed. School officials, students, and police reported the positive effects of the new construction on the school.

The most important items of information at this stage are:

1. _____

2. _____

3. _____

Your Views: Using the SARA checklists presented above, assess whether you feel the problem-solving intervention was carried out well.

_____

_____

_____

_____

_____

_____

What were the strengths of the approach?

_____

_____

_____

_____

_____

What improvements would you suggest?

_____

_____

_____

_____

_____

_____

Case Study 3. Traffic Accidents Involving Schoolchildren

Scanning: In 1990, there were 252 collisions involving pedestrians or cyclists under the age of 16. Eighty percent of the collisions involving children aged six to eight were "dart out" collisions resulting from children running out into traffic from between parked cars. The results were surprising because one of the seven rules first graders were routinely taught was not to play between parked cars. Records from 1985 to 1989 revealed the same statistics. In 1991, the Community Service Traffic Safety Branch of the local police service decided it was time to evaluate school traffic safety programs.

The most important items of information at this stage are:

1. _____

2. _____

3. _____

Analysis: Discussions of the Traffic Safety Advisory Committee revealed that several organizations were teaching completely different programs, which resulted in a scattered and inconsistent approach. Parents were identified as the best teachers because they had the most access to their children and were often willing to spend the time required for children to learn traffic safety. However, they often lacked the proper information or knowledge to take on this role. Moreover, in some family settings, traffic safety was not taught at all. Additional findings from a traffic safety research study confirmed the following conclusions:

1. Community agencies must work together to address traffic safety issues.
2. Police officers are not the best safety educators.
3. Dart-out collisions are a major cause for concern.
4. Parents often fail to become involved in teaching traffic safety.
5. Parents are an important part of any safety program.

Data analysis found that 250 collisions between cars and pedestrians or cyclists under the age of 16 occurred annually.

A previous traffic safety program—"Elmer's Safety Rules"—existed at the time the project was initiated. This 30-year-old program involved an elephant mascot who educated first graders on the seven rules to follow when around traffic.

Citizen representatives from city traffic departments, public health departments, early education organizations, and parents' groups participated in an advisory committee meeting in which they voiced their concerns about traffic safety education for children.

The most important items of information at this stage are:

1. _____

2. _____

3. _____

Response: Police collaborated with community members and organization representatives to adapt the "KIDestrian Book and Education Program," which was developed in Germany and consisted of simple and fun lessons which parents or other caregivers could teach their children. The program was then field-tested by parents at two local schools and by public health nurses. The officers then solicited corporations for sponsorship of the book. The team also sent letters and order forms to particular groups of people connected to the children. In addition, the police video training branch produced a promotional video. A media event was scheduled to launch the KIDestrian program. The goal of the project was to promote a consistent and effective form of traffic safety education in order to reduce the number of traffic accidents involving children.

To prepare, officers met with residents and various organization members to increase their knowledge of the problem and involve them in finding a solution to the problem of educating children on traffic safety. The advisory committee also obtained a copy of the original German program book and sought permission to use the material in order to develop a similar program.

Parents' groups, traffic engineers, health department officials, educators, and public health nurses provided available resources. Canadian Tire, an automotive, sporting goods, and hardware retailer, provided the finances to produce prototypes of the book in both English and French. Canada Post offered to package and distribute the materials at no cost, mailed out a fundraising request, provided a cash donation, purchased sidewalk chalk to accompany the books, and put advertising posters on postal trucks. *Today's Parent,* a national magazine, offered to print the books at a reduced cost and used their marketing expertise to enhance the book's layout. Finally, the video training branch of the police service contributed their resources as needed.

Citizen involvement occurred in the following manner. Two volunteer authors from the advisory committee worked with two police officers to develop the KIDestrian program and adapt the German book *Traffic Training: Parents Practise with Their Children* (English translation). Additional community members assisted in launching the program and in making further additions and revisions.

The most important items of information at this stage are:

1. _____

2. _____

3. _____

Evaluation (Assessment): At the time of this study, no quantifiable data existed to illustrate the impact of the program on reducing child traffic injuries. No correlation could be determined between the safety program and the number of child traffic accidents. However, qualitative measures found that the KIDestrian program reached the intended audience and that it was well received. As a result of feedback, the books were redesigned to include sections on rural and railroad-crossing safety. In addition, a new KIDestrian manual was developed to publicize the program.

The program was evaluated for approximately one year. Program evaluations were distributed to parents, daycare workers, teachers, community groups, and the Canadian Association of Chiefs of Police.

The most important items of information at this stage are:

1. _____

2. _____

3. _____

Your Views: Using the SARA checklists presented above, assess whether you feel the problem-solving intervention was carried out well.

_____

_____

_____

_____

_____

_____

What were the strengths of the approach?

_____

_____

_____

_____

_____

What improvements would you suggest?

_____

_____

_____

_____

_____

_____

Case Study 4. Convenience Store Robberies

Scanning: An internal year-end report produced by the Police Service Robbery Unit identified one major convenience store chain as the target of 44 percent of total convenience store robberies. By February the following year, the same convenience store chain represented 49 percent of the total number of robberies for the year. The police service decided to initiate a community-based approach to resolving the problem.

The most important items of information at this stage are:

1. _____

2. _____

3. _____

Analysis: Through crime analysis it was found that several clerks had been victimized. Two clerks required hospital treatment after having been slashed with knives. Three males had been identified as suspects in the robberies. The director of employee safety and training was consulted. Both the director and a detective attended all the high-risk and high-incident stores in the city, where physical security surveys and internal procedural reports were completed. The analysis showed that there were physical problems with security associated with the lighting and that there was a lack of adherence to cash-handling techniques and policies regarding cigarette lock-up and inventory control. The region became a first priority for security upgrading and store retrofitting.

The analysis concluded that the large numbers of robberies were consuming a significant percentage of police time. In addition, staff and customers at these stores were targets of violence. Moreover, the parent company was losing a great deal of money.

The most important items of information at this stage are:

1. _____

2. _____

3. _____

Response: Based on recommendations from the police and safety director, the company agreed to change the physical environment of the stores in order to discourage further robberies. Changes and upgrades included the following: a 24-hour time-lapse video recorder and camera; a video monitor to be displayed publicly near an entrance to educate the public that observation and recording were occurring; a locked cash-dispensing unit, cigarette safe, and locked safes for the counter area; additional alarms to be used in the event of personal threat or injury; computer upgrades to monitor entrances, exit tills, and storage areas; new, aggressive signage (large red and white signs placed in conspicuous areas alerting the public to video and security programs); upgraded levels of light; and revised robbery prevention manuals for all the dealers and stores.

Future outlined goals included corporate involvement in the Crime Stoppers program, corporate financing of additional projects undertaken by the robbery unit, public announcements highlighting the liaison with the police as well as crime prevention measures, and an improved cigarette disposal unit allowing removal of only a single package of cigarettes at a time, thus eliminating the "scoop and run" aspect of the robberies.

The goal of the community problem-solving plan was to reduce the number of armed robberies by increasing community, corporate, and police involvement and by educating community residents through media and corporate advertising. The police hoped to create a safer working environment for the convenience store employees and customers, and decrease the parent company's losses.

The most important items of information at this stage are:

1. _____

2. _____

3. _____

Evaluation (Assessment): Details of the evaluation have not been provided. Evaluate the problem-solving process. What outcomes are predictable? What impact do you think the problem-solving process would have in this case?

The most important items of information at this stage are:

1. _____

2. _____

3. _____

Your Views: Using the SARA checklists presented above, assess whether you feel the problem-solving intervention was carried out well.

_____

_____

_____

_____

_____

_____

What were the strengths of the approach?

_____

_____

_____

_____

_____

_____

What improvements would you suggest?

_____

_____

_____

_____

_____

_____

Case Study 5. Dealing with a Person Suffering from a Mental Illness

Scanning: Over a period of eight months, a person dealing with a mental illness repeatedly escaped from a group home and broke into hair salons to satisfy a fetish for shaving his head and pubic hair. In addition, he would expose himself and masturbate in public without concern for others watching.

The most important items of information at this stage are:

1. _____

2. _____

3. _____

Analysis: A beat officer responded to a break-and-enter call still in progress at a hair salon. He later checked police records and found 22 files concerning the same individual. Each call tied up police resources. Property owners who were the victims of the break-and-enters suffered without any hope of compensation. The police met with the subject's parents, psychiatrist, and caseworkers, and executive members from Social Services, to understand the nature of the problem and possible response options. He learned that the subject posed a serious challenge for the caseworkers attempting to control his activities.

The goal was to identify strategies that would eliminate, or at least reduce, police response and public concern regarding the mischief to property and indecent exposure.

The most important items of information at this stage are:

1. _____

2. _____

3. _____

Response: Police met again with the subject's parents, psychiatrist, and caseworkers, as well as with executives from Social Services. All parties agreed to implement the following strategies: (1) a buzzer system was put in place to enable caseworkers to restrict the subject's comings and goings, (2) a plan was developed that would help the subject burn off excess energy by involving him in household chores and sporting events, and (3) the subject was permitted to use his own hair clippers to shave his head and pubic hair.

The most important items of information at this stage are:

1. _____

2. _____

3. _____

Evaluation (Assessment): As a result of the targeted response, there were no further calls in relation to this individual for the duration of the eight-month evaluation period. Following this period, the subject experienced several relapses in his behaviour and was charged with a mischief offence. Once police resumed their vigilance, however, there were only isolated incidents, and the subject did not appear on the police database for the following 12 months. The problem-solving process drastically reduced, though it did not eliminate, the subject's offensive behaviour.

The most important items of information at this stage are:

1. _____

2. _____

3. _____

Your Views: Using the SARA checklists presented above, assess whether you feel the problem-solving intervention was carried out well.

_____

_____

_____

_____

_____

_____

What were the strengths of the approach?

_____

_____

_____

_____

_____

_____

What improvements would you suggest?

_____

_____

_____

_____

Case Study 6. The Methamphetamine Lab

Scanning: The fire department responded to a call to extinguish a small fire at a fenced compound. Other workers from the neighbourhood had responded previously when the occupant had set his clothing and footwear on fire while working with some chemicals. Emergency response found a fenced-in "fortress" that contained run-down buildings and a significant amount of toxic and volatile chemicals. Police involvement occurred when it became apparent that this was, in all probability, a clandestine methamphetamine laboratory. Several months later, neighbourhood residents reported unusual circumstances at this location. An ominous-looking, dense white cloud had formed over the compound. The occupant was reluctant to grant access to the emergency response team, but they entered nevertheless under the authority of the provincial *Health Safety Act*. The team quickly determined that the smoke resulted from another chemical experiment gone awry.

The most important items of information at this stage are:

1. _____

2. _____

3. _____

Analysis: Once the police concluded that the location was likely a meth lab, forensic experts were called in to examine the property. Unfortunately, they were unable to support this hypothesis. Various environmental agencies then assumed the case and served several control and access orders against the occupant. Because no charges were laid, all seized items had to be returned to the property owner.

Conversations with neighbourhood residents confirmed that the occupant had purchased an old abandoned house on an oversized city lot several years earlier. He had constructed a three-metre solid fence with a reinforced gate that blocked any view of the interior grounds. With his mysterious comings and goings at all hours of the night, the occupant had become known as the neighbourhood eccentric. Area residents had become accustomed to occasional clouds of smoke, colourful gaseous clouds, and strange noises. The police also learned that the science department at a local university had unknowingly supplied a good portion of the chemicals found at this location.

Among the agencies available to solve the problem were the environmental protection ministry and members of emergency response. Independent contractors from the Dangerous Goods Team of the Ministry of Environment were also called in to clean up the location at a cost of nearly $100,000.

The most important items of information at this stage are:

1. _____

2. _____

3. _____

Response: The goal was to stop the occupant's experimentation with potentially hazardous materials and to ensure that the area was safe for local residents. To achieve this objective the following steps were taken.

A charge of common nuisance was laid against the occupant. The occupant remained silent throughout the entire investigation. The police began to work closely with the provincial Environmental Protection Ministry. Consultants to the ministry provided the expertise to conduct the safety investigation and to interpret the installation. Emergency response and their dangerous goods team dealt with the *Safety Codes Act*. A private company was assigned responsibility for the clean-up and the storage of unsafe substances. A multitude of city departments got involved as well, including water and sanitation, which used robotics to document the damage done to the drainage system downstream.

The most important items of information at this stage are:

1. _____

2. _____

3. _____

Evaluation (Assessment): The long-standing problem was brought to a halt. There is no longer a chemical laboratory at this location, and all noxious substances have been purged. Results were measured through direct observation, and no ongoing effort is required as there are no longer noxious chemicals on the site and utilities have been suspended.

The most important items of information at this stage are:

1. _____

2. _____

3. _____

Your Views: Using the SARA checklists presented above, assess whether you feel the problem-solving intervention was carried out well.

_____

_____

_____

_____

_____

What were the strengths of the approach?

_____

_____

_____

_____

_____

What improvements would you suggest?

_____

_____

_____

_____

_____

EXERCISES: KNOWLEDGE INTO PRACTICE

Exercise 1: When Is Problem Solving an Appropriate Response? The Case of *Doe v. the Metropolitan Toronto Board of Commissioners of Police*

In 1986, a serial rapist attacked Jane Doe. She sued the chief of police, the Board of Commissioners of Police, and the two investigators, alleging that they were responsible for her injuries. Doe argued that she was part of a narrow and distinct group of potential victims. The victims were all single, white women who resided in second- or third-floor apartments with accessible balconies that had been used to gain access. The serial rapist confined his attacks to a small geographic area and an easily identifiable class of victims.

Doe claimed that the police were negligent in that they failed to warn her of a danger that they knew (or ought to have known) existed or, in the absence of such a warning, that they failed to adequately protect her against the danger.

The Ontario Court ruled:

> The police failed in their duty to protect these women and [Jane Doe] in particular from the serial rapist the police knew to be in their midst by failing to warn so that they may have had the opportunity to take steps to protect themselves.
>
> It is no answer for the police to say women are always at risk and as an urban adult living in downtown Toronto they have an obligation to look out for themselves. Women generally do, every day of their lives, conduct themselves and their lives in such a way as to avoid the general pervasive threat of male violence which exists in out society. Here the police were aware of a specific threat or risk to a specific group of women and they did nothing to warn those women of the danger they were in, nor did they take any measures to protect them. (Ontario Court [General Division] 1998:61, quoted in Ceyssens and Childs 1998:103)

It is important to note that during this investigation, there was another investigation going on in another part of the city involving more violent attacks, regarding which the police from the same department had issued a series of effective public warnings.

Questions

1. How would you have handled this investigation?
2. Would your response have been different if you knew who the offender was but did not have reasonable evidence on which to base an arrest? If so, how would it have been different?
3. Would the problem-solving process have been useful in this investigation? If so, what problems would it have addressed? If not, why not?

4. Which segments of the community were affected by this problem? What would have been an appropriate role for those communities?
5. Was there an appropriate role for the police to play in this investigation? What arguments would they have made for not informing the public?

Exercise 2. Identify a Problem in Your Community

1. Identify a current problem in your community.
2. Apply the problem-solving process to it.
3. Identify who is affected by the problem. What are the consequences related to the problem?
4. Make a detailed list of agencies and stakeholders that have an interest in resolving the problem. This may involve contacting the agency to determine whether it has a specific mandate to be involved in the problem.
5. Which groups have a mutual interest in improving the problem?
6. What are the objectives of your problem-solving process? If there are several aspects to the problem, what are the priorities, and why?
7. Where would you look to find more information about the problem?
8. In the assessment stage, what are the probable outcomes of your response (e.g., displacement, new problem)?
9. What steps or actions would you take to ensure that the problem does not appear again or manifest itself in a different way?

Exercise 3. The Criminal Apartment Building

Complete the SARA form for the following scenario. In your area, there is a rundown apartment building housing a mix of welfare tenants, new immigrants, elderly citizens, and criminals. Patrol officers have encountered several drug dealers, prostitutes, and other offenders with extensive backgrounds involving both property and violent crime. Over the last six months, you have noticed a dramatic increase in calls for service to or near this building, many of them coming through the 911 system as disturbances. The situation has now reached a point where the problems have spilled over into the surrounding area and nearby residents are becoming extremely frustrated and are complaining to the police chief and the mayor's office. You are directed to deal with this situation.

   What approach would you take to address this problem, and what measures would you initiate? What difficulties might be encountered? How would you measure the effectiveness of your efforts?

The Problem-Solving Process

Scanning

Describe the problem (be specific):

_____

_____

_____

_____

_____

_____

List the person(s) and/or groups affected by the problem:

_____

_____

_____

_____

_____

_____

Analysis

List the questions you have about this problem and the sources you would go to for the answers:

Question	Source

1. _____

_____

2. _____

_____

3. _____

_____

4. _____

_____

5. _____

_____

6. _____

_____

Goals (Short and Long Term)

Short Term	Long Term

_____

_____

_____

Responses

What strategies would you apply to solve this problem?

_____

_____

_____

_____

_____

Assessment

How would you measure the effectiveness of your problem-solving effort?

_____

_____

_____

_____

_____

Additional Notes on the Case

_____

_____

_____

_____

_____

Exercise 4. Drug Trafficking in the Park

Complete the SARA form for the following scenario. The unemployed, the homeless, and new immigrants are more heavily frequenting a large public park. Drug dealing, public drinking, littering, and the occasional disturbance have resulted in several complaints to the police. Some elderly people who have traditionally used the park are now too frightened to enter it, and a local newspaper has started publicizing their concerns, exacerbating already high levels of fear in the neighbourhood. Park officials and community activists have asked for more police attention, but aggressive patrol tactics have led to complaints from political minority groups and street workers, who say that the park is for everyone. Summer is approaching, and the resulting increased use of the park holds the potential for even greater problems. This park is located within your zone of responsibility. Design a plan to address the problem.

What approach would you take to address this problem, and what measures would you initiate? What difficulties might be encountered? How would you measure the effectiveness of your efforts?

The Problem-Solving Process

Scanning

Describe the problem (be specific):

_____

_____

_____

_____

_____

List the person(s) and/or groups affected by the problem:

_____

_____

_____

_____

_____

Analysis

List the questions you have about this problem and the sources you would go to for the answers:

Question	Source

1. _____

_____

2. _____

_____

3. _____

_____

4. _____

_____

5. _____

_____

6. _____

_____

Goals (Short and Long Term)

_____

_____

_____

_____

_____

Responses

What strategies would you apply to solve this problem?

_____

_____

_____

_____

_____

Assessment

How would you measure the effectiveness of your problem-solving effort?

_____

_____

_____

_____

_____

Additional Notes on the Case

_____

_____

_____

_____

_____

Exercise 5. Trouble in the Nightclub District

Complete the SARA form for the following scenario. A trendy nightclub district has created many problems for the police in the last few months. Residents of a nearby exclusive downtown apartment complex have phoned in numerous complaints about drunks on the street and frequent fights, and police checks of the premises have found problems with overcrowding and serving liquor to minors. Patrol officers in the area have been so busy processing the large number of impaired drivers in club parking lots that they have lacked the time to give sufficient attention to the street disturbances that have been occurring.

After bar closing time the supply of taxis is very limited and there is no public transit service at this time either. Concerns exist that unless the situation is brought under control, it will become totally and permanently unmanageable. You are the team sergeant of the zone in which these incidents are occurring. Devise a plan to respond to and solve this problem.

What approach would you take to address this problem, and what measures would you initiate? What difficulties might be encountered? How would you measure the effectiveness of your efforts?

The Problem-Solving Process

Scanning

Describe the problem (be specific):

_____

_____

_____

_____

_____

List the person(s) and/or groups affected by the problem:

_____

_____

_____

_____

_____

Analysis

List the questions you have about this problem and the sources you would go to for the answers:

Question   Source

1. _____

_____

2. _____

_____

3. _____

_____

4. _____

_____

5. _____

_____

6. _____

_____

Goals (Short and Long Term)

Short Term   Long Term

_____

_____

_____

_____

Responses

What strategies would you apply to solve this problem?

_____

_____

_____

_____

Assessment

How would you measure the effectiveness of your problem-solving effort?

_____

_____

_____

_____

Additional Notes on the Case

_____

_____

_____

_____

Exercise 6. Loitering Youths

A local convenience store has become a hangout for youths in the area. The shopping complex in which the store is situated also contains a fast-food restaurant and a gas station. The complex is situated within two blocks of a high school, and all these services are open until midnight. Serious crimes in the complex are rare, but there are an increasing number of calls related to disturbances, shoplifting, and fights. On most occasions, by the time police officers arrive on the scene, the youths have fled. Both the convenience store and the fast-food outlet have expressed an interest in solving the problem, as the situation is affecting their business. The gas station owner has stated that he is not concerned about the issue because the youths do not frequent his station, and he does not believe they detrimentally affect his business.

What approach would you take to address this problem, and what measures would you initiate? What difficulties might be encountered? How would you measure the effectiveness of your efforts?

The Problem-Solving Process

Scanning

Describe the problem (be specific):

_____

_____

_____

_____

_____

List the person(s) and/or groups affected by the problem:

_____

_____

_____

_____

Analysis

List the questions you have about this problem and the sources you would go to for the answers:

Question   Source

1. _____

_____

2. _____

_____

3. _____

_____

4. _____

_____

5. _____

_____

6. _____

_____

Goals (Short and Long Term)

Short Term Goals   Long Term Goals

_____

_____

_____

_____

Responses

What strategies would you apply to solve this problem?

_____

_____

_____

_____

Assessment

How would you measure the effectiveness of your problem-solving effort?

_____

_____

_____

_____

Additional Notes on the Case

_____

_____

_____

_____

Exercise 7. Social Disorder in a Remote Community

Complete the SARA form for the following scenario. A remote northwestern Ontario community is experiencing a high rate of solvent abuse among teenagers. This includes sniffing "white-out" correction fluid stolen from the school and gasoline siphoned from snowmobiles and other equipment in the community. Within the past year, three teenagers have committed suicide while under the influence of solvents and two others have been evacuated for medical treatment.

Except during the summer months, this community is accessible only by air. Although the population is around 200, there is widespread crime, and there are other social problems. The community has acknowledged that problems exist among the teenagers and that action is required. A new chief and council have indicated an interest in addressing the solvent abuse problem among the teenagers.

You have recently been posted to this community for a two-year tour of duty. What approach would you take to address this problem, and what measures would you initiate? What difficulties might be encountered? How would you measure the effectiveness of your efforts?

The Problem-Solving Process

Scanning

Describe the problem (be specific):

_____

_____

_____

_____

_____

List the person(s) and/or groups affected by the problem:

_____

_____

_____

_____

_____

Analysis

List the questions you have about this problem and the sources you would go to for the answers:

Question	Source
1. _____	_____
_____	_____
2. _____	_____
_____	_____
3. _____	_____
_____	_____
4. _____	_____
_____	_____
5. _____	_____
_____	_____
6. _____	_____
_____	_____

Goals (Short and Long Term)

Short Term Goals   Long Term Goals

_____

_____

_____

_____

Responses

What strategies would you apply to solve this problem?

_____

_____

_____

_____

_____

Assessment

How would you measure the effectiveness of your problem-solving effort?

_____

_____

_____

_____

_____

Additional Notes on the Case

_____

_____

_____

_____

_____

REFERENCES

Ceyssens, P. and S. Childs. 1998. "*Doe v. Metropolitan Toronto Board of Commissioners of Police* and the Status of Public Oversight of the Police in Canada." *Alberta Law Review* 36(4):1000.

Eck, J.E. and W. Spelman. 1987a. *Problem-Solving: Problem-Oriented Policing in Newport News.* Washington, DC: Police Executive Research Forum.

Eck, J.E. and W. Spelman. 1987b. "Who Ya Gonna Call? The Police as Problem-Busters." *Crime and Delinquency* 33(1):31–52.

Goldstein, H. 1987. "Toward Community-Oriented Policing: Potential, Basic Requirements, and Threshold Questions." *Crime and Delinquency* 3:6–30.

Goldstein, H. 1990. *Problem-Oriented Policing.* New York: McGraw-Hill.

Hough, M. and N. Tilley. 1998. *Getting the Grease to the Squeak: Research Lessons for Crime Prevention.* London, UK: Police Research Group, Home Office.

Ontario Provincial Police. 1997. *The "How Do We Do It" Manual.* Orillia, ON: Community Policing Development Centre.

Osborne, D. and T. Gaebler. 1993. *Reinventing Government: How the Entrepreneurial Spirit Is Transforming the Public Sector.* New York: Penguin.

Scott, M. 2000. *Problem-Oriented Policing: Reflections on the First 20 Years.* Washington, DC: U.S. Department of Justice, Office of Community-Oriented Policing Services.

UNIT

4

The Key Players in Community Policing

The Community Policing Police Service

Community Policing: providing community-oriented police services in a manner that reflects the needs of the community. A community policing approach involves partnering with other members of the community to gain their assistance in reducing crime, maintaining peace and order, and promoting safety.

Source: © Peter Power/Toronto Star/Getstock.com

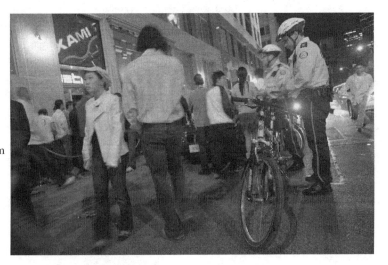

Learning Objectives

After completing this chapter, you should be able to:

- Discuss how community policing has affected the way police services are organized;

- Discuss the role of mission, value, and vision statements in policing;

- Describe the techniques of environmental scans, benchmarking, best practices, growth positions, and performance indicators;

- Discuss what is meant by the police service as a learning organization;

- Describe the Policing for Results Survey used by the Ontario Provincial Police;

- Discuss the role of teams in community policing;

- Describe the role of strategic planning and business plans in community policing; and

- Discuss the Ontario Provincial Police's customized approach and delivery process.

INTRODUCTION

Community policing requires both a philosophical shift in the way that police departments think about their mission, as well as a commitment to structural changes this new form of policing demands.

—R. Trojanowicz and B. Bucqueroux (1990)

Police services across the country have often struggled with the question of how to redesign the organization and delivery of police services in order to incorporate the philosophy and principles of community policing. Many of those principles require rethinking how police services are organized. Community policing is about much more than merely introducing new programs in the community; it involves a substantial shift in organization and delivery, as well as an expansion of the roles and responsibilities of line officers.

In reviewing the experience of many Canadian police services with community policing, there has often been a "cart before the horse" problem. Initiatives have been undertaken without a clear understanding of the organizational and operational changes required to institutionalize this new model of service delivery. In the absence of a blueprint for how to implement these principles, individual police leaders and police organizations have been left on their own to craft the structural, policy, and program changes required to "do" community policing (Rosenbaum, Yeh, and Wilkinson 1994). This has resulted in considerable diversity across the country in how the concept of community policing has been interpreted and implemented. A key element of community policing is recording the lessons of the past so that future efforts make substantive improvements rather than simply "reinvent the wheel" or even make the same mistakes again.

In this chapter, we will examine the organizational and institutional changes required by community policing as well as the tools and techniques used by police services to deliver services within a community policing framework.

ORGANIZATIONAL REQUIREMENTS FOR COMMUNITY POLICING

The perfect community policing department does not exist. No department is a paragon of the values represented by the concept of community policing, nor is there one model of community policing.

—F. Hartmann, L. Brown, and D. Stephens (1988)

Organizational change is difficult under the best of circumstances. Community policing requires that police services re-examine all aspects of the organization, administration, and delivery of policing services. This requires time, vision, commitment, planning, and an ability to question and assess outcomes constantly. In this chapter, we will examine the key organizational requirements for implementing the principles of community policing.

In the words of R.D. Hunter and T. Barker (1993), two U.S. police scholars, discussions of community policing tend to be afflicted by a considerable amount of "BS and buzzwords." Trendy terms are applied to traditional practices, and new programs are developed in the absence of any framework for the delivery of policing services. To fulfill the philosophy and the principles of community policing, police services must make a number of significant changes in how police services are organized, administered, and delivered.

A number of key ingredients are required in any effort to implement community policing. Many of these are discussed throughout this chapter.

Table 6.1 presents a matrix used by the Seattle Police Department that can be used to determine the particular stage of development in the process of moving toward adopting and implementing the principles of community policing. As an organization

Table 6.1 Community Policing Stage Assessment Matrix: Development Stages

Development Stage	Program Components/Elements	
Stage 1: Awareness/Discovery Initial interest in the new style of policing from magazine articles/conferences/exchange of information with other police personnel; take action to learn more about new community policing approach; discuss use of new programs in meetings and formulate tentative new program ideas	*Problem-Solving Approach* General discussions about how projects are selected held between police and citizens; concerns about involvement of citizens and security issues addressed; concerns about police workload and limited resources addressed; little or no interaction with public about problems	*Program Evaluation* No specific evaluation questions considered relevant at this stage; basic process evaluations of planning and information-gathering timeliness (if formal project designation) considered
Stage 2: Experimental/Exploratory Police agency and/or city identify potential applications of community policing model; acquire more information about specific programs and plan/implement pilot efforts; begin limited discussions with other city personnel to familiarize them with new problem-solving approach; evaluate pilot projects	*Problem-Solving Approach* Initial problem-solving meetings on how to set agendas/select problems and procedures; solution approaches reflect little creativity or involvement of other (non-police) resources; feedback on outcomes requested by citizens but viewed as time consuming by police	*Program Evaluation* Process evaluations and tracking of activities; report actions/successes of problem-solving projects; initial use of customer surveys to identify needs/priorities
Stage 3: Commitment/Understanding More in-depth analysis of information about community policing programs and requirements; review results of pilot programs; establish open communications links with other city departments and provide educational materials; develop and conduct extensive training programs; expand involvement of citizens/business groups and build trust; police agency, city officials, and other departments analyze required organizational and managerial changes; commit resources and begin coordinated implementation	*Problem-Solving Approach* Working relationships among police/citizens/other city departments built on trust and respect; problem targets selected by community; long-term problems addressed; level of creative and innovative solutions increases; amount and quality of analysis increase	*Program Evaluation* Develop outcome/impact measures for performance evaluations tied to goals; use customer surveys to assess priorities and satisfaction with results of city/police efforts
Stage 4: Proficiency/Renewal The new approach to police service delivery and community/business partnership becomes ingrained in police agency operations and management style; most city departments focus on coordinated service delivery; ongoing and automatic processes for service improvement and innovation are operational; innovative managerial approaches and structural changes to the organization completed (and revised as necessary) based on the new mission and vision	*Problem-Solving Approach* Joint city-wide problem-solving program involves regular meetings and open communications process; private sector and regional resources are part of process; coordinated service delivery is city-wide standard	*Program Evaluation* Continuous process, impact, and project monitoring part of normal operations; constant "fine tuning" of performance measures with focus on service improvement

Source: Fleissner, D.W., 1997. Community Policing Stage Assessment Model for Implementation Planning and Organizational Measurement. Seattle: Seattle Police Department and National Institute of Justice, p. 62.

evolves through each stage, the principles and practices of community-based policing become more embedded in the organization. By the time a police organization has evolved to the fourth stage (and many, if not most, do not get this far!), the organization is now practising community policing in a strategic way.

The Police Leader and Community Policing

[T]he task facing modern police leadership oriented to CPB [community-based policing] is obviously daunting. Added to the typical leadership responsibilities is the challenge of effecting major organizational transformation.

—D. Clairmont (1996)

There is little doubt that police leaders are in the spotlight as never before. They must be oriented toward action and results rather than merely to maintaining the status quo. Police leaders must be educated, be creative, have vision, be able to communicate that vision, and be willing to take risks and break with tradition. All this must be accomplished at a time when increasing demands are being placed upon the police, including significant human resource pressures and a broadened security policing mandate. The priorities and challenges of contemporary police leaders can be summarized as needing to be focused on three C's: cost of policing, conduct of police officers and crime control.

Police chiefs and chief constables play a critical role in implementing the principles of community policing and building the organizational capacity to facilitate community-based policing. Section 41(1) of the Ontario Police Services Act lists the duties of the chief of police, two of which are ensuring that members of the police force carry out their duties in accordance with the Act in a manner that reflects the needs of the community, and ensuring that the police force provides community-oriented police services. The Canadian Association of Chiefs of Police has actively developed initiatives to improve the quality of police leadership in Canada. In Ontario, the Ontario Association of Chiefs of Police has declared the improvement of police leadership in the province to be a major part of its mandate. The 2007 Task Force Report on Governance and Cultural Change in the RCMP—Rebuilding the Trust—focuses on the leadership challenges and change necessary to modernize the RCMP.

Implementing community policing presents police leaders with a formidable management challenge. Police leaders must abandon traditional command and control practices and decentralize power in order to create a much more participatory organizational environment within which the ideas and requirements of line officers can be incorporated into the decision-making process. Table 6.2 illustrates some of the changes in management that are required for community policing.

The task for senior police leadership is to create a framework within which the role of the line officer can be transformed from one of reacting to incidents and "crime fighting" to that of actively solving problems and understanding the needs and issues of the community, and working in partnership with the community to address these issues.

Table 6.2 Changes in Management Required for Community Policing

From	To
Bureaucratic management	Strategic management
Administrative management	People management
Maintenance management	Change management

Source: Murphy, C., and C.T. Griffiths, 1994. "Community Based Policing —A Review of the Issues, Research, and Development of a Provincial Policy." Unpublished research report prepared for the Commission of Inquiry, Policing in British Columbia. Victoria: Ministry of Attorney General. p. 8.

There are key differences between managing a police service and leading a police service:

- The manager administers; the leader innovates.
- The manager is a copy; the leader is an original.
- The manager maintains; the leader develops.
- The manager focuses on systems and structures; the leader focuses on people.
- The manager relies on control; the leader inspires trust.
- The manager has a short-range view; the leader has a long-range perspective.
- The manager asks how and when; the leader asks what and why.
- The manager has an eye on the bottom line; the leader has an eye on the horizon. (Bennis 1989:44).

In describing the transition required to implement a management philosophy of total integrated policing in the Halton Regional Police Service, the Chief of Police stated: "Our managers will become coaches and team leaders rather than drivers and bosses and will help contribute to the team building and problem solving at lower levels. . . . Our success and real solutions to everyday problems will only come from staff involvement" (Halton Regional Police Service 2000).

Undermining Community Policing

The failure of senior police leaders to "walk the talk" can significantly undermine the implementation of the principles of community policing and the development of a community policing service. The community policing scholar John Eck has written a slightly tongue-in-cheek checklist of the actions that tradition-bound police chiefs can engage in to undermine community policing. These are listed in Box 6.1.

Mission, Value, and Vision Statements

Police organizations today have developed **mission, value, and vision statements** that set out the general principles for providing policing services. These statements generally incorporate the basic tenets of community policing and reflect the general orientation of the police service. The motto of the Halton Regional Police Service, for example, is "Progress Through Participation," and its Mission is "To Provide Effective and Efficient Community-Based Policing." Check out the vision and value statements of the Royal Newfoundland Constabulary in Box 6.2 and the mission statement of the Calgary Police Service in Box 6.3. Notice any resemblance between this mission statement and Sir Robert Peel's principles? Now, compare these mission statements to that of the Anishinabek Police Service, an Aboriginal police service in Ontario, in Box 6.4.

Redesigning the Organizational Structure

Community policing requires that police services make significant changes to their traditional, hierarchical organizational structures. These include decentralizing decision making and giving line officers more authority and autonomy to work collaboratively with community residents, reducing the amount of bureaucracy that often hinders officer initiatives, reducing specialization in the police service and expanding the role of police constables as generalists, and "flattening" the organizational structure by reducing the levels of management and supervision. Over the past decade, police services across Canada have undertaken a number of efforts designed to reorganize and restructure the delivery of police services and to improve the effectiveness of service delivery.

The effect of reorganization on police personnel should not be underestimated. It is, potentially, a major obstacle to the implementation of community policing. Flattening the organizational structure and increasing the emphasis on line-level police work has direct implications for the careers of many police personnel, particularly those officers

BOX 6.1

HELPFUL HINTS FOR THE TRADITION-BOUND CHIEF

Things that tradition-bound, enforcement-oriented chiefs of police can do to undermine community policing:

1. **Oversell it.** Community policing should be sold as the panacea for every ill that plagues the community, including crime, fear of crime, racism, unemployment, domestic violence, and bad government.

2. **Don't be specific.** Never define what is meant by the terms such as "community," "service," "effectiveness," "neighbourhood," "problem solving," and "partnership." These terms should be used indiscriminately. When scrutinized, the amorphous nature of community policing can be blamed.

3. **Create a special unit or group.** Less than 10 percent of the department should be engaged in the community policing effort. This makes it appear that community policing is being adopted by the police service but at the same time undercuts the potential effectiveness of community policing.

4. **Create a soft image.** The best image for community policing is a uniformed female officer hugging a small child. This will undermine community policing by playing to traditional stereotypes of sexism within policing and create cynicism among line officers.

5. **Separate community policing officers from "real" police work.** Assigning officers to community policing tasks such as visiting schools, speaking to community groups, and working in store-front operations will undermine their credibility and ability to accomplish anything of significance. These officers will not be perceived as "real" police officers by their colleagues, further undermining community policing.

6. **Never try to understand why problems occur.** Having officers gather information on the possible causes of problems will lead to successful interventions. Problem solving should not involve any analysis of the problem and no information should be sought from other agencies, the community, or departmental records. To maintain ignorance of community problems: (a) make sure crime analysis produces only management reports, (b) do not respond to requests from line officers for crime analysis, (c) keep officers away from computer terminals, (d) suppress listening skills, and (e) prevent access to research conducted on similar problems.

7. **Never publicize a success.** In situations where, despite your best efforts as chief, an officer has developed a successful problem-solving strategy, ignore that individual and make sure there is no publicity and that the project is spoken of only in the least meaningful way.

Source: From "Helpful Hints for the Tradition-Bound Chief," *Fresh Perspectives*, 1992, June. Eck, J.E., pg. 7.

in middle management. Reform often involves eliminating or reducing senior-level positions and streamlining the organizational hierarchy.

The management structure of the traditional police services was a hierarchical pyramid, reflecting a top-down system in which senior management issued directives to be carried out by line officers at the bottom. A one-way flow of information—from senior officers to line officers—ensured obedience to the goals and objectives established by senior officers. Community policing turns the traditional pyramid on its head. The role of senior police managers is to provide leadership and support for line officers, who implement the principles of community policing daily. The focus shifts from achieving the goals set by senior managers to community building and problem solving. In short, implementing community policing requires police services to invert the **police pyramid** (see Figure 6.1).

The Halton Regional Police Service has developed a philosophy it calls Total Integrated Policing (TIP). The Chief of Police describes the philosophy as empowering officers to address issues at the local level while at the same time holding them

BOX 6.2

THE ROYAL NEWFOUNDLAND CONSTABULARY: VISION AND VALUES

Vision

Safer communities through policing excellence.

Values

In accomplishing its vision the Royal Newfoundland Constabulary believes in:

- Foremost, protecting and helping people;

- Treating people with respect;

- Delivering police services compassionately, ethically and free of bias;

- Using police authority judiciously;

- Seeking the truth;

- Working with the community to identify and resolve crime and disorder problems; and

- Being approachable, accessible, and of service to every individual.

Within the organization, the Royal Newfoundland Constabulary believes in:

- Embracing change;

- Approaching duty diligently and enthusiastically;

- Continuing the professional development of each individual through education and training;

- Being a team player—acting in harmony, being respectful and supportive of individuals; and

- Upholding the proud traditions of policing and the Royal Newfoundland Constabulary.

Source: Royal Newfoundland Constabulary, 2011. Corporate Plan 2011-2014. http://www.rnc.gov.nl.ca retrieved 2012 May 12.

BOX 6.3

MISSION STATEMENT AND GUIDING PRINCIPLES OF THE CALGARY POLICE SERVICE

Mission Statement—To maximize public safety in Calgary

With a mission to "maximize public safety in Calgary," the Calgary Police Service is committed to working with the community to maintain this city as a safe place to live, work and visit.

As we continue to utilize community policing, in which collaboration and co-operation with partners is essential to public safety, we remain focused on our vision of "working together for a safe community". We are committed to doing this by remaining true to our core values of respect, honesty, integrity, fairness, compassion and courage.

We work to provide the best quality of service paired with cost effectiveness. We also strive to ensure that the type of policing, and the services we provide, reflect what the community needs. Because these needs can shift as the community evolves, we consistently review and evolve our policing methods. Ongoing review of workload and deployment is required to meet the changing face of our city, in order to ensure modern, effective and efficient policing.

Source: Calgary Police Service (2012) 2012–2014 Business Plan

---

BOX 6.4

ANISHINABEK POLICE SERVICE MISSION STATEMENT

Providing for the safety, security and protection of first nation communities through the provision of culturally sensitive, proactive, professional, unbiased enforcement strategies. We encourage community involvement, public education, and transparent accountability.
    We support victims of crime and are committed to the protection of inherent rights and freedoms.

Source: Anishinabek Police Service 2012 (http://www.apscops.org/)

---

accountable for the tasks performed. The result is a flattened, top-down organizational hierarchy. The TIP approach, for example, has resulted in a 35 percent reduction in the number of supervisors and a 24 percent reduction in staff sergeants and sergeants in the Halton Regional Police Service, which now has the smallest ratio of supervisors-to-constables in Ontario. This trend is consistent across Canada among almost all police organizations, where the absolute numbers of personnel remain essentially the same but upper levels of management have been trimmed in order to place more officers in operational, front-line positions.

What does the organizational structure of a community policing police service look like? Each municipal or regional force has taken a different approach to changing its organizational structure to incorporate the principles and practice of community policing. Figure 6.2 illustrates the organizational structure of the York Regional Police Service. Notice how the organization addresses contemporary demands for police service within its structure and how sections are grouped together to maximize organizational effectiveness.

Reorienting the Organization: The Police Service as a Learning Organization

For an organization to learn, its systems for learning from its own experiences and those of other organizations must be explicit as well as understood by all employees . . . Organizations must value and recognize learning, be intentional about learning, or be ones that have discovered how to learn . . . [This] will enable

Figure 6.1 Inverting the Police Pyramid

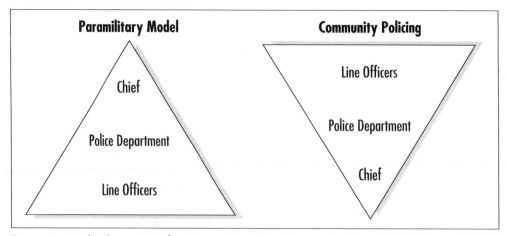

Figure 6.2 York Regional Police Organizational Structure

POLICE SERVICES BOARD

Executive Director

CHIEF OF POLICE

EXECUTIVE SERVICES

- Freedom of Information
- Legal
- Diversity, Equity & Inclusion
  - Chaplains
  - Hate Crime
  - Diversity & Cultural Resources
- Corporate Communications
- Professional Standards
  - Public Complaints
  - SIU Liaison
- Health & Safety
- Strategic Services
  - Risk Management
  - Quality Assurance
  - Planning & Research — Statistics
  - Capital Projects & Facilities Management
  - Property/Evidence & Records Retention

DEPUTY CHIEF Administration Branch

COURT SERVICES
- Court Operations
  - Prisoner Management
  - Court Security
  - Prisoner Transportation
  - POA Courts
- Court Administration
  - Case Management
    - Disclosure Management
    - Document Service
  - Court Management
    - Court Support
    - Victim Notification
    - Witness Management

COMMUNITY SERVICES
- Community Mobilization
  - Crime Prevention
  - Guns & Gangs Prevention
  - Personal Safety
  - Persons with Disabilities Safety
  - Seniors Safety
  - Victims Assistance
- Community Partnerships
  - Auxiliary
  - Crime Stoppers
  - Mental Health Resources
  - Volunteers
- Youth Programs
  - Community Liaison
  - Community Safety Village
  - School Resources
  - Youth Education

STAFF SERVICES
- Human Resources
  - Civilian Recruiting
  - Compensation & Benefits
  - Employee Relations
- Professional Development
  - Staff Development
  - Uniform Recruiting
- Training & Education
  - Academics
  - Technology & Skills Development
  - Use of Force
  - Police Vehicle Operations

FINANCIAL SERVICES
- Budget & Control
  - Accounting
  - Alarms
  - Budget
  - Paid Duty Administration
- Procurement & Fleet Management
  - Purchasing
  - Stores
  - Fleet

INFORMATION SERVICES
- Communications
  - 911 / Call Centre
  - Community Resource Centre
  - Technical Support
- Information Management
  - Crown Folder Processing
  - Customer Service
  - Data Quality Verification
  - Document Control
  - General Occurrence Reader
  - Transcription/ Validation
- Information Technology
  - Application Support
  - Business Continuity
  - Enterprise Architect
  - Help Desk
  - Network Support

DEPUTY CHIEF Operations Branch

INVESTIGATIVE SERVICES
- Special Investigations & Support
  - Auto/Cargo Theft
  - Forensic Identification
    - Archaeological Recovery
    - Technical Data Recovery
    - Video Support
  - High Risk Offenders
  - Hold Up
- Intelligence
  - Integrated Crime Analysis
  - Mobile Support
  - Special Services
  - Strategic Intelligence
- Major Crimes
  - Crimes Against Children
    - Internet Child Exploitation
  - Homicide
  - Integrated Domestic Violence
  - Major Case Management
    - ViCLAS
  - Polygraph
  - Sexual Assault
- Organized Crime
  - Drugs & Vice
  - Guns & Gangs Enforcement
  - Major Fraud

SUPPORT SERVICES
- Field Support
  - Emergency Response
    - Critical Incident Management
  - Operational Support
    - Air Support
    - Canine
    - Firearms
    - Incident Response
- Traffic
  - Commercial Motor Vehicle Safety
  - Enforcement
  - Road Safety Programs
  - Collision Investigation

Duty Inspectors

1 DISTRICT
- Patrol
- Criminal Investigations
- Community Oriented Response

2 DISTRICT
- Patrol
- Criminal Investigations
- Community Oriented Response
- Marine
  - Underwater Recovery

3 DISTRICT
- Patrol
- Criminal Investigations
- Community Oriented Response

4 DISTRICT
- Patrol
- Criminal Investigations
- Community Oriented Response

5 DISTRICT
- Patrol
- Criminal Investigations
- Community Oriented Response

Source: Courtesy of York Regional Police

them to adapt quickly notwithstanding rapid technological, social and economic changes . . . Learning also has to do with "unlearning" . . . the ability to cast off those practices determined by experience to be redundant and counterproductive.
—D.S. Campbell (1992)

A key component in community policing is the concept of the **police service as a learning organization**. A learning organization is "an organization that is continually expanding its capacity to create its future" (Senge 1994:14). This involves creating an organizational environment that interacts with its external environment, rather than being isolated from it. The goal is greater organizational effectiveness through the use of a number of systems or processes, including:

- *generating a holistic view of the organization*: ensuring that police personnel understand the objectives of the organization and their role in achieving them;
- *obtaining and using information about the "external" environment*: developing networks with other agency personnel, such as social workers and community groups, and conducting research and incorporating research findings into operational policy and practice;
- *encouraging the development of new knowledge*: encouraging officers to think creatively and independently and take risks, and ensuring that new recruits have an opportunity to contribute ideas;
- *learning from other organizations*: forging alliances with public- and private-sector organizations to facilitate sharing information;
- *providing feedback to officers about their performance*: considering the results from community surveys, using different criteria to assess officers' contributions to overall objectives, and using roll calls and debriefings effectively; and
- *questioning assumptions*: giving officers the opportunity to question longstanding policies and practices and the rationale for them (Campbell 1992:253–62).

In the learning organization, employees continually expand their knowledge base and improve their performance and the effectiveness of their activities. The province of Ontario has given considerable attention to developing the capacity for police services to become learning organizations. The Police Learning System (PLS) was implemented in 1995 and redesigned the training, education, and development programs for police personnel. The PLS Advisory Committee is charged with identifying new trends and strategies to enhance the learning capabilities of police services throughout the province.

Another key resource in Ontario is the Ontario Provincial Police Community Issues Unit, described in Box 6.5.

The creation of learning organizations is key to the success of a community-policing police service. At the heart of the learning organization is *continuous learning*, which helps an organization to innovate, to learn from past experience, and to manage the change process rather than simply react to it.

A concept related to the learning organization is called "intelligence-led policing." Intelligence-led policing can be defined as:

[A] collaborative enterprise based on improved intelligence operations and community-oriented policing and problem solving. . . . To implement intelligence-led policing, police organizations need to reevaluate their current policies and protocols. Intelligence must be incorporated into the planning process to reflect community problems and issues. Information sharing must become a policy, not an informal practice. Most important, intelligence must be contingent on quality analysis of data. The development of analytical techniques, training, and technical assistance needs to be supported. (Bureau of Justice Assistance [U.S.] 2005)

BOX 6.5

THE ONTARIO PROVINCIAL POLICE COMMUNITY ISSUES UNIT

The Ontario Provincial Police Community Issues Unit was established around the principle of "Crime Prevention through Community Engagement." To achieve this, the Community Issues Unit, part of the OPP's Crime Prevention Section, works closely with communities to develop sustainable strategic partnerships that encourage crime prevention at the community level and results in the development of community capacity to build a safe community. The Community Issues Unit works with other government agencies, regional community policing coordinators, and community services coordinators in the development and distribution of new initiatives that are designed to enhance relationships between the police and the community.

The Unit supports ongoing evaluation of crime-prevention activities and takes a lead role in the coordination of large programs—such as Community Watch, Cottage Watch, and so on—to ensure that the delivery of these programs is consistent throughout the province. The Unit is designed to support the development of police–community partnerships, enhance the problem-solving capacities of line officers, and identify and encourage the use of best practices in preventing and responding to crime and disorder. Developing strategies to assist with community engagement is a key service provided by the Unit.

The development of resources such as the OPP's Community Issues Unit increases the capacity of the OPP to develop and implement community policing models and plans. You can learn more about the OPP's Community Issues Unit at www.opp.ca.

It is similar in the attempt to ensure the organization learns in an institutional way from its experiences. It is dependent on technology and the IT resources of police services. You will recall that one trend is to integrate databases in an effort to improve knowledge acquisition and make better decisions based on business intelligence. For this reason, we are seeing steps to do the following:

• Integrate police databases to share information between police services
• Integrate justice system databases to ensure more comprehensive decision making throughout the justice system.

Adopting a Corporate Model: Strategies and Measures

Increasingly, police services are adopting strategies and measures traditionally found in the private sector. The language of modern policing includes terms that were virtually unheard of a decade ago—environmental scans, benchmarking, intelligence-led, best practices, balanced scorecard, strategic planning, community surveying, growth positions, performance indicators, and performance outcomes. These efforts are designed to improve the efficiency, effectiveness, and accountability of police services while responding to increased public demands for service, despite budgetary constraints. This has become known as the **corporate model of policing**, and it complements the requirements of community policing as well as meeting the needs of municipal governments that allocate the funds for police services.

Within this framework, Kernaghan and Seigal (1995) note that governments can frequently accomplish more by entering into a partnership with private-sector or not-for-profit organizations, or by reducing their role so as to allow other organizations to do things better. This trend is largely a response by government agencies in general to reduce the direct delivery of some services and to become facilitators rather than doers. Some of the key components of the corporate model are discussed below.

Strategic Planning

Strategic planning isn't an "event" or "exercise" in TPS [the Toronto Police Service]. It's a dynamic and continuous process that helps the organization and its units set objectives, develop programs to achieve them, and arrange its resources to make that happen.

—*Toronto Police Service (1999)*

As police services adopt the principles of community policing and make more effective and efficient use of their resources, the functions of planning and research assume even more importance. They provide the organization with the capacity not only to assess the effectiveness of specific policy and programmatic initiatives but also to anticipate future demands that are likely to be made upon the department.

A key component of the planning process is the **business plan**, also known as the **strategic plan**. In Ontario, the Adequacy and Effectiveness of Police Services standards (Section 30(1) and 30(2)) require all police service boards to produce a business plan for their police force at least once every three years. This plan must set out the core business and function of the police force, and include how it will provide adequate and effective police services. It must also establish quantitative and qualitative performance objectives and indicators relating to:

- the provision of community-based crime-prevention initiatives,
- community patrol,
- criminal investigation,
- community satisfaction with police services,
- emergency calls for service,
- violent crime and clearance rates for violent crime,
- property crime and clearance rates for property crime,
- youth crime and clearance rates for youth crime,
- police assistance to the victims of crime,
- resource planning,
- information technology,
- police facilities,
- revictimization rates, and
- road safety.

Note that several of the above-noted areas are most often associated with traditional police practice, again illustrating that the strategies and approaches in community policing are best viewed as an expansion of police activities, rather than a replacement of them.

Taylor (1999:14) has identified the requirements and benefits of strategic planning. The requirements include:

- an accurate assessment of the strengths and weaknesses of the service;
- the opportunities for improved service and the threats to its effectiveness;
- a comprehensive review of the operational environment, including incident statistics and demographic data;
- consideration of provincial standards;
- opportunities for collaborative efforts with other agencies or private industry;
- a thorough understanding of service parameters and of the extent to which the agency meets demands for service; and
- a clear understanding of the strategic direction of the agency.

As for benefits, a good strategic plan provides:

- a focus for the organizational framework that determines organization needs and practices,
- a basis for assessing the effectiveness and efficiency of organizational practices,
- a long-term perspective, and
- information from people in all parts of the organization (Taylor 1999:15).

BOX 6.6

STRATEGIC PRIORITIES OF THE ROYAL CANADIAN MOUNTED POLICE 2012–2017

The strategic priorities of the RCMP are selected based on a thorough scan and analysis of the external environment and crime trends.

Identifying these issues as priorities across the entire organization allows employees to focus operations in a more strategic manner in order to enhance public safety.

Each strategic priority has outcomes and objectives which are developed and evaluated by a working group led by a Deputy Commissioner.

The detailed plans and performance indicators for each priority are articulated to employees and external partners on the RCMP's performance management tool, the Balanced Scorecard.

In June 2011, the RCMP Senior Executive Committee reviewed and confirmed that the following would continue to be the strategic priorities for the period from 2012 to 2017:

- reducing the threat and impact of serious and organized crime,

- countering criminal threats to Canada's economic integrity,

- reducing youth crime,

- countering criminal threats to the security of Canada, and

- contributing to safer and healthier Aboriginal communities.

The RCMP has also established management priorities to strengthen professional integrity and redress, to support employee wellness, and to provide strong talent management. Key performance indicators for the priorities are available on the RCMP website.

Each year the Treasury Board Secretariat completes a Departmental Performance Report for the Royal Canadian Mounted Police. This document sets out how well the Royal Canadian Mounted Police is doing in relation to its strategic priorities. You can link to this report through www.rcmp-grc.gc.ca or go to the Treasury Board of Canada Secretariat website at www.tbs-sct.gc.ca.

Source: © Royal Canadian Mounted Police, Report on Plans and Priorities 2012–2013 [Online] http://publications.gc.ca/collections/collection_2012/grc-rcmp/PS61-20-2012-eng.pdf (p. 8). Retrieved June 12, 2012.

Taylor also notes that strategic plans have the potential for greatest impact when the plan and its performance measures are understood and applied by personnel at all levels of the organization. Check out the RCMP's strategic priorities, which are highlighted in Box 6.6.

The (Ontario) Adequacy Standards (Section 32(2)) also require the police service boards to consult with the local municipal council, school boards, community organizations and groups, businesses, and community residents in developing its business plan. **Forecasting** involves using the information gathered to anticipate future demands on the police service and to identify the resources that will be required to meet these demands.

The increasing use of strategic planning and forecasting indicates that police organizations are adopting many of the techniques used by private-sector companies and are becoming more corporate in their structure and activities. All of this is occurring against a backdrop of increasing fiscal accountability and a philosophy that what gets measured counts. Virtually all Canadian police agencies publish their strategic plans on their websites. For example, see the Ottawa Police Service's strategic plan at www.ottawapolice.ca, under the "Media/Publications" link.

Audits

Audits provide a valuable barometer of the health of the organization. They identify areas of concern that may render the agency vulnerable. They monitor and maintain a balance between those tasks that contribute to agency objectives and those which meet the public demand for protection and reassurance. At the same time, they assure police managers and oversight bodies that the agency is acting in a fiscally responsible way and conforming to provincial or legislative guidelines.

—*K. Taylor (1999)*

Ontario's Adequacy Standards require that police services conduct audits of their administrative and operational activities as well as of specific programs and policing initiatives.

Environmental Scans

A key role in the planning process, **environmental scans** are studies that identify forces in the community (environment) that may affect the demands that will be made upon the police. A typical environmental scan involves gathering information, from a wide range of sources, on topics such as:

- demographic, social, and economic trends;
- crime trends;
- public perceptions of and satisfaction with the police;
- the impact of federal legislation, including the *Youth Criminal Justice Act* and the *Charter of Rights and Freedoms,* and provincial legislation, including police acts;
- the impact of technology;
- human resources;
- finances;
- the goals and objectives of the police service; and
- a profile of police personnel.

Many police services conduct scans annually or semi-annually in order to maintain a continual flow of information on critical issues that may require changes in policies and operational practice. Both the Ontario Provincial Police and Toronto Police Service have very detailed environmental scans available at their respective websites.

Service Performance Indicators

The public expects the Police Service to provide quality service and to be accountable. Performance measures can both indicate how well we are doing in providing that service and provide a vehicle for accountability.

—*Toronto Police Service (1999)*

The move away from traditional styles of policing has necessitated the development of performance measures that more accurately measure the activities and accomplishments of the police service and its officers. **Performance indicators** are specific numerical measurements for each aspect of performance (i.e., output or outcome) under consideration.

In Toronto, the municipal government has identified and defined three types of performance indicators, as follows.

- *Condition/demand indicators.* These are indicators of environmental conditions and include the population served, the number of calls for service, traffic accident statistics, reported criminal victimization, and information volunteered to the police by community residents through programs such as Crime Stoppers.

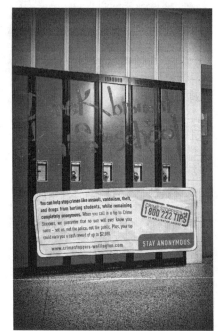

Media-based crime prevention programs such as Crime Stoppers offer cash rewards for information leading to the arrest and conviction of offenders. These programs also serve to educate the public about crimes occurring in their community.

Source: Neal/Wickware/Ciccocioppo/Tour. Reproduced with Permission of Crime Stoppers of Wellington County Inc.

- *Units of service.* These are measurable components that indicate how much service is provided and include the number of police and civilian members, the number of police officers per population, the ratio of constables to *Criminal Code* offences, the number of uniformed officers on the street, the proportion of plainclothes officers (detectives) to uniformed officers, the ratio of supervisors to police officers, and community participation in programs, including Neighbourhood Watch.
- *Effectiveness/efficiency measures.* These are indicators of how well the organization is doing in various areas, and include crime rates in the various divisions, number of arrests, clearance rates, response times to critical incidents, and the per capita costs of policing.

Traditionally, the most commonly used performance indicators for police services were costs per capita, the number of citizens per sworn police officer, and the number of citizens per police employee (all employees). However, a police service that is cost efficient is not necessarily an effective police service. For example, the police service may have a very limited budget for drug enforcement, yet a large number of community crimes may have their origins rooted in drug-related problems. Community policing requires that police services expand the range of performance indicators for both the police service and individual officers. One such indicator is discussed in Box 6.7.

Best Practices and Benchmarking

Best practices refer to those organizational, administrative, and operational strategies that have proven successful in preventing and responding to crime and disorder. Many were first developed in the corporate sector and have been adapted for use in police services. Best practices are activities—implementing a philosophy, policy, strategy, program, process, and/or practice—that an organization does better than other organizations and that serve as models for other organizations that want to enhance their performance. The process of searching for best-practice organizations is called **benchmarking**.

Benchmarking is a tool used to improve performance. It is a process whereby an organization continually measures and compares its activities and performance with other organizations in order to improve its effectiveness.

BOX 6.7

IMPLEMENTING COMMUNITY POLICING BY "STAFFING TO WORKLOAD"

While "pop to cop" ratios tell us how many police officers there are per number of citizens, they generally tell us very little about the quality of police service. What does it mean if one community has 1 officer per 530 residents, while another community has 1 officer for every 425 residents? Does it mean the community with more police per capita receives better police service or has a lower crime rate? Several Canadian municipalities have established service-level targets as a better approach to delivering community police service. Calgary and Edmonton police services, for example, try to ensure there are enough police officers to provide the following patrol performance targets:

1. Seven-minute average response time to high-priority calls.

2. Forty percent of a shift available for problem solving activities.

3. One two-person unit available in each specified geographic location to provide back-up.

Staffing to workload assesses how many work demands are placed upon officers and then it redistributes it in order that all officers have essentially the same amount of reactive workload as well as time available to engage in proactive, preventive activities. Durham Regional Police Service, Vancouver Police Department, and Edmonton and Calgary Police Services have all moved to patrol performance deployment models, which staff according to workload.

In Canada, the International Centre for the Prevention of Crime (ICPC) performs important crime-prevention benchmarking both nationally and internationally. You can see their work at www.crime-prevention-intl.org.

Community Surveys

A valuable tool for defining police priorities within a community policing framework is the community survey. **Community surveys** generally seek information in relation to the following three areas:

- Overall citizen satisfaction with the police;
- Policing problems in the community; and
- Questions related to criminal victimization, including the fear of crime.

In Chapter 7, we will see how the corporate model used by the police services in Guelph and Calgary improves the effectiveness and efficiency of those services. In our discussion in Chapter 10, we will also see that community surveys can be used to determine the concerns and perceptions of the residents of a particular neighbourhood or area. If you are interested in community surveys, you can find actual surveys at a number of Canadian police websites including the Ottawa Police Service and Calgary Police Service.

In addition to community surveys, police services also gain important information from **victimization surveys**; these serve to identify rates of self-reported victimization, which are typically higher than rates of reported crime. For example, the rate of reported domestic violence in a community will be lower than the self-reported victimization rate, which is one indicator of how well police and community initiatives are addressing this critical issue. During every federal census, Statistics Canada administers the General Social Survey (GSS) to determine victim reporting rates for numerous criminal offences. Results for the most recent survey, conducted in 2009, can be found at the Statistics Canada website, http://statcan.gc.ca (search for the document *Criminal Victimization in Canada, 2009*).

Organization for Service Delivery

The adoption of community policing has changed how service delivery is organized.

Community Policing Teams

In contrast to the traditional model of police work, officers in community policing police services are assigned a zone or turf. This geographic assignment of officers is referred to as **geopolicing**. The term is relatively new to Canada, but you can learn more about it through the Seattle Police Service's Neighbourhood Policing Staffing Plan at www.seattle.gov/police/programs/NPP.htm. It is the responsibility of officers to work together in **community policing teams** to develop partnerships with the community, to engage in problem solving, and to respond to incidents that occur within the zone. The Edmonton Police Service implemented a new patrol service delivery model in 2007 incorporating community policing teams with geographic assignments. We will examine this initiative in greater detail in Chapter 7.

Community policing teams, depicted in Figure 6.3, represent a departure from the structure of police platoons in traditional police work.

Sergeants in charge of the community policing teams have two primary sets of relationships: to their specific platoon or shift, and to members of other platoons that are responsible for the zone or area being policed. The sergeants are also responsible for initiating and maintaining contact with community groups, participating in setting goals and objectives for the zone, and evaluating the performance of individual officers

Figure 6.3 Traditional Platoon Structure versus Community Policing Team
Structure

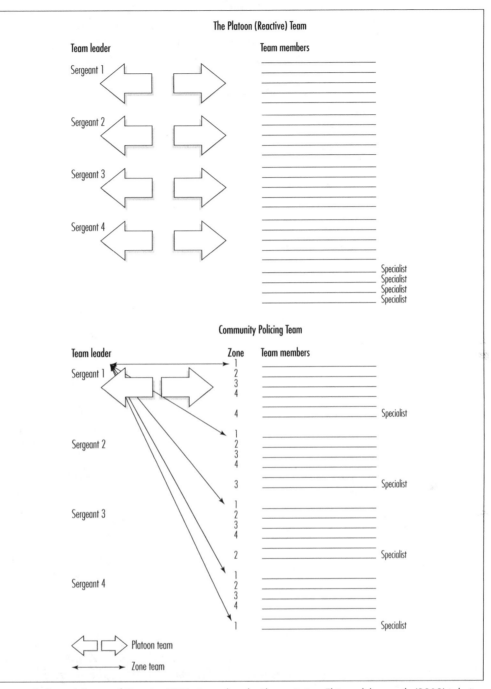

and the entire team. As well, the sergeants are accountable for the successes and the shortcomings of the community policing team.

Community policing teams provide an opportunity for officers to work both individually and collectively to set goals and objectives for the zone, to identify community resources and establish partnerships with the community, and to address community priorities and concerns within a problem-solving framework (Ontario Provincial Police 1997a:5).

Community Policing in Winnipeg

The Winnipeg Police Service uses the deployment of community support foot patrol officers, providing proactive policing services that involve solving problems rather than simply reporting incidents. The police officer provides a service that is community-based rather than criminal justice–based, acting as a community team leader in identifying problems. The officer then works through community resources, identifying and applying solutions to the problems.

Objectives

- To reduce the number of repeat calls for service
- To solve community problems
- To improve the public's satisfaction with the police
- To increase the job satisfaction of constables
- To increase the reporting of intelligence and sharing of information

Strategies

- Target police services to "hot spots"
- Decentralize the service
- Increase constables' autonomy and problem-solving abilities
- Involve the community in defining and solving problems
- Increase constables' knowledge of the community
- Increase police visibility

How Does It Work?

An analysis of the calls for service is completed, identifying small geographical areas that require additional police resources. A constable is assigned to patrol this area, encouraging accessibility and community involvement. The constable is also encouraged to form community liaison committees that are organized to identify community ownership problems. Together, the police officer and the community use innovative problem-solving strategies to address the concerns of the particular community.

CUSTOMIZED POLICING SERVICES: THE OPP SERVICE DELIVERY PROCESS

A primary requirement of community policing is that police services tailor the delivery of services to the specific needs and requirements of the communities. To do this effectively requires that the police service determine what those needs and requirements are.

To ensure that detachments across the province know the communities they police, the OPP has designed a process for customizing the specific needs of individual communities that are policed under contract. This process is administered by the Contract Policing Section. This process is depicted in Figure 6.4 on next page.

There are three stages to the **community policing service delivery process**.

Stage 1. Preparation: Preparing for a Customized Police Service

The first stage involves constructing a profile of the community, including population and demographics, demands on police services, and information on community resources, thus creating a **customized police service**. This profile provides the OPP detachment with important information about the community and the potential for developing police–community partnerships. It helps ensure that the organization and delivery of police services focus on the community.

From the information compiled for the community profile, the detachment establishes community policing committees and determines specific policing areas.

Figure 6.4 OPP Service Delivery Process

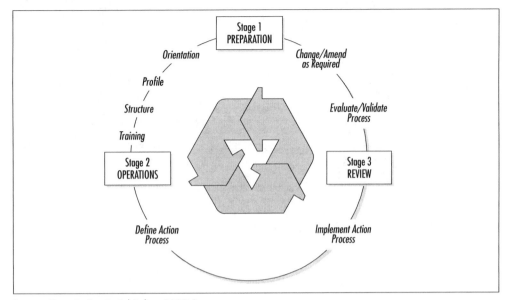

Source: Ontario Provincial Police 1998:2.

Officers are assigned to work in teams under the supervision of a team leader, and each team is, in turn, responsible for developing partnerships with the neighbourhoods and residents in the area.

Stage 2. Operations: The Delivery of Customized Policing Services

In the second stage, the community policing teams work with the community in defined community zones to solve problems of crime and disorder. The police–community partnership facilitates the identification of problems, a determination of the resources that are available to address the problems, the use of specific problem-solving strategies, and an assessment of the outcomes of the interventions. A key objective of this stage is for the community to assume ownership of the problem and work with officers assigned to the area.

In order to collect information on police–community initiatives and make this information available to OPP officers and communities throughout the province, the OPP established the **Community Policing Network**, more commonly referred to as **CP Net**. CP Net is a computer-based program for community policing and problem solving that is a repository for information on past and current projects, both successful and unsuccessful. It is a valuable resource for OPP officers across the province, and is accessible by officers, police managers, and municipal authorities. OPP officers enter a specific community problem into the database, and CP Net analyzes it and suggests possible solutions based on previous problem-solving situations. CP Net has a number of very positive attributes; for example, it provides a cumulative database on problem solving and is accessible province-wide. It is also a good example of a strategy that promotes the OPP as a learning organization.

Stage 3. Review: The Customized Policing Report Card

The third stage of the service delivery process focuses on evaluating the initiatives taken by the police and communities working together, with the goal of determining whether the objectives of the interventions were achieved. This involves assessing the outcome of the interventions and whether the appropriate resources were used.

A key component of the evaluation process is the **Policing for Results Survey**, profiled in Box 6.8.

BOX 6.8

THE OPP POLICING FOR RESULTS SURVEY

The Policing for Results program operated by the OPP is designed to enhance police–community partnerships by providing community residents with the opportunity to express their views on policing services and to identify community concerns, needs, and priorities.

The program starts with a telephone survey of a sample of community residents conducted by trained volunteers. Respondents are queried on a wide range of topics, including perceptions of safety, victimization experiences, satisfaction with the police, and awareness of police programs in the community. The responses of residents are entered into a computer database and then analyzed at OPP headquarters. The findings are then relayed back to the OPP detachment and to community authorities and are used to improve policing services and to enhance the development of police–community partnerships. In recent years the process has evolved to serve a much stronger accountability role.

Source: "Customizing Your Public Service Delivery." **CPDC News 3** (June). Ontario Provincial Police 1998:5.

Among the questions that are asked in this evaluative stage are:

- "What is the problem?"
- "What are we doing about it?"
- "Were we successful?"
- "Are community residents satisfied with the services being provided?"

The results of this report card are shared with police service boards and with Community Policing Advisory Committees, municipal councils, and the community.

This is part of an overall organizational strategy called **Results Driven Policing (RDP)**, which is designed to improve community safety through targeted crime reduction strategies, traffic enforcement, and greater support for field and frontline service delivery and frontline policing. Ongoing evaluation and assessment ensures strategies are effective—in short, that they are achieving results.

How They Do It: How the OPP Delivers Community Policing

We have just reviewed the three major stages of the **OPP community policing service delivery process**—preparation, operation, and review. Now, let's take a closer look at the various components of each of these stages, which gets down to the nitty-gritty of doing community policing. You may want to refer back to Figure 6.4 to refresh your memory of the OPP service delivery process.

Stage 1. Preparation

Step 1—Orientation

Define: what is community policing
Understand: the service delivery process
Identify: partnership requirements to do the process

Step 2—Community Profile

Identify: what are the

- demographics
- economic/physical characteristics
- incident trends
- agency/community resources

Analyze: information to develop structure (go to step 3)

Step 3—Structure

Develop:

- teams
- community zones
- community policing committee partnerships
- community liaison

Step 4—Training

Educate the following on their roles and responsibilities, problem solving, and planning:

- team leaders
- team members
- community leaders
- community committees

Stage 2. Operations

Step 5—Defining Action

Identify:

- reactive requirements
- incidents, motor vehicle accidents

Develop: local community/police plans including:

- traffic management
- crime management
- other local issues

Identify:

- resources
- methods/strategies
- time lines
- plan evaluations

Step 6—Implement Action

Respond: to reactive requirements

Implement: community/police plans dealing with:
- traffic management
- crime management
- other local issues

Evaluate: actions

Stage 3. Review

Step 7—Service Delivery Evaluation

Measure/Evaluate:

- reactive and proactive operations
- impact of preparation stage on operational results
- community satisfaction levels

Identify: required changes

Step 8—Change

Implement:

• actions to effect required changes

Source: Ontario Provincial Police 1997b:4–5.

CHAPTER SUMMARY

Our discussion in this chapter has focused on the issues related to the police organization and community policing. For police services to translate the model of community policing successfully from an idea or philosophy to the operational level requires a number of changes, including modifying how police services are organized, administered, and delivered. A promising approach is the adoption of a corporate model of police work and the use of a number of key tools, including mission, value, and vision statements, strategic planning, benchmarking, and environmental scans. Using these strategies, police services can assess the effectiveness of their current practices, discard those approaches that are not effective, and adopt best practices whenever possible.

In conclusion, however, it is important to note the discrepancy between how police organizations are structured to deliver services and the ever increasing and changing demands that are being placed on them. This includes the increasing sophistication and globalization of crime, which requires the police to have access to the latest technologies as well as officers who are comfortable with that technology. The strategies for combating transnational fraud, for example, are considerably different from those required to implement community policing at the neighbourhood level, yet the community can be overlooked in seeking solutions to these issues. This suggests that over the next decade, urban police services will be required to re-examine whether the generalist model is effective or whether greater specialization may be required to meet the complex demands of many calls for service.

CHAPTER REVIEW

Key Terms

• benchmarking, p. 183
• best practices, p. 183
• business or strategic plan, p. 180
• Community Policing Network (CP Net), p.187
• community policing service delivery process, p. 186
• community policing teams, p. 184
• community surveys, p.184
• corporate model of policing, p. 179
• customized police service, p. 186
• environmental scans, p. 182
• forecasting, p. 181
• geopolicing, p. 184
• mission, value, and vision statements, p. 173
• OPP community policing service delivery process, p. 188
• performance indicators, p. 182
• police pyramid, p. 174
• police service as a learning organization, p. 178
• Policing for Results Survey, p. 187
• Results Driven Policing (RDP), p. 188
• victimization surveys, p. 184

Key Points

- Adoption of the community policing model requires significant changes to all facets of the police organization.
- Police chiefs and chief constables play a critical role in community policing, although one that is much different from the traditional model of police work.
- Mission, value, and vision statements are a core component of the community policing police service.
- Key changes required for community policing include inverting the police pyramid, decentralizing command and control functions, and adopting appropriate organizational strategies from the private sector.
- Community policing police services are learning organizations that have the capacity to continually gather and analyze information, assess performance, and make the adjustments required in order to deliver effective police services.
- Business or strategic plans are a core component of the community policing police service.
- Environmental scans are used by police services to gather information that can be used in planning and in developing police–community partnerships.
- Community policing teams are a primary way to deliver community-based policing.
- The OPP Service Delivery Process provides a good illustration of how to do community policing.

Self-Evaluation

QUESTIONS

1. What are **mission, value,** and **vision statements** in policing, and what role do they play in community policing?
2. What is the **police pyramid**, and how is it affected by the community policing model?
3. Describe what it means for a police service to be a **learning organization**, and identify the characteristics of a police service that is a learning organization.
4. What is a **business** or **strategic plan**, and what role does it play in community policing?
5. What is an **environmental scan**, and what role does it play in community policing?
6. Identify and discuss the types of **performance indicators** used by community police services.
7. Define and describe the role of the following in community policing: **benchmarking, best practices, forecasting, audits,** and **community policing teams**.
8. Define and describe what is meant by the term **geopolicing** and explain its importance to community-based service delivery.
9. Explain why **staffing to workload** is a better method for calculating police resources than "pop-to-cop" ratios.
10. Why is it said that the OPP delivers **customized policing services**?
11. Summarize the **OPP community policing service delivery process**—"How They Do It."
12. What is **CP Net** and what role does it play in the OPP model of community policing?
13. Describe the **Policing for Results Survey** and discuss the role it plays in the OPP model of community policing.
14. Explain what **Results Driven Policing (RDP)** is, and discuss how it contributes to more effective and efficient policing.

KEY IDEAS

1. Which of the following is a characteristic of police leadership within a community policing model?
   ✓ a. change management
   b. bureaucratic management
   c. administrative management
   d. maintenance management

2. Where are words such as "honesty," "integrity," "respect," and "fairness" most often found within the administrative components of a community policing service?
   a. in audits
   ✓ b. in core value statements
   c. in emergency response guidelines
   d. in forecasting scans

3. Which of the following does NOT occur when a police service alters its organizational structure to incorporate the principles of community policing?
   a. decentralization of command and control
   b. more autonomy and discretion to line police officers
   c. flattening of the organizational structure
   ✓ d. increased specialization of line police officers

4. Which documents typically provide general principles for providing policing services?
   a. legislation provided by the provincial government
   ✓ b. the mission, value, and vision statements of the police agency
   c. the policy and procedures manuals of the police agency
   d. the Criminal Code of Canada

5. What is Ontario's Police Learning System?
   a. a pre-training program for police recruits
   b. a system of teaching the community about community policing
   ✓ c. a program of training and education for police personnel
   d. a system for identifying potential trouble spots in the community

6. What is the term for the community policing strategy designed to identify forces in the community that may have an impact on police services?
   ✓ a. environmental scan
   b. benchmarking
   c. auditing
   d. best practices

7. Which of the following describes the Policing for Results Survey?
   a. it is a survey conducted by all police services involved in community policing
   b. it has been discarded by Ontario police services due to its ineffectiveness in determining community needs and priorities
   ✓ c. it is part of the OPP customized policing services approach
   d. it is conducted annually by the Ontario Ministry of the Attorney General

8. Which of the following is typically given to officers in community policing police services?
   a. a partner to coordinate activities in the community
   b. police motor vehicles that display community decals and have the ability to transport several volunteers
   c. training in a second language that is reflective of what is spoken in the community
   ✓ d. a geographic assignment known as a zone or turf

9. In the context of community policing, what are performance indicators?
    a. the criteria used for promoting officers from one rank to another
    b. the criteria used to determine the effectiveness of police technology
    c. the criteria used to compare the effectiveness of the police with other components of the criminal justice system
    ✓ d. the criteria that is used to measure the activities and accomplishments of a police service and its officers

10. Which of the following is an accurate statement about the current state of policing in Ontario in terms of the requirements of community policing?
    a. Only a very few police services in Ontario have redesigned the organization and delivery of policing services.
    ✓ b. The *Police Services Act* and the Adequacy Standards have had a major impact on Ontario police services.
    c. Attempts to legislate change in Ontario police services have not been very successful.
    d. There have been modest changes in the organization of police services and in how police services are delivered.

The Police Organization: Situations and Strategies

Community Policing Implementation Checklist

There are a number of key questions that can be asked to determine whether a police service has adopted the principles of community policing. Note that these are general points and that more specific questions should be asked, depending upon the particular police service and the community it polices.

Mission and Value Statements

- Does the police service have a current mission statement?
- Does the mission statement refer to a police–community partnership?
- Is the mission statement widely published in the community, both on the police service's website and in print material?
- Is there a value statement that indicates the priorities and focus of the police service?
- Does the value statement refer to community involvement?
- Does the value statement indicate support for officers?

Decentralization of Command and Control

- Has the police service decentralized its command and decision-making authority?
- Are line officers given the discretion and autonomy to solve problems?
- Are officers assigned to specific zones or turfs for an extended period of time?
- Are the principles of community policing reflected in the organization, administration, and delivery of police services?
- Have lines of communication between line officers and their superiors been created so that information from the community can flow upward?

Building Organizational Capacity to Do Community Policing

- Has the police service developed the capacity to be a learning organization?
- Does the police service conduct environmental scans and use this information in the planning process?
- Does the police service use a corporate model for planning and for implementing goals and objectives?

- Does the police service use growth positions and performance indicators in its planning process and in annual evaluations of organizational effectiveness?
- Is there an attempt to integrate best practices into the administration and delivery of police services?

Partnering with the Community

- Is the police service successful in communicating its goals and objectives to the community?
- Does the police service have a media strategy to promote police–community partnerships and highlight program successes, as well as to respond to criticisms and incidents involving officers?

EXERCISES: KNOWLEDGE INTO PRACTICE

Exercise 1. The Mission Statement

Develop a mission statement for the police service in the community where you spent the most time while growing up. Address the following:

- What is the purpose of the mission statement?
- How does the mission statement reflect the unique attributes of your community, the demands made on the police service, and the current and potential role of the community?
- How will the extent to which the mission statement is reflected in the policies, strategies, and operational delivery of policing services be assessed?
- Take a look at the Ontario Provincial Police's Promise (http://www.opp.ca/ecms/ index.php?id=20). Would your community benefit from a similar statement? Why or why not?

Exercise 2. Using the World Wide Web

Select four police departments, one each in the United States, Canada, Asia, and Europe.

1. Print out and read through the website materials for each service.
2. Then, for each police service, consider what the materials on the website tell you about:
   - how the particular police service is organized;
   - what its goals and objectives are;
   - what its orientation is;
   - how it recruits and trains officers;
   - how it deploys its resources;
   - the community it polices, and the demands made upon it by the community; and
   - how it carries out patrol and general duty.

3. Assess each police service as to whether it is a community policing organization, noting the reasons why or why not.

Exercise 3. Providing Policing Services under Contract: The RCMP and the OPP

When a municipality in Ontario considers having the OPP as the local police service, a request for costing of police services is made to the Ministry of Community Safety and Correctional Services.

This initiates a process of community profiling, workload analysis, and community consultations to build a picture of the community and its specific needs. The primary objective is to develop a policing contract tailored to the community. This process is referred to as *Customized* or *Community First Policing*. In Ontario a reference manual called *Restructuring Police Services in Ontario: A Guidebook and Resource Kit for Municipalities from Ontario's Police Community* provides guidance on disbanding police services and contracting with the OPP.

The Royal Canadian Mounted Police also contract their service to communities. Contract Policing is authorized under the federal *RCMP Act*. The current Provincial Police Services Agreement (PPSA) is the umbrella under which the RCMP provides contract policing services to three territories and all provinces except Ontario and Quebec. This amounts to approximately 198 municipalities and, under 172 agreements, to 192 First Nations communities. The RCMP, in contrast, applies a standard agreement to all communities, although in the last several years, the RCMP process has incorporated a more community-based approach.

The approach taken by the OPP is due in large measure to the fact that the OPP is establishing many first-time contracts, whereas the RCMP tends to be involved primarily in the renewal of existing contracts.

List what you consider to be the advantages and disadvantages associated with the process by which the RCMP and OPP create a contract for a municipality.

Exercise 4. Contract Policing versus Independent Municipal Police Service

Consider the following scenario: The former Town of New Liskeard established a municipal police service on July 1, 1963. That service was renamed the Temiskaming Shores Police Service following amalgamation. It polices the portion of the City that was the Town of New Liskeard. Under current policing arrangements, the former town of New Liskeard is policed by a municipal service, while the rest of the city is policed by the OPP from the Temiskaming OPP Detachment Temiskaming Shores. Like many communities in northern Ontario, New Liskeard is faced with economic setbacks including declines in traditional resource-based industries and economic indicators such as housing demand, while the proportion of seniors is expected to double from 16 percent (2006) to 34 percent (2026). Faced with these challenges, and the requirement for a significant expenditure of funds to bring the current police facility up to standard, Council has been considering policing options for some time. The municipal council of New Liskeard is considering the disbandment of the Temiskaming Shores Police Service to bring it under a policing contract with the OPP. This has many residents of New Liskeard feeling they will not receive the same level of policing service as they did in the past and that they will not have control over local policing decisions. They have formed an advocacy group called "Keep Our Police Service (KOPS)." A consultant has been hired to advise this group on practical and technical matters.

You are a member of New Liskeard Municipal Council, and the mayor has asked you to prepare a short paper outlining the benefits, limitations, and implications of dismantling the independent municipal force in favour of a contractual policing arrangement with the OPP, with specific reference to the implications for community policing. Once you have considered the issues, check your responses to the real life scenario available on the Ontario Civilian Commission on Police Services website at www.occps.on.ca, where you will find the actual Temiskamnig Shores Police integration application.

Exercise 5. Selecting a Detachment Commander in the RCMP and OPP

One of the concerns a community has when they opt to have the RCMP or OPP deliver policing services is whether the community has a say in the selection of the detachment commander. The process for identifying a detachment commander in the RCMP has traditionally been an internal process carried out by senior management at RCMP headquarters in Ottawa. That process has begun to change, where internal processes identify two or three potential candidates for a detachment posting. These candidates are then presented to the town council or municipal government for their input. In the Yukon, the Royal Canadian Mounted Police recently developed a process that formalizes community participation in the selection of a detachment commander (Finding Common Ground 2011). Similarly, the OPP provides an opportunity for the municipality to state a preference between potential candidates. The OPP thus provides some opportunity for the municipality to participate in selecting the detachment commander and to maintain a degree of control over who will in effect become the next police chief (even though the list of candidates is provided by the OPP). This is set out by statute in the *Police Services Act* [section 10(9)]. Similarly with independent municipal police departments, local police commissions and police boards use a process of community consultation to identify and select police chiefs (Section 31(1)(d) *Police Services Act*).

Identify advantages and disadvantages to having the OPP or Royal Canadian Mounted Police select a detachment commander. What could be a disadvantage of inviting community participation in the selection of a detachment commander?

Advantages	Disadvantages

In your view, which process best exemplifies the principles and practices of community policing? Provide reasons for your response.

_____

_____

_____

_____

Source: Ontario Provincial Police 2004.

Exercise 6. Selecting a Police Leader

Place yourself in the position of a member of a municipal police board that has the authority to hire and fire the chief of police in the municipality. Your committee has been charged with developing a set of criteria for hiring the next chief of police. The goal is to hire a person with strong leadership skills who will implement the principles of community policing.

List the criteria that should be used in recruiting the new police chief. Then list the criteria that should be used to assess the performance of the chief of police in the annual performance review conducted by the municipal police board.

_____

_____

_____

_____

_____

REFERENCES

Anishinabek Police Service. 2008. "Mission Statement." Online. http://www.apscops.org/.

Arnold, S., P. Clark, and D. Cooley. 2011. *Sharing Common Ground: Review of Yukon's Police Force—Final Report.* Yukon, NWT: Government of Yukon, 2011.

Bennis, W. 1989. *On Becoming a Leader.* New York: Addison-Wesley.

Black, L., D. Brown, R. Drouin, N. Inkster, and L. Murray. 2007. *Rebuilding the Trust: Task Force on Governance and Cultural Change in the RCMP.* Online. http://www.publicsafety.gc.ca/rcmp-grc/_fl/Task_Force_Report-English.pdf. Cat. No.: PS4-53/2007E-PDF. Ottawa: Public Safety Canada.

Bureau of Justice Assistance. 2005. *Intelligence-Led Policing—The New Policing Architecture.* Washington, DC: U.S. Department of Justice.

Calgary Police Service. 2012. *2012–2014 Strategic Plan.* Calgary, Alberta.

Campbell, D.S. (Chair). 1992. *A Police Learning System for Ontario: Final Report and Recommendations.* Toronto: Strategic Planning Committee on Police Training and Education, Ministry of the Solicitor General.

Clairmont, D. 1996. *Community-Based Policing at Halton Regional: The Years 1980 to 1995.* Ottawa: Solicitor General Canada.

Eck, J.E. 1992. "Helpful Hints for the Tradition-Bound Chief." *Fresh Perspectives.* June. Washington, DC: Police Executive Research Forum.

Fleissner, D.W. 1997. *Community Policing Stage Assessment Model for Implementation Planning and Organizational Measurement.* Seattle: Seattle Police Department.

Guelph Police Service. 2000. *Services and Administration.* Online. http://fp.police.guelph.on.ca/gps_adm.html. (October).

Halton Regional Police Service. 2000. *Team Policing.* Online. http://www.hrps.on.ca/teampol.htm (October).

Halton Regional Police Service. 2011. *Corporate Business Plan 2011–2013.* Online. Retrieved May 12, 2012 (http://hrps.on.ca).

Healey, S. and L. Bradburn. 2000. *Our Policing Future: Business Plan 2001–2003.* Guelph: Guelph Police Service.

Hartmann, Francis X., Lee Brown, and Darrel Stephens. 1988. *Community Policing: Would You Know It If You Saw It?* Community Policing Series No. 16. East Lansing, MI: The National Neighborhood Foot Patrol Center.

Hunter, R.D. and T. Barker. 1993. "BS and Buzzwords: The New Police Operational Style." *American Journal of Police* 12(3):157–68.

Kelly, W. and N. Kelly. 1976. *Policing in Canada.* Toronto: Macmillan of Canada.

Kernaghan, K. and D. Siegel. 1995. *Public Administration in Canada,* 3rd ed. Scarborough, ON: Nelson.

Lymburner, M. 1997. "The Protection of the Bear." *Blue Line Magazine* 9(8):9–11.

Murphy, C. and C.T. Griffiths. 1994. "Community Based Policing—A Review of the Issues, Research, and Development of a Provincial Policy." Unpublished research report prepared for the Commission of Inquiry, Policing in British Columbia. Victoria: Ministry of Attorney General.

Murphy, C. and P. McKenna. 2007. *Rethinking Police Governance, Culture and Management, A Summary Review of the Literature.* Online. http://www.publicsafety. gc.ca/rcmp-grc/_fl/eng/rethinkingpolice.pdf (May 11).

Ontario Provincial Police. 1997a. "What's a Community Policing Team?" *CPDC News* 1 (June):4–5.

Ontario Provincial Police. 1997b. *Community Policing "How Do We Do It" Manual.* Orillia, ON: Ontario Provincial Police Community Policing Development Centre.

Ontario Provincial Police. 1997c. "Civilian Governance: Is There a Difference?" *Ontario Provincial Police Focus: A Police Service to Call Your Own*, November.

Ontario Provincial Police. 1998. "Customizing Your Police Service Delivery." *CPDC News* 3 (June).

Ontario Provincial Police. 2004. *Ontario Provincial Police Focus, A Police Service to Call Your Own.* October.

Ontario Provincial Police. 2011a. *2010 Annual Report.* Orillia, ON: Ontario Provincial Police.

Ontario Provincial Police. 2011b. *Environmental Scan.*

Ontario Provincial Police. 2011c. *Strategic Plan 2011–2013.* Orillia, ON: Ontario Provincial Police.

Perreault, Samuel, and Shannon Brennan. 2010. "Criminal Victimization in Canada, 2009." *Juristat.* Vol. 30, no. 2. Statistics Canada Catalogue No. 85-002-X (accessed May 12, 2012).

Rosenbaum, D.P., S. Yeh, and D.L. Wilkinson. 1994. "Impact of Community Policing on Police Personnel: A Quasi-Experimental Test." *Crime and Delinquency* 40(3):331–53.

Royal Canadian Mounted Police. 2004. *The Canada We Want—Speech from the Throne.* Online. http://www.rcmp-grc.gc.ca/rpp/rpp_2003_b_e.htm (March).

Royal Canadian Mounted Police. 2012. *Report on Plans and Priorities 2012–2013.* Online. Retrieved June 12, 2012 (http://publications.gc.ca/collections/collection_2012/ grc-rcmp/PS61-20-2012-eng.pdf).

Royal Newfoundland Constabulary. 2011. *Corporate Plan 2011–2014.* Online. Retrieved May 12, 2012 (http://www. www.rnc.gov.nl.ca).

Senge, P.M. 1994. *The Fifth Discipline: The Art and Practice of the Learning Organization.* New York: Doubleday.

Taylor, K. 1999. *Bringing into Focus—Policing in Halton Region: The Executive Summary*. Oakville, ON: Halton Regional Police Service.

Toronto Police Service. 2011. *Environmental Scan.*

Trojanowicz, R. and B. Bucqueroux. 1990. *Community Policing: A Contemporary Perspective*. Cincinnati, OH: Anderson Publishing Company.

Trojanowicz, R. and B. Bucqueroux. 1998. *Community Policing: How to Get Started*, 2nd ed. Cincinnati, OH: Anderson Publishing Company.

Winnipeg Police Service. 2004. *What Is Community Policing? Neighbourhood Foot Patrol*. Online. http://www.city.winnipeg.mb.ca/police/About The Service/neighbourhood foot patrol.htm (March).

York Regional Police. 1999. *Strategic Plan*. Newmarket: York Regional Police.

Implementing Community Policing

A decentralized community police station is designed to improve community access to police services and allow police to be informed about local conditions of crime and disorder.

Source: © Granville Police Services

Learning Objectives

After completing this chapter, you should be able to:

- Describe the key stages of transforming a traditional policing service into one centred on community policing;

- Discuss how the Edmonton Police Service, the City of Montreal Police Service, and the Surrey (B.C.) RCMP altered the organization and delivery of their police services to implement the principles of community policing;

- Describe the Edmonton Police Service's transformation to community policing;

- Identify the phases the Halton Regional Police Service went through in implementing community policing;

- Identify the difficulties encountered and the lessons learned by the Halton Regional Police Service in implementing community policing;

- Discuss the role of police leaders and patrol officers in the Halton Regional Police Service transformation to community policing;

- Discuss the Organizational Renewal Project of the Durham Regional Police;

- Identify issues relating to regional police services and community policing;

- Discuss the ways in which the Ottawa Police Service addressed the issue of community policing when the service was created; and

- Describe how the Guelph Police Service and the Calgary Police Service use a corporate model to organize, deliver, and assess the effectiveness and efficiency of policing services.

INTRODUCTION

Across Canada, there are a number of excellent examples of police services undertaking the organizational and operational reforms required to implement the principles of community policing. Often, when a department hires a new Chief of Police, the Chief initiates an intensive examination of the overall effectiveness and efficiency of the department. In this chapter, we will examine how several departments have restructured the organization and delivery of their police services. Among the case studies are an independent municipal police service, regional police services, and an RCMP detachment.

We will then consider how two police services—the Guelph Police Service and the Vancouver Police Department—use a corporate model to improve the effectiveness and efficiency of policing services. All of the police services examined demonstrate a high level of commitment to the principles of community-based policing. You will also notice how each department uses research and evaluation to provide a more strategic approach to the delivery of police service.

As you read each case study, it is important to keep in mind that these police services are presented only for illustrative purposes. The nature and extent of organizational reform required by an individual police service will depend, to a great extent, upon the types of demands that are placed on the service, the community it serves, and the level of interest among community residents. These case illustrations do, however, provide insights into the types of organizational initiatives that are involved as a police service moves toward a model of operational community policing.

WHY A CORPORATE MODEL?

Why do many Canadian police services adopt a corporate model? In Chapter 6 we examined how some police services have tried to become learning organizations, a corporate model borrowed from Dr. Peter Senge, author of *The Fifth Discipline—The Art and Practice of the Learning Organization*. Other corporate models are also being applied to police operations, including total quality management (TQM), Six Sigma, the balanced scorecard, and SWOT analysis (which stands for strengths, weaknesses, opportunities, and threats).

The reason for the adoption of corporate models is that they provide a framework for police organizations to:

- manage costs and resources more effectively and efficiently,
- demonstrate organizational effectiveness and efficiency,
- model the practices put in place by the local government(who ultimately fund policing in the jurisdiction),
- foster a highly motivated and empowered work environment, and
- empower police personnel.

All of these objectives help make police officers' careers much more satisfying. If you listen to a manager or police executive, you will hear the buzzwords and catchphrases that illustrate the adoption of these models.

Adoption of corporate models is not unique to policing. The entire public sector, including the Canadian civil service, has also undergone significant change, with a number of parallels to policing. The public service has developed a model called **new public management**. Table 7.1 reflects the priorities and principles of new public management. This shift in the management of police organizations from a paramilitary system to a bureaucratic, corporate model establishes the framework for modern police service delivery. The evolving community-based policing model is shaped by the management principles and practices of the corporate model.

Before taking a look at specific examples, an important point needs to be addressed. There are many elements of police work that do not easily fit the corporate model.

Table 7.1 Comparison of New Public Management and Traditional Public Administration

Components	New Public Management	Traditional Public Administration
Focus	Clients	Citizens and communities
Principal means	Management	Policy making
Characteristics of public servants	Entrepreneur (acting)	Analyst (thinking)
Values	Entrepreneurship, freedom for managers, flexibility, creativity, enthusiasm, risk taking	Ministerial responsibility, prudence, stability, ethics, probity, fairness, transparency
Vocabulary	Service to clients, quality skills, managerialism, empowerment, privatization	Public interest, democracy, social equity, due process
Culture	Private sector, innovation, business management, accountability by results, politics administration dichotomy	Bureaucratic (hierarchical), functionalism stability, process accountability, politics administration continuum
Structures	Civil service as organizational units, simple and frugal government, introduction to quasi-market mechanism, decentralization	Civil service as an institution, large departments, government-wide systems, central authority resource allocation

Source: Charih, M., and L. Rouillard, 1997. "The New Public Management", in Charih, M. and A. Daniels (eds.), *New Public Management*, p. 31. Reprinted with permission of The Institute of Public Administration of Canada, d'Administration Publique du Canada.

Notably, people who access police services are not necessarily consumers or customers; generating revenue and profits is not a police service goal, and many of the indicators of performance are considerably different in public organizations than in private organizations. There are essential differences between public- and private-sector management models that should not get lost in the rhetoric!

THE TRANSFORMATION OF THE EDMONTON POLICE SERVICE

In our discussion of community policing in Chapter 3, we noted that police services often experience difficulties in translating the philosophy and principles of community policing into practice. The transformation of the Edmonton Police Service from a traditional, reactive police service to a community-policing police service helps us understand the many challenges that police services encounter and the strategies that can be used to overcome these challenges.

The Edmonton Police Service (EPS) took its first cautious steps toward reform in 1988, at a time when demands on the police service were increasing and available resources were declining. It was not unusual for the service to receive 500 calls per day, and the response time for nonemergency calls often exceeded three hours.

Table 7.2 is an overview of the types of demands that were being made on the EPS from 1980 to 1990. In the years since these figures were compiled, demands on the EPS have accelerated and are even more severe, particularly in relation to the decline in available police resources. Not only have overall demands grown for police service, but actual calls for service have also been increasing.

A further indication of the pressures on the EPS and the inadequacy of the police response is illustrated by the fact that in 1991, 60,000 callers to the police complaint line hung up before being answered. Many would then call the 911 emergency line, tying up this emergency system.

Table 7.2 Demands on the Edmonton Police Service, 1980–1990

Subject	Indicator	Outcome
Demographics	Population	19 percent increase
Reported crime	Annual criminal occurrences	44 percent increase
Communications division workload	Complaint-line calls answered	No change
	Calls dispatched	16 percent increase
Police service strength	Crime reports taken over phone	67 percent increase
Authorized civilian strength	Authorized sworn strength	2 percent decrease
	Authorized patrol constables	1 percent decrease
		12.4 percent increase
Self-initiated work	Impaired driving charges	101 percent increase
	Drug charges	51 percent decrease
Budget	Portion of operating budget allocated to communications and patrol divisions	41 percent of budget
Time-oriented measures of effectiveness	Consumed time and response (on scene) time	15 percent increase to April 1990

Source: Veitch, D., 1995. *Community Policing in Edmonton*, 3rd edition. Edmonton: Community and Organizational Support. pg.18. © Edmonton Police Services

Responding to the Challenge: The Development of a New Model of Service Delivery

These pressures were the catalyst for the EPS to examine new ways of delivering police services. Like many police organizations, the EPS had traditionally been hierarchical and was characterized by a high degree of specialization. In 1969, there were 64 different units in the department; by 1991, the number of units had grown to 120.

As part of its restructuring, EPS conducted a thorough review of all units in the organization, asking five basic questions:

1. What is the unit intended to do?
2. What is it actually doing at this time?
3. Should it be doing what it is actually doing?
4. What should it be doing?
5. How should it do what it should be doing?

EPS then identified 21 "hot spots" in the city. It was discovered that 81 percent of calls in these areas were from repeat addresses. Twenty-one members of the newly formed Neighbourhood Foot Patrol Program (NFPP) began walking the beat in these areas, becoming familiar with the residents and solving their problems. The success of this initial approach resulted in the development of a core value that would guide the entire service: "Committed to Community Needs."

Organizational changes were structured using a modified **differential response model**, supported by decentralized reporting outlets, face-to-face interactions when reporting crimes, problem solving, and public involvement in policing (see Figure 7.1).

In addition, police officers were given ownership of areas and problems, decision making was decentralized, and efforts were made to "despecialize" officers' activities. Calls for service which were not resolved at the initial stages by the dispatch centre or at the community police station were referred to officers with knowledge of the area or

Figure 7.1 Edmonton Police Service Differential Response Model

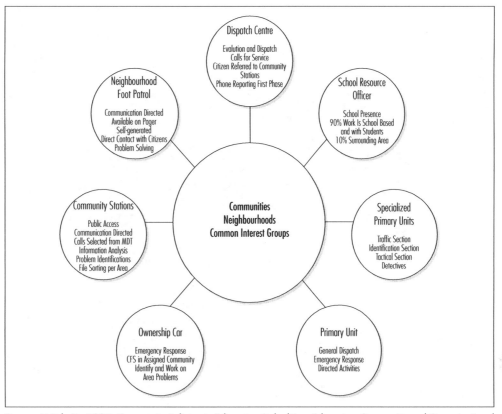

Source: Veitch, D., 1995. *Community Policing in Edmonton,* 3rd edition. Edmonton: Community and Organizational Support. pg. 35. © Edmonton Police Services

issue. These policies maximized police resources while increasing the likelihood that a solution would be found to the problem at hand.

In 2004, the Edmonton Police Service underwent a second wave of organizational renewal. An Organizational Review was conducted between 2004 and 2005 resulting in the release of the document *Agenda for Change,* which made 123 recommendations for organizational improvement based on the findings of extensive research and the examination of best practices from both the public and private sector. In 2006, following a series of high-profile scandals, including allegations of police corruption, infiltration into the EPS by organized crime, and improper use of authority, the EPS released its Professional Committee Report making 58 recommendations aimed at increasing public trust and confidence in the EPS by enhancing ethics and professionalism.

Later in 2006, the Edmonton Police Commission (EPC) hired Chief Boyd following an extensive talent search for a new Chief. The new Chief of Police had to strengthen public confidence in the EPS, and, shortly after taking office, released a 100-Day Plan (2006) as a first step toward rebuilding trust with citizens. The plan involved extensive consultation with the "Big 5" (residential and business community, social and government agencies, political leaders, media, and police), and identified 57 recommendations to enhance service and to move the organization forward.

As a result of the extensive consultation, the following five strategic directions for 2006 to 2008 were established:

1. Reduce victimization;
2. Improve service;
3. Improve effectiveness, efficiency, and innovative business processes;

4. Improve financial investment, sustainability, and accountability;
5. Enhance professionalism.

Under these five strategic directions, 27 priorities were identified which would provide the framework for prioritizing those needs and ideas that stemmed from the 100-Day Plan, as well as past needs outlined in the 2004 organizational review and the 2005 Professionalism Committee. In the end, the EPS and Police Commission created a working document with 143 recommendations charting the course for future policing in the city of Edmonton.

Today, the EPS operates a number of full-service community police stations, each staffed by uniformed officers who are assisted by community volunteers. EPS ran a marketing campaign to encourage community residents to report incidents and problems directly to the community police stations. At all times, the focus was on the community and its needs, rather than the needs of the police organization. There are also neighbourhood foot-patrol officers who staff offices located in areas throughout the city.

Empowerment and Ownership: A New Role for Patrol Officers

Two of the critical components of the model of community policing developed by EPS are **empowerment** and **ownership**. Approximately 75 percent of officers in the service have been given ownership responsibilities in communities, regardless of whether community is defined by specific geographic boundaries or by other attributes, such as residents who are members of visible or cultural minorities. Ownership members, including foot-patrol officers, are responsible for developing contacts with the community and working with community residents (including businesses) to identify, address, and solve problems. Ownership officers are given the authority and discretion to address the issues and to respond to the calls for service that arise in their area. The remaining EPS officers are considered primary response officers, answering emergency calls. All officers in the EPS are encouraged to be innovative, to take risks, and to work with community residents.

For the reorganization to succeed, both police officers of the EPS and community residents had to understand the changes that were occurring. This required internal and external communication strategies. The **internal communication strategy** exposed police officers to the principles of community policing, and their participation in redesigning the model of service delivery was solicited. In recent years, the EPS has also partnered with local post-secondary institutions to provide advanced education opportunities to learn about community policing. In addition, the process of recruiting and training new officers was altered. The **external communication strategy** was designed to inform the general public about the changes in how police services would be delivered and to solicit public participation and involvement as active partners in the process and in the new policing model.

Outcomes and Effectiveness of the EPS Model of Service Delivery

Over the past decade, the EPS has assessed the effectiveness of the new model of service delivery. These assessments have been carried out both by the EPS itself and by external researchers. The results of the studies that have been conducted to date indicate, conclusively, that the reforms have produced positive outcomes on a number of measures. These include:

- *Increased citizen satisfaction with the police.* The results of annual surveys of community residents, covering a wide range of issues from fear of crime to attitudes toward the police, reveal that citizens support the police and have a high level of confidence in the EPS. In addition, there is widespread support for community policing as practised by EPS: a survey conducted in 2007 by the EPS indicated that 85 percent of those residents surveyed were satisfied or very satisfied with police. In addition, 17 percent of residents said their confidence in the EPS had gone up in the previous year, compared to only 10 percent in the 2004 citizen survey. This is an important measure of trust and support for the EPS.

- *Improved officer morale, motivation, and job satisfaction.* Community police officers and foot-patrol officers have responded favourably to being empowered to address and resolve issues and problems in the areas in which they work.
- *Reduction in levels of crime.* The city of Edmonton, in sharp contrast to other western urban centres, has recorded reductions in the total number of *Criminal Code* occurrences as well as in the level of person-related offences and property crime in recent years. Key crime indicators have for the most part seen decreases; however, there have been marginal increases in auto theft and violent youth crime.
- *Increases in clearance rates.* In 1995, the clearance rate for person and violent crimes was 66 percent, a 12.5 percent improvement over 1991. For property-related crimes (which traditionally have a very low clearance rate), the clearance rate in 1995 was 27 percent, an improvement of nearly 39 percent from 1991. The overall clearance rate for all crime in 2010 was 39 percent and there was a 7 percent decrease in reported crime compared to 2005. From 1997 to 2007, the crime rate (measured as reported crime per 100,000 population) increased by 12 percent. Nationally, clearance rates have been improving since 2004, and while violent crime clearance rates have followed the same upward shorter term trend, they have decreased since the mid-1990s.
- *Reductions in complaint-line calls and decreases in dispatches.* Between 1991 and 1993, dispatched calls declined 18 percent while at the same time the number of contacts with community citizens rose dramatically. More specifically, from 1991 to 1995, there were the following reductions relating to calls to the communications centre: 911 police (–37 percent), calls answered (–40 percent), abandoned calls (–70 percent), average speed of answer of calls (–69 percent), total calls (–44 percent), and dispatched calls (–32 percent). In recent years the EPS has created **specialty units** such as the Derelict Housing Unit to target specific crimes and disorder that would typically result in numerous complaints to the police communication centre requesting police attendance. By adopting a broader problem-solving approach the EPS has reduced the demand on its communication section to dispatch units to repeat calls for service to the same address.

Previously, the primary ways of assessing the effectiveness of the police were the levels of criminal activity and the clearance rates. It is interesting to note that the implementation of a service delivery model based on community policing has had a significant impact on these two factors, and has resulted in positive outcomes on a number of other measures.

The EPS and Organizational Reform

Identifying the principles of community policing and paying them "lip service" is easy. It is making the organizational changes that are actually required to implement community policing that is the most difficult part.

There were several identifiable stages through which the EPS passed in developing and implementing its model of community policing. In each stage, senior police administrators in the department played a critical role in instigating the reform effort, yet line officers participated actively in the process.

Stage 1: Recognition of a Performance Gap

Senior administrators acknowledged that the department, as it was traditionally structured, did not effectively meet the demands and expectations being placed upon it. This performance gap was exemplified by the volume of calls on the complaint line, the high percentage of abandoned calls, the slow response time to requests for service, and the apparent ineffectiveness of the police in reducing levels of crime. Added to this was a crisis in confidence in the EPS from many of its citizens.

Stage 2: Recognition of a Need for Organizational Change

The inability of a police service to respond effectively to demands does not automatically result in senior administrators undertaking reform. Rather, there is often a tendency to rely on traditional responses, such as increasing police personnel or seeking additional fiscal resources. For the reform process to begin, senior police leaders must recognize that fundamental changes are required in the structure and delivery of policing services. The EPS conducted a thorough review of all facets of the police service, and the results provided impetus to the reform movement.

Stage 3: Creating an Organizational Climate Receptive to Reform

It is the responsibility of the senior police leadership in a department to create an atmosphere conducive to change. Since the implementation of the principles of community policing requires change at all levels of the organization, a commitment to change (or, at the very minimum, a receptiveness to change) must be secured from senior administrators, middle managers, and line officers. Significantly, the EPS's senior administration used the findings of a complete organizational review to flatten and decentralize the organizational structure and to reduce or eliminate the traditional boundaries between the different levels and units of the EPS.

The EPS's internal communication strategy informed police members at all levels of the organization of the principles of community policing and solicited their participation in the development of a new model of service delivery. According to the results of surveys on job satisfaction and morale among EPS officers, it is clear that the senior administration was successful in creating a positive environment in which officers made use of the new model of service delivery. This success is also reflected in the other positive outcomes produced by evaluations and assessments.

Stage 4: Creating a Community Climate Receptive to Reform

Given the importance of the community in any model of community policing, residents must be told about the reforms and their impact on the delivery of policing services. In addition, community residents must be educated about the role of the community in the new model of service delivery. To accomplish this, the EPS's external communication strategy was designed to promote the idea of community policing and the new service delivery model to the citizens of Edmonton.

Stage 5: Creating a New Model of Service Delivery and Call Response

If the well-entrenched, reactive model of police service delivery is to be replaced, it is essential that the organization develop a viable alternative. The EPS model of service delivery provides for line officers to assume ownership of problems in the areas they police and thus empowers them to work with community residents to solve those problems. In short, new roles and responsibilities have been created for line officers, and these have resulted in greater autonomy being vested in officers on the street.

The model also identifies a key role for the community, and highlights the importance of community police stations and neighbourhood foot patrol as strategies for service delivery.

You will also recall from Chapter 6 that the Edmonton Police Service changed the way it deploys its resources by implementing a "staffing to workload" model that attempts to match resourcing requirements to predicted call volumes and tasks and evenly distribute the workload in an effort to free up time for police officers to work on preventative initiatives.

Stage 6: Conducting Ongoing Analyses and Evaluations of the Service Delivery Model

To ensure that organizational reforms and the model of service delivery are effective in meeting the demands placed on the police service, ongoing analyses and evaluations are essential. In recognition of this, the EPS has a substantial in-house capacity to carry out surveys and studies. These include assessments on the impact of various policing strategies on the rates of criminal activity in Edmonton, and surveys of police members to record their levels of job satisfaction and issues of concern, as well as surveys to determine the levels of citizen satisfaction with the police. In 2002, the Edmonton Police Service committed itself to becoming an **intelligence-led police organization**, taking its commitment to research and evaluation to a new level. While we will examine this idea in more detail in Chapter 10, the EPS defines "intelligence-led policing" as follows:

Intelligence-led policing involves the collection and analysis of information to produce an intelligence product designed to inform police decision making at both the tactical and strategic levels. In this model, intelligence serves as a guide to operations, rather than the reverse. It begins with the notion that a principal task of the police is to prevent and detect crime rather than simply react to it. (Edmonton Police Service 2002)

The EPS has also been supportive of external evaluations conducted by university-based scholars and by representatives of internationally recognized organizations such as the Police Executive Research Forum, located in Washington, D.C. Rather than viewing these external evaluations and assessments as a threat, the EPS considers such studies and reviews as part of its continuing efforts to excel in the provision of police services to the city of Edmonton.

Final Thoughts on the EPS and Community Policing

The experience of the EPS illustrates conclusively that it is possible for police services to reform their organizational and operational structures and to adopt new models of service delivery based on the principles of community policing. The EPS's reform was undertaken very deliberately and with considerable planning, and its experience provides an example for police services and communities across the country as to what is possible. What is particularly significant for our focus in this text is that not only were line officers involved in all phases of the reform process, but the new model of service delivery resulted in a major transformation of the role of police members.

Furthermore, both internal and external assessments of the effectiveness of the activities and initiatives of the EPS, using a variety of performance indicators, provide strong and consistent evidence that service delivery based on community policing is a "win–win" situation—for the community, which experiences reduced levels of criminal activity and positive relationships with and perceptions of the police, and for police officers, who are given the autonomy and authority to use their skills and imagination to address and solve problems at the neighbourhood level.

It is important to note that the EPS continues to evolve to meet the changing demands and needs of the communities it serves. In 2011, soaring numbers of homicides in Edmonton required the organization to adapt its processes and capacities, something it was capable of doing based on the foundation and trust it had built with its communities. Although the experiences of this police service may serve as an example of what is possible in the realm of policing, each police service must chart its own course, depending on the demands placed upon it, the capabilities of its personnel, and the interests and abilities of the citizens it serves.

THE CITY OF MONTREAL POLICE SERVICE NEIGHBOURHOOD POLICING PROJECT: REORGANIZATION FOR COMMUNITY POLICING

In December 1996, after five years of analysis, debate, and union negotiations, the Montreal Police Service (MPS) implemented the first phase of a major reform of the organization and delivery of policing services in the greater Montreal Urban Community region. The reform included the following changes:

- *Organizational decentralization:* a shift from a traditional, centralized command and control structure with 24 precincts to a decentralized service delivery structure with 49 precincts.
- *The creation of 49 neighbourhood police stations:* "mini stations" staffed by a small number of civilian employees and a uniformed officer complement ranging from 30 to 98, depending on the size of the population served.
- *Four operations centres, one in each region:* centres containing prisoner cells, detectives' offices, and specialized units such as SWAT teams.

Planning for the reorganization involved recruiting, selecting, and training commanders for the neighbourhood police stations and for the operations centres; reviewing and evaluating potential locations for the neighbourhood stations and two of the operations centres; restructuring the call-response procedures; and training police constables and their supervisors in community policing methods. Extensive improvements were also made to the telecommunications systems; this included providing patrol officers with cellular telephones and pagers.

The external marketing strategy involved a promotional campaign featuring posters placed on buses and in other public places. In addition, a newsletter on neighbourhood policing was mailed to 900–1,000 homes and businesses in the region (Communauté urbaine de Montréal 1997).

The changes put officers in closer contact with the community, with the goal of increasing the involvement of community residents in identifying and responding to crime and disorder, and, by having citizens use the neighbourhood police station to complete reports, of reducing the amount of paperwork for officers. Also, each station has an advisory committee that meets monthly to discuss community concerns.

The neighbourhood stations provide basic police services, while case investigations and specialized police services such as crime-scene analysis and traffic control are delivered by the four operations centres, which are situated in each of the police regions. The mini-stations are situated mainly in shopping districts and in areas of heavy pedestrian traffic.

For cases that are not urgent, community residents file a report at the neighbourhood station. At least one officer at each station serves as a liaison with the local community, providing citizens with the opportunity to express their concerns and problems. Emergency calls are still handled by MPS dispatch, which forwards them to the appropriate police district.

Since the inception of the Neighbourhood Policing Project there has been ongoing evaluation. In 2003, a significant review of the project established a number of priorities for the years ahead. These priorities, determined through an extensive consultative process with the community and municipal government, identified six areas of focus: (1) meeting residents' expectations, (2) establishing closer ties between the constabulary and investigations, (3) strengthening neighbourhood stations, (4) valuing individuals and integrating culture, (5) optimizing processes, and (6) structure and management. Box 7.1 describes both police and community perceptions of the Neighbourhood Policing Project.

BOX 7.1

THE MONTREAL POLICE SERVICE EXPERIENCE

"It's more than just us talking—it's listening to the citizens and finding out how to improve the quality of life here."

—Sylvan Brouillette, Commander, Neighbourhood Police Station 8

"It's not up to the police to solve all the problems. We're here to work with partners in the community."

—Pierre Richer, Commander, Neighbourhood Police Station 2

"They [merchants] all know me here and they're not shy to tell me if they don't like the way things are going."

—Officer Michel Deziel, Neighbourhood Police Station 8

"This is very, very good now, to have the police station closer. It's important that they be local. They'll know the community better and there is also an economic impact because the officers shop and eat in the area."

—Ghislain Dufour, merchant and member, Citizens Advisory Committee for Station 8.

Source: Material reprinted with the express permission of: *Montreal Gazette*, a division of Postmedia Network Inc.

THE EVOLUTION OF COMMUNITY POLICING IN SURREY, B.C.

Surrey is very culturally, socio-economically, and geographically diverse. By decentralizing our operations to five district policing offices, our members can better meet the needs and concerns of each unique community, while still maintaining a consistent quality of service throughout Surrey.

—Chief Superintendent T. Smith, former Surrey RCMP (1997)

The Surrey RCMP community policing project in British Columbia began in 1997, focusing upon the decentralization of policing services. The Surrey Detachment is the largest RCMP detachment in Canada with nearly 600 police personnel (including civilian members) and a support staff of over 200 municipal employees. As the largest and busiest RCMP detachment in Canada (in 2011, the population was over 468,251, of which 191,000 were visible minorities [Statistics Canada 2012]), the municipality has been divided into five districts, based on an analysis of call levels. Each district office is under the command of a district commander, who has the authority to arrange shift schedules and officer assignments to respond to the policing needs of each district. Taking a page out of the Edmonton Police Service approach to service delivery, patrol officers are assigned to one of the five district offices and work with their colleagues and community residents to address the specific needs and concerns of each area.

The original main detachment remains open to the public and continues to house all plainclothes units, including the drug and break-and-enter sections as well as victim services and administrative offices. In addition, patrol strategies are adapted to the requirements of each district. For example, unique to District 1 is the RCMP's only full-time "Footbeat Section," which deals with a number of special community concerns, including a needle exchange and drop-in centre, prostitution, welfare offices, methadone clinics, and drug recovery houses. The 11-person, full-time foot-patrol section represents a return to strategic street-level community policing with zero tolerance for crime. Through increased visibility and an "up close and personal" policing style, the Footbeat Section is attempting to restore the community's sense of safety within the area. In 2006, a community storefront station was also added.

In 2006, a delegation consisting of representatives from the RCMP, Office of the Attorney General of B.C., Office of the Solicitor General of B.C., School Board, Fire Department, and Social Service agencies went to the U.K. to learn first hand how their crime rates had dropped by as much as 44 percent in some jurisdictions. They also went to New York City to study community courts. Based on their observations, focused particularly on root causes of crime, the municipality of Surrey established the Mayor's Task Force on Public Safety and Crime Reduction. Over 100 individuals representing over 50 different organizations, including the RCMP, non-profits, provincial and federal governments, Parole, Crown Counsel, School Board, Board of Trade, and numerous community organizations, brought their expertise and resources to the creation of the **Surrey Crime Reduction Strategy**.

The Crime Reduction Strategy is broken down into four components:

1. Prevent and Deter Crime
2. Apprehend and Prosecute Offenders
3. Rehabilitate and Reintegrate Offenders
4. Reality and Perceptions of Crime

Under each component are a number of strategies and recommendations that arose from meetings of the Mayor's Task Force on Public Safety and Crime Reduction.

1. Prevent and Deter Crime

- Community Safety Officers
- Skytrain and Transit safety
- Education and awareness programs
- CRS website in three most common languages in Surrey
- Community drug action teams
- CCTV pilot program
- Crime free multi housing
- Parenting orders
- Youth intervention programs

2. Apprehend and Prosecute Offenders

- Identifying prolific offenders and crime hot spots
- Dismantling grow op and drug houses
- Community Court model
- Night Court
- Stiffer penalties for priority crimes
- Prolific Offender Management Teams
- Enhanced treatment in provincial corrections facilities

3. Rehabilitate and Reintegrate Offenders

- Expanded treatment through the private sectors
- Regional approach to treatment
- Recovery house accreditation
- Homelessness and housing foundation ($8.4 million)
- Sobering centre
- Transitional housing

- Full-time homelessness outreach workers
- Education and job training
- Community support teams

4. Reality and Perceptions of Crime

- Communications strategy
- Community action groups
- Working with seniors and the most vulnerable
- Leaflet drops in neighbourhoods after drug houses are taken down (City of Surrey 2006)

Implementation of the crime reduction strategy has produced some promising results, including reductions in auto theft (22 percent in 2006) and business break-and-enters in the Whalley area (45 percent reduction).

The evolution of community policing in Surrey, B.C. has gone from being the first RCMP detachment to decentralize its service delivery model to the creation and implementation of a crime reduction strategy which incorporates a number of community partnerships designed to address underlying causes of crime and disorder. Many RCMP detachments are too small for this type of reorganization; however, there are a number of large detachments in urban areas where similar changes have been made, including the creation of specialized units to better address the needs of the community.

You will recall in our discussion of community policing that it is the particular relationship between the police and the community that gives the model of policing its own distinct character, and accounts for why some strategies work and others do not. Surrey is no exception and it is worth keeping up to date with policing developments in British Columbia, particularly in relation to evaluations of the crime reduction strategy.

The Surrey RCMP strategic service delivery model depicted in Figure 7.2 incorporates the following three elements:

- Community Policing: *Based on the belief that the community plays an integral role in crime reduction and through collaborative working relationships the underlying cause of crime and disorder can be addressed.*

Figure 7.2 Surrey RCMP Strategic Service Delivery Model

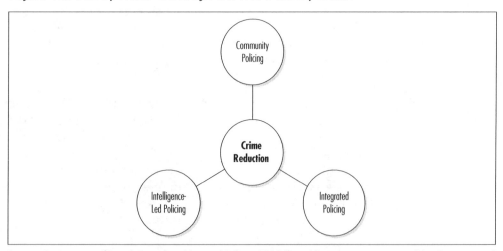

Source: Department of Royal Canadian Mounted Police, 2012 (http://surrey.rcmp-grc.gc.ca/ViewPage.action?siteNodeId=93&languageId=1&contentId=855). Reproduced with the permission of the Minister of Public Works and Government Services Canada, 2012.

- Intelligence-Led Policing: *Acknowledges that research, analysis, and evidence-based decision-making are critical to effective and efficient policing and that reliable and timely crime analysis are critical in the utilization of both police and community resources (i.e. enforcement, investigation and prevention measures proactively targeting habitual offenders, high crime areas, and crime causation factors).*
- Integrated Policing: *Recognizes that success in crime reduction can better be achieved by partnering with other organizations that also contribute to public safety, either directly or indirectly, which ensures combined efforts are better equipped to address complex community problems.**

THE EVOLUTION OF COMMUNITY POLICING IN THE HALTON REGIONAL POLICE SERVICE

To transform an organization from one that is traditionally oriented, quasi-militaristically managed and relatively impermeable to external policy collaboration, to one that can fully embody the community-based policing philosophy is clearly a formidable task.

—D. Clairmont (1996)

The changes that were made in the Halton Regional Police Service (HRPS) as it moved from a traditional police service to one centred on community-based policing are another good illustration of the various stages of adopting and implementing the principles of community policing. The Halton Regional Police Service was one of the earliest and most comprehensive community policing programs to be implemented in North America and is considered to be a leading-edge police service (Clairmont 1996:6).

As fate would have it, there have been a number of studies conducted on the HRPS covering the period from the 1970s to the year 2000. A composite picture of the phases the HRPS went through in implementing community policing is provided by the work of Donald Loree of the Canadian Police College (1988), Don Clairmont of the Atlantic Institute of Criminology in Halifax (1996), Lori Cooke-Scott (1998), and K. Taylor (1999). Taken together, the studies provide unique insight into the evolution of a police service. And without doubt, these investigations make the HRPS one of the most, if not the most, studied police services in Canada.

Among the highlights of the evolution of community policing in the Halton Regional Police Service (written in present tense) are the following:

The 1970s

- *1974–1980:* Following the creation of the HRPS in 1974, team policing and other components of what was to become known as "community policing" are used.
- *1975:* HRPS establishes a team-policing program in Burlington. Teams of 10 officers work together in designated areas. Police administrators support the approach, which is viewed as a way to increase police–community contact and to improve officer awareness and understanding of community problems. A year later, the *Burlington Post* writes: "This system gets people closer to the people they serve by giving constables more of a chance to leave their cars and mingle with the public, getting

to know them and their problems on a less formal basis" (1976:3, 5). The project collapses several years later due to a lack of resources.

- *1979:* James Harding becomes Chief of Police and announces a commitment to crime prevention and community policing, a proactive approach to policing, and the adoption of a participatory management style. Although reception to this approach among officers appears to be mixed, Harding's leadership style plants the seeds of significant changes in the organization and delivery of police services by HRPS.

The 1980s

A variety of innovative approaches to policing are implemented, including the Village Constable Program and a number of specific proactive initiatives.

- *1982:* A proactive policing squad is created in Aldershot, a high-crime area in the city of Burlington. Platoons in this area are split into proactive and reactive squads, each under the supervision of a sergeant. Proactive officers do problem-solving police work in collaboration with the community. This approach reduces the crime rate and receives strong support from community residents. A year later the program is implemented throughout the city of Burlington. The split-platoon approach suffers from a number of operational difficulties, including a general absence of input from the community, and line officers receive little direction. This results in officers not fully supporting the initiative or being confused about management expectations. In short, "planning and implementation were limited and the impact uncertain" (Clairmont 1996:43).
- *1982–1985:* Other programs are gradually phased in. Community conference committees are established and administered by constables. These are designed to give community members opportunities to interact with officers, discuss community problems, and voice their concerns. An auxiliary unit composed of volunteers is created, along with a summer youth program and special community events. The Children's Safety Village is established to educate children on safety practices.

   Also, a mission statement is created to reflect the new philosophy of policing. It states: "The Halton Regional Police Force [later changed to 'Service'] will respond to community needs through a combined strategy of preventative, proactive and reactive policing programs, using the concept of the Constable Generalist, the whole of which will be supported by a participatory management environment" (Halton Regional Police Force 1982).
- *1984:* The **Village Constable Program** is created. Officers are assigned to specific geographic areas, and partnerships are developed between officers and the community. Positive results are obtained, particularly in high-trouble neighbourhoods such as Warwick Court, a low-income housing complex. This program peaks in 1990–91, with 13 sites and 17 constables involved in community-directed patrol. Officers participating in the program experience marginalization within the organization.
- *End of the 1980s:* Studies suggest that despite all the above-noted initiatives, "the organization only modestly featured a participatory management style, the field officers were not particularly trained in or committed to CBP [community-based policing], and, apart from the village constables, there was little collaboration between the police and community in the sense of community-directed policing" (Clairmont 1996:57). Commenting on the difficulties in developing substantive links with the community, Donald Loree (1988:207) stated: "[the idea that] the community itself becomes a real partner in the provision of police services, not merely the recipient of programs developed and delivered in isolation . . . is probably the most difficult of the community policing ideas for police forces and their members to accept."

The 1990s

- *1990–1995:* A distinctive HRPS community-based policing model emerges. The commitment to CBP is widespread in the organization. HRPS continues to be a leading-edge police service, although concerns are expressed that the term CBP itself may carry too much historical baggage and may hinder the implementation of key principles, such as problem-oriented policing.

- *1990:* The HRPS community-based policing model is implemented and focuses on several key initiatives: the Village Constable Program, which involves officers working out of storefronts, community-directed patrol involving officers assigned to specific areas, and community consultation committees (CCCs). The adoption of this model is precipitated by a number of factors, including the following: village constables were only a small portion of the service and were at risk of being marginalized; the directive that patrol officers divide their time equally between proactive and reactive police work was not working; and many patrol officers still did not have a close relationship with the residents in the areas to which they were assigned. Efforts to create a service-wide community policing approach are hindered by insufficient training for officers and an absence of officer participation in decision making. Clairmont (1996:67) notes the "widespread view that management policies in practice did not overly encourage strong officer-CCC linkages and that officers experienced both ambivalence and uncertainty with respect to their roles in the CBP system."

- *1993:* Reductions in provincial transfer payments and social contract legislation result in major changes in the police service. A comprehensive Organizational Review Project (ORP) is undertaken to eliminate, combine, or automate those activities of the police service that hinder effective policing.

- *1994:* A Community Policing Committee, an internal committee within the HRPS, examines the state of CBP in the police service and notes that, although the HRPS is widely recognized as a CBP police service, there are still problems in implementing CBP. Clairmont notes: "By the end of 1994 there were discernible cracks in HRPS's model of CBP. The number of village constables had declined … the CCCs in at least one district no longer had specific named constables assigned to them … participatory management among patrol constables … was at a low ebb … the stress level had reached as high as 15 percent of the members" (Clairmont 1996:78–79).

- *1995:* The ORP concludes and contains 170 recommendations. The Chief of HRPS states: "We believe that we must create a learning environment in which our employees will become increasingly empowered to provide service to the public without management interference. We will encourage them to participate more in designing changes to the way we do business" (Clairmont 1996). This provides the basis for what becomes known as **Total Integrated Policing** (TIP), an approach designed to empower employees while at the same time holding them accountable for their work. To accomplish this, the organization is flattened and the traditional top-down command and control structure is altered.

    A community survey is conducted, soliciting feedback on citizens' perceptions of crime, experiences with the police, levels of satisfaction with the police, policing priorities, and expectations of the police service.

    A service delivery philosophy is developed, centred on proactive, reactive, and preventive policing and the development of police–community partnerships. The core components of the philosophy are problem solving, continuity of service, communication among officers assigned to areas, and an ability to adjust to a changing environment. Officers are assigned to teams that concentrate on specific areas. Direction is provided by the Service Delivery Design Team (SDDT), which is to implement the TIP approach and the recommendations from the ORP.

- *1995–2000:* A continuing emphasis on enhancing the organizational and operational requirements for community policing. As HRPS heads into the remaining years of the decade (and the century), there is increased emphasis on communication between management and patrol officers and on the participation of officers in decision making. Team policing is becoming a cornerstone of service delivery.

Clairmont (1996:102–03) notes that it may be useful to downplay the generic term *community policing* and focus instead on those of its components that have widespread support in the community and among officers. These include police–community partnerships, problem-oriented policing, and team policing.

Nearly all of the 170 recommendations from the 1995 ORP report are implemented. A revised planning process is developed that includes a framework for producing a business plan. This includes environmental scans, an annual consultative process within the police service for identifying issues and goals, and business plans for each unit of the service.

The team concept has widespread support among officers and has been successfully implemented. An evaluation reveals that understaffing compromises its success and that, to be successful, teams require time and the support of supervisors. A comprehensive evaluation of all facets of HRPS concludes in 1999 that "the HRPS has demonstrated a successful community service orientation. Community consultation committees, periodic public surveys, the introduction of village constables, and the team approach have all buttressed the community-police partnership" (Taylor 1999:59).

Lessons from the Halton Regional Police Service Experience

The HRPS experience illustrates the difficulty of effecting integrated, thorough-going CBP even in a very favorable policing environment where resources have been fairly plentiful, crime and reactive pressures fairly low, the population well-educated and appreciative, management positive and able, and the staff well-trained and young.

—*D. Clairmont (1996)*

Some important lessons can be drawn from the experience of the Halton Regional Police Service:

1. Community policing cannot be merely a set of programs; it must be built on a vision of what a police service should be. This vision must be communicated throughout the organization. It must be adopted as a philosophy governing the delivery of all policing services.
2. Implementing community policing does not occur overnight. It is a slow and gradual process that requires support and commitment. The Halton experience indicates that it is a combination of patience, commitment, ideas, and creatively constructed programs that allows for the success of a comprehensive community-based policing approach (Cooke-Scott 1998:42).
3. Community policing requires significant changes in the organization of police services. Flattening the police organization by trimming upper-level management personnel displaces decision making to front-line officers; this, in turn, empowers patrol officers to do community policing.
4. Implementing community policing requires police services to take risks, to learn from their mistakes, and to develop the capacity to adapt to changes in legislation, community expectations, and available resources. It is important that the police service document its efforts, thereby developing an organizational memory from which others may learn.

5. The innovation required for community policing must come from within the police service, and an organizational structure must be created to allow for change to be initiated from the bottom up, rather than from the top down. Line officers in the HRPS often felt they were "thrown to the wolves" when upper management "imposed a program [on them] from above without any input from them, without any details about how or why they were supposed to go about implementing it . . . They expected us to carry something out that they [upper management] didn't even understand" (Cooke-Scott 1998:130).

PLANNING FOR CHANGE: THE DURHAM REGIONAL POLICE SERVICE ORGANIZATIONAL RENEWAL PROJECT

The Adequacy and Effectiveness of Police Services Regulations have been in effect since January 1, 2001. We previously noted that these standards set out specific requirements for Ontario police services in a number of areas, including community policing. In anticipation of these new regulations, police services across the province engaged in planning exercises to develop the capacity for compliance. These exercises provide us with further insight into how organizational change can be initiated and directed. The **Organizational Renewal Project** of the Durham Regional Police (which is available at www.drps.ca/internet_explorer/businessplan.asp) illustrates how one police service planned to meet the new requirements.

At the outset, Durham's Police Services Board retained the services of a management research organization. The group followed a plan that addressed a number of implementation issues, each with sections on "What We Intend to Do" and "How We Intend to Do It." The approach taken by the Durham Regional Police (2004), which flowed from the consultants' report, is summarized below.

Implementation Issue 1. Defining Community Policing

- *What We Intend to Do:* Assist the Police Services Board to define, develop, communicate, and implement a stated board policy setting our approach to community policing and how it will be sustained.
- *How We Intend to Do It:* A research team will be established to meet this objective. Its role will be to create a definition of community policing so that the police service can measure programs and initiatives. This process will involve consultation with the community, community office, and unit leaders, and will include all our stakeholders. It will also review unit mandates, current practices, and resource materials.

Implementation Issue 2. Structural Changes

- *What We Intend to Do:* Establish accountability statements, competencies, and skills required for all positions listed in the consultant's report. Develop accountability statements, competencies, and skills required for all other roles within the organization.
- *How We Intend to Do It:* Establish a research team to examine each position identified on the organizational chart in the consultant's report and develop broad accountability statements, competencies, and skills required for all positions to the level of unit leader, in consultation with current incumbents, human resources, and involved stakeholders.

Implementation Issue 3. Communication

- *What We Intend to Do:* Develop a strategy for ensuring that effective internal and external communication can take place.

- *How We Intend to Do It:* Designate an internal/external communications research team with the responsibility for ensuring that the communication issues identified in the consultant's report are responded to.

Implementation Issue 4. Relationships with Associations

- *What We Intend to Do:* Address the issue of relationships with the two Durham Regional Police Associations, by identifying specific positions within the organization that will be responsible for improving the relationship with the associations through effective communication.
- *How We Intend to Do It:* For the positions of executive director of the Police Services Board, director of employee environment, and the chief of police, place specific tasks in the accountability statements to ensure effective communication with the associations. A research team will be established to meet this objective and the team will consult with the two associations to include their knowledge and expertise.

Implementation Issue 5. Leadership Development

- *What We Intend to Do:* Address the need of the police service to formulate a plan of leadership and career development for all members (both civilian and police) who aspire to meet its current and future succession needs. The plan will ensure that developmental roles are treated on a rotational basis to ensure optimal development and readiness of members to assume key leadership roles when they become available.
- *How We Intend to Do It:* Establish a research team that will be charged with formulating a plan of leadership and career development for the police service. This team will work closely with the team identified under Implementation Issue 6 (Training Development/Certification), because leadership development will have a direct impact on the strategies of Team 6.

Implementation Issue 6. Training Development/Certification

- *What We Intend to Do:* The Learning Centre will be tasked with performing a needs analysis for formal learning and certification training requirements for each level within the organization, and with developing a strategy to present to the service to meet those requirements.
- *How We Intend to Do It:* Establish a research team tasked with developing a strategy to meet the identified formal learning and training requirements for each level, as well as identifying requirement standards. This team will work closely with the group identified under Implementation Issue 5 (Leadership Development), as the input of the team will have a direct impact on its work.

Implementation Issue 7. Resourcing Requirements

- *What We Intend to Do:* Ensure that the resourcing requirements under the five-year staffing and facilities plans are addressed.
- *How We Intend to Do It:* Establish a research team to analyze resource requirements and to make recommendations to the Police Services Board regarding the increased resource needs that will result from these initiatives. Develop a five-year resource plan to correspond to the five-year staffing and facilities plans and all demographic changes that are anticipated to occur within the region during the next five years. This will put the police service's administration and infrastructure in a better position for supporting all resource areas as the service grows. This team will consult with and involve human resources, planning, information technology, the learning centre, the deputy chief of administration, and all operational units.

Implementation Issue 8. Change Management

- *What We Intend to Do:* Establish a project steering committee to ensure that change management issues are addressed on an ongoing basis. This team will ensure that new and existing initiatives work co-operatively and not in conflict with one another, and that they are in harmony with the spirit of the consultant's recommendations.
- *How We Intend to Do It:* Every quarter, the project steering committee will analyze the progress of the implementation of the recommendations from the consultant's report. It will also audit results and regularly review the position of the police service in relation to the Adequacy Standards, and it will plan for the police service's ability to respond to future internal and external changes.

As of 2003, Durham Regional Police Service call response had increased by 37 percent and overall calls to the police service had increased by 24 percent over the previous five-year period. Demands on policing had also increased by expanding legislative requirements requiring the police to deal with increasingly complex criminal investigations. By 2010 the population of Durham region was 620,427 and is expected to reach over 1 million by 2031. Durham Region's economic prospects also continued to grow as evidenced by $1.7 billion in building permits issued in 2003, the highest in the Region's 30-year history.

It will be interesting to track the progress of the Durham Regional Police Service as it progresses through the various stages of organizational renewal, and the successes as well as the trials and tribulations that it will encounter on the path to implementing community policing. Our previous examination of the HRPS suggests that the journey of a police service to becoming a full-fledged community policing service is often filled with successes as well as setbacks, and that good intentions alone are not sufficient to achieve the ultimate objective.

REGIONAL POLICE SERVICES AND COMMUNITY POLICING

Regional police forces are a key feature of policing in the eastern regions of Canada. In Chapter 2 we discussed the large number of independent municipal police services that have been amalgamated into regional police services over the past 40 years in Ontario. A major issue concerning regionalization is compatibility among regional police services and the requirements of community policing. When a regional police service is created, a previously smaller, independent municipal police service becomes part of a much larger organization, and its officers are mixed with those from other police services.

Proponents of regional police services argue that these larger entities are more effective in providing a full range of services to the community, are more cost effective than smaller independent police services, and create an equity situation where all of the municipalities involved contribute to the costs of policing services and receive equal protection. Critics argue that regionalization actually increases the costs of policing, both during the start-up phase when multiple police services are melded into one organization and later, when large regional police services have difficulty establishing partnerships with the community. Research suggests, however, that regional police services can achieve a number of efficiencies, including a reduction in per capita policing costs, increased police coverage, higher clearance rates, and increased flexibility in deploying officers (Griffiths, Whitelaw, and Parent 1999:50).

Regionalization has not occurred without some difficulties. A report on the Niagara Regional Police Force documented a number of problem areas, including lack of lead time in planning regionalization, difficulties integrating officers from different police services into one organizational and operational structure, and an absence of loyalty to the regional police service (cited in Oppal 1994:D9–10). However, the report also found that over time, with strong leadership from senior administrators, these problems could be successfully addressed. Similar problems were encountered, and resolved, in the amalgamation of the police services in Halifax, Dartmouth, and Bedford, Nova Scotia.

Integrated Policing

In response to the difficulties noted with regionalization, many police services in Canada are electing to integrate specific sections of their police service with those of a neighbouring police service. Integration of police services and resources is increasingly becoming a much more common approach in delivering police services. Box 7.2 describes strategies many police services are implementing in an effort to enhance service. For example, by integrating key sections such as forensic services, emergency response teams, K-9 units, and other common specialized areas of policing, it becomes possible to provide a more efficient and effective response to the community's needs. This process also allows the policing service to retain its autonomy and loyalty to the local community, and in some instances, a cost-saving factor is also achieved. For example, in the metropolitan area of Vancouver, the independent police services of Abbotsford, Delta, New Westminster, and Port Moody recently integrated their emergency response personnel and hostage negotiators into one team. This integrated approach eliminated the duplication of these highly specialized services, providing an enhanced service delivery to a population of roughly 300,000. Similarly, the Halifax Regional Police and Royal Canadian Mounted Police have integrated their forensic functions.

For purposes of this text, a major question is to what extent the regionalization of police services facilitates or hinders the implementation of community policing strategies and programs. However, sensitivity to this issue is reflected by the Ottawa Police Service, which is discussed below.

Lower Vancouver Island has integrated traffic safety unit called the Vancouver Island Integrated Road Safety Unit (IRSU). This is one example of integrated strategic policing which is responsive to a very common citizen concern of road safety.

Source: © Saanich Police Department

BOX 7.2

NEW ARRANGEMENTS FOR SERVICE DELIVERY: INTEGRATIONS, CONSOLIDATIONS, AND INTEROPERABILITY

Many police departments are exploring new and improved arrangements for the delivery of police services. In British Columbia, RCMP Communication Centres consolidated from several centres into three Operational Communications Centres (OCCs). In Calgary, Alberta the Calgary Police Service, Calgary Fire Department, and Emergency Medical Services integrated their emergency 9-1-1 communications centre into one, called Public Safety Communications (PSC). Through the use of various technologies and training, the goal is to develop the knowledge and skills among employees to manage any type of emergency or nonemergency call regardless of whether they previously worked for fire, police, or emergency medical services. Across Canada, agencies like the RCMP in British Columbia are incorporating lower priced personnel, called Community Safety Officers (CSOs), into their service delivery models to increase police visibility and provide dedicated resources for crime prevention initiatives. Alberta (as discussed in Chapter 3) has established provincial sheriffs with limited authority to perform traffic enforcement duties on rural highways as well as fugitive apprehension and province-wide surveillance.

Following September 11, 2001, recommendations made by the 911 Commission Inquiry called for greatly improved interoperability or the ability for emergency services to communicate with one another using shared radio systems. In British Columbia, a common radio system (called BC PRIME) became a legislated requirement. Similar efforts are currently underway in Alberta.

Since September 11, 2001, integrated policing has also taken on a global scale, requiring the alliance of law enforcement agencies locally, federally, and internationally. According to former RCMP Commissioner Giuliano Zaccardelli, integrated policing requires that police agencies work together in five key areas:

1. The concentration of developing shared priorities, both domestically and internationally, to determine the best way to leverage and maximize police efforts and resources toward common objectives.

2. The free flow of intelligence, obtaining the right information, and providing it to the right people.

3. Implementing interoperable systems to ensure that intelligence and information systems are able to communicate across organizations and geographic locations.

4. Taking advantage of economies of scale to make the most out of the resources dedicated to policing, and focusing efforts on what police do best.

5. Ensuring seamless service delivery and eliminating duplicate services and activities as well as the fragmentation of functions.

As of 2012, there were a number of integrated teams across Canada, including integrated proceeds of crime units (IPOCs), which target money laundering; integrated border enforcement teams (IBETs), which protect the security of Canadian borders; integrated market enforcement units (IMETs), which are designed to protect the integrity of Canada's capital markets; and integrated national security enforcement teams, which investigate terrorist and extremist threats. As of 2008, and as part of the National Counterfeit Enforcement Strategy, the RCMP had established three Integrated Counterfeit Enforcement Teams (ICETs) to protect the integrity of Canadian currency. These teams, located in Montreal, Toronto, and Vancouver, also illustrate the RCMP's commitment to its strategic priorities (recall Box 6.6).

The Ottawa Police Service and Community Policing

The Ottawa Police Service was created on January 1, 1995, bringing together police services from Gloucester, Nepean, and Ottawa. One of the biggest challenges facing the new police service, as noted by the first Chief of Police, was to work together as a unified and integrated police service, while at the same time providing a decentralized police service through the deployment and delivery of services at the district and neighbourhood levels.

The formal submission to the Ontario Civilian Commission on Police Services (OCCPS) described the foundations upon which police service delivery would be based. Problem-oriented policing was selected as the community policing philosophy for the new service, and a three-pronged approach was developed to incorporate this approach into the organization and delivery of policing services:

- to move in the direction of implementing a problem-oriented policing organization;
- to move as rapidly as possible to include the community as an active partner in problem solving and prevention;
- to reassess the current community-based activities of the Ottawa Police Service; and
- to retain only those that advance progress in the achievement of the above two priorities.

In addition, district-level policing was incorporated as a key strategy. This resulted in the decentralization of command and control structures and provided increased autonomy to line officers.

The new police service then set out a number of **service delivery principles** to provide the framework for providing police services to the new, expanded community, as follows:

1. The Ottawa Police Service is organized around problem-oriented policing. Officers will work in teams to develop internal and external partnerships. These teams will be led by sergeants and staff sergeants and will engage in reactive and proactive and preventive activities.
2. The Ottawa Police Service is moving to district-level policing. Responsibility for policing, including patrol, resources, staffing decisions and hours of work, crime analysis, and general investigation, will reside at the district level. Front-line officers will be generalists and will assume responsibility for many types of investigations.
3. The Ottawa Police Service is front-loading supports. Front-loading support involves increased analytical and research support, improved technology, and increased training for officers in areas such as problem solving, conflict resolution, and interpersonal skills.
4. The Ottawa Police Service is focusing on partnerships. The community will be involved in the design, delivery, and evaluation of policing services. Partnerships will enhance the problem-solving capacities of the police service.
5. The Ottawa Police Service is emphasizing its commitment to administrative efficiency. This commitment involves exploring ways to provide front-line officers with the time and support required to develop partnerships in the community, the use of auxiliaries and volunteers, and equitable distribution of workloads (Ottawa-Carleton Regional Police Service 1996:25–27).

APPLICATION OF THE CORPORATE MODEL IN POLICING

In our discussion in Chapter 6, we noted that a key component of community policing is the use of strategies from the private sector. Police services are making increasing use of the corporate model for administrative and operational planning and performance assessment, as seen in materials from the Guelph Police Service and the Vancouver Police Department described below.

Planning within a Community Policing Framework: The Guelph Police Service

The *Guelph Police Service Business Plan: 2010–2012* details the planning process carried out by a community-policing police service. The introduction, written by Chief Rob Davis, states that:

This Plan helps guide our response to the current issues of our community and our members. Moreover, it also assists us in preparing for future challenges that are likely to affect policing and the overall safety of our community. We cannot rest upon our past successes but instead need to continue striving to be a leader in developing new and innovative ways of addressing emerging issues. . . . As recently documented in the new Statistics Canada "Crime Severity Index" data, Guelph is recognized as the safest city of its size in our Country which was mirrored in the responses of our community survey respondents, the majority of whom feel very safe in our community. As always, there are issues we need to be constantly mindful of and which are likely to be part of our long term focus. These include the positive development of our youth; maintaining a respectable standard for road and pedestrian safety; and continuing to develop strategies to address drug and associated crime through enforcement and as partners in the Wellington/Guelph Community Drug Strategy. (Guelph Police Service 2010)

The Guelph *Business Plan* contains a number of sections, including:

- a review of the 2007–2009 business plan;
- an analysis of the socioeconomic trends in the community, including population and development trends, crime patterns and projections, and community priorities;
- discussions of police resource and workload trends, labour market and staffing issues, legislative changes, and changes in information and technology;
- a budget forecast, including a trends summary and implications for policing; and
- recommended corporate goals for 2010–2012.

Let's take a brief look at each of these areas of the report to gain a better idea of how a community-policing police service does business.

A Review of the 2007–2009 Business Plan

A key part of the police service as a learning organization involves examining the outcomes of previous plans and initiatives. In fact, the 2007–2009 *Business Plan* clearly states the business plan builds on the work of previous business plans—which is why the name, "Partners in Excellence," remained unchanged from previous plans. In this section, the Guelph Police Service reviews its previous business plan and annual reports, lists the individual **corporate goals**, notes the major accomplishments found in yearly accomplishment reports, and identifies outstanding issues that remain to be addressed. The Guelph Police Service also reviewed its vision, mission, and values statements to ensure they were in line with the current philosophy and strategic direction of the department. In the 2004–2006 *Business Plan,* the vision, mission, and values were changed to ensure alignment with philosophy and strategic direction.

One corporate goal in the 2007–2009 business plan, under the heading "Neighbourhood Policing," was "Continue to seek solutions to neighbourhood issues in partnership with the community through crime prevention, education and enforcement."

Indicators of success included:

- A multi-language survey was conducted in partnership with community agencies to determine the police-related needs of multicultural communities.
- The Traffic unit undertook successful initiatives targeting high-risk locations where pedestrian and/or motorist safety were jeopardized.
- A pre-charge diversion protocol was developed with local partners to facilitate referrals of persons with mental health issues to a diversion program, where appropriate, instead of being charged.
- The role of police in domestic violence and/or sexual assault incidents and investigations was discussed with community partners unit in 2008.

Socioeconomic Trends, Crime Patterns and Projections, and Community Priorities

Socioeconomic data presented in the *Business Plan* for 2010–2012 include:

- *Information on population*: population projections, population and age structures of the City of Guelph, population projections by age, and ethnocultural characteristics of the City of Guelph.
- *Residential, commercial, and industrial growth*: new residential units by type, including single detached, semidetached, townhouses, and apartments; industrial and commercial building construction.

    Crime data presented include:

- *Rates of police-reported criminal behaviour*: a summary of crime trends comparing national trends with trends in the City of Guelph relating to total crime, violent crime, property crime, and youth crime.
- *Crime severity rates*: an overview of the severity of crime in the City of Guelph.
- *Information on community perceptions and priorities*: as determined by community surveys and information from partner agencies.

Police Resource and Service Delivery Trends

Information presented on police resources and service delivery trends includes:

- Police resource and workload comparison, including population per police officer, per capita policing costs, and *Criminal Code* incidents per officer.
- Labour market and staffing issues, including changes in the labour force population and the anticipated shortage of police officers, changes in the occupations and industries in which people work, changes in the educational level of workers, and the alternative forms of work that are emerging.
- Legislative changes, including the impact of federal legislation (changes in the *Criminal Code,* sentencing reform, and gun control registration) and provincial legislation (the Adequacy Standards, downloading of the *Provincial Offences Act,* changes to seatbelt laws, and the *Law Enforcement and Forfeited Property Management Statute Law Amendment Act*).
- Information and technology changes and their impact on the delivery of policing services, including the growth of the Internet; the use of computers to gather, store, and process information; and the resource and financial implications of these changes for the police service.

    Table 7.3 outlines the policing resource indicators for the Guelph Police Service in a comparative context.

Trends Summary and Implications for Policing

Highlights include population and commercial and industrial growth in the community; the need for increased training of police officers to meet the requirements of legislation, changes in technology, and career enhancement; and the need for continuing to adapt policies and procedures to ensure effective police services.

    A business plan includes a list of the corporate goals, key strategies for achieving these goals, and identification of the parties responsible for implementation of the goals and strategies.

    Table 7.4 presents materials on one of the corporate goals identified by the Guelph Police Service, called "neighbourhood policing," where the corporate goal focuses on seeking solutions to neighbourhood issues in partnership with the community through crime prevention, education, and enforcement.

Table 7.3 Municipal Policing Resource Indicators, Guelph and Selected Comparators

City	Population	Total police officers	Number of police per 100,000 population	Crime Severity Index	Clearance Rate
Barrie	139,050	228	164	67.5	42.5
Chatham-Kent	109,048	166	152	86.6	39.3
Durham Regional	620,427	920	148	51.3	48.2
Greater Sudbury	164,357	260	158	84.2	39.7
Guelph	124,130	190	153	50.4	46.8
Halton Regional	506,900	637	126	37.5	38.3
Hamilton	533,280	816	153	82.3	31.6
Kingston	125,354	201	160	70.9	41.3
London	378,809	587	155	92.8	46.7
Niagara Regional	443,866	728	164	69.5	35.5
Ottawa	896,529	1,273	142	61.3	41.2
Peel Regional	1,273,348	1,908	150	51.9	42.3
Thunder Bay	116,937	228	195	113.2	44.9
Toronto	2,720,024	5,776	212	74.0	38.5
Waterloo Regional	522,968	725	139	67.6	44.4
Windsor	221,310	466	211	85.3	38.4
York Regional	1,040,165	1,466	141	43.2	46.7

Source: Statistics Canada, Canadian Centre for Justice Statistics, 2011. Police Resources in Canada, 2011, Cat. No. 85-225-X , Ottawa: Statistics Canada.

Table 7.4 2010 Guelph Police Service Neighbourhood Policing Accomplishments

The Guelph Police Service reports in its 2010 Accomplishments report that it achieved 26 objectives within its corporate goal of "neighbourhood policing." Here are three samples from that report.

Objective: Assist in the improvement of clearance rates for violent crime and property crime.

Importance: Guelph's clearance rate appears to be quite low in comparison to others, giving the appearance that the Service does not solve crimes as effectively as other police services.

Corporate Goal: Neighbourhood Policing

Objective Status: Achieved

Synopsis:

A working group was formed early in 2010 to examine how crime statistics were being collected and forwarded to Statistics Canada and to examine how other police services were recording these data to ensure consistency in comparisons across services. The results did show some minor irregularities that could affect the final clearance rates. As a result of the review, new processes have been put in place that should improve clearance rates and response times to calls. A review of the changes to date shows an increase in clearance rates after the first six months of 2010, particularly in property crime where Guelph tended to be lower than comparators. The specialty units (persons crime and property crime) in the detective division are working well and the consistency in staffing and investigative processes is improving clearance. The GPS's clearance rates for violent crime are some of the highest in the province. The crime analyst is also increasing the information collected and shared with operational units on active crime types and locations leading to increased targeted enforcement and focused patrol. The overall results will be examined in more detail when the year-end review of crime data is conducted.

Objective: Ensure the GPS has excellent risk management procedures and processes in place.

Importance: It is important to identify and address high-risk activities to reduce organizational and member liability and increase member and community safety, both of which contribute to providing excellent service to the community.

Corporate Goal: Neighbourhood Policing

Objective Status: Achieved

Synopsis:

The Risk Management Committee held regularly scheduled meetings during the year and the committee membership was updated to ensure adequate representation of the various work units. The minutes of the meetings were made available to all members of the GPS. A number of committee members attended a risk management training session presented by Gordon Graham.

The committee also spearheaded a proposal to provide patrol rifles to the platoons. This proposal was approved by the executive, and has been successfully implemented. The patrol rifles have the potential to assist our members and the community in critical firearms incidents.

In 2010 the Service complied with the implementation of the Bill 168 legislation (Workplace Violence and Harassment), including training our members and having an external risk assessment of the GPS conducted.

In addition, for the past year this Inspector (now overseeing a different division) has represented the Service on a community advisory committee for Project Wisdom, which has the goal to examine and understand elder abuse from a cultural perspective, thereby increasing cultural understanding and sensitivity to issues of elder abuse within ethno-specific communities. The project is made possible with funding from the New Horizon for Seniors Program, Human Resources and Skills Development Canada, and has partners from Trellis, Immigrant Services, County of Wellington Social Services, Women in Crisis, and the GPS. This work primarily supports the Service's Social Responsibility corporate goal.

Objective: Strengthen ties with formal Neighbourhood Groups by holding a series of Town Hall style meetings (community forums).

Importance: The discussion during these forums will build the collaborative relationship between the Police Service and the neighbourhoods.

Corporate Goal: Neighbourhood Policing

Objective Status: Achieved

Synopsis:

Four community forums were conducted throughout the year, and issues and solutions raised during those forums were incorporated into operational planning for the Neighbourhood Services Division. All Neighbourhood Groups were invited to these forums, and representation from each group was achieved. City councilors and staff also attended the forums. Very positive feedback from the community, city councilors, and city staff about these forums was received.

To review all accomplishments see *Guelph Police Service, Business Plan 2010–2012, 2010 Unit Accomplishments.*

Source: Courtesy of Guelph Police Services

Appendices

- Results of city service quality studies, conducted on households and businesses and comparing city services on a number of key performance indicators.
- Priorities identified by community partners in workshops, focus groups, and forums held in the community.

Guelph Police Service 2010 Accomplishments

The Guelph Police Service prepares an Accomplishments report to assess how well they are meeting their corporate goals. This level of accountability to the community is a key feature of community-based police organizations. Table 7.5 outlines the Guelph Police Services self-assessment of some its accomplishments for 2010.

Table 7.5 Meeting the Needs of the Community: Strategies and Accountability

Objectives	Performance Measure
1. Review cruiser, foot and bike patrol patterns and resources available for community policing efforts along with an exploration of alternative scheduling and staffing models.	• Review of patrol & community policing patterns & demands (2010–2011) • Research alternative scheduling & staffing models (2010) • Strategies allowing for enhanced patrol & community policing initiatives developed (2010–2011), implemented & evaluated (2011–2012) • Amount of overtime hours* • Number and quality of community policing initiatives*
2. Maintain or improve violent and property crime clearance rates.	• Percent of members trained in investigations* • Resources available for investigations* • Clearance rates*
3. Maintain or improve response times for Priority One Calls for Service	• Percent of Priority One calls in queue • Response times • Alternate response strategies explored (2010) & implemented & evaluated as appropriate (2011–2012)
4. Enhance our collaboration with neighbourhood stakeholders on crime prevention, including Problem Oriented Policing (POP) initiatives.	• Number of members on committees* • Number of successful POPs* • Number of successful strategies implemented through partnerships*
5. Continue to improve the efficiency and effectiveness of officer involvement with mental health patients.	• Number of successful strategies developed by mental health partnerships* • Percent of members trained in mental health issues* • Amount of resources, including officer time, spent at hospitals*
6. Ensure the Guelph Police Service has excellent Risk Management and Emergency Preparedness procedures and processes in place.	• Quality of training, including training in relevant policies & procedures (2011) • Feedback received by Risk Management Committee*

*will be assessed annually
Source: Guelph Police Service, Business Plan 2010–2012, from http://www.guelphpolice.com/business-plan/, p. 11

The Vancouver Police Department Strategic Plan

The Vancouver Police Department is an excellent example of a "best practices" police service organized on a corporate model. From the period of 2003 to 2007, the Vancouver Police Department undertook a thorough review of all aspects of its service delivery model including demands for service, ratio of civilian and sworn positions, clearance rates, and an overall service-wide analysis of effectiveness and efficiencies. As a result of this extensive evaluation, the Vancouver Police Department adjusted a number of its call response performance targets, and identified a number of positions that could be staffed by civilian employees as opposed to police officers.

Demands on policing in Vancouver, combined with the results of a very through analysis, made a strong case for change. These indicators, while specific to the municipality of Vancouver, are very similar to those experienced by the Edmonton Police Service in the 1980s (refer to Table 7.2) and they required the VPD to balance its resources and services effectively to meet these current demands while at the same time adapting to future demands brought on by growth. The *2012–2016 Strategic*

Plan: Vancouver Police Department incorporates the research and findings into a comprehensive plan, setting the stage for future growth.

The main purposes of the VPD Strategic Plan are to:

- Serve as an agreement about the policing priorities for the City of Vancouver among the Vancouver Police Board, the Chief Constable, and the Senior Management Team;
- Inform the citizens of Vancouver about the policing services and standards they can expect;
- Support performance measurement by the Police Board, the Chief Constable, the Senior Management Team, and the British Columbia Ministry of Public Safety and Solicitor General;
- Establish the basis for inter-agency discussion on coordination of services, with respect to community safety;
- Direct the annual business plans and current budgets of the divisions and individual sections; and
- Outline and demonstrate our commitment to being the safest major city in Canada.

The *2012–2016 Strategic Plan: Vancouver Police Department* sets out a number of key strategic goals to be addressed. The goals are as follows:

Crime Reduction Goals

- reduce violent crime by 2.5% a year for a total reduction of 12.5% over the next five years
- reduce property crime by 5% a year for a total reduction of 25% over the next five years
- combat low-level crimes and problems that impact perceptions of neighbourhood safety
- reduce motor vehicle collisions that result in injury or death by 12.5% over the next five years

Community Focused Goals

- develop and maintain positive working relationships, including sharing information, within the VPD and with stakeholder agencies in the community
- provide public educational outreach on policing and police related issues
- provide socially responsible programs and initiatives that benefit youth
- Manage resources in an environmentally sustainable manner

Organizational Development Goals

- encourage and support career development and succession planning for all staff
- ensure that the VPD has the human resources and training needed to meet objectives
- support and foster employee wellness
- develop and implement initiatives that streamline administrative processes
- research, acquire and utilize the best technology and infrastructure to assist officers in the investigation and enforcement of crime

For each goal there are a number of strategies, as illustrated in the examples that follow.

Goal: Reduce violent crime by 2.5% a year for a total reduction of 12.5% over the next five years.

Strategies: The VPD's plan involves three components to address violent crimes:

- reducing the number of violent incidents through preventative measures,
- investigating the violent incidents that do occur in an effective manner, and
- communicating when appropriate with the public about incidents that have occurred and the resulting police response.

VPD also intends to reduce organized crime activities, which in turn impact violent crime, through

- seizures of assets under provisions of the *Criminal Code* and
- referrals to the BC Civil Forfeiture office where property can be forfeited if it was used, or acquired, in an unlawful manner.
- Utilizing administrative laws, when criminal charges are not possible to interfere or disrupt a group's operations
- Crime analysis
- Programs such as BarWatch and Restaurant Watch, two examples of proactive measures that interfere with violent criminals' ability to gather within Vancouver to reduce the likelihood of violent incidents occuring.
- The Gang Crime Unit's partnership with the Marine Unit during the summer months ensures this disruption tactic is taken to the marine environment, further interfering with gang members' ability to gather without police interference.

Goal: combat low-level crimes and problems that impact perceptions of neighbourhood safety

Strategies:

- Reduce behaviours that have a negative impact on the quality of life of those living in the area through advocacy and enforcement.
- Manage "quality of life" problems, to promote improved perceptions of safety.

Goal: reduce motor vehicle collisions that result in injury or death by 12.5% over the next five years

Strategies:

- Developing approaches incorporating enforcement, engineering, and education.
- Targeting enforcement and education approaches for all classes of road users (drivers, cyclists, and pedestrians).
- Work in partnership with the Insurance Bureau of British Columbia and City of Vancouver.

Goal: develop and maintain positive working relationships, including sharing information, within the VPD and with stakeholder agencies in the community

Strategies:

- Continue collaborating with external agencies, e.g. mental health agencies, Aboriginal groups, women's groups.
- Develop new relationships or improve existing ones.
- Develop an internal communication strategy to improve internal working relationships by facilitating communication and information sharing between senior management and front-line staff.
- Ensure communication between all units to improve front-line service effectiveness.

Goal: provide public educational outreach on policing and police related issues

Strategies:

- Increase outreach and public education for Vancouver communities.
- Proactively share information about investigations and public safety issues, through the VPD website and regular media releases.

- Develop new communication mediums such as Crime Alerts Program, Twitter, and Facebook.
- Develop a social media strategy to ensure the community learns more about the VPD, its services, and its staff, which assists in managing community expectations.
- Engage the community in crime prevention efforts by addressing root causes of crime. Programs designed to reduce auto theft, violent crime, and drug-facilitated sexual assaults serve to educate and enhance community safety.

Goal: provide socially responsible programs and initiatives that benefit youth

- Build respect among youth for the law and criminal justice system, by ensuring positive role models, support services, and programs to assist them. Programs include Eastside Aboriginal Space for at-risk aboriginal youth (EASy), School Liaison programs at Vancouver schools, Car 86 for child welfare matters, the Police Athletic League (PAL), and high-risk youth/street youth intervention team. These programs assist youth by providing the skills necessary to allow them to make better life choices and reduce their chances of becoming entrenched in criminal lifestyles.

Goal: Manage resources in an environmentally sustainable manner

Strategies:

- Seek improvements to the vehicle fleet and facilities to reduce the VPD's carbon footprint.
- Develop and sustain a waste diversion program.
- Develop "Green" practices that increase efficiencies and reduce operating costs.
- Focus on reducing, reusing, recycling, and using innovative methods to better utilize resources through its Code Green program.

Goal: encourage and support career development and succession planning for all staff

Strategies:

- Improve and expand on current succession planning strategies.
- Strengthen performance development, mentorship, and access to development opportunities.

Goal: ensure that the VPD has the human resources and training needed to meet objectives

Strategies:

- Ensure the VPD is staffed to its authorized strength to meet demands, achieve the goals in the Business Plan and better ensure community safety.
- Improve training opportunities to ensure excellent service.

Goal: support and foster employee wellness

Strategies:

- Continue the operation of the Critical Incident Stress Management Team and Employee Services.
- The VPD will work to improve awareness of and access to various assistance programs such as the annual debrief for employees in high stress units through the Employee Wellness Program.
- The VPD will continue to develop and expand current employee wellness programs.

Goal: develop and implement initiatives that streamline administrative processes

Strategies:

- Strive to make administrative processes more effective and efficient, increasing time available for operational policing.

- Further analysis will be conducted to identify additional inefficiencies and projects developed to solve administrative challenges.

Goal: research, acquire, and utilize the best technology and infrastructure to assist officers in the investigation and enforcement of crime.

Strategies:

- Use technology as a force multiplier to make front-line officers more effective and support staff more efficient.
- Use technologies to increase the efforts of volunteers and partners.
- Providing staff with the facilities, equipment, and technology they require to do their jobs at the highest level of performance.

Source: © Vancouver Police Department 2010.

CHAPTER SUMMARY

In this chapter, we have presented several case studies that illustrate the organizational and operational changes made by police services across the country to incorporate the principles of community policing. The Edmonton Police Service was one police service to embark on a major organizational reform, the outcomes of which have been positive for both the police service and the community. The Montreal Police Service and the Surrey, B.C. detachment of the RCMP have undertaken similar structural reforms, and, although it is too early to assess the impact of these changes, it can be assumed that there will be positive outcomes in these jurisdictions as well.

In another case study the successes and setbacks of the Halton Regional Police Service were traced through the decades-long implementation of community policing. Among the lessons of the Halton experience were that transforming police organizations takes time, patience, and vision on the part of leaders and front-line officers, as well as a capacity to adapt to changing demands.

The Organizational Renewal Project of the Durham Regional Police was then examined to illustrate the planning process of one police service designed to meet the requirements of the Adequacy Standards. This process involved identifying a number of implementation issues; for each issue the police service then set out a course of action for how the issue would be addressed.

The issue of regionalization, integrated policing, and community policing was examined, and the efforts of one regional police service—the Ottawa Police Service—to ensure that the principles and practices of community policing were at the core of the police service were discussed. Finally, the business plans of the Guelph Police Service and the Vancouver Police Department were presented to illustrate the planning process involved in implementing community policing.

These case studies provide important insights into the challenges that police services encounter in changing their organizational structures and their strategies for delivering police services. The experiences of the police services that have been presented in this chapter leave little doubt that transforming police organizations is an all-encompassing process that does not happen overnight.

CHAPTER REVIEW

Key Terms

- corporate goals, p. 224
- differential response model (Edmonton Police Service), p. 204

Key Points

- The experience of the Edmonton Police Service provides key insights into the challenges and outcomes of altering the organization and delivery of policing services.
- The Montreal Police Service and the Surrey RCMP detachment have recently undertaken major reforms in an attempt to implement the principles of community policing.
- The experience of the Halton Regional Police over three decades provides several lessons in the requirements for successfully adopting and implementing community policing.
- The Organizational Renewal Project of the Durham Regional Police is a good illustration of how a police service can plan to meet the requirements of the *Police Services Act* and the Adequacy Standards in the area of community policing.
- The regionalization of police services raises questions about the ability of amalgamated police services to implement the principles of community policing effectively.
- The service delivery principles established by the Ottawa Police Service illustrate how one regional police service set out to ensure that amalgamation did not prevent the development of a decentralized, community-focused police service.
- The planning approaches used by the Guelph Police Service and the Vancouver Police Department illustrate the use of a corporate model for the organization and delivery of policing services.

Self-Evaluation

QUESTIONS

1. Describe the components of the Edmonton **Police Service differential response model**.
2. What role does **empowerment** of line officers play in the transformation to a community-policing police service?
3. What is meant by **ownership**, and what role does it play in a community-policing police service?
4. Define what is meant by an **internal marketing strategy**, and discuss the role that this strategy plays in implementing community policing. Provide examples.
5. Define what is meant by an **external marketing strategy**, and discuss the role that this strategy plays in implementing community policing. Provide examples.
6. Describe the **Village Constable Program** and the role this program played in the transformation of Halton Regional Police Service to community policing.
7. What is **Total Integrated Policing**, and how is this approach to the delivery of police services illustrative of community policing?
8. Describe the key components of the **Organizational Renewal Project** of the Durham Regional Police.

9. What are the **service delivery principles** of the Ottawa Police, and how do they reflect community policing?

10. What are **corporate goals**, and what role do these play in a community-policing police service?

KEY IDEAS

1. Which demand on the Edmonton Police Service during 1980–1990 led the EPS to begin the process of transforming itself into a community-policing police service?
   a. an increase in reported crime
   b. an increase in the number of patrol constables
   c. an increase in the elderly population
   d. an increase in the number of motor vehicle incidents

2. Which of the following was found by evaluations of the Edmonton Police Service?
   a. a decrease in citizen satisfaction with the police
   b. an increase in officer morale, motivation, and job satisfaction
   c. an increase in the levels of crime
   d. a decrease in clearance rates

3. In the Edmonton Police Service, senior police administrators secured the support and participation of line officers in the transformation into a community-policing police service. What strategy did they use in order to do this?
   a. co-optation strategy
   b. external marketing strategy
   c. internal marketing strategy
   d. devolution strategy

4. Which statement is true about the Montreal Police Service Neighbourhood Policing Project?
   a. it encountered considerable resistance from community residents
   b. it is designed to increase foot and bicycle patrols in the community
   c. it involved the creation of nearly 50 neighbourhood police stations
   d. it was abandoned after a one-year trial period

5. Which statement is true about the Village Constable Program?
   a. it was used by police services in Ontario until the mid 1970s
   b. it was a key component of the Halton Regional Police community policing effort
   c. it has been used by the Ontario Provincial Police for many years
   d. it involves citizen volunteers patrolling the community

6. Which of the following is indicated by the experience of the Halton Regional Police with community policing?
   a. Implementing community policing requires corporate sponsorship during the initial stages more than programs.
   b. Implementing community policing is a slow and gradual process.
   c. Implementing community policing requires federal funding to be successful.
   d. Implementing community policing can occur in a quick and efficient manner with proper planning.

7. In its Organizational Renewal Project, how did the Durham Regional Police Service propose to address its identified implementation issues?
   a. by creating audit teams
   b. by creating statements of accountability
   c. by contracting out certain police services
   d. by using more volunteers

8. What do research studies indicate about regional police services?
    a. that they increase the costs of police services
    b. that they have difficulty establishing partnerships with the communities they police
    c. that they reduce per capita policing costs
    d. that they are able to provide more traffic enforcement than smaller police services

9. What did the Ottawa Police Service do upon its creation in 1995?
    a. it based its policing philosophy on problem-oriented policing
    b. it implemented district-level policing
    c. it focused on building community partnerships
    d. it focused on providing patrol officers with support and resources

10. Which of the following is used by the Guelph Police Service and the Vancouver Police Department in applying the corporate model to the organization and delivery of police services?
    a. business partnerships
    b. environmental scans
    c. budgetary goals
    d. tactical response plans

11. Which of the following best exemplifies integrated policing?
    a. a strategic patrol technique
    b. shared computer-based systems and radio frequencies
    c. an example of strategic policing
    d. a traditional, paramilitary style of policing

12. Which of the following factors is most important in terms of implementing a corporate model?
    a. a corporate model solves longstanding organizational problems
    b. corporate models indicate a police service has implemented a highly evolved community policing model
    c. corporate models need to be adapted to the realities of police work
    d. corporate models are necessary for generating revenue in policing

EXERCISES: KNOWLEDGE INTO PRACTICE

Exercise 1. Leading-Edge Policing

The Halton Regional Police Service is widely regarded as a leading-edge police service, particularly in relation to community policing. From a review of the materials presented on the HRPS covering the 1970s to the 1990s, list what you would consider to be the elements that contribute to this police service being leading edge.

Now, using the same materials, list what you would consider to be the major obstacles confronted by the HRPS in transforming itself from a traditional police service into community policing.

Exercise 2. The Durham Regional Police Service Organizational Renewal Project

To prepare for the guidelines imposed by the Adequacy Standards as of January 1, 2001, the Durham Regional Police Service undertook the Organizational Renewal Project. This project identified a number of implementation issues and then set out what the police service planned to do about each of the issues and how it planned to do it. Four implementation issues are reproduced below.

Review the plans of the Durham Regional Police for addressing each of the implementation issues. Then, using the experience of the Halton Regional Police Service as a resource:

1. Identify what you would consider to be the major challenge(s) that the implementation issue poses;
2. Identify the potential difficulties that the Durham Regional Police might encounter in addressing each implementation issue; and
3. Suggest how the potential difficulties that might be encountered could be either avoided or successfully addressed.

Implementation Issue 1. Defining Community Policing

Challenges posed by this issue:

_____

_____

_____

_____

_____

Difficulties that may be encountered in addressing this issue:

_____

_____

_____

_____

_____

How these difficulties could be avoided or successfully addressed:

_____

_____

_____

_____

_____

Implementation Issue 2. Structural Changes

Challenges posed by this issue:

_____

_____

_____

_____

_____

Difficulties that may be encountered in addressing this issue:

_____

_____

_____

_____

_____

How these difficulties could be avoided or successfully addressed:

_____

_____

_____

_____

_____

_____

Implementation Issue 3. Communication

Challenges posed by this issue:

_____

_____

_____

_____

_____

Difficulties that may be encountered in addressing this issue:

_____

_____

_____

_____

_____

How these difficulties could be avoided or successfully addressed:

_____

_____

_____

_____

_____

Implementation Issue 4. Relationships with associations

Challenges posed by this issue:

_____

_____

_____

_____

_____

Difficulties that may be encountered in addressing this issue:

_____

_____

_____

_____

How these difficulties could be avoided or successfully addressed:

_____

_____

_____

_____

_____

The Durham Regional Police Service 2005–2007 Business Report includes messages from the Chief of Police, Chair of the Durham Regional Police Services Board, and the Durham Regional Police Service Police Association, in addition to the message from the Chief of Police and Director of the police board. How do you feel about the police association providing a statement in a corporate document? What do you think this suggests about the strength of the relationship between the regional police service and the police association?

_____

_____

_____

_____

_____

REFERENCES

Burlington Post. 1976. "Experiment Spreads to Cover the Entire City." February 4:3, 5.

Charih, M. and L. Rouillard. 1997. "The New Public Management." In M. Charih and A. Daniels (eds.), *New Public Management and Public Administration in Canada.* Toronto: The Institute of Public Administration of Canada.

City of Surrey. 2006. *Surrey Crime Reduction Strategy.* Online (http://www.surrey.ca/NR/rdonlyres/4D63836D-9691-44EA-9393-41320D92C105/33777/SurreyCrimeReduction Strategyweb.pdf).

Clairmont, D. 1996. *Community-Based Policing at Halton Regional: The Years 1980 to 1995.* Ottawa: Solicitor General Canada.

Communauté urbaine de Montréal. 1997. *Evolution.* Montreal: Communauté urbaine de Montréal.

Cooke-Scott, L.A. 1998. "Community-based Policing in Ontario: Lessons from the Halton Regional Police Service." *Canadian Public Administration* 41(1):120–46.

Durham Regional Police Service. 2004. *2005–2007 Business Plan.* Whitby: Durham Regional Police Service.

Edmonton Police Service. 1996. *Community Policing in Edmonton, 1996.* Edmonton: Community and Organizational Support Section.

Edmonton Police Service. 2002. *Project Archimedes, Developing an Intelligence-led Policing Model for the Edmonton Police Service.* Edmonton: Edmonton Police Services.

Edmonton Police Service. 2007a. *Delivering Service, Achieving Results: A New Patrol Service Delivery Model.* Edmonton: Community Policing Bureau.

Edmonton Police Service. 2007b. *Edmonton Police Service Citizen Survey: Highlights.* Edmonton: Edmonton Police Service Research and Evaluation Unit.

Griffiths, C.T., B. Whitelaw, and R. Parent. 1999. *Canadian Police Work.* Toronto: ITP Nelson.

Guelph Police Service. 2007. *Partners in Excellence 2007–2009.* Guelph, ON: Business Plan of the Guelph Police Service.

Guelph Police Service. 2010. *Business Plan 2010–2012.* Guelph, ON: Guelph Police Service.

Guelph Police Service. 2011a. *2010 Annual Report.* Guelph, ON: Annual Report of the Guelph Police Service.

Guelph Police Service. 2011b. *Business Plan 2010–2012, 2010 Unit Accomplishments.* Online. Retrieved May 20, 2012 (http://www.guelphpolice.com/assets/2010-Accomplishments-Report-Yr-1-of-2010-2012-Business-Plan.pdf).

Halton Regional Police Force. 1982. *Policing Philosophy* [internal document].

Healey, S. and L. Bradburn. 2000. *Our Policing Future: Business Plan 2001–2003.* Guelph, ON: Guelph Police Service.

Loree, D. 1988. "Innovation and Change in a Regional Police Force." *Canadian Police College Journal* 12(4):205–39.

Montreal Police Service. 2002. *Annual Report.* Montreal, Quebec.

Montreal Police Service. 2003. *Annual Report*. Montreal, Quebec.

Oppal, W.T. (Commissioner). 1994. *Closing the Gap: Policing and the Community*. Policing in British Columbia Commission of Inquiry, Final Report, vol. 1. Victoria: Attorney General of British Columbia.

Ottawa-Carleton Regional Police Service. 1996. *Ottawa-Carleton Police Amalgamation Report*. Ottawa: Ontario Civilian Commission on Police Services.

Royal Canadian Mounted Police. 2003. "Integrated Policing." *Gazette* 65(3).

Royal Canadian Mounted Police. 2004. *Community Policing Surrey Style*. Surrey Royal Canadian Mounted Police.

Statistics Canada. 2011. *Police Resources in Canada, 2011*. Cat. No. 85-225-X. Ottawa: Statistics Canada, Canadian Centre for Justice Statistics.

Statistics Canada. 2012. *Surrey, British Columbia (Code 5915004) and Greater Vancouver, British Columbia (Code 5915)* (table). *Census Profile*. 2011 Census. Statistics Canada Catalogue no. 98-316-XWE. Ottawa. Released May 29, 2012.

Sutherland, A. 1997a. "Right Up Their Alley: More Street Patrols Suits Officers, Residents and Merchants Just Fine." *The Gazette* (Montreal), February 20:G6.

Sutherland, A. 1997b. "New Station Brings Policing Down to Street Level." *The Gazette* (Montreal), March 13:F10.

Taylor, K. 1999. *Bringing into Focus—Policing in Halton Region: The Executive Summary*. Oakville: Halton Regional Police Service.

Vancouver Police Department. 2012. *2012–2016 Strategic Plan*. Vancouver: Vancouver Police Department.

Veitch, D. 1995. *Community Policing in Edmonton*, 3rd ed. Edmonton: Community and Organizational Support Section, Edmonton Police Service.

The Community Police Officer

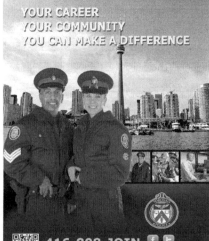

Police services across Canada strive to ensure the recruitment of police officers reflects the cultural and ethnic diversity of the communities they serve. "Branding" police work as an exciting and rewarding career is a key challenge faced by all police services.

Source: Courtesy of Toronto Public Service

Learning Objectives

After completing this chapter, you should be able to:

- Discuss how recruitment and training of police officers has changed in recent years;
- Identify the basic and preferred qualifications for police recruits;
- Discuss the role of diversity in police recruitment;
- Identify and discuss the issues related to recruitment of gays, lesbians, bisexual, and transgender individuals, members of First Nations, visible or cultural minorities, and women;
- Discuss the controversy over qualifications for women and members of cultural or visible minorities;
- Discuss the Recruit Training Program for Constables;
- Discuss the importance of in-service training;
- Describe the working personality of a police officer and its importance to the discussion of community policing;
- Describe what is meant by the community police officer as a generalist;
- Describe the relationship between reactive, proactive, and coactive policing; and
- Identify and discuss the sources of resistance to community policing.

INTRODUCTION

The success of community policing depends on the police officers who are responsible for implementing the programs. In essence, their attitudes, perceptions, and behaviors must be substantially changed before community policing can be put into practice.
—*A.J. Lurigio and W.G. Skogan (1994)*

The cornerstone of community policing is the line patrol officer, and it is this officer who ultimately plays a major role in the success of community policing. The task for senior police administrators is to create an organizational climate within which the line officer's role can be transformed from one of reacting to incidents and "crime fighting" to that of a proactive problem-solver who knows and understands the needs of the community he or she polices, and who works in partnership with the community to address these issues.

Community policing schemes result in more discretion and authority being vested in line officers who, as a result, are engaged in solving problems rather than merely reacting to them. This makes it imperative that line patrol officers have an intimate knowledge of the communities and neighbourhoods they police and also have the time and opportunity to develop working partnerships with community residents.

RECRUITING POLICE OFFICERS

Community police officers must be creative in thinking and problem solving. They must listen to community residents and mobilize them to address areas of concern, to identify the core issues related to a problem, and to develop intervention strategies for solving that problem. Understanding the root causes of crime and disorder, not to mention the complexity of social issues, has added to the difficulty of policing. Thus, applicants to police services should have some exposure to a university or college education that will assist them in developing research and critical thinking skills.

In addition, applicants should display good judgment and an ability to communicate. This will help the officer establish rapport with community residents and work collaboratively to solve problems. It is also essential that applicants have the personality and disposition to carry out the broad mandate given to community police officers, including the ability to work independently, take initiative, and be receptive to the varied duties of community policing officers (Carter 2000:1).

For anyone considering a career in a police service, there are certain **basic qualifications** and, while some variation exists around the country (e.g., minimum age and post-secondary education requirements), generally an applicant must:

- be a Canadian citizen;
- be at least 18 years of age (although most applicants are between 25 and 32);
- be physically fit, in good health, and with the appropriate weight and height;
- be a grade 12 graduate or equivalent, supplemented with accredited post-secondary education (typically a minimum of two years of university or college);
- possess a valid Canadian driver's licence;
- be of good character and have a personal background of proper conduct; and
- show common sense and good judgment.

Preferred qualifications may result in an applicant's ranking being raised; knowledge of a second language or culture, related volunteer experience, and a university degree or college diploma may all serve to do this.

Education and the Community Police Officer

In Chapter 6 we discussed the police service as a learning organization. Related to this topic is the role of education in policing generally and, more specifically, how education can enhance the performance of line officers. In a thorough examination of the issues relating to post-secondary education and strategic learning requirements for police officers, Donald Campbell (1992:113) identified a number of benefits that post-secondary education should provide to a police service:

- Improved performance by individual officers due to enhanced job skills, improved attitudes, or both, and an interest on the part of officers to pursue continuing education opportunities throughout their policing careers; and
- Improvements to the police service, including greater flexibility and adaptability, the capacity to anticipate, accommodate, and plan for change, and increased prestige.

The extent to which these expectations for individual officers and for police organizations are actually met by post-secondary education is unclear. On the one hand, it would be expected that regardless of the discipline pursued, successful completion of a college or university degree requires the ability to incorporate knowledge, think critically, express oneself orally and in writing, and appreciate the complexity of the issues that arise in society.

Research evidence, primarily from studies of policing in the United States, suggests that officers with higher levels of education:

- are more culturally sensitive to visible minorities;
- exhibit greater flexibility in carrying out policing tasks;
- generate fewer complaints from citizens than their less educated police colleagues;
- have a greater ability to process information; and
- have better relations with the community (Fischer, Golden, and Heininger 1985).

Although the associations between higher education and these outcomes may be weak or, at best, moderate, they appear to be consistent: "The overall conclusion is that higher education is a generally beneficial but not highly significant factor in improving the performance of front-line officers" (Campbell 1992:114). There is certainly a need for more research on the impact of education on police officer perspectives and performance, as well as on the types of educational experiences that are more beneficial to police officers working in various policing environments (Tomovich and Loree 1989).

Table 8.1 presents data on the education levels of Ontario police recruits.

The principal advantage of recruiting mature individuals is that they are more likely to have acquired significant life skills prior to joining the police. An individual with broader life experience is arguably more capable of coping with the various stressors of police work. Life skills also appear to be an important factor in an officer's ability to empathize with many of

Table 8.1 Educational Attainment of OPC Recruits, 1996–2011

	Frequency	Percent
No college or university courses completed	1,497	9.1
Some college or university courses completed	1,741	10.6
Other college program completed	2,778	16.9
Law and Security Administration and/or Police Foundations completed	2,559	15.5
Law and Security Administration and/or Police Foundations and other college program completed	2,284	13.9
University completed	3,894	23.7
University and college completed	1,706	10.4
Total	16,459	100.0

Source: Morris 2011. © Queen's Printer for Ontario, 2011. Reproduced with permission.

the troubled individuals encountered by the police. Additionally, length of service, maturity, and general life experience may be important factors in the police use of deadly force.

In concluding the discussion of post-secondary education and policing, Campbell states:

The justification of educational upgrading should not be linked to the impact on the performance of traditionally defined policing roles and functions. Rather, the emphasis must be on what these roles and functions will become, and on the types of holistic knowledge, skills, and abilities that will be needed by police officers to perform these new duties in a competent manner. On the basis of the available empirical evidence, there seems to be support for the value of increased educational requirements, in the successful performance of the types of work associated with policing needs of the future. (1992:116)

The Changing Practice of Recruiting: Promoting Diversity

One of Sir Robert Peel's fundamental principles of modern policing expounded in the early 1800s, and a key principle of community policing, is that police services should reflect the diversity of the communities they police. Historically, police officers have been overwhelming Anglo-Saxon males, and police services displayed little interest in recruiting visible and cultural minorities, Aboriginal people, and gays. Today, **diversity** is a key concept in policing (see Box 8.1).

The adoption of community policing as the model for police service delivery has resulted in major changes in recruiting. In contrast to previous decades, police services are actively seeking female applicants and applicants from visible ethnic minorities. Police services are also recognizing that diverse groups such as gays, lesbians, bisexual, and transgender individuals are part of the communities they serve. Police recruits today tend to be from a variety of educational backgrounds—many police services have officers who have law degrees and college and university degrees in fields as diverse as business and biology. On average, a police recruit is typically in his or her late 20s. Today's police recruit is a mature individual who brings a set of life skills and practical experience to policing (see Table 8.2).

Within the framework of community policing, recruitment assumes a very important role. Police services must recruit individuals who have an interest in policing

BOX 8.1

RCMP RECRUITMENT: COMMITMENT TO CULTURAL DIVERSITY AND EMPLOYMENT EQUITY

Employment Equity is of crucial importance in ensuring that the Royal Canadian Mounted Police has a diverse, innovative and responsible work force fully capable of achieving its mission. The RCMP remains committed to the principle that it should reflect the diverse population of Canada to ensure effective police/community relations and the effective delivery of police services. The RCMP has committed to ensure that all employment policies, practices, and standards are fully inclusive and provide all Canadians with equal and fair opportunities within the spirit of employment equity policies and legislation.

The RCMP is undergoing profound operational and organizational change. RCMP employment equity resources and actions continue to focus on practical measures in which employment equity contributes directly to effective community policing, quality of service and police/minority relations. Community Policing is a partnership between the police and the community in sharing the delivery of police services. The RCMP will continue to strive towards fully incorporating this policing philosophy in its strategic objectives, both external and internal.

For further information about employment equity in the RCMP you can access the following reports online through the Royal Canadian Mounted Police website at http://www.rcmp-grc.gc.ca/ee-eme/index-eng.htm.

Source: Royal Canadian Mounted Police (http://www.rcmp-grc.gc.ca/recruiting-recrutement/rec/requirements-exigences-eng.htm)

Table 8.2 Age Distribution of Ontario Police College Recruits, 1996–2011

		Frequency	Percent
Valid	24 years or younger	3,978	24.4
	25–29 years	6,995	43.0
	30–34 years	3,362	20.7
	35–39 years	1,386	8.5
	40 or older	558	3.4
	Total	16,279	100.0

Source: Morris 2011. © Queen's Printer for Ontario, 2011. Reproduced with permission.

beyond the traditional "blue lights and siren" role and who understand the challenges that police officers encounter in policing in a multicultural society.

Demographic trends also play a significant role in police recruitment. During the period from roughly 2004 through to 2009, many police services were conducting aggressive hiring campaigns in response to the replacement of a retirement bulge faced by several police services. While recruitment has since slowed in response to recent economic changes, including government austerity, it is safe to assume that recruitment levels will continue to remain steady due to continued retirements and modest growth. You will recall from our review of trends in Chapter 2 that recruiting and retaining police personnel ranks in the top three objectives for almost all Canadian police agencies. Besides retirements, the difficulty of keeping police services fully staffed is compounded by the following factors:

- Competition among all public safety agencies—for example, Canadian Border Services Agency, Alberta Sheriffs—from a limited resource pool of potential candidates;
- Limited federal and provincial funding support for police officer growth positions; and,
- Police personnel choosing to join another police agency or leave the police profession altogether (called the **attrition rate**).

Competition for qualified recruits, particularly women and members of visible minorities, remains steady. Box 8.2 highlights an innovative approach to recruitment in the virtual world.

BOX 8.2

VANCOUVER POLICE RECRUITING IN THE CYBERWORLD

May 30, 2007

The Vancouver Police Department is taking recruitment to a wider, more tech-savvy audience in a first-of-its kind initiative. This recruitment drive is taking place on the worldwide web in Second Life, a virtual world of over 6.7 million people from around the globe.

The VPD partnered with the masters of digital media program at the Great Northern Way Campus for assistance in making it happen. Together, the police officers involved and some of the campus staff, created their own avatars, which are the characters that inhabit this world. A meeting space for an information and recruitment seminar was designed inside the virtual campus already created by the Great Northern Way Campus. VPD recruitment officers have the ability to show video and Powerpoint presentations to the avatars that come to learn about what it takes to be a Vancouver Police officer in the real world.

"All police officers must meet eligibility requirements, but if we can get applicants with the added bonus of technology skills, that's a very good thing in this day and age," says Inspector Kevin McQuiggin, who spear-headed the initiative within the department. "Technology is changing so fast. It's important we explore new audiences for recruiting our officers."

Source: © Vancouver Police Services (http://mediareleases.vpd.ca/2007/05/30/vancouver-police-recruiting-in-the-cyberworld/)

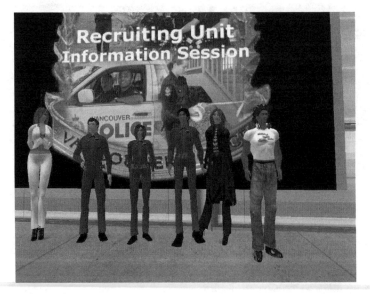

Cyber police recruits

Source: http://mediareleases.vpd.ca/2007/05/30/vancouver-police-recruiting-in-the-cyberworld/ © Vancouver Police Services

As well, there is greater competition among police services to recruit already-serving police officers. Increasingly, municipal and provincial police services and the RCMP welcome experienced and trained officers from other agencies. An experienced and trained police officer is usually exempt from a complete recruit training program and can often negotiate his or her entry level of pay, vacation leave, and a preferred posting with the new police service. The experienced officer can readily be deployed in the field with minimal training, and minimal cost, thereby providing a substantial benefit to the new police service. While it was uncommon in the past for police officers to leave their police agency and join another, many are doing just that because of flexible hiring processes and career incentives. In addition, retirement-eligible police officers continue to retire and then rejoin another law enforcement agency in order to receive both their pension and a new law enforcement salary, a practice referred to as **double dipping**. Box 8.3 describes the basic steps in the RCMP recruitment process.

There is increasing political pressure on police services to reflect the diversity of the communities they serve (recall Peel's principles from Chapter 1). This has resulted in several fundamental changes in recruitment. In particular, demographic groups such as visible ethnic minorities and women are generally in high demand by recruiting officers, who are often under pressure from senior police administrators, politicians, and community groups to increase the numbers of these groups in policing. Police services, recognizing

---

BOX 8.3

THE RCMP APPLICATION PROCESS

The Royal Canadian Mounted Police, like all Canadian police agencies, includes information about its recruitment process on its website. To apply for a job as a Regular Member of the RCMP, you **must** meet the following basic requirements:

- Be a Canadian citizen;

- Be of good character;

- Be proficient in English or French;

- Have a Canadian secondary school (high school) diploma or equivalent;

- Possess a valid, unrestricted Canadian driver's licence;

- Be at least 19 years of age at the time of engagement (may apply at 18 years of age);

- Meet medical/health standards;

- Be willing to relocate anywhere in Canada; and

- Be physically fit.

Source: Basic Requirements URL: http://www.rcmp-grc.gc.ca/recruiting-recrutement/rec/requirements-exigences-eng.htm, Department of Royal Canadian Mounted Police, 2012. Reproduced with the permission of the Minister of Public Works and Government Services Canada, 2012.

Officers in action.

Source: THE CANADIAN PRESS/John Ulan

the potential recruitment pool among visible minorities and Aboriginal people, have established a number of outreach programs with future recruitment as a primary goal. In Box 8.4, you can read about the RCMP's Aboriginal Pre-Cadet Training Program.

While minority groups have always existed within mainstream society, past recruiting practices generally promoted an all–white male profession. During the 1970s, this practice was so systemic that recruiting officers often made only minor attempts to recruit women and visible ethnic minorities. Although police services across the country have made great strides in broadening out the recruiting process, they still fall far short of reflecting the diversity of Canadian society.

BOX 8.4

THE ABORIGINAL PRE-CADET TRAINING PROGRAM

The Aboriginal Pre-Cadet Training Program (APTP) offers Canadian Aboriginal people aged 19–29 the opportunity to **experience daily police work** with the RCMP. This 17 week summer program provides candidates with hands-on experience at the RCMP Academy (Depot) and a unique opportunity to **work in or near their home community** at a detachment with RCMP police officers.

About the Program

APTP candidates attend a **three week training session** at the RCMP Academy (Depot) in Regina, Saskatchewan. The training includes collaborative problem-solving skills, law enforcement techniques, public speaking and cultural diversity. Elements of physical fitness and drill are incorporated into the training, which promote team work and provide candidates with long-term strategies to meet their personal fitness goals.

After successful completion of the APTP course, candidates are posted to an RCMP **detachment in or near their home community** where they will work with police officers for **14 weeks**. Activities and duties vary depending on the need of the detachment but they will include crime prevention and community policing initiatives.

Basic requirements:

- Be between 19–29 years of age;

- Be of First Nation, Métis or Inuit descent;

- Be a Canadian citizen;

- Be of good character;

- Be able to pass an enhanced reliability security check;

- Be in good physical condition;

- Possess a Canadian secondary school (high school) diploma or equivalent; and

- Possess and maintain a valid, unrestricted Canadian driver's licence.

Source: Aboriginal Pre-Cadet Training Program—About the Program URL: http://www.rcmp-grc.gc.ca/recruiting-recrutement/aboriginal-autochtone/aboriginal-autochtone-cadet-eng.htm Department of Royal Canadian Mounted Police, 2012. Reproduced with the permission of the Minister of Public Works and Government Services, 2012.

Today, the vast majority of recruiting officers are actively seeking out these minority groups as well as recognizing the diversity in sexual orientation in an attempt to rectify the practices of the past and to ensure adequate staffing within police organizations. As the Canadian landscape continues to change, police recruiting officers must make important inroads into communities that are underrepresented in the police population.

Canadian police agencies have adopted employment equity practices in their recruitment of police officers. Employment equity is the practice of giving preference to a visible minority or member of a target group where two equally qualified candidates, one a visible minority and the other a male Caucasian police officer, are ideally suited to a career in policing. Section 2 of the federal *Employment Equity Act* sets out the purpose and meaning of employment equity as follows:

The purpose of this Act is to achieve equality in the workplace so that no person shall be denied employment opportunities or benefits for reasons unrelated to ability and, in the fulfillment of that goal, to correct the conditions of disadvantage in employment experienced by women, Aboriginal peoples, persons with disabilities, and members of visible minorities by giving effect to the principle that employment equity means more than treating persons in the same way but also requires special measures and the accommodation of differences.

Employment equity is different from the practice of "affirmative action" (legislatively mandated hiring quotas), which was prevalent at one time in the United States. Despite employment equity practices, the demand for new police recruits, and the relatively limited supply, means virtually all suitable candidates are hired.

Gays, Lesbians, Bisexual, and Transgender Individuals

Since the 1990s, police agencies have recognized that gays, lesbians, bisexual, and transgender individuals are a part of the community they serve, and several Canadian police services are actively recruiting officers from these communities. Due to historical attitudes, this is not an easy task. At one time, police personnel often referred to gays and lesbians as deviants, and as a result it was unthinkable that such persons could be police officers. Police services did not recruit anyone who was openly homosexual. During the 1980s, this attitude slowly softened to the point that gays and lesbians were generally tolerated within police organizations, provided they did not openly disclose their sexual orientation. There do appear to be differences among police services across the country in the extent to which gays, lesbians, bisexual, and transgender individuals are actively sought as recruits and in the degree to which the officers feel comfortable with having their co-workers know about their sexual orientation.

Today, most police leaders acknowledge and support gay, lesbian, bisexual, and transgender police personnel in the workplace. This acceptance has been facilitated by human rights legislation and positive workplace laws and policies, and has been accompanied by the creation of Hate and Bias Crime units in many police services. Even with this support, however, many gay, lesbian, bisexual, and transgender officers are fearful and cautious of coming out—that is, publicly revealing their sexual orientation. Many of these officers feel that their sexual orientation is a very private matter. In addition, there is also the concern that some police officers would not work with an openly gay, lesbian, bisexual, or transgender police officer on the street. In an extreme case, they might not provide the necessary back-up that could literally save a police officer's life.

Even after these significant inroads into the police subculture, there are stereotypes that have yet to be dismantled. Interestingly, it may be considered somewhat positive to hire a lesbian police officer because she is perceived as being more macho and tougher than her straight female counterpart. The lesbian police officer may also be viewed as a more reliable employee; she is less likely to become pregnant and to leave the agency to raise a family.

In contrast, there remains the general perception within police circles that the gay male police officer is soft and not macho. Given this, gay male officers may have difficulty assimilating into a police service comprised primarily of heterosexual males.

Members of First Nations

Due to a long history of suspicion and distrust, Aboriginal people traditionally showed little interest in policing as a career. In addition, they were often categorized by police agencies as visible minorities and were thus rarely recruited. This situation has changed somewhat in recent years, and many police services are now actively seeking Aboriginal recruits. The RCMP has perhaps been the most successful, having developed and expanded its Aboriginal Policing Program, which was designed to recruit Aboriginal members. The OPP, through its Aboriginal Policing Bureau, assists First Nations police services to be self-sufficient. This includes administering policing in 19 communities that have not yet elected self-directed policing pursuant to the Ontario First Nations Policing Agreement.

You can read more information on this situation at www.opp.ca/ecms/index .php?id=80. This growth of autonomous Aboriginal police forces has also contributed to the opportunities available to Aboriginal persons interested in a policing career.

Visible and Cultural Minorities

Depending on the police agency, an individual who is a visible ethnic minority may be considered a preferred applicant. Police agencies are under increasing pressure to hire, retain, and advance visible minorities. It has been argued that in order for a police force to be effective, it must represent the community it serves. For example, a police agency serving a large Indo-Canadian population will be less than effective in dealing with policing issues related to Indo-Canadians if it does not employ police officers with a similar background. Thus, if a community has a population base in which roughly 10 percent of the individuals are visible ethnic minorities, then 10 percent of its police officers should reflect those minorities. While this idea makes sense, more research needs to be done to test whether this belief is valid. For now, it is a guiding principle in a community-based policing recruitment process.

An applicant who meets all of the qualifications necessary to be a police officer and who is a visible ethnic minority may be considered an asset to the police agency due to his or her ethnic heritage. While this may seem discriminatory on the surface, it is nonetheless a reality faced by police agencies across Canada. The principles of community policing require police services to meet this challenge. However, there is no guarantee that the community from which the visible-minority officers were recruited will openly accept them back into the community.

Even so, there is widespread agreement that minority hiring targets must not be achieved by lowering entrance standards. Both visible-minority group representatives and police leaders agree that only the best applicants should be hired. Anything else would be a disservice to the community and to the visible ethnic group represented by that individual. All applicants must therefore meet the minimum entrance standards, which are not lowered or compromised.

However, if two individuals are considered equal during this process, the tie will likely be broken in favour of the visible-minority applicant. Of course, this will depend on the specific needs of the police service and on the extent to which the composition of the service already reflects the make-up of the community that it serves.

Women

Similar to the realities facing applicants who are visible ethnic minorities, a female may now be considered a preferred applicant. In the past 15 years most police services have made great strides in hiring, retaining, and advancing female police officers. However, although women comprise approximately 45 percent of the labour force and roughly 51 percent of the population, female police officers accounted for just 20 percent (13,605) of the national police population in 2011 (Statistics Canada 2011).

Interestingly, the number of female officers in police services across Canada continued to grow in 2011, while the number of male officers decreased. There were 285 more female officers in 2011 than in 2010, while the number of male officers decreased by 97. The growth in the number of female officers recorded in recent years, especially within the higher ranks, represents a continuation of a longer-term trend. For example, in 2001 women represented 14 percent of all officers; by 2011, that proportion had risen to 20 percent. In 2011, Quebec had the highest percentage of female police officers at 24 percent. The lowest proportions were found in the Yukon, Northwest Territories, and Nunavut, with women accounting for about 13 to 14 percent of total police officers in each jurisdiction (Statistics Canada 2011).

While lowering entrance standards has generally not occurred, a number of challenges to the recruitment process have resulted in changes to entrance requirements, particularly in relation to physical fitness standards. As a result, systemic barriers for visible minorities and women have been successfully challenged and removed from the selection process. Traditionally, while the best applicant has been hired regardless of gender, employment equity considerations allow for the selection of a female candidate or an applicant who is a member of a cultural or ethnic minority over another applicant, all other qualification being equal.

For all the increasing recognition that police services should reflect the diversity of the communities they serve, this is easier said than done. A look at the official record reveals some encouraging developments, but also reveals the difficulties that police services have had in recruiting women and persons from cultural and ethnic minorities:

- Female officers are underrepresented at the senior management levels. However, over the last several years there has been a steady increase of female officers, particularly in the ranks of non-commissioned and senior officers. Over the past decade, the proportion of female officers within these ranks has almost tripled.
- Women continue to increase their overall representation in police services: while the total number of police officers has increased marginally since 1990 (14.5 percent), the number of female officers has risen from 6.4 percent of the police population in 1990 to 19.6 percent of the police population in 2011. Females now account for roughly one in five officers in Canada, compared to approximately one in ten a decade ago.
- In Toronto, female officers make up roughly 18 percent of police personnel. Diversity hiring has also increased over the past few years and currently 12.5 percent of the police officers in Toronto are visible minorities (Statistics Canada 2011; Toronto Police Service 2011).

These outcomes indicate that, overall, the recruitment strategies designed to attract more women and members of visible minorities into policing have met with moderate success. The reasons for this are complex: the failure of police services to devote the necessary resources to attract non-Anglo and female recruits; the negative perceptions of the police held by many visible minorities, based on experiences with the police in their country of origin; and the view that policing is not an honourable profession (Jain 1994).

The Controversy over Recruiting Standards for Women and Visible Minorities

A number of suggestions have been made for increasing the numbers of women and visible minorities in policing. One is the imposition of **hiring quotas**. These require police services to give hiring priority to these individuals in the recruitment and selection process and, if need be, to waive or modify traditional hiring criteria, such as physical fitness requirements, that may act to discriminate against women and visible minorities. In the past decade, police services have abolished restrictions on height, minimum weight, and age that most likely would have been found to be discriminatory in a court of law.

Critics have argued that in an attempt to catch up in recruiting members of cultural and ethnic minorities, entry requirements and training standards have been relaxed. This is certainly an accusation that would cause police administrators and recruiting officers to bristle.

An internal survey of a sample of RCMP officers from all ranks found a widespread perception that entrance standards had been lowered to accommodate women, Aboriginal peoples, and members of cultural minorities (Mofina 1996). And for several years beginning in 1997, the RCMP did modify its recruiting standards, highlighting what is a very contentious issue in policing. Today this practice has changed, although hiring practices can be modified in keeping with the federal *Employment Equity Act*, which requires the Royal Canadian Mounted Police to eliminate systemic recruitment barriers and to strive for a workforce that mirrors the complexion of the Canadian population. Recently the Supreme Court of Canada has ruled a criminal conviction cannot serve as a bar to employment in a police service (*Montréal [City] v. Quebec [Commission des droits de la personne et des droits de la jeunesse]*) 2008 SCC 48).

RECRUIT TRAINING

The big strong silent type who drives a race car and shoots straight is not the profile of tomorrow's police professional.
—*The Honourable Mr. Justice W.T. Oppal (1994)*

Training is also a cornerstone of community policing. As previously noted, it is important that officers receive the training to equip them to carry out their tasks within a community-based strategic policing framework. An underlying theme that appears throughout the training and promotion process in police services is **competency-based training**, which focuses on the acquisition of specific, measurable skills and knowledge that can then be transferred to the operational level.

To be effective, the training of police recruits in community policing should be based on a number of factors:

1. *Police officers should possess a sense of social history.* They should understand police history and the dominant approaches to policing. An understanding of the past allows the police to learn from history and, more importantly, not repeat the mistakes of the past.
2. *Police officers should have a sense of society and community.* Police should know about changes that are occurring around them that affect the decisions they make. By being made aware of trends as well as local community factors, the police will be better at developing solutions for the community.
3. *Police officers should be equipped with the skills and knowledge for incorporating community policing into their work* (Palmiotto et al. 2000). The development of knowledge and skills requires an understanding of the broadened police role, including how to implement effective working relationships with community members. The goal is to achieve a mobilized community where the police provide support, guidance, and assistance.

Subject areas in the "ideal" curriculum for recruits would include:

- a philosophy of the police department;
- organizational structure of the police department;
- social, economic, and political make-up of the community;
- cultural diversity of the community;
- police history;
- police operations;
- police mission;
- police culture;
- police discretion;
- police misconduct;
- police values and ethics;
- problem-oriented policing;
- alternative dispute resolution;
- crime prevention; and
- community-oriented policing.

Box 8.5 describes the Police Academy at the Justice Institute of British Columbia and the Recruit Training Program for Constables, and Box 8.6 outlines the four "blocks"

BOX 8.5

THE JUSTICE INSTITUTE OF BRITISH COLUMBIA—POLICE ACADEMY

The Justice Institute of British Columbia (www.jibc.bc.ca) is located in the greater Vancouver area and was established in 1978 with a mandate to train people working in the areas of justice, public safety, and human services. Within the Justice Institute, the Police Academy provides training programs to B.C. municipal police departments. The curriculum is designed upon a series of "building blocks" to ensure a balanced mix of skill training, academic education, and practical field experience relevant to policing in today's complex society.

The Recruit Training Program for Constables

In the Recruit Training Program for Constables, the candidate initially undergoes a selection process by the police service. This will typically include a written test, interviews, physical abilities and psychological testing, and successfully passing a background check and polygraph examination. Upon being hired by the police service, the candidate is then sent to the designated police academy/college for training. Although the candidate is hired and receives a salary during training, the candidate is typically expected to pay the tuition fees and other costs associated with recruit training, which can be as high as $10,000.

While at the police academy/college, the recruit will receive training in:

- driver training and traffic;
- firearms;
- arrest and control;
- investigation;
- patrol techniques;
- legal studies;
- physical fitness;
- foot drill (dress and deportment);
- the social sciences;
- report writing and police computer programs;
- use of force;
- tactical communications;
- officer safety; and
- contemporary issues, including ethics, racism, and violence against women.

Source: © JIBC - Justice Institute of British Columbia (http://www.jibc.ca/programs-courses/schools-departments/school-public-safety-security/policeacademy/programs/recruit-training)

BOX 8.6

RECRUIT TRAINING AT THE JUSTICE INSTITUTE OF B.C.—POLICE ACADEMY

The JIBC–Police Academy training program for recruit constables is structured in a series of "blocks" that serve to provide the police recruit with both formalized training and interaction with the community:

Training

The Recruit Training program is composed of three separate "blocks" of training.

- Block I: The first block of training (13 weeks) takes place at the Police Academy. It places heavy emphasis on police skills (such as driver training, firearms, arrest and control, investigation and patrol techniques), legal studies, physical fitness, foot drill (dress and deportment), and an introduction to the social sciences. The intent of Block I is to develop a relevant knowledge base for the Block II field training

- Block II: In Block II, the recruit constable returns to their home police department for a period of 13 to 17 weeks. During this field-training component, the recruit works under the guidance and continuous assistance of an experienced, specially trained constable (known as a field trainer). The field trainer is responsible for ensuring that the recruit receives a wide exposure to general police work. As a result, the recruit has the opportunity to apply the knowledge gained in Block I within an operational setting

- Block III: In Block III (8 weeks), the recruit constable returns to the Police Academy, bringing experience from the "street scene." This block builds on the knowledge of Block I, and the practical experience of Block II, to prepare the recruit to function independently upon graduation. After successfully completing Block III, the recruit graduates as a "Qualified Municipal Constable" that is designated by regulation, pursuant to the Police Act

During Blocks I and III the police recruit is trained within a classroom setting. However, during Block II, the recruit is assigned to a field trainer with the police service in the community that he or she will police upon graduation. During this critical Block II phase of training, the recruit learns the applied components of policing that include understanding the community that he or she will serve.

Source: © JIBC - Justice Institute of British Columbia (http://jibc.ca/programs-courses/schools-departments/school-public-safety-security/policeacademy/programs/recruit-training)

of a new police officer's learning development through the Justice Institute of British Columbia.

Although community policing was once only one of many specialty subjects taught to recruits, today the philosophy and practice of community policing permeates all facets of recruit training. There are, as well, core areas in recruit training where community policing and problem solving are reinforced. The Royal Canadian Mounted Police integrates the CAPRA problem-based model throughout their cadet curriculum (recall from Chapter 5, page 126, that CAPRA stands for *clients, acquire/analyze* information, *partnerships, response,* and *assessment*). The goal of this approach is to have police officers apply CAPRA to operational and organizational problems.

The community policing philosophy focuses on a number of questions, including the following:

- What is the best way to resolve this complex issue within the parameters of the law?
- What is best for the community and the individual?
- How can the police, as only one component of society, solve this problem best?
- How can the police best meet the needs of the community they serve?

The underlying theme of the training is problem solving or problem-based learning and understanding the community that they serve.

From the Academy to the Street: Operational Field Training

Becoming a police officer involves two distinct socialization processes: formal socialization is accomplished through the selection process and police training programs. These provide the new recruit with a vast amount of information on myriad subjects related to policing. Informal socialization takes place as recruits interact with older, more experienced officers and with their peers on the job.

These two processes of socialization may conflict with one another, if only because of the differences between classroom learning and the skill development that comes with experience on the street. It was not uncommon in the past for new recruits to be told by veteran officers to forget what they learned in the training academy because they were now street cops. Somehow, street officers perceived an incompatibility with what was taught in the training academy and the way it "really" was on the street.

Today, police services give increasing attention to ensuring continuity between the training that a recruit receives in the academy and the supervision that is provided once the new recruit is involved in operational policing. A model of instruction, called **problem-based learning**, has been implemented across Canada, including at RCMP Depot, Justice Institute of British Columbia, and both Calgary and Edmonton Police Services. The model presents actual problems a police officer would encounter on patrol and encourages the police officer to apply their knowledge across a number of subject areas to solve the problem. This also assists in establishing limits on the acceptable use of police discretion.

Upon completing recruit training, the individual officer is usually assigned to general patrol duties for three to five years. After this initial indoctrination to the fundamentals of policing, the individual officer will receive additional in-service training. For the most part, in-service training is designed to teach the basic skills of police work by complementing both recruit training and the hands-on experience that the new officer has received in the field.

It is during this second component of the training process, known as **operational field training**, when the recruit will learn to apply the basic principles taught at the training academy. Under the guidance of a senior officer, the recruit is exposed to a wide variety of general police work. During this critical phase, the specially trained senior officer (often referred to as the "field trainer," "officer coach," or mentor) ensures that the recruit can handle the demands and challenges of police work. A primary objective of the field trainer is to enhance the skills and knowledge the recruit has learned at the academy. While the selection of the field trainer is critical for the ongoing learning and professional development of the new officer, it is not uncommon to find very inexperienced officers acting as coaches. This is due primarily to the significant levels of recruitment over the last several years, resulting in very limited levels of experience among frontline patrol officers. In many instances this is also occurring among supervisory levels as well, causing many to observe a crisis in experience where it is needed most.

IN-SERVICE TRAINING

Training provided to police officers during the course of their career—variously referred to as **in-service training**, refresher training, requalification training, advanced training, and career development training—is usually conducted by individual police agencies, provincial training centres, or at the Canadian Police College in Ottawa.

A high level of demonstrated skill is expected during firearms training for recruit constables at the Police Academy and during annual firearm qualifications for all police personnel.

Source: © Atlantic Police Academy. P.E.I.

The purpose of in-service training is to provide police personnel with ongoing professional development in operational, investigative, and administrative skills that are relevant to their current assignment or one that they will soon be filling. Typically, these training courses are highly sought after and are often viewed as a reward for competent and dedicated service to the police agency. In some instances, the in-service training may be a necessary component for the re-assignment of the officer to a specialized section such as traffic enforcement or the drug section.

Advanced in-service training may include the following:

- *Administrative skills for police supervisors.* A course designed for police personnel that have recently been promoted or are soon to be promoted to a supervisory position.
- *Basic collision investigation.* A course designed to provide advanced skills and recommended techniques in traffic collision investigation.
- *Advanced collision investigation.* A course designed to provide technical knowledge in the area of crash sciences by facilitating investigative skills in collision analysis and collision reconstruction.
- *Control tactics instructor.* An instructor-level course designed to develop expertise in the area of use of force, handcuffing, weapons, compliance tools (e.g., pepper spray, baton), and handgun retention.
- *Crisis (hostage) negotiator.* A course designed to develop skills and techniques in negotiating the release of hostages or in the surrender of barricaded persons.
- *Drug investigator training.* A course designed to provide prospective drug investigators with the knowledge, skills, and techniques that relate to the search and seizure of drugs, including informant control, statements and confessions, and undercover operations.
- *Firearms instructor program.* An instructor-level course designed to develop expertise in the area of firearms and the instructional techniques needed to conduct firearms training in the police service.
- *Forensic DNA evidence.* A course designed to provide police officers with the necessary skills to investigate serious violent crimes and to accurately collect and process DNA evidence.
- *Forensic interviewing techniques.* A course designed to enable police officers to interview complainants, victims, witnesses, and suspects to obtain accurate, detailed, and relevant information that will aid in an investigation and will be admissible in court.

- *General investigative skills.* A course designed for plainclothes police officers (detectives) in an investigative role, providing skills that include evidence handling, crime scene management, interviewing or interrogation, and forensic identification.
- *Media relations.* A course designed to enable police officers to disseminate information to the community via the print and electronic media, including skills to utilize when interacting with the media in general.
- *Police supervisors.* A course designed to provide training in the necessary abilities, skills, and knowledge that are required for effective supervision and leadership.
- *Problem-oriented policing.* A course designed to enhance the operational police officer's skills and knowledge of community policing, the SARA model of problem-oriented policing, and crime analysis.
- *School liaison officers.* A course designed to provide police officers with the necessary intervention and prevention techniques related to youths, including skills that foster informal and formal interaction with youth in the classroom and in the community.
- *Search and seizure.* A course designed to provide police officers with knowledge pertaining to the search warrant process and skills essential to conducting a lawful search and seizure.

It is also important that officers have access to continuing education and information once they are on the job. There is a trend in Canadian police services toward integrating in-service training with career development and requiring that officers achieve certain educational and training competencies in order to apply for promotion. Many police services have developed in-service training programs to ensure that officers keep abreast of changes in legislation, policy, court decisions, and departmental procedures. This includes the use of learning technology, referred to as **e-learning**, to provide continual training to officers in the field. The Calgary Police Service, like most police services across Canada, has utilized a computer program, called TRACCESS, in which organizationally important learning modules are developed. Police officers must work their way through the interactive programs and complete a test at the end of each module. Officers can work their way through a module any hour of the day. This mode of learning is ideal for ensuring police officers clearly understand critical aspects of policing, such as pursuit policy, civil property disputes, and domestic violence.

Similarly, the Canadian Police Knowledge Network (CPKN) is a not-for-profit organization providing online in-service training for Canadian police officers. CPKN was created by, and specifically for, members of the Canadian police community. Working with subject matter experts from police training academies and police services across Canada, CPKN provides training to meet police-specific situations, protocols, and tactics and is available to all police officers across Canada. The Canadian Police Knowledge Network is available online at www.cpkn.ca.

The Royal Canadian Mounted Police also has developed an online learning system to better serve its members, which is accessible at www.rcmp-grc.gc.ca/ctb-fc/index-eng.htm. This "distance delivery" approach is excellent for reaching all members of the RCMP, whether in remote parts of Canada or involved in international assignments.

ON THE LINE: THE NEW COMMUNITY POLICE OFFICER

The new police officer becomes a thinking professional, utilizing imagination and creativity to identify and solve problems ... the police officer is encouraged to develop co-operative relationships in the community, guided by values and purposes, rather than constrained by rules and excessive supervision.

—*E. Meese (1993)*

Two key elements of community policing are the decentralization of decision making and the empowerment of line officers to collaborate with community residents in

Figure 8.1 Modes of Response

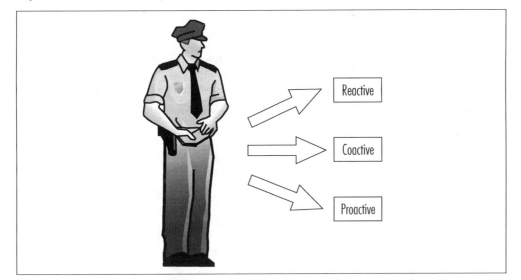

Source: Modes of Response from *Personnel Performance Evaluations in the Community Policing Context,* 1997. Oettmeier and Wycoff pg.22

problem solving. This has been described as a coactive response. This term recognizes the importance of citizen–police partnerships. Either party can identify conditions that need to be addressed to increase the safety of a neighbourhood. It is coactive because citizens and police work collaboratively to define and design the response to threatening conditions. The coactive role of police officers in a community policing framework does not replace the reactive and proactive roles of the police; rather, it expands the role of the police by broadening the capacity of police officers to address the causes of crime and disorder (see Figure 8.1). It is therefore essential that the necessary reforms be made to provide an opportunity for officers to assume a new role.

The Community Police Officer as a Generalist

Within the framework of community policing, the community police officer (CPO) is viewed as a **generalist** who is supported by specialists within the police service. The term "generalist" means that line officers have the authority, discretion, and skills to develop partnerships with the community in the area they are assigned and to apply various strategies to solve problems of crime and social disorder. In many police services, of course, patrol constables have always been generalists, particularly officers in smaller police services. In large, urban police services, however, the trend over the past several decades has been toward increasing the specialization of officers.

The CPO is the primary conduit through which the police service reaches out to the community and engages residents in identifying and responding to problems. As well, CPOs are a primary referral source to other agencies and organizations that may be able to address specific concerns and issues. CPOs, however, cannot be expected to be experts in all areas, and the police service must provide the support of specialists when required. Also, CPOs must have access to information gathered and analyzed by the police service. As Taylor (1999:66) notes, "Good community policing depends on gathering and analyzing accurate information."

For CPOs to be successful, the police service must meet a number of conditions:

- It must take a client-oriented approach to dealing with the community.
- It must focus on solving community problems.
- It must deploy patrol officers based on clear objectives.
- It must assign officers to defined areas where they can consult with residents and other agencies.

- It must provide resources and specialist expertise in support of patrol officers.
- It must embrace demand-driven policing that considers short-, medium-, and long-term demands on police services (Taylor 1999:28–29).

Placing police officers in the role of generalists is, in the words of a certain baseball hall-of-famer, Yogi Berra, "déjà vu all over again." Check back to the description of the various roles that police constables played in communities in the early days of police forces. These officers were generalists as well, and had an even wider range of responsibilities and activities, such as tax collector, chimney inspector, and animal pound keeper. And officers in rural and remote areas of the country have always assumed a variety of roles, both out of necessity and because many RCMP, OPP, and Sûreté du Québec detachments are quite small. It was mainly in the larger urban police services that officers slowly drifted away from contact with the community and tended toward increasing specialization. As noted in Chapter 1, the loss of contact with the community was precipitated largely by the introduction of the police patrol car and the demise of beat policing, which has now made a comeback within the framework of community policing.

THE POLICE PERSONALITY AND COMMUNITY POLICING

After completing academy and field training, the new officer becomes a full-fledged member of the police service and begins the process of adopting the attitudes that distinguish the occupation of police work. Research on the police occupation has resulted in the development of a number of key concepts that provide insights into the attitudes, perceptions, and behaviour of police officers. Many of these concepts are components of what Jerome Skolnick (1966) labelled the **working personality of police officers**, a set of attitudinal and behavioural attributes that develop as a consequence of the unique role that police officers play and the duties they are asked to perform. While the work may be dated, it remains relevant today.

Attributes of the Police Working Personality

Characteristics of the working personality include a preoccupation with danger, excessive suspiciousness of people and activities, a protective cynicism, and difficulties in exercising authority—that is, in balancing the rights of citizens under the *Canadian Charter of Rights and Freedoms* with the need to maintain order.

As a consequence of these personality attributes, many police officers:

- tend to view policing as a career and a way of life, rather than merely a nine-to-five job;
- value secrecy and practise a code of silence to protect fellow officers;
- exhibit strong in-group solidarity—often referred to as the *blue wall*—with other police officers due to job-related stresses, shift work, and an "us versus them" division between police and nonpolice (Goldsmith 1990);
- tend to hold conservative political and moral views; and
- exhibit attitudes that emphasize the high-risk/action component of police work—often referred to as the *blue-light syndrome*.

Although individual patrol officers have their own styles of policing, and although not every officer exhibits all of the characteristics of the working personality, it is a useful concept for understanding the police occupation and the behaviour of officers in certain situations, especially if the police organization is seeking to establish a major change initiative.

The extent to which this typology is useful for studying Canadian police services cannot be determined at this time. Not all police services are the same, and the police organizations in which officers carry out their tasks may differ on a number of key dimensions. What is clear, however, is that police officers and their style of policing are influenced by a number of environmental factors that combine to shape their perceptions. For example, following the terrorist acts of September 11, 2001, a much stronger commitment to national security, images of terrorism and terrorists, and perceptions of safety have imprinted themselves on the psyche of modern Canadian police in ways that have not been studied but need to be understood. If attitudes drive behaviours, then many contemporary examples of police misconduct, particularly in relation to the use of force, are likely rooted in the "working personality" of police officers.

The Occupational Subculture of Police and Community Policing

In the four decades since Skolnick first proposed the existence of an occupational subculture of police and identified the components of the working personality of police officers, there has been a considerable amount of debate about the validity of his arguments.

One question relates to the extent to which the isolation of police officers, their in-group solidarity, and their traditional distrust and suspicion of the general public are undermined by emerging trends in policing. These trends include the move toward community policing, the decentralization of traditional command and control structures, the empowerment of line officers, the growing number of partnerships being developed between police and communities, the increasing reliance on restorative justice approaches (see Chapter 9), and the changing face of police recruits. To counter negative aspects of the occupational subculture, police organizations have spent considerable time and effort developing codes of professional conduct and values statements, as well as ethics training to serve as guideposts for professional police conduct and service to the community. Box 8.7 examines the core values of Canadian police officers.

A second question relates to how the organizational and operational environment in which police officers carry out their work affects the various attributes of a police personality. Police officers assigned to community police stations or posted to small detachments in remote areas of the country, for example, have little choice but to interact with community residents. We have previously noted that police officers carry out their tasks in a variety of environments, ranging from small Inuit villages to large metropolitan areas.

Also, there may be two distinct subcultures within police services: one of senior police managers focused on delivering services within the framework of community policing, and the other of line officers focused on the operational realities of day-to-day police work (Dean 1995; Goldsmith 1990). There may be considerable distance between

---

BOX 8.7

CORE VALUES IN POLICE SERVICES ACROSS CANADA

In Chapter 6 we examined mission statements as well as organizational values. The values of various Canadian departments are included below. Do you see similarities between them?

- Toronto Police Service: "Honesty, Integrity, Fairness, Respect, Reliability, Teamwork, Positive Attitude"

- Edmonton Police Service: "Integrity, Accountability, Respect, Innovation, Courage, and Community"

- Ontario Provincial Police: "Professionalism, Accountability, Diversity, Respect, Excellence." In 2010, the OPP added a sixth value: Leadership.

- Vancouver Police: "Integrity, Professionalism, Accountability, Respect"

- Royal Canadian Mounted Police: "Integrity, Honesty, Professionalism, Compassion, Respect and Accountability" these two, even within the same police service. The success of police managers is often measured by the extent to which they can convince patrol officers to support the goals of the organization and incorporate its objectives into daily patrol practice.

In sum, the "us (police) versus them (public)" dichotomy is much too general to capture the variety of relationships that exist between the public and the police and the differences that exist among police officers themselves in how the police role is carried out (Herbert 1998).

The Positive and Negative Features of the Police Subculture

The subculture that exists among police officers has many positive features. Given the unpredictability of their work and the potential for violence, officers must develop camaraderie among themselves. Such group solidarity helps individual officers cope with the more stressful aspects of police work, and is also a source of support.

Even so, there are a number of drawbacks, such as:

- police alienation from the general public and other agencies and organizations;
- police officer alienation from management;
- establishment of "symbolic" criminals; that is, people who "look like" criminals or terrorists; and
- resistance to change, including community policing, that could assist in addressing personal and organizational problems.

In sum, while it may not be possible to document the existence of a distinct police personality statistically, and while a considerable amount of mythology surrounds police work, many police officers believe that they have a working personality that sets them apart as an occupational group. This belief in itself may make the working personality of police a reality. The occupational perspectives of police officers may have a significant impact on operational patrol work and decision making (police discretion) in situations on the street and in case investigations.

This decision-making process and the influence of the police subculture upon the individual community police officer is a growing concern. Throughout Canada, there is a heightened awareness, and visibility, regarding the ethical conduct and professionalism of police officers.

For the new recruit, one factor in reducing the "inward" influence of the police subculture is in maintaining outside friendships and taking part in community life outside of policing:

Outside friendships help to bring down the "blue wall" between police and those they serve, and to combat the insular nature of the police culture that can help corruption to breed. If you want to be a well-rounded officer, you must understand your community. Your community will keep you grounded (Toronto Police Superintendent Keith Forde, Officer I/C, Charles O. Bick Police College).

PATROL OFFICER RESISTANCE TO COMMUNITY POLICING

Departments converting to community policing might ... be wise to recognize that there is a large body of research which suggests that rank and file police officers prefer the "law enforcement" role over the "order maintenance" and "service delivery roles."

—*K. Polowek (1995)*

Experience suggests that many front-line patrol officers may resist the concept of community policing. This opposition may have several sources.

Distrust of Senior Police Leaders

Officers often distrust pronouncements about community policing made by senior police administrators. This response is based, in part, on experiences with past reforms and projects that produced few tangible results. In a survey of a sample of police officers in British Columbia, 29 percent felt that community policing was "just a public relations" exercise (Murphy and Griffiths 1994). In a secret ballot conducted in Halifax in 1996, 87 percent of police officers indicated that they were in favour of returning to a "more traditional" style of policing (*Halifax Daily News* 1996:4).

Fear of Being Marginalized

Patrol officers often fear being marginalized by other officers and certain of their supervisors. Those officers who are extensively involved in community policing initiatives are often facetiously referred to as "the rubber gun squad" by other police officers who subscribe to a more traditional, crime-control model of police work. The term originated in the New York City police department, where officers who experience stress-related disorders have their working guns replaced with rubber ones. It can be anticipated that as the culture of police services changes from one centred on traditional police practices to one focused on community policing, the levels of marginalization will decrease.

Lack of Time

Many patrol officers feel that they do not have time to do community policing—a perception that is often grounded in reality. In the absence of a clear framework for implementation and clearly stated objectives, patrol officers may view community policing as merely adding to their workload. In fact, increasing call loads, excessive paperwork, and cutbacks in resources and in the number of police personnel may make it difficult for officers to work on establishing partnerships with the community and to solve problems. Generally speaking, if the police service has not adopted corporate practices such as strategic plans, business plans, and service performance indicators, and created the conditions for police to engage in proactive activities, then patrol officers are probably correct in feeling they don't have time.

In a study of community policing in British Columbia, a high percentage of a sample of RCMP and municipal police officers indicated that they did not have time to do community policing, due to already heavy workloads (Murphy and Griffiths 1994). This reflects the widespread view that community policing is a programmatic "add-on" to the core activities of the police. And it also reflects the reality that patrol officers are often not provided with the organizational and operational frameworks within which to become community police officers. Many police organizations across Canada have begun to address this issue by engaging in workload analysis studies to determine how busy police officers actually are, and how workload can be redistributed to make more available time for police officers. You will recall our discussion in Chapter 7 about staffing to workload as opposed to staffing based on population to police officer ratios ("pop to cop"). The RCMP, Vancouver Police Department, Calgary and Edmonton Police Services, and Durham Regional Police Service have all developed staffing models based on an analysis of workload.

Performance Evaluations

Most performance evaluations currently used by police agencies do not reflect the work officers do. Evaluations typically consist of compliance audits, statistical comparisons, or descriptive summaries of events.

—*T.N. Oettmeier and M.A. Wycoff (1997)*

The implementation of community policing has resulted in an expansion of the role and activities of many police patrol officers, and of the expectations of both community residents and senior police administrators. The criteria used to assess the performance of line officers must reflect the myriad tasks and activities they are involved in. Many police services have implemented **competency-based performance evaluations**, which assess observable behaviours, knowledge, and skills directed toward the achievement of organizational objectives. The *National Diagnostic on Human Resources in Policing, 2007* describes competency-based performance management in the following way:

… a competency as any skill, knowledge or other attribute, which leads to superior performance at work. The principle is that if we understand what separates "the best" from "the rest," then we can:

- focus recruitment on finding people who will have what it takes to be a strong performer,
- focus performance management system towards individual acquisition of missing competencies so that they can be more like the best performers, and
- develop talent for the future that will leverage people's strengths and place them in roles where they are more likely to be successful thus developing a high performance organization (Hay Group 2007).

While consensus among police human resource professionals favours a competency-based developmental approach (see Box 8.8), there is still a tendency to recognize and reward officer performance based on reactive, law enforcement–oriented police work—despite the creation of mission and value statements that incorporate the principles of community policing, and despite the development of new programs in the community.

In a study in British Columbia, municipal police officers were asked to assign a relative weight (low, medium, high) to a number of factors they felt should be used in evaluating their performance. The responses of the officers for each factor are presented in Table 8.3.

The officers surveyed generally felt that the traditional measures of police performance, such as the number of tickets issued and arrests made and the number of criminal convictions, should not be used in evaluating their performance. Rather, the officers believed that more emphasis should be placed on the skills required to do the job and on the effectiveness of officers in solving community problems. When these same officers were asked to rank the importance of a number of police activities, 98 percent ranked "responding to emergency calls" and 65 percent ranked "building better relationships with the community" as "most important" or "important."

BOX 8.8

THE CANADIAN POLICING COMPETENCY FRAMEWORK

The Police Sector Council recently collaborated with policing executives from across Canada to develop a competency framework and tools to support all aspects of strategic human resource management for the policing industry as a whole. This work involved leveraging existing best practices and knowledge within the policing sector to develop a nationally relevant system.

The **Policing Competency Framework** provides the policing industry with a common language and understanding of the work and underlying competency requirements associated with general policing duties for all ranks: Constable, Sergeant, Staff Sergeant, Inspector, Superintendent, Chief Superintendent, Deputy Chief, and Chief. This framework was developed by leveraging the best practices from police services across Canada and working with the policing community to fully analyze and document the job responsibilities of each rank. The resulting Framework includes Job Descriptions, Task Lists, Competency Profiles and a Policing Competency Dictionary.

Source: Police Sector Council (http://www.policecouncil.ca/pages/research.html)

Table 8.3 Officer Ratings of the Importance of Criteria for Assessing Performance

	Low	Medium	High
Number of tickets/arrests	26 percent	55 percent	17 percent
Number of criminal convictions	33 percent	47 percent	17 percent
Community involvement	16 percent	59 percent	22 percent
Skills (interviewing, report writing, etc.)	0.9 percent	27 percent	70 percent
Appearance	10 percent	55 percent	34 percent
Lack of citizen complaints	33 percent	43 percent	22 percent
Effectiveness in solving community problems	12 percent	45 percent	40 percent

Source: Copyright © Province of British Columbia. All Rights Reserved. Reprinted with permission of the Province of British Columbia. www.ipp.gov.bc.ca

In an effort to develop more relevant criteria for performance evaluation, a task force in Houston, Texas, gathered information from a representative sample of officers, who kept a record of their actual work during shifts. This information was in turn used to create new performance criteria based on the work the officers did in the neighbourhoods to which they were assigned. The tasks and activities of the officers are presented in Table 8.4.

Table 8.4 Tasks and Activities of Patrol Officers

1. Learn characteristics of area, residents, businesses
   a. Study beat books
   b. Analyze crime and calls-for-service data
   c. Drive, walk area, and make notes
   d. Talk with community representatives
   e. Conduct area surveys
   f. Maintain area/suspect logs
   g. Read area papers (e.g., "shopper" papers)
   h. Discuss area with citizens when answering calls
   i. Talk with private security personnel in area
   j. Talk with area business owners/managers
2. Become acquainted with leaders in area
   a. Attend community meetings, including service club meetings
   b. Ask questions in surveys about who formal and informal area leaders are
   c. Ask area leaders for names of other leaders
3. Make residents aware of who officer is and what he or she is trying to accomplish in area
   a. Initiate citizen contacts
   b. Distribute business cards
   c. Discuss purpose at community meeting
   d. Discuss purpose when answering calls
   e. Write article for local paper
   f. Contact home-bound elderly
   g. Encourage citizens to contact officer directly
4. Identify area problems
   a. Attend community meetings
   b. Analyze crime and calls-for-service data
   c. Contact citizens and businesses
   d. Conduct business and residential surveys
   e. Ask about other problems when answering calls

(continues)

5. Communicate with supervisors, other officers, and citizens about the nature of the area and its problems
   a. Maintain beat bulletin board in station
   b. Leave notes in boxes of other officers
   c. Discuss area with supervisor
6. Investigate/do research to determine sources of problems
   a. Talk to people involved
   b. Analyze crime data
   c. Observe situation if possible (stakeout)
7. Plan ways of dealing with problems
   a. Analyze resources
   b. Discuss with supervisor, other officers
   c. Write patrol management plan, review with supervisor
8. Provide citizens information about ways they can handle problems (educate/ empower)
   a. Distribute crime prevention information
   b. Provide names and number of other responsible agencies; tell citizens how to approach these agencies
9. Help citizens develop appropriate expectations about what police can do and teach them how to interact effectively with police
   a. Attend community meetings/make presentations
   b. Present school programs
   c. Write article for area paper
   d. Hold discussions with community leaders
10. Develop resources for responding to problem
    a. Talk with other officers, detectives, supervisors
    b. Talk with other agencies or individuals who could help
11. Implement problem solution
    a. Take whatever actions are called for
12. Assess effectiveness of solution
    a. Use data, feedback from persons who experienced the problem, and/or personal observation to determine whether problem has been solved
13. Keep citizens informed
    a. Officers tell citizens what steps have been taken to address a problem and with what results
    b. Detectives tell citizens what is happening with their cases

Source: Oettmeier, T.N., and M.A. Wycoff, 1997. *Personnel Performance Evaluations in the Community Policing Context.* Washington, DC: Police Executive Research Forum. pp. 382–83.

Lack of Training or Experience with Community Policing

Patrol officers may have little training or experience in how to do community policing and the strategies and skills required to work with community residents and organizations. Community police officers must have a variety of skills, ranging from those associated with case investigation and apprehending offenders to the ability to build partnerships with the community, to engage in problem-solving policing, and to meet the demands of policing in specific types of neighbourhoods. Officers without the personal attributes compatible with community policing, or without the necessary training to do community policing, may become frustrated and turn into an obstacle to the efforts of the police service. Initial and in-service training, combined with a supportive organizational environment, are critical to the success of individual CPOs. Also, many officers still equate crime prevention and community relations activities with community policing—a misperception that can only be corrected by education and training. In response to this deficiency, several Canadian police services have worked with post-secondary institutions to develop community policing courses. Dalhousie

University in Halifax, Nova Scotia, offers a Police Leadership Certificate, which includes two courses on community-based strategic policing. Across Canada, there are a number of post-secondary institutions that have partnered with police agencies to augment learning opportunities in community-based policing. You can find more information out about some of these programs at the following websites: Management Development for Police Services, at www.extension.ualberta.ca/study/management/mdps/; a police studies program through Simon Fraser University, at www.sfu.ca/criminology/ugrad/ PoliceStudies.html; and B.A. Police Studies, offered by the University of Regina, at www.uregina.ca/gencal/ugcal/facultyofArts/ugcal_209.shtml.

Absence of Patrol Officer Input into Community Strategies and Plans

Patrol officers may not have participated in the development of plans for service delivery, and there may be an absence of direction from senior management. Front-line officers must be intimately involved in the development of policing policies and programs. Often, police leaders have attempted to impose community policing and to implement various programs without adequate consultation with patrol officers. Senior police managers and line patrol officers may disagree about the extent to which community policing should be implemented. Officers in some police services feel they have not been empowered to identify and resolve problems in the communities they police.

Our discussion of community policing in Ontario in Chapter 3 revealed that there has often been a lack of communication between senior management and front-line officers, as well as a lack of training to provide patrol officers with the skills required to develop partnerships with the community and do problem-solving policing. As a result, patrol officers have often been confused about what exactly they are supposed to be doing and what expectations senior management and the community have of them. Ultimately, these problems will undermine attempts to adopt and implement community policing.

CHAPTER SUMMARY

In this chapter, we have focused on the community policing officer. Community policing places specific types of demands on police officers. This is reflected in the significant changes that have occurred in the recruitment of new police officers. Police services are increasingly expected to reflect the diversity of the communities they police, and this has resulted in an emphasis on hiring women, members of First Nations, and visible and cultural minorities, as well as gays, lesbians, bisexual, and transgender individuals. There has also been an emphasis on promoting women within the ranks and into senior officer positions.

Police training has also changed. Community policing permeates all facets of recruit training at the Justice Institute of British Columbia–Police Academy and other police training facilities across the country. Despite this major change, the characteristics of the occupational subculture of police and the resistance of officers may undermine community policing efforts. For those officers with the necessary skills, motivation, and organizational support, however, a number of tools and techniques can be used to implement community policing in the areas to which they have been assigned.

In Chapter 10, we will focus on how police officers can work with communities to establish partnerships and to identify and solve problems of crime and social disorder.

CHAPTER REVIEW

Key Terms
- attrition rate, p. 245
- basic qualifications, p. 242

- competency-based performance evaluations, p. 262
- competency-based training, p. 251
- diversity, p. 244
- double dipping, p. 246
- e-learning, p. 256
- generalist, p. 257
- hiring quotas, p. 251
- in-service training, p. 254
- operational field training, p. 254
- Policing Competency Framework, p. 262
- preferred qualifications, p. 242
- problem-based learning, p. 254
- working personality of police officers, p. 258

Key Points

- There is increasing pressure on police services to reflect the diversity of the communities they police.
- Police services are attempting with moderate success to recruit more women, members of First Nations, and visible and cultural minorities.
- Police services are competing with other law enforcement/public safety agencies for a limited pool of suitable applicants.
- Police training is becoming more centred on community policing and problems.
- Operational field training must complement the training received by recruits at the police academy/college.
- Community police officers are generalists who have the skills and knowledge to carry out a number of roles and mandates within the framework of community policing.
- CPOs can be effective only if they have the support of their police service and are given the discretion, autonomy, and resources they need to carry out their tasks.
- There are a number of sources of resistance to community policing among police officers that can undermine efforts of a police service to develop partnerships with the community and have officers be problem solvers.

Self-Evaluation

QUESTIONS

1. What role does the concept of **diversity** play in the recruitment of police officers?
2. What is meant by **hiring quotas**, and why is this term often mentioned in discussions of police recruiting?
3. Describe the components of the **Recruit Training Program**.
4. What are the **basic qualifications** required by police services in the recruitment process?
5. Discuss what is meant by **preferred qualifications**, and note what role these play in the recruitment process.
6. What is **competency-based training**, and what role does it play in police training?
7. Describe the importance of **operational field training**.
8. What is **in-service training**, what type of courses are offered, and what role does it play in the training of police officers?
9. Discuss how the **decentralization** of decision making and the **empowerment** of line officers can result in effective problem-solving.
10. Describe what is meant by the **working personality of police officers**, and then note the importance of this concept for our study of community policing.
11. What is meant by the community police officer as **generalist?**
12. Discuss how core values within a police service serve to influence the police **subculture**.

KEY IDEAS

1. In the police recruiting process, what is the term for things like citizenship, age, physical abilities, and common sense and good judgment?
   a. nonessential abilities
   b. preferred qualifications
   c. standard abilities
   d. basic qualifications

2. Which of the following have Canadian police services done in recent years?
   a. attempted to avoid hiring people who are visible minorities
   b. continued to maintain regulations that prohibit the hiring of gays, lesbians, bisexual, and transgender individuals
   c. experienced moderate success in attracting qualified women and members of visible minorities
   d. hired large numbers of women, so that female officers now comprise nearly 30 percent of police personnel across the country

3. According to recent figures, what percentage of police officers nationwide are women?
   a. 10 percent to 15 percent
   b. 16 percent to 20 percent
   c. 21 percent to 25 percent
   d. 26 percent to 30 percent

4. What percentage of police officers nationwide are members of First Nations and visible and cultural minorities?
   a. fewer than 10 percent
   b. about 15 percent
   c. 20 percent
   d. 25 percent

5. Overall, recruitment strategies designed to attract more women and members of visible minorities into policing have had moderate success. This is because of which of the following factors?
   a. the general lack of "specialty incentives" that exist once an individual is hired
   b. difficulties encountered in the physical testing process
   c. the failure of police services to devote the necessary resources to attract non-Anglo and female recruits
   d. height requirements that tend to prevent many individuals from applying to become police officers

6. How have some police services increased the numbers of women and visible and cultural minorities in policing?
   a. reducing the entrance standards
   b. establishing hiring quotas
   c. raising pay levels
   d. offering a hiring bonus and covering expenses related to relocating

7. What is the term for police training that focuses on the acquisition of specific, measurable skills and knowledge that can be transferred to the operational level?
   a. competency-based training
   b. hard skills training
   c. soft skills training
   d. intensive, professional training

8. Which of the following is true according to research studies on police services?
   a. Officers in some police services who participate in community policing initiatives are paid a bonus.
   b. Officers who participate in community police initiatives are guaranteed a high status among patrol officers.
   c. In some police services, officer performance assessments are still based on traditional police work.
   d. In some police services, officer promotions are based upon community policing initiatives.

9. Which statement best defines the "working personality" of police officers?
   a. a term used to describe the attitudes and behaviours of police officers
   b. one of many personalities that police officers may have while on duty
   c. a discredited term that cannot be used to describe why police officers behave the way they do
   d. the personality changes that occur from initial recruit training to working in the field

10. What statement best describes "employment equity" hiring practices?
    a. a legislated "quota"-based hiring practice
    b. a preferential hiring system focusing on visible minorities and other identified groups
    c. a form of affirmative action to right the wrongs of systemic discrimination
    d. a salary policy of "like pay for like work"

11. The RCMP integrates the CAPRA model throughout its recruit-training curriculum. The goal of this approach is to have police recruits deal with operational and organizational challenges by utilizing which of the following models?
    a. a theoretical model toward community-based policing
    b. a problem-solving model
    c. an individual decision-making model based upon education and experience
    d. a corporate business practice model

The Community Police Officer: Situations and Strategies

Community Policing Implementation Checklist

There are a number of questions that should be asked to determine whether officers in a police service are recruited, trained, and deployed within a community policing framework. These include:

Recruiting and Training

- In recruiting and screening prospective officers, does the police service emphasize individuals with the skills and interest to do community policing?
- Are new recruits trained in the principles and practices of community policing, including problem-solving skills, strategies for identifying and mobilizing community residents and resources, and communication skills?
- Do new recruits learn about a variety of crime attack strategies and crime prevention approaches and their effectiveness?
- Do new recruits receive cultural sensitivity training on the specific challenges in policing visible minority communities and neighbourhoods, and strategies for involving residents in these communities in police–community partnerships?
- Do new recruits learn about Aboriginal history and cultures and how to police communities with Aboriginal residents effectively?

Deployment of Officers

- Are officers responsible for policing, problem solving, and establishing partnerships with residents in a specific zone or turf?
- Are officers assigned to a specific area for an extended period of time so that they have the opportunity to become familiar with the neighbourhoods and their residents?
- Do the residents in the community or neighbourhood know any of the officers by name?
- Do officers have the authority to establish committees composed of community members and to engage in problem-solving activities?
- Are officers familiar with the key strategies of community policing, including problem-oriented policing, situational crime prevention, and crime prevention through social development (see Chapter 9)?
- Do line officers understand the principles and practice of community policing, and do officers have access to ongoing training and information sessions?
- Do officers have the opportunity to participate in integrated service teams, working with professionals from other agencies and organizations?
- Are officers familiar with the resources and sources of support available within the community, including shelters, safe houses, youth street workers, and mental health workers?
- Are officers familiar with the philosophy and practices of community policing and how the principles of this model can be adapted to meet the needs and concerns of individual communities and neighbourhoods?
- If the officers are assigned to a neighbourhood with a high population of visible minorities or to a predominately Aboriginal community, do the officers have an understanding of the history, culture, and dynamics of the particular community?
- Do officers receive departmental recognition for accomplishments in the community?
- Apart from the ordinary cynicism that arises on the job, do officers respect the communities and residents they police?
- Are officers highly motivated to make a difference in their policing activities, or are they more focused on working toward their retirement?

Performance Assessment

- Does the officer's performance review include assessments of problem-solving activities, contacts with the community, and involvement in specific crime prevention and response initiatives?

Case Studies

Case Study 1: Project Shock

The RCMP's response to 9/11 was called "Project Shock." It was one of the RCMP's first investigative and enforcement initiatives that was national in scope, with implications in one form or another in all divisions across the country. Under Project Shock, the RCMP worked closely with other government departments in the fight against terrorism—the Canadian Security Intelligence Service, the Department of Foreign Affairs and International Trade, Canada Customs and Revenue Agency, the Department of Justice, Transport Canada, Criminal Intelligence Service Canada, the Department of National Defence, and the Privy Council Office, among others.

This collaboration was underscored in the December 2001 federal budget, which funded a number of initiatives including lawful access; emergency preparedness; marine security; border infrastructure; and chemical, biological, radiological, and nuclear (CBRN) technology.

The RCMP received $576 million under this budget, to be spread over six years. The funding from the December 2001 budget was earmarked for 17 specific national security projects and programs. Many of these initiatives leverage the expertise and resources of other federal government departments.

One such initiative was the creation of Integrated National Security Enforcement Teams (INSETs), comprised of representatives from across the RCMP and partner agencies at the municipal, provincial, and federal levels.

After September 11, 2001, the RCMP also created the Financial Intelligence Task Force, which has now expanded to become the Financial Intelligence Branch. This group tracks the criminal misuse of Canadian financial systems that may facilitate terrorist acts here and in other countries.

The task force works in close co-operation with the new Financial Transactions and Reports Analysis Centre of Canada (FINTRAC) to analyze terrorist funding information and prosecute those individuals or groups.

Situation

You are in charge of an INSET when a prominent member of a Middle Eastern community comes forward and alleges you are profiling his community based on race. How do you respond to this criticism? Justify your answer in terms of the main ideas you have learned about community-based strategic policing.

_____

_____

_____

_____

_____

_____

Case Study 2: *R. v. Meiorin*

In the case of *R. v. Meiorin* ([1999] 3 S.C.R. 3), Ms. Meiorin was an employee of the B.C. Ministry of Forests and worked as a member of an initial attack forest firefighting crew. To ensure safe and productive work, employees in this category must be aerobically fit and have adequate levels of muscular strength and endurance to help combat fatigue, recover from high-intensity work, and cope with the added demands of heat and altitude.

In 1988 the B.C. Ministry of Forests instituted the U.S. Forest Service Smoke Jumpers Test as the standard for physical fitness for its forest firefighters. The ministry contracted with the University of Victoria to see if other testing methods were available that would be more appropriate, and the university attempted to establish a test that reflected actual firefighting activities and the minimum fitness levels necessary to perform them properly. One element of the test was aerobic fitness, which was measured to a standard of 50 VO_2 max. Evidence submitted in the course of this arbitration showed that, due to physiological differences, women are on average less able to do aerobic work than men, and would therefore have more difficulty meeting the required standard than would men. In 1995 there were 800 to 900 initial attack crew personnel, of which 100 to 150 were female. Thirty-five percent of females passed the test the first time, as compared to 65 to 70 percent of males.

In 1994, the new fitness standard was introduced as mandatory. Recalled employees such as Ms. Meiorin were allowed to take the old test if they failed the new fitness test. Ms. Meiorin was given four opportunities to pass the aerobic aspect of the old test (a 2.5-kilometre run in 11 minutes or less) and failed on each occasion. As a result of her failure to meet the required physical fitness standard, she was suspended from work and, after further review, was laid off. The matter made its way through various appeals to the Supreme Court of Canada.

The Supreme Court ruled a three-step test should be adopted for determining whether an employer has established, on a balance of probabilities, that a *prima facie* discriminatory standard is a *bona fide occupational requirement* (BFOR). First, the employer must show that it adopted the standard for a purpose rationally connected to the performance of the job. Second, the employer must establish that it adopted the particular standard in an honest and good-faith belief that it was necessary for the fulfillment of that legitimate work-related purpose. Third, the employer must establish that the standard is reasonably necessary to the accomplishment of that legitimate work-related purpose. To show that the standard is reasonably necessary, it must be demonstrated that it is impossible to accommodate individual employees sharing the characteristics of the claimant without imposing undue hardship upon the employer. The Supreme Court allowed Ms. Meiorin's appeal and reinstated her to her previous position.

This decision has had an important impact on the physical testing of prospective police officers. As a result, police agencies have had to ensure they can meet the three-part test established by the Supreme Court and that physical entrance requirements do not discriminate against women. The full text of the Meiorin decision is available through the Supreme Court's website at www.scc-csc.gc.ca.

EXERCISES: KNOWLEDGE INTO PRACTICE

Exercise 1. Recruiting Criteria

You are a member of a recruitment team for your police service. Your department has recently adopted a new mission and value statement based on the principles of community policing. You and your colleagues on the recruiting team must develop a new set of criteria for recruiting new members to the department. List what you would consider to be the most important criteria for hiring new recruits. Then, for each item, provide a rationale for why you feel it is important.

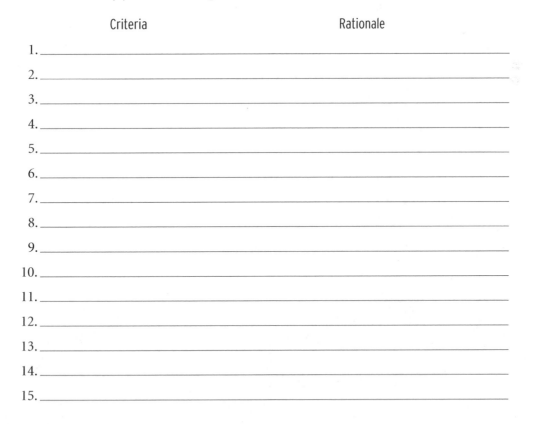

	Criteria	Rationale
1.		
2.		
3.		
4.		
5.		
6.		
7.		
8.		
9.		
10.		
11.		
12.		
13.		
14.		
15.		

Exercise 2. Assessing Officer Performance

Your police service has recently adopted a new mission and value statement based on the principles of community policing. You have been appointed by your chief to a committee charged with developing new standards for the review and assessment of the performance of officers in the department. Develop a list of the criteria that you feel should be used to assess officer performance. Then, for each item, provide an example.

	Criteria	Rationale
1.		
2.		
3.		
4.		
5.		
6.		
7.		
8.		
9.		
10.		

Exercise 3. Policing Remote Communities

As a member of the personnel division of the RCMP, you have responsibility for selecting officers to serve in remote Northern communities. Develop a list of criteria that you feel should be used for assigning officers to police these communities. Then, for each item, provide a rationale for why it is important.

	Criteria	Rationale
1.		
2.		
3.		
4.		
5.		
6.		
7.		
8.		
9.		
10.		

Now, explain how these criteria differ from those used in selecting officers to police communities in more urban communities.

_____

_____

_____

_____

_____

Exercise 4. Recruiting Standards

Question: Should recruiting standards be modified in an attempt to attract more women and visible and cultural minorities to policing?

In 1997, the RCMP relaxed its fitness requirements in an attempt to allow more women to join. This was done in response to a review that indicated that a high percentage of female applicants were failing the Physical Abilities Requirement Evaluation (PARE), primarily due to a lack of upper-body strength. Up to 50 percent of the women who took the test during the review period failed, even after repeated attempts; 80 percent of the male applicants passed, most on the first attempt. At the time the decision was made, the Canadian Human Rights Commission was considering a complaint by a woman that the PARE test was discriminatory.

In 1998, the RCMP rewrote portions of its entrance exam in response to a concern that some Aboriginal applicants and members of visible minorities scored lower than other potential recruits.

Consider the issues that have been raised by the actions of the RCMP and then answer the following questions:

1. Do you support or oppose the decision by the RCMP to modify the fitness rules for female applicants?

Support   Oppose

☐   ☐

A. What are the primary reasons for your opinion?

_____

_____

_____

_____

_____

B. What assumptions about policing are reflected in your response?

_____

_____

_____

_____

_____

2. Do you support or oppose the decision by the RCMP to alter its entrance examination in response to lower scores by some groups of applicants?

Support   Oppose

□   □

A. What are the primary reasons for your opinion?

_____

_____

_____

_____

_____

B. What assumptions about policing are reflected in your response?

_____

_____

_____

_____

_____

REFERENCES

Abernethy, T. 1995. *Community Policing Review: Report.* Ottawa: Corporate Management, Royal Canadian Mounted Police.

Campbell, D.S. 1992. *A Police Learning System for Ontario—Final Report and Recommendations.* Toronto: Ministry of the Solicitor General.

Carter, D.L. 2000. "Human Resource Issues for Community Policing." University of Michigan: Community Policing Center. Online (http://www.ssc.msu.edu).

Dean, G. 1995. "Police Reform: Rethinking Operational Policing." *Journal of Criminal Justice* 23(4):337–47.

Employment Equity Act. Online (http://laws.justice.gc.ca/en/showdoc/cs/E-5.401/// en?page=1).

Eustace, C. 2007. "VPD: Virtual Police Department." *Vancouver Sun,* May 29.

Fischer, R.J., K.M. Golden, and B.L. Heininger. 1985. "Issues in Higher Education for Law Enforcement Officers: An Illinois Study." *Journal of Criminal Justice* 13:329–38.

Goldsmith, A. 1990. "Taking Police Culture Seriously: Police Discretion and the Limits of the Law." *Policing and Security* 1(1):91–114.

Halifax Daily News. 1996. "Officers Also Want Return to 'More Traditional' Policing." December 6:4.

Hay Group. 2007. *A National Diagnostic on Human Resources in Policing, 2007*. Police Sector Council.

Herbert, S. 1998. "Police Subculture Reconsidered." *Criminology* 36(2):343–69.

Jain, H.C. 1994. "An Assessment of the Strategies of Recruiting Visible-Minority Police Officers in Canada: 1985–1990." pp. 138–64 in *Police Powers in Canada: The Evolution of Practice and Authority*, edited by R.C. MacLeod and D. Schneiderman. Toronto: University of Toronto Press.

Justice Institute of British Columbia. 2012. *Police Academy Training Calendar 2012*.

Lurigio, Arthur J. and Wesley G. Skogan. 1994. *Winning the Hearts and Minds of Police Officers: An Assessment of Staff Perceptions of Community Policing in Chicago Crime & Delinquency* 40(3):315–330.

Meese, E. 1993. "Community Policing and the Police Officer." In *Perspectives on Policing, National Institute of Justice* 15:1–11.

Mofina, R. 1996. "Force Fights Racism, Survey Reveals Problems." *Calgary Herald*. September 27:A1.

Montréal (City) v. Quebec (Commission des droits de la personne et des droits de la jeunesse), 2008 SCC 48.

Morris, R. 2005. *Ontario Police College Basic Constable Training Program Student Demographics 1996–2005*. Policing Services Division, Ministry of Community Safety and Correctional Services Research and Evaluation Unit, Ontario Police College (Ontario). Online (http://www.opconline.ca/res/BCT/BCTdemographicprofile2005.pdf).

Murphy, C. and C.T. Griffiths. 1994. "Community Based Policing—A Review of the Issues, Research, and Development of a Provincial Policy." Unpublished research report prepared for the Commission of Inquiry, Policing in British Columbia. Victoria: Ministry of Attorney General.

Oettmeier, T.N. and M.A. Wycoff. 1997. *Personnel Performance Evaluations in the Community Policing Context*. Washington, DC: Police Executive Research Forum.

Palmiotto, M.J., M. Birzer, L. Unnithan, and N. Prabha. 2000. "Training in Community Policing: A Suggested Curriculum." *Policing: An International Journal of Police Strategies and Management* 1:8–21.

Police Sector Council. Policing Competency Framework. Online (http://www.police-council.ca/pages/hr2.html).

Royal Canadian Mounted Police. 2012a. *The Aboriginal Pre-Cadet Training Program*. Online (http://www.rcmp-grc.gc.ca/recruiting-recrutement/aboriginal-autochtone/aboriginal-autochtone-cadet-eng.htm).

Royal Canadian Mounted Police. 2012b. "RCMP-GRC Recruiting." Online (http://www.rcmp-grc.gc.ca/recruiting-recrutement/rec/requirements-exigences-eng.htm).

Skolnick, J. 1966. *Justice without Trial: Law Enforcement in a Democratic Society*. New York: John Wiley and Sons.

Statistics Canada. 2011. *Police Resources in Canada, 2011*. Cat. No. 85-225-X. Ottawa: Minister Responsible for Statistics Canada.

Swol, K. 1999. *Police Personnel and Expenditures in Canada–1997 and 1998*. Ottawa: Canadian Centre for Justice Statistics.

Taylor, K. 1999. *Bringing into Focus—Policing in Halton Region: The Executive Summary*. Oakville, ON: Halton Regional Police Service.

Tomovich, V.A. and D.J. Loree. 1989. "In Search of New Directions: Policing in the Niagara Region." *Canadian Police College Journal* 13:29–54.

Toronto Police Service. 2011. *More Minority Police*. Online (http://www.torontopolice .on.ca/modules.php?op=modload&name=News&file=article&sid=1219).

CHAPTER 9

Restorative Justice within a Community Policing Framework

A component of restorative justice includes a healing process. Traditional healing practices in the Aboriginal community attempt to restore peace and harmony in the community, the family, and the individual. The response to criminal behaviour occurs within a broader, holistic framework placing an emphasis on healing the victim, the offender, and, where required, the community.

Source: CP PHOTO/Winnipeg Free Press - Ken Gigliotti

Learning Objectives

After completing this chapter, you should be able to:

- Define restorative justice;
- Compare the principles of retributive justice and restorative justice;
- Compare the community decision-making models of circle sentencing, family group conferencing, and victim–offender mediation;
- Describe how victim–offender mediation works, including the four phases of mediation;
- Describe circle sentencing;
- Compare the adversarial criminal court process with the restorative justice process;
- Discuss the differences between criminal courts and community circles;
- Describe how family group conferencing works; and
- Describe how the *Youth Criminal Justice Act* includes principles of restorative justice.

INTRODUCTION

Our discussion of police strategies for responding to and preventing crime would not be complete without considering the emergence of restorative justice. Among the nations of the world, Canada has long assumed a lead role in the development and implementation of alternative justice policies and programs, including a number of innovative initiatives that place Canadian communities and jurisdictions at the forefront of the community and restorative justice movement. For example, the first modern-day victim–offender reconciliation project was established in Elmira, Ontario, in 1974, and since that time numerous jurisdictions worldwide have adopted and expanded on this practice. There are many victim–offender mediation programs operating across Canada and nearly 300 in Germany and 130 in Finland. Canada has also contributed significantly to the development of restorative justice policy and practice for the United Nations.

More recently, Aboriginal peoples and communities have served as the catalysts for the development of a wide range of innovative, community-based restorative justice practices. The *Youth Criminal Justice Act* also incorporates a number of the principles of restorative justice. Another factor that provides the impetus for the development of community-based restorative justice programs is the fiscal situation of governments. These programs hold the promise of addressing the needs of victims, communities, and offenders more effectively, and of doing so at less expense than the formal justice system (see Church Council on Justice and Corrections 1996; Galaway and Hudson 1996; Zehr 1995).

WHAT IS RESTORATIVE JUSTICE?

Restorative justice is an approach to problem solving that involves the victim, the offender, their social networks, justice agencies, and the community. It rests on the fundamental principle that criminal behaviour injures not only victims but also communities and offenders, and that any efforts to address and resolve the problems created by the criminal behaviour should involve all these parties. A widely used definition of restorative justice states: "Restorative justice is a process whereby parties with a stake in a specific offence collectively resolve how to deal with the aftermath of the offence and its implications for the future" (Marshall 1999:5). The Canadian Resource Centre for Victims of Crime defines restorative justice as follows:

Restorative Justice (RJ) is not a program, but a way of looking at crime. It can be defined as a response to crime that focuses on restoring the losses suffered by victims, holding offenders accountable for the harm they have caused, and building peace within communities. (Canadian Resource Centre for Victims of Crime 2011:n.p.)

Principles and Objectives of Restorative Justice

Restorative justice is not a specific practice, but rather a set of principles that provides the basis for both a community and the justice system to respond to crime and social disorder. These general principles include:

- providing for the involvement of offenders, victims, their families, the community, and justice personnel;
- viewing crimes in a broad social context;
- a preventive and problem-solving orientation; and
- flexibility and adaptability (Marshall 1999:5).

Table 9.1 Principles of Retributive Justice and Restorative Justice

Retributive Justice	Restorative Justice
Crime violates the state and its laws.	Crime violates people and relationships.
Justice focuses on establishing guilt....	Justice aims to identify needs and obligations...
...so that doses of pain can be meted out.	...so that things can be made right.
Justice is sought through conflict between adversaries...	Justice encourages dialogue and mutual agreement...
...in which the offender is pitted against the state rules and intentions outweigh outcomes, and...	...gives victims and offenders central roles, and...
...one side wins and the other loses.	...the outcome is judged by the extent to which responsibilities are assumed, needs are met, and healing (of individuals and relationships) is encouraged.

Source: From *Changing Lenses: A New Focus for Crime and Justice* by Howard Zehr. Copyright © 1995, 2005 by Herald Press, Harrisonburg, VA 22802. Used by permission.

The primary objectives of restorative justice are:

- to address the needs of victims of crime,
- to prevent reoffending by reintegrating offenders into the community,
- to enable offenders to acknowledge and assume responsibility for their behaviour,
- to create a "community" of support and assistance for the victim and the offender and for the long-term interests of the community, and
- to provide an alternative to the adversarial system of justice (Marshall 1999:6).

A key feature of restorative justice is that the response to criminal behaviour focuses on more than just the offender and the offence. There is also the involvement of crime victims and their families, the offender's family, community residents, and justice personnel, including police officers, both in the response to the behaviour and in the formulation of a sanction that will address the needs of all parties.

Retributive and Restorative Justice Compared

The concept of restorative justice is best illustrated by comparing it to the principles of **retributive justice**, upon which our adversarial system of criminal justice is based. Several of these key differences are listed in Table 9.1.

THE DIMENSIONS OF RESTORATIVE JUSTICE

Among the more common restorative justice initiatives are victim–offender mediation, circle sentencing, community holistic healing programs, and family group conferences. There are critical differences among the various models of restorative and community justice, relating to their mandates and relationships to the formal adversarial system, the role of the crime victim and other co-participants, and the provisions and procedures for preparing for the event and for monitoring and enforcing the agreement (Van Ness and Strong 1997). The models also differ in terms of their objectives, the degree to which the model requires that the justice system share power with community residents, and the extent to which the model empowers the community and addresses the specific incident and behaviour in question. Also, some restorative justice programs provide for police participation; others do not.

Victim-Offender Mediation

Victim–offender mediation programs (VOMP)—also often referred to as victim–offender reconciliation programs, or VORP—have been operating in Canada since the early 1970s and are widely used across the country. VOM takes a restorative approach by giving both the victim and the offender the opportunity to express their feelings and concerns. With the assistance of a mediator, who is a neutral third party, the offender and the victim resolve the conflict and the consequences caused by the offence, and ultimately learn to understand each other.

There are generally four phases of mediation: (1) intake of the case from a referral source; (2) preparation for the mediation, which involves the mediator meeting separately with the victim and the offender; (3) the mediation session; and (4) post-session activities, including ensuring the fulfillment of any agreement reached during the mediation session.

In recent years, VOM has been used in cases involving crimes of violence and in situations where the offender is incarcerated in a correctional facility. A recent analysis of VOM finds both victims and offenders report greater satisfaction with restorative justice principles than traditional non-restorative approaches (Latimer, Dowden, and Muise 2001).

Circle Sentencing: A Partnership between the Community and the Criminal Justice System

Circle sentencing originally developed in several Yukon communities as a collaborative initiative between community residents and territorial justice personnel—primarily RCMP officers and judges from the Territorial Court of Yukon (Stuart 1996).

In **circle sentencing**, all the participants, including the judge, defence lawyer, prosecutor, police officer, victim and his or her family, offender and his or her family, and community residents, sit facing one another in a circle. Discussions are designed to reach a consensus about the best way to dispose of the case, taking into account the need to protect the community as well as the rehabilitation and punishment of the offender. There are a number of important stages in the circle sentencing process, each critical to its overall success. An actual case that was handled in a sentencing circle is included as a case study at the end of this chapter.

Circle sentencing is premised on traditional Aboriginal healing practices and has multifaceted objectives, including addressing the needs of communities and the families of victims and offenders through a process of reconciliation, restitution, and reparation. A fundamental principle is that the sentence is less important than the process used to select it.

There are a number of important stages in the circle sentencing process, each of which is critical to its overall success. It is generally only available to those offenders who plead guilty. The process is community-specific, meaning that it may (and should) vary between communities, and it relies heavily upon community volunteers for its success (Stuart 1996). Offenders whose cases are heard in a sentencing circle may still be sent for a period of incarceration; however, many other sanctions are available, including banishment (generally to a wilderness location), house arrest, and community service.

Table 9.2 compares formal, adversarial criminal courts with the community-based, restorative approach. As you can see, there are some very significant differences between the two.

Circle Sentencing versus Adversarial Justice

There are some very significant differences between circle sentencing and the formal, adversarial system of criminal justice. These differences are outlined in Table 9.3.

Table 9.2 Formal Criminal Court Context and the Restorative Justice Process

	Court	**Restorative Justice**
People	Experts, nonresidents	Local people
Process	Adversarial (state versus offender)	Consensus (community versus problem)
Issues	Laws broken	Relationship broken
Focus	Guilt	Identification of needs of the victim, offender, and community, and solution to the problem
Tools	Punishment and control	Healing and support
Procedure	Fixed rules	Flexible

Table 9.3 Differences between Criminal Courts and Community Circles

Criminal Courts	**Community Circles**
The conflict is the crime	Crime is a small part of a larger conflict
The sentence resolves the conflict	The sentence is a small part of the solution
Focus on past conduct	Focus on present and future conduct
Take a narrow view of behaviour	Take a larger, holistic view
Avoid concern with social conflict	Focus on social conflict
Result (the sentence) is most important	Result is least important—the process is most important, as the process shapes the relationship among all parties

Source: From HATCH. *CRIMINAL JUSTICE PRIMER.* © 1997 Nelson Education Ltd. Reproduced by permission. www.cengage.com/permissions

The Potential of Circle Sentencing

Circle sentencing is an example of how the principles of restorative justice can be applied within a holistic framework in which justice system personnel share power and authority with community residents. In contrast to the adversarial approach to justice, circle sentencing:

- reacquaints individuals, families, and communities with problem-solving skills;
- rebuilds relationships within communities;
- promotes awareness of and respect for the values and the lives of others;
- addresses the needs and interests of all parties, including the victim;
- focuses on causes, not just symptoms, of problems;
- recognizes existing healing resources and creates new ones;
- coordinates the use of local and government resources; and
- generates preventive measures (Hatch-Cunningham and Griffiths 1997:240).

The majority of offenders whose cases have been heard by sentencing circles have been adults; however, an increasing number of young offenders' cases are being handled by way of the legislated provisions contained in the *Youth Criminal Justice Act*. Circle sentencing has spawned a number of variations, including community sentence advisory committees, sentencing panels, and community mediation panels. Preliminary analysis suggests that this technique may be very effective in reducing or eliminating criminal and disruptive behaviour, particularly on the part of offenders who have lengthy records in the formal criminal justice system.

Judge Barry Stuart (1996) of the Territorial Court of Yukon, a pioneer in the development of circle sentencing, cautions that this approach is not appropriate for all offenders or crimes; the success of the circles depends upon the co-operation of community residents and justice professionals, and it is imperative that the needs, rights, and interests of crime victims and offenders be protected. These concerns are particularly important in considering restorative justice initiatives for young offenders, who, due to their age and status in communities, often have many vulnerabilities.

Circle sentencing is a superb example of how the principles of restorative justice can be applied within a framework in which justice system personnel share power and authority with community residents. For police officers, it provides two important opportunities: (1) to participate in a community-based approach to addressing crime and disorder, and (2) to shift from a reactive mode to a coactive, problem-solving one. The principles and processes of circle sentencing complement those of community policing.

Although circle sentencing originated in the North, its principles and processes can be adapted to larger communities. In the Yukon, both Aboriginal and non-Aboriginal residents have participated in circles, as victims and offenders, and in community support roles. Furthermore, as a point of interest, with the assistance of justice and community representatives from the Yukon, a circle-sentencing program has been successfully established in Minneapolis, Minnesota.

Family Group Conferencing

Family group conferencing (FGC) originated in New Zealand, was "exported" to Australia, and is now appearing in discussions of restorative justice in several Canadian jurisdictions. In 1989, Australia's *Children, Young Persons, and Their Families Act* identified the youth's family and extended family as key participants in addressing the problems of young people in conflict. The forum for discussing the issues surrounding the youth and his or her behaviour is the FGC, which incorporates the traditional restorative approach of the indigenous Maori people. Through the above-noted legislation, it is now used as the basis of the entire youth justice system.

In Edmonton, a **community conferencing** program has been established to divert young offenders away from the justice system into a forum where they can be held accountable and where the victims of the offence can express their feelings and participate in the decision-making process. Personnel trained in mediation and communication techniques operate the program in conjunction with a community-based diversion program. The program is based on a partnership between the police service and a number of community agencies, including the Legal Aid Youth Office, the John Howard Society, the Victim Offender Mediation Society, and the Native Youth Justice Committee.

This program illustrates the potential for police involvement in restorative justice initiatives in urban and suburban areas, and is an excellent example of the type of police–community partnerships possible within an overall framework of community policing (Griffiths, Whitelaw, and Parent 1999). An actual case heard in a community conference is presented as a case study at the end of this chapter.

RESTORATIVE JUSTICE INITIATIVES IN ABORIGINAL COMMUNITIES

In recent years, Aboriginal communities have become increasingly involved in developing community-based justice services and programs designed to address the specific needs of community residents, victims, and offenders. These initiatives have often been developed as part of a process of cultural and community revitalization and are part of the increasing efforts by Aboriginal peoples and communities to reassert their authority over all facets of community life (Griffiths and Hamilton 1996). There has also been an attempt to explore alternatives to confinement in order to decrease the large numbers of Aboriginal persons incarcerated in provincial and territorial correctional institutions. Box 9.1 outlines Canada's Aboriginal Justice Strategy.

BOX 9.1

THE ABORIGINAL JUSTICE STRATEGY

The Aboriginal Justice Strategy (AJS) enables Aboriginal communities to have increased involvement in the local administration of justice and, as such, provides timely and effective alternatives to mainstream justice processes in appropriate circumstances. AJS programs are also aimed at reducing the rates of victimization, crime and incarceration among Aboriginal people in communities operating AJS programs, and helping the mainstream justice system become more responsive and sensitive to the needs and culture of Aboriginal communities.

Objectives of the AJS:

• To contribute to a decrease in the rates of victimization, crime and incarceration among Aboriginal people in communities operating AJS programs;

• To assist Aboriginal people to assume greater responsibility for the administration of justice in their communities;

• To provide better and more timely information about community justice programs funded by the AJS; and

• To reflect and include relevant Aboriginal values within the justice system.

During the 2007–2008 fiscal year, the AJS funded approximately 113 programs that served nearly 400 Aboriginal communities.

The Aboriginal Justice Strategy is comprised of two funding components:

• The Community-Based Justice Programs Fund; and

• The Capacity Building Fund.

1. Community-Based Justice Programs

Community-based justice programs continue to be the centerpiece of the AJS. The Community-Based Justice Programs Fund provides support to community-based justice programs in partnership with Aboriginal communities. Programs are cost-shared with provincial and territorial governments and are designed to reflect the culture and values of the communities in which they are situated.

The objectives of the Community-Based Justice Programs Fund are:

• to help reduce the rates of crime and incarceration among Aboriginal people in communities with cost-shared programs;

• to allow Aboriginal people the opportunity to assume greater responsibility for the administration of justice in their communities; and,

• to foster improved responsiveness, fairness, inclusiveness, and effectiveness of the justice system with respect to justice and its administration so as to meet the needs and aspirations of Aboriginal people in the areas of appropriate models for:

  a. diversion;

  b. the development of pre-sentencing options;

  c. community sentencing alternatives (circles);

  d. the use of Justices of the Peace;

  e. family and civil mediation; and,

  f. additional community justice services such as victims support or offender-reintegration services which support the overall goals of the AJS.

2. Capacity Building Fund

The Capacity Building Fund is designed to support capacity-building efforts in Aboriginal communities, particularly as they relate to building increased knowledge and skills for the establishment and management of community-based justice programs.

(continues)

The objectives of the Capacity Building Fund are:

- to support the training and/or developmental needs of Aboriginal communities that currently do not have community-based justice programs;

- on-going training needs of current community-based justice programs, including supporting evaluation activities, data collection, sharing of best practices and useful models, where the cost-shared budget does not adequately meet these needs;

- to support activities targeted at improved community reporting in AJS communities and the development of data management systems;

- to support the development of new justice programs, paying particular attention to:

  - the current geographic/regional imbalance in programming;

  - the commitment to develop new programs in the under-represented program models, such as dispute resolution for civil and family/child welfare; and,

- to support one-time or annual events and initiatives that build bridges, trust and partnerships between the mainstream justice system and Aboriginal communities.

Source: The Aboriginal Justice Strategy, URL: http://canada.justice.gc.ca/eng/pi/ajs-sja/, Department of Justice Canada, 2012. Reproduced with the permission of the Minister of Public Works and Government Services Canada, 2012.

Recently the Supreme Court of Canada recognized the importance of restorative justice approaches in its landmark decisions of *R. v. Gladue* (1999) and *R. v. Proulx* (2000). In *Gladue*, the Supreme Court supported restorative approaches found in the sentencing principles of section 718.2 (e) of the *Criminal Code*, which states:

718.2 A court that imposes a sentence shall also take into consideration the following principles: . . . (e) all available sanctions other than imprisonment that are reasonable in the circumstances should be considered for all offenders, with particular attention to the circumstances of aboriginal offenders.

The *Gladue* decision directed the court system to take meaningful steps to counter the increasing reliance on incarceration in the sentencing of Aboriginal offenders. Sentencing judges must consider the assessment of the Aboriginal offender and all non-jail options that are appropriate and available in the local community. Recently the Supreme Court of Canada applied it earlier decision in *Gladue* to the sentencing of violent offenders. In *R. v. Ipeelee* (2012 S.C.C. 13), Justice LeBel, writing for the majority of the court, stated:

To be clear, courts must take judicial notice of such matters as the history of colonialism, displacement and residential schools and how that history continues to translate into lower educational attainment, lower incomes, higher unemployment, higher rates of substance abuse and suicide and, of course, higher levels of incarceration for Aboriginal Peoples[.]

Failing to take these circumstances into account would violate the fundamental principle of sentencing.

Restorative or community justice initiatives in Aboriginal communities are often premised on customary law and traditional practices and may contain aspects of spirituality. Many involve elders and place a strong emphasis on healing the victim, the offender, and, where required, the community. Rather than focusing only on the offender and the offence, the response to criminal behaviour occurs within a broader, holistic framework. This facilitates the inclusion of crime victims and their families, the offender's family, and community residents in the response and also in the formulation of a sanction that accommodates the needs of all parties (Green 1997; 1998).

Another attribute of these initiatives is that the Aboriginal band or community maintains a high degree of control over the disposition and sanctioning process, or

BOX 9.2

INDIAN RESIDENTIAL SCHOOLS: A NATIONAL DISGRACE

Library and Archives Canada a123707

As part of the Government of Canada's policy of "aggressive assimilation," Aboriginal children were forced to leave their homes on Indian reservations and forced to attend Indian residential schools. This policy existed from the late 19th century until 1996.

In the 19th century, the Canadian government believed it was responsible for educating and caring for the country's Aboriginal people. The government of the day believed that an English education and the adoption of Christianity and white customs would result in the transmission of new customs, serving to diminish and eventually abolish native culture. This belief was premised on the underlying assumption that Aboriginal culture could not adapt to a rapidly modernizing Canadian society.

Relying upon a policy called "aggressive assimilation," Indian children were bused to church-run, government-funded industrial boarding schools, later called "residential schools," operated under the federal Department of Indian Affairs. They stayed there for 10 months of the year, and when they returned home to their reserves they had difficulty assimilating. In 1931, there were approximately 130 residential schools. The last residential school closed in 1996. In all, about 150,000 Aboriginal, Inuit, and Métis children were removed from their communities and forced to attend the schools.

Following the Royal Commission on Aboriginal Peoples initiated in 1991, Canadian churches apologized to Aboriginal people. Archbishop Michael Peers offered an apology on behalf of the Anglican Church of Canada in 1993, stating "I am sorry, more than I can say, that we were part of a system which took you and your children from home and family."

In 2007, two years after it was first announced, the federal government formalized a $1.9 billion compensation package for those who were forced to attend residential schools. Following the establishment of a Truth and Reconciliation Commission in 2008, Prime Minster Stephen Harper apologized to residential school students in Parliament on June 11, 2008.

Source: "Residential Schools: A History of Residential Schools in Canada," CBC.ca (http://www.cbc.ca/news/canada/story/2008/05/16/f-faqs-residential-schools.html)

these are shared, on a partnership basis, with justice system personnel. This represents a significant departure from the manner in which justice services are typically provided by the criminal justice system.

Hollow Water's Community Holistic Circle Healing

Community Holistic Circle Healing was initiated in 1986 by the Hollow Water First Nation in Manitoba and was designed as a community-based response to the high rates of sexual and family abuse in the community. It consists of a 13-phase process, depicted in Figure 9.1.

Figure 9.1 The Thirteen Phases of the Hollow Water Community Holistic Circle Healing Process

Source: Community Holistic Circle Healing: The process, a model. URL: http://www.publicsafety.gc.ca/res/cor/apc/apc-15-eng.aspx#holistic Public Safety Canada, 1996. Reproduced with the permission of the Minister of Public Works and Government Services, 2012

One of the phases of **community holistic healing** is the special gathering, which is a public event that shares many similarities with the traditional justice case described in detail below. Traditional healing practices attempt to restore peace and harmony in the community, the family, and the individual. A healing contract is signed, and offenders apologize publicly to the victims and to the community for the harm done. The circle healing process is designed to consider the needs of all of the parties to the abuse—the victim, the offender, and the community—and is directed beyond merely punishing the offender for a specific behaviour. The notion of forgiveness may also be part of the healing process, allowing all of the involved individuals to come to terms with the offence that has occurred.

Preliminary research findings suggest that the program may have a positive impact on offenders, victims, their respective families, and the community (Lajeunesse and Associates Ltd. 1996; Latimer et al. 2001).

Traditional Aboriginal Justice

While many restorative justice initiatives such as circle sentencing involve partnerships between criminal justice system personnel and communities, there are instances in which communities themselves assume total control and take responsibility for the resolution of conflicts. These events are often not publicized, nor do they receive outside attention. And although local justice system personnel, such as the police, may be aware of the case and of the activities of the community in resolving it, there is little or no official intervention. One such case is presented as a case study at the end of this chapter.

RESTORATIVE JUSTICE PRINCIPLES IN THE *YOUTH CRIMINAL JUSTICE ACT*

On April 1, 2003, Canada's *Youth Criminal Justice Act* (YCJA) became law, requiring the criminal justice system to distinguish between violent and nonviolent offenders, with a focus upon prevention and meaningful consequences for youth. One important aspect of this legislation is the provision of **extrajudicial measures** that serve as means (other than court proceedings) to deal with young people who have committed offences.

Before using the formal youth justice court system, police in Canada are now directed to consider whether one of the following options would be sufficient:

- to take no further action;
- to warn the young person;
- to administer a caution;

- to refer the young person to a program such as a community accountability program, a police-based diversion program, or an agency in the community that may assist the young person not to commit offences; or
- to refer the young person to an extrajudicial sanctions program due to the seriousness of the offence and the nature and number of previous offences committed, or other aggravating circumstances.

In keeping with the principles and objectives of restorative justice, the extrajudicial measures contained within the *YCJA* are designed to provide an effective and timely response to offending behaviour and to encourage young offenders to acknowledge and repair the harm caused to the victim and the community. Extrajudicial measures also encourage the involvement of families and members of the community in designing and implementing measures directed at the offending young person. Victims can also participate in these decisions and receive reparation.

CRITICAL ISSUES IN RESTORATIVE/COMMUNITY JUSTICE

Despite the success of many initiatives in restorative and community justice, both within a collaborative framework involving justice system personnel and community residents, such as circle sentencing, and within Aboriginal communities on their own, there are a number of critical issues that must be addressed. Some of these are described below.

Restorative Justice in Urban Centres

In discussions about the potential for developing restorative justice initiatives, it is often argued that programs such as circle sentencing, which involve substantive community participation in a holistic framework, are suited only to rural and remote communities with a strong cultural identity and foundation. This assertion is often used to deflect suggestions that justice personnel in suburban and urban areas should explore the development of system–community partnerships for addressing the needs of offenders, their victims, and the community.

However, as was mentioned earlier, there is a community conferencing program in Edmonton, operated by non-profit community organizations and staffed by volunteers trained in mediation and communication skills and techniques. There are also a number of successful restorative justice initiatives currently operating in urban and suburban areas of Canada that, with additional funding, could be easily adapted to accommodate offenders (see Roberts and LaPrairie 1996 and www.publicsafety.gc.ca [search "restorative justice"]).

Crime Victims and Restorative Justice

Although crime victims are often excluded from the formal adversarial system of criminal justice, concerns have been expressed that restorative and community justice initiatives may not give adequate attention to the rights and needs of vulnerable groups, specifically women and female adolescents. As a consequence, crime victims may be "revictimized" by the process of restorative and community justice. Aboriginal women, for example, have voiced concerns about the high rates of sexual and physical abuse in communities and have questioned whether restorative and community justice initiatives provide adequate protection for the victims of violence and abuse and also whether the sanctions imposed are appropriate.

Assessing the Effectiveness of Restorative Justice

There have been few evaluations of whether restorative justice strategies have achieved their stated objectives. Despite receiving widespread publicity at the national and international levels, for example, there have been no controlled evaluations of circle sentencing. Concluding a critique of circle sentencing, Roberts and LaPrairie (1996:82–83) stated: "It has been claimed that sentencing circles have the following benefits: (a) they reduce recidivism; (b) prevent crime; (c) reduce costs; (d) advance the interests of victims; and (e) promote solidarity among community members. These are all measurable objectives and they should be put to empirical test."

Promising Canadian research suggests restorative justice approaches have been more successful than traditional, non–restorative approaches in the following areas:

- they are a more effective method of improving victim/offender satisfaction;
- they increase offender compliance with restitution; and
- they decrease the recidivism of offenders when compared to the more traditional criminal justice responses of incarceration, probation, and court-ordered restitution (Latimer et al. 2001).

In one Canadian study examining whether restorative justice approaches could be suitable in addressing serious crimes it was found that it could successfully be applied in the *pre-sentence stage* in serious crimes. Participants reported higher levels of satisfaction with the restorative approach, especially when compared to participants who experienced only the traditional criminal justice system. Victims and offenders were offered the opportunity to actively participate in the decision-making process, in developing a reparation plan and, in some cases, providing a sentencing recommendation. Overall, individuals affected by serious crime were empowered to achieve satisfying justice through a restorative approach

The Restorative Action Program (RAP) is a community-driven initiative providing conflict resolution training and services, leadership development, and life skills to more than 4,675 youth in Saskatoon. RAP directly deals with issues of bullying, relationship breakdown, violence, and crime that stand in the way of academic success and personal growth. The goal is to transform the cycle of conflict so that youth can contribute and live in safer communities. See http://www.rapsaskatoon.org/.

Source: Courtesy of Restorative Action Program (RAP).

(Rugge, Bonta, and Wallace-Capretta 2005). Another study examining recidivism rates and restorative justice found that restorative justice programs can have a small but positive impact on rates of recidivism: anywhere from two to eight percent reductions in recidivism. More research is required to validate these findings.

Attempts to assess the effectiveness of restorative and community justice programs will face a number of problems. One such problem is that the holistic approach and multifaceted objectives of many restorative justice programs require a broader evaluative framework than is used for traditional crime-control initiatives. Program objectives may encompass macro-level dimensions such as cultural and community revitalization and empowerment, as well as community, family, and individual healing.

The Dynamics of Community Justice

The significant role assumed by communities in restorative justice initiatives requires a close consideration of both the strengths and the potential pitfalls of community justice. Canadian observers have identified several critical issues, which, if unaddressed, may undermine the efficacy of restorative justice initiatives. These issues include the general "health" of the community, including community leaders and those who would assume key roles in any restorative justice initiatives; the circumstance that within all communities there are power and status hierarchies that may threaten consensus building and place certain residents, be they victims or offenders, in positions of vulnerability; and the need to protect the legal rights of offenders (Griffiths and Hamilton 1996).

There are often competing and conflicting goals in community justice, and even in relatively small communities it may be difficult to establish and maintain a consensus about how to respond to an offender.

THE ROLE OF THE POLICE IN RESTORATIVE JUSTICE

With the advent of community policing, the opportunities for patrol officers to become involved in restorative and community justice programs has increased. In fact, officers may assume a primary role in organizing and facilitating community conferences. This role can be described as coactive, because of the relationship it establishes between the police and community. Patrol officers not only need to understand the principles of restorative and community justice, but also must develop the skills to bring together the various stakeholder groups, including the offender and the victim, their respective support groups, and other parties. We provide a case illustration of how to facilitate a community conference in one of the case studies at the end of this chapter.

CHAPTER SUMMARY

In this chapter, we have examined restorative justice and considered its role within the framework of community policing. Restorative justice is based on the fundamental principle that in order to be effective, efforts to address and resolve the problems created by criminal behaviour must consider the victim, the offender, and the community. There are significant differences between restorative justice and the adversarial approach to responding to crime and offenders. Among the restorative justice initiatives developed over the past several decades are victim–offender mediation, circle sentencing, and family group conferencing. Canada's recent *Youth Criminal Justice Act* has embraced many of the principles and concepts found within restorative justice. In addition, many First Nations communities have developed programs premised on the principles of restorative justice. The philosophy and practices of restorative justice complement community policing and provide patrol officers with an opportunity to participate in alternative forums for addressing crime. Restorative justice interventions also provide officers with the opportunity to engage in problem solving and to partner with communities to address issues of crime and social disorder.

Chapter Review

Key Terms

- circle sentencing, p. 280
- community conferencing, p. 282
- community holistic healing, p. 286
- extrajudicial measures, p. 286
- family group conferencing, p. 282
- restorative justice, p. 278
- retributive justice, p. 279
- victim–offender mediation programs, p. 280
- *Youth Criminal Justice Act*, p. 286

Key Points

- Canada has long assumed a lead role in the development of restorative justice programs.
- Restorative justice is based on the principle that criminal behaviour injures victims, offenders, and communities, and that all three parties must be involved in resolving problems created by criminal behaviour.
- There are a wide variety of restorative justice programs across the country and within the legislated provisions of the *Youth Criminal Justice Act*.
- There are significant differences between retributive and restorative justice.
- Victim–offender mediation, circle sentencing, and family group conferencing are three common restorative justice initiatives.
- There are significant differences between the formal, adversarial process in the criminal courts and the community-based, restorative approach of circle sentencing.
- Many First Nations communities have developed community-based alternatives to the justice system based on the principles of restorative justice.
- There are a number of critical issues related to restorative justice that must be addressed in order to enhance its effectiveness as a response to crime and social disorder in communities.

Self-Evaluation

QUESTIONS

1. Define **restorative justice**.
2. Compare **retributive justice** and restorative justice.
3. Describe how **victim–offender mediation programs** operate.
4. Describe **circle sentencing** and then compare it to the adversarial court process.
5. What is **community holistic healing** and how does this program reflect the principles of restorative justice?
6. Describe the key features of **family group conferencing**.
7. What is **community conferencing**?
8. Discuss the use of **extrajudicial measures** within the *Youth Criminal Justice Act*.
9. Canadian research suggests that **restorative justice approaches** have been more successful than traditional, non-restorative approaches in which areas?
10. Discuss the critical issues that exist within the current framework of **restorative and community justice**.

KEY IDEAS

1. Which statement best describes restorative justice programs in Canada?
   a. they generally exclude the police
   b. they have only been developed in the past five years
   ✓ c. they vary widely in the types of offences and offenders processed
   d. they operate primarily as diversion programs

2. One approach to justice views crime as a violation of the state and its laws, focuses on establishing guilt, and results in one side winning and the other losing. What is the term for this approach?
   ✓ a. retributive justice
   b. winner-take-all justice
   c. restorative justice
   d. community justice

3. One approach to restorative justice approach provides an opportunity for the key individuals in this process to express their feelings and concerns with the assistance of a mediator. What is the term for this approach?
   a. circle sentencing
   b. family group conferencing
   c. crisis counselling
   ✓ d. victim–offender mediation

4. Where did circle sentencing originate?
   ✓ a. Yukon
   b. Minnesota
   c. Ontario
   d. Newfoundland

5. One restorative approach views crime as part of a larger conflict and the sentence as a small part of the solution. What is the term for this approach?
   a. victim–offender mediation
   b. retributive justice
   ✓ c. community circle sentencing
   d. distributive justice

6. Which statement describes the experience of restorative justice programs in Canada?
   a. They are generally unsuccessful in dealing with serious offences.
   b. They work best in rural and remote communities.
   c. Their participants have been generally limited to the residents of First Nations.
   ✓ d. They can work in both rural and urban areas.

7. Which of the following has been found by research studies on restorative justice initiatives?
   a. Restorative justice programs are highly successful with young offenders, but less successful with adult offenders.
   b. Restorative justice programs are most successful when the police are not involved.
   ✓ c. Due to a lack of research it is difficult to determine the extent to which restorative justice programs have achieved their objectives.
   d. Circle sentencing is not effective with serious offenders.

8. Which of the following factors can undermine the effectiveness of restorative justice programs?
   ✓ a. power and status hierarchies in communities
   b. protecting the legal rights of offenders

   c. strong community leadership
   d. a healthy, vibrant community

9. What are police officers directed to do when considering extrajudicial measures within the *Youth Criminal Justice Act*?
   a. take no further action
   b. warn the young person
   c. administer a caution
   ✓ d. refer the young person to a program, or agency, that may assist him or her to not commit offences

10. Which of the following things did the *Gladue* decision direct the Canadian court system to do?
    a. provide separate holding cells for individuals arrested by the police that fall within the jurisdiction of the *Youth Criminal Justice Act*
    b. utilize community conferencing principles when dealing with young persons
    ✓ c. take meaningful steps to counter the increasing reliance on incarceration in the sentencing of Aboriginal offenders
    d. utilize victim–offender mediation programs (VOMP) in cases involving domestic violence

Restorative Justice: Situations and Strategies

Case Studies

Case Study 1. Community Conferencing in an Urban Centre

The following is the report of a community conference facilitated by a police officer in a Canadian urban centre.

The Case

The case involved a 14-year-old boy who sprayed pepper spray in the hallway of his school. At the time, there were approximately 50 students and 10 staff members in the school, most of whom were affected by the spray. After discharging the substance, the boy gave the pepper spray container to another student, who was unaware of the incident. This student subsequently led police to the boy who admitted spraying the pepper spray. A police constable discussed the option of community conferencing with the principal, who was interested in the idea. The offender agreed to participate and gave the officer the names of several people he wanted to attend.

The Offences

Sec. 90, Canadian Criminal Code—Possession of a Prohibited Weapon
Sec. 430 (1)(a), Canadian Criminal Code—Mischief

The Offender

The Aboriginal youth came from a broken home and had had three different stepfathers and two different stepmothers. He had 12 siblings and, at the time of the offence, was living with his 23-year-old sister, who was providing him with a stable home. The constable's impression of the youth was that he was a good boy who had very difficult issues to deal with, including the substance abuse by his parents. In his case study report, the constable wrote: "He is struggling to do the right thing most of the time, and I believe he needs people in his life to support him. He has no criminal record."

The Process

On the date of the offence, the constable met with all the staff at the school and explained the concept of community conferencing. He gathered the names of six staff members who were affected by the incident and were willing to participate in a conference. The names of six mature and responsible students who were affected by the incident were also obtained. The following morning, the constable met with the students and explained the concept of community conferencing. The students were all interested and willing to be involved.

The offender had informed the constable that he wanted his birth father, his sister, and a good friend of the family to be at the conference. The constable met with these three individuals, described the incident, and prepared them for the conference. The conference was scheduled to be held approximately 48 hours after the offence had occurred.

The Conference

The conference lasted 1.5 hours. Almost all of the participants were Aboriginal and were aware of traditional Aboriginal ways. Two Aboriginal elders (wife and husband) attended the conference and provided invaluable input. One conducted a sweetgrass ceremony to begin the conference. This ceremony was significant because it gave the process a sense of legitimacy and respect.

The offender was the first to speak and said he had found a canister of pepper spray earlier that day. He openly admitted that he brought the spray to school and sprayed it, in a hallway near some exit doors, in front of two unidentified students. He then ran upstairs and gave the spray to an acquaintance and told him to hold on to it until the end of the day. When the constable questioned him about whom he thought was affected, he indicated he did not know.

After the offender had spoken, the constable asked each of the victims (staff and students) to describe how they were affected by the incident and how they felt at the time. Some people were very expressive and eloquent in their description of their experience with the pepper spray. One teacher, who had asthma, disclosed how she urinated during severe coughing. Another teacher described how her special needs students were extremely traumatized by the disruption in their normally routine day. The students described how the spray made them feel physically and also described the initial anxiety they felt as a result of not knowing what was happening.

The offender's father spoke after the victims. He described the fear and anxiety he felt when the constable had first contacted him to tell him about the incident. He also became emotional when he talked about how, in some way, he was responsible for his son's actions. The participants were all moved by what the father had to say. The offender's sister then spoke and described her reaction to finding out about the incident. She was also very supportive of the offender and spoke about how responsible he usually was.

After all the participants had the opportunity to speak, it was time for the group to decide on an appropriate outcome. An agreement had to be reached regarding how the offender would be responsible for "making things better." After discussions, the following agreement was arrived at:

1. The offender would make a public apology to the student body and staff at an assembly to be held in the school's library.
2. He would meet with the principal every morning 45 minutes before class for counselling and work projects.
3. He would meet with the arts and crafts teacher one day per week for one-on-one counselling.
4. He would assist the janitor in his duties for one week.

The offender agreed to the noted sanctions, which resulted from group consultation and consensus. No time limit was specified for the second and third items because the group wanted the offender to prove himself. The time limit would be set by the offender's behaviour and progress.

When the formal part of the conference was completed, there was a symbolic "breaking of bread." This part of the process was very meaningful because it provided the opportunity for the participants to talk informally. The principal had prepared some bannock (traditional Aboriginal bread). This event allowed the individuals involved to move on from the incident and look toward a more positive future. It also provided the constable with the time to prepare the written agreement with the four sanctions, which all participants subsequently signed. Copies of the agreement were given to the offender, his father, and the principal.

Summary of the Conference (the Constable's Observations)

I believe this community conference was a success. Time will tell, however, if the four outcomes will be completed by the offender. A positive outcome of this process is the many people who have agreed to monitor the offender's progress and, as a result of this, the offender has a newfound community within the school. Prior to the incident he had only attended this school for a couple of months and had not established much of a support network. In fact, this offender has now established a new peer group made up of some of the more responsible students in the school. This is a peer group that, under normal circumstances, this offender would not have associated with. During the informal snack time after the conference, it was clear that he had made some new friends, both among his peers and the staff. It was also interesting to note that the offender's father connected with one of the teachers. This teacher will attempt to provide some counselling for him and his son in the future.

General feedback from the participants was very positive. The sense that the victims of this incident could actually have a say in the justice process proved to be very satisfying for them. They believed they were ensuring that the offender took responsibility for his actions and that he was correcting the wrong. Victim satisfaction was very real and tangible. I sensed that the offender believed he had his work cut out for him; however, it was not so much a punishment he felt but an accountability to his community. That community I speak of is the community within his school and those who care for him.

On a personal note, I was surprised by my own reaction as I heard the many different ways that people had been affected by this incident. I had no idea that they had suffered in the ways that they described during the conference. In conclusion, compared to the mainstream justice system where this youth would most likely have received a sentence of 20 to 30 hours of community service, I believe this approach is much more meaningful to the offender, the victims, and the supporters of the victims and offender. Community conferencing made a positive difference in the participants' lives. This approach will not be appropriate in all cases; however, I feel we can divert many youths to this model and thereby create a system of responding to youth crime that is meaningful and will hopefully prevent future criminal behaviour.

Source: International Review of Victimology, September 1999, Vol 6, No 4, 297–294. Copyright © 1999 by *International Review of Victimology*. Reprinted by Permission of SAGE.

Case Study 2. Family Group Conferencing in an Aboriginal Community

The following describes a successful family group conference that was held in Lennox Island Reserve after the theft of candy vending machines from the reserve's main building.

Since one of the two offenders connected to the incident was on probation, the constable convinced community members to attempt to resolve the issue through restorative justice. After hearing how paying restitution would financially affect the offenders' families and the band, the vending machine company representative dropped the price of machine repairs by $200. "The session was very emotional and the offenders heard the disappointment, embarrassment, and lack of trust they had caused," stated the constable. "At the end of the session, the whole mood of the group was relief. There was no pent-up anger or unresolved feelings." The penalty determined by the community was 10 hours of community service and repayment of repair costs.

Source: Ramsey, K., 1997. "A Return to Wisdom: Restorative Justice Revisited." *Pony Express*, the RCMP's National News Magazine (April): 16–19.

Case Study 3. Circle Sentencing: A Case Study

The following is an actual case that was resolved through the use of circle sentencing.

The victim—the wife of the offender, who admitted to abusing her physically during two recent drunken episodes—spoke about the pain and embarrassment her husband had caused her and her family. After she had finished, the ceremonial feather (used to signify who would be allowed to speak next) was passed to the next person in the circle, a young man who spoke about the contributions the offender had made to the community, the kindness he had shown toward the elders by sharing fish and game with them, and the offender's willingness to help others with home repairs. An elder then took the feather and spoke about the shame the offender's behaviour had caused to his clan, noting that in the old days the offender would have been required to pay the woman's family a substantial compensation.

Having heard all this, the judge confirmed that the victim still felt that she wanted to try and work things out with her estranged husband and that she was receiving help from her own support group (including a victims' advocate). Summarizing the case by again stressing the seriousness of the offence and repeating the Crown counsel's opening remarks that a jail sentence was required, the judge then proposed that sentencing be delayed for six weeks until the time of the next circuit court hearing. If, during that time, the offender had (1) met the requirements presented earlier by a friend of the offender who had agreed to lead a support group, (2) met with the community justice committee to work out an alcohol and anger management treatment plan, (3) fulfilled the expectations of the victim and her support group, and (4) completed 40 hours of service to be supervised by the group, he would forgo the jail sentence. After a prayer in which the entire group held hands, the circle disbanded and everyone retreated to the kitchen area of the community centre for refreshments.

Source: Bazemore, G., and C.T. Griffiths, 1997. "Conferences, Circles, Boards, and Mediations: The 'New Wave' of Community Justice Decision Making." Federal Probation (June) 61(2): 25–37. Canadian Resource Centre for Victims of Crime, 2000. Online. http://www.crcvc.ca/docs/ restjust.pdf. (Retrieved May 30, 2008). p. 25.

Case Study 4. A Traditional Aboriginal Justice Ceremony

On December 4, 1993, a significant event was held in the gymnasium of an Aboriginal community on the west coast of Vancouver Island in British Columbia. The community held a traditional justice ceremony and potlatch (ceremonial feast), during which a man from the community who had sexually abused women in the community over a 35-year period faced his victims, their families, and invited witnesses. The event was made possible by one of the man's victims, known as The One Who Broke the Silence, who could no longer bear to return to the community, see the offender, or endure the pain of silence.

The One Who Broke the Silence approached her eldest brother and the speaker and told them of her desire to resolve this long-standing crisis through a traditional justice ceremony rather than through the Canadian justice system. Subsequently, three additional women publicly disclosed that they, too, had been sexually assaulted by the offender and that they would also participate in the ceremony. At the time of the ceremony, the age of the four victims ranged from late teens to mid-40s. All now had children, and three were married.

Prior to the start of the ceremony, three chairs were situated at one end of the gymnasium: one for the speaker, one for the eldest brother of The One Who Broke the Silence, and one for the offender. The victims, female elders, and female relatives sat in the front row of a semicircle. Behind them, in ever-widening semicircles, sat the witnesses from the village and from neighbouring Aboriginal communities. Witnesses play a very important role in this Aboriginal nation. The proceedings were initiated by the speaker, who explained to the assembly both the reasons for the ceremony and the sequence of events that would occur during the ceremony. He then presented his cousin, the offender, to the assembly. The offender entered and took a seat between the speaker and the eldest brother of The One Who Broke the Silence. It was the desire of The One Who Broke the Silence that the entire ceremony should be videotaped so as to provide a record for the community and for others.

The offender in this case was a highly respected member of the community, a historian and a ritualist, singer, mask carver, dancer, painter, and name giver. He was also highly respected in the Aboriginal communities along the west coast of Vancouver Island. He rose and spoke to the assembly, admitting guilt for his offences, describing in detail the crimes he had perpetrated upon the four victims, and relating how, through intimidation of the victims and their families, he had managed to silence their pain and suffering for so many years. The offender then begged for their forgiveness—not for them to forget but, within the traditions and customs of the First Nation, to forgive.

Following this, the offender approached each of the victims individually. Next to their feet stood a washbasin filled with water and, at the side, a towel. In the culture of this nation, the feet of women are washed during puberty ceremonies to signify their ascension to womanhood. Because of the pain and anguish inflicted on them by the offender, to that day the women had been denied their full womanhood. Now, in a symbolic gesture, the offender would wash the feet of the four victims, beginning with The One Who Broke the Silence.

The offender approached each of the victims individually, spoke to them, and apologized. The washing of the victim's feet followed. The washing began the process of transformation for each of the women from sexual assault victim to sexual assault survivor. The washing was the beginning of the process of renewal, a process that would allow the women to live full lives within the village. The washings took place before all of the assembled witnesses. The water from the washings was then transported outside, where it was placed in a fire, along with the basins and towels.

Following this, The One Who Broke the Silence approached the offender and removed a mask from his face. This mask, which had been carved by the offender, symbolized the persona of the offender at the time the offences were committed and until the present moment. Masks are among the most highly treasured possessions in this Aboriginal culture and are normally used in dances to demonstrate social status. The One Who Broke the Silence took this mask and placed it, face up, on the fire. As the fire consumed the mask, the speaker, accompanied by a rattle, chanted a prayer. The burning of the mask was the pivotal moment of the entire ceremony. At this juncture the ceremonial conversation involving the speaker, the victims, and the offender ended and the public conversation began. The victims were now survivors of sexual abuse and were spoken of as such. The mask burning terminated the ceremonial formalities of the event.

The offender, survivors, and witnesses then returned to the gymnasium, at which time the witnesses were asked to ratify the events that had occurred. For the next several hours, women in attendance spoke about the crimes and the victims, and offered support for the victims and the action they had taken. A feast was then held, and then the men in attendance spoke.

This ceremony was planned and carried out by the people in the community, without the assistance of the police, lawyers, the judiciary, or outside government. The objectives and process of this ceremony could not be more different from the adversarial system of criminal justice. The offender was held directly accountable to the victims of his crimes and was required to come before them and an assembly of witnesses to confess these crimes and to ask for forgiveness. The ceremony also provided an opportunity to begin the healing process for the victims, the offender, and the community. The victims were supported by their families, community members, and witnesses from neighbouring bands. The offender had the support of his family.

Source: Griffiths, C.T., and R. Hamilton, 1996. "Sanctioning and Healing: Restorative Justice in Canadian Aboriginal Communities." In J. Hudson and B. Galaway, eds., Restorative Justice: Theory, Practice, and Research, pp. 175–91. Monsey, NY: Criminal Justice Press.

Case Study 5. How to Run a Community Conference

One of the biggest obstacles to the use of community conferences is the inexperience of line officers with this form of dispute resolution. Once the participants have been identified, it is important that the officer create a forum where the interests of all of the parties to the incident can be heard and addressed. The following is a suggested "script" that gives an idea of how to organize a successful conference.

"Welcome, everyone. My name is ___. Before the conference begins, I would like to introduce everybody here and indicate their reason for being here." [Introduce each participant and indicate his or her relationship to the victim and the offender.]

"At this stage, I would like to thank you all for making the effort to attend this conference. This is difficult for all concerned and your presence here will help us deal with the matter that has brought us together.

"This conference will focus on an incident that happened on ___. It is important to understand that we will focus on what ___ did and how his/her unacceptable behaviour has affected others.

"___ has admitted his/her part in the incident and so we are not here to determine guilt or innocence. Our primary objective is to explore the ways in which people have been affected by the behaviour and, hopefully, work toward repairing the harm that has resulted from his/her actions. As well, we need to consider the interests of the general community or neighbourhood. We also want to try to ensure that no further harm is done to the victim or to the community and that the needs of ___ are addressed as well.

"If at any stage of the conference, [offender], you no longer wish to participate, you are free to leave; however, you must understand that if you do, the matter will then have to be dealt with by other means. If you participate to the end, this matter will be finalized subject to your satisfaction and your compliance with the conference agreement. Do you understand?" [Ask offender's parents and caregivers also.]

"This conference is an opportunity for all of you here to be involved in repairing the harm that has been done and to formulate a plan that will decrease the likelihood of it happening again in the future."

Offender

Ask the perpetrator to tell the story of what happened. If there is more than one perpetrator, each is asked to speak in turn, taking up the story at different intervals:

- "To help us understand what happened and who has been affected by this incident, we'll begin by asking ___ to tell us what happened. How did you come to be involved?"
- "Tell us what happened."
- "What were you thinking at the time?"
- "What have you thought about since the incident?"
- "Who do you think has been affected by your actions?"
- "In what way do you think they have been affected?"

Victim

The victim is then asked to describe the incident as he or she experienced it. If there is more than one victim, each is asked to speak.
    Key questions include:

- "What did you think at the time? Immediately afterwards?"
- "How has this incident affected you (in terms of health, emotions, physical harm, employment, relations with others, patterns of activity)?"
- "How did your family and friends react when they heard about the incident?"

Victim's Supporters

The victim's supporters, in turn, are then asked:

- "How did you find out about the incident?"
- "What did you think when you heard about it?"
- "What has happened since?"
- "In your view, how has the incident affected the victim?"

Offenders' Supporters

The offender's supporters are then asked for their reactions. Begin with the parents (keep mother for last unless father is very angry), caregivers, and then the other supporters in turn.
    To the parents/caregivers:

- "It must be very difficult for you to hear this." [Give the person time to respond at this point. Do not interrupt until he or she has finished speaking.]
- "What did you think when you heard that this had happened?"
- "What has happened since?"

Offender

Give the offender a chance to respond, having heard the stories from all participants.

- "Before we move on, is there anything you want to say to ___ or anyone else here?"

Agreement

Restitution and reparation are now negotiated.

1. Begin with the victim. "You've heard all that has been said here. What do you want to see happen out of this conference?"
2. Ask the same question of the victim's supporters. Allow plenty of time for discussion at this point. Plans to repair the harm may begin to develop.
3. As the group begins to develop a plan, be sure to ask the offender if he or she thinks it is fair.
4. To the offender's supporters, ask if they think it is a fair arrangement.

5. Ask the group if everyone is happy with the plan.
6. Make sure the agreement includes arrangements for monitoring and follow-up.

Closing the Conference

The facilitator summarizes the outcome(s) of the conference regarding restitution and reparation:

"Allow me to read back what you have agreed upon [at this point read the agreement aloud]. Completion of this agreement will go a long way to putting right the wrong and allowing all of us to learn from this unhappy experience. Is there anything else you want to say? No? Thank you all, again, for coming and participating in the conference. Although it has been difficult at times, we hope it's been worthwhile for everyone."

The facilitator writes up the agreement, which the participants sign, and then makes photocopies for anyone related to the incident or just for the key people. Where appropriate, refreshments can be served while the agreement is being written up, signed, and photocopied. Do not hurry participants out of the conference room, as informal reintegration can begin after the conclusion of the conference.

Case Study 6. Graffiti Vandalism: The Art of Tagging

Graffiti, known as mischief under S.430.[1] of the *Canadian Criminal Code,* has serious financial and emotional costs to victims, businesses, and communities. If left unchecked it can seriously damage the reputation of a community and adversely impact the economy and quality of life enjoyed by the residents. It may open the door for other property crimes and create an environment that tolerates more serious crimes.

The vast majority of graffiti vandalism is the result of "tagging," committed by juveniles for the main reason of recognition. Taggers are not necessarily gang members, they do not reflect any specific socio-economic background, and they come from all neighbourhoods. In some instances, the individuals responsible for writing illegal graffiti are expressing complex behaviour, requiring intervention and help.

The Vancouver Police Department's Anti-Graffiti Unit (AGU) found that the driving force behind individuals engaged in graffiti outweighed the deterrent effect of the criminal justice system. Given the high rates of recidivism and the complicated nature of the problem, the AGU collaborated with researchers from Simon Fraser University and restorative justice advocates to create a unique response to graffiti. The resulting program, entitled "RestART," is based upon successful restorative justice practices in correctional and community settings, as well as the AGU's work within the graffiti subculture.

The RestART initiative is a restorative justice response to graffiti and is a collaborative effort by the Vancouver Police Department, the City of Vancouver, and community members.

Source: © Vancouver Police Department

There are three main objectives of RestART:

1. To use processes based on the values and principles of restorative justice to:

   - bring together varying perspectives including youth, art community, victims, police, local business representatives, community and social service resources, legal graffiti artists, restorative justice advocates, academics;
   - create an environment where all participants feel safe, equal, and respected;
   - raise awareness of the impacts of graffiti;
   - create an sense of connection that can facilitate reintegration and acceptance into community; and
   - promote collective responsibility in finding solutions to the current situation of illegal graffiti.

2. To increase youths' skills and channel these abilities and talents towards legal opportunities.
3. To use a creative, interactive, experiential approach to learning.

   When police apprehend a youth or adult for illegal graffiti and it is decided that the formal court process is not appropriate, the following steps may occur:

   - The individual can be referred to additional programs such as drug and alcohol counseling, psychological testing, or art therapy.
   - The individual may be asked to complete various tasks related to their offense, such as an apology letter to the victim, cleaning up graffiti, victim reconciliation, or forms of related volunteer work.
   - The individual participates in the four-day RestART workshop, which includes the production of a mural on a public wall commissioned by the city.

REFERENCES

Abramson, A. and R. Chauhan. 2006. "RestART Information Package." City of Vancouver.

Bazemore, G. and C.T. Griffiths. 1997. "Conferences, Circles, Boards, and Mediations: The 'New Wave' of Community Justice Decision Making." *Federal Probation* (June) 61(2):25–37.

Canadian Resource Centre for Victims of Crime. 2011. "Restorative Justice in Canada— What Victims Should Know." Online. Retrieved June 10, 2012 (http://www.crcvc.ca/docs/restjust.pdf).

Church Council on Justice and Corrections. 1996. *Satisfying Justice: Safe Community Options That Attempt to Repair Harm from Crime and Reduce the Use or Length of Imprisonment.* Ottawa: Church Council on Justice and Corrections.

Department of Justice. 2008. *Aboriginal Justice Strategy.* Online. http://www.justice.gc.ca.

Galaway, B. and J. Hudson. 1996. *Restorative Justice: International Perspectives.* Monsey, NY: Criminal Justice Press.

Green, R.G. 1997. "Aboriginal Community Sentencing and Mediation: Within and Without the Circle." *Manitoba Law Journal* 25(1):77–125.

Green, R.G. 1998. *Justice in Aboriginal Communities: Sentencing Alternatives.* Saskatoon: Purich Publishing.

Griffiths, C.T. and R. Hamilton. 1996. "Sanctioning and Healing: Restorative Justice in Canadian Aboriginal Communities." pp. 175–91 in J. Hudson and B. Galaway, eds., *Restorative Justice: Theory, Practice, and Research*. Monsey, NY: Criminal Justice Press.

Griffiths, C.T., B. Whitelaw, and R. Parent. 1999. *Canadian Police Work*. Toronto: ITP Nelson.

Hatch-Cunningham, A. and C.T. Griffiths. 1997. *Canadian Criminal Justice: A Primer*. Toronto: Harcourt Brace.

Lajeunesse, T. and Associates Ltd. 1996. *Evaluation of Community Holistic Circle Healing: Hollow Water First Nation*. Volume 1. Final Report. Winnipeg: Manitoba Department of Justice.

Latimer, J., C. Dowden, and D. Muise. 2001. *The Effectiveness of Restorative Justice Practices: A Meta-analysis*. Ottawa: Department of Justice.

Marshall, T.F. 1999. *Restorative Justice: An Overview*. London: Research Development and Statistics Directorate, Home Office.

Ramsey, K. 1997. "A Return to Wisdom: Restorative Justice Revisited." *Pony Express, the RCMP's National News Magazine* (April):16–19.

Regina v. Gladue [1999] S.C.R. 688.

Regina v. Ipeelee [2012] 1 S.C.R. 433.

Regina v. Proulx [2000] 1 S.C.R. 61.

Roberts, J.V. and C. LaPrairie. 1996. "Sentencing Circles: Some Unanswered Questions." *Criminal Law Quarterly* 39(1):69–83.

Rugge, T., J. Bonta, and S. Wallace-Capretta. 2005. *Evaluation of the Collaborative Justice Project: A Restorative Justice Program for Serious Crime*. (User Report 2005-02). Ottawa: Public Safety Canada.

Spicer, V. 2005. "Couch Surfing in Vancouver: An Aggregate Study of the Vancouver Graffiti Suspect Network." Unpublished MA dissertation, School of Criminology, Simon Fraser University.

Stuart, B. 1996. "Circle Sentencing: Turning Swords into Ploughshares." pp. 193–206 in B. Galaway and J. Hudson, eds., *Restorative Justice: International Perspectives*. Monsey, NY: Criminal Justice Press.

Truth and Reconciliation Commission of Canada. 2012. Online. Retrieved May 23, 2012 (http://www.trc.ca).

Van Ness, D. and K.H. Strong. 1997. *Restoring Justice*. Cincinnati, OH: Anderson Publishing Co.

Wickins, R. 1998. *Community Conferencing: The Edmonton Model. Justice for Victims, Justice for Offenders, Justice for Citizens*. Edmonton: Edmonton Police Services.

Youth Criminal Justice Act. S.C. 2002, c.1. Online. http://www.canlii.org/ca/sta/y-1.5/

Zehr, H. 1995. *Changing Lenses: A New Focus for Crime and Justice*. Scottsdale, PA: Herald Press.

CHAPTER 10

The Community and Community Policing

Gang violence has become common in most Canadian communities. Combating gang violence requires community awareness. The Calgary Police Service invited students to participate in gang suppression strategies by designing posters such as this one.

Source: © Calgary Police Service

Learning Objectives

After completing this chapter, you should be able to:

- Identify the key issues relating to community involvement in community policing,

- Describe Ontario's Mobilization and Engagement Model of Community Policing and explain its purpose.

- Discuss the issues relating to cultural and visible minority and Aboriginal communities and community policing,

- Describe the nine steps for building working relationships with the community,

- Describe the strategies used to gather information on and facilitate partnerships with the community,

- Discuss the role of integrated service teams in community policing,

- Identify and discuss the potential obstacles to police–community partnerships,

- Describe the role of volunteers in community policing, and

- Describe the various types of community policing committees.

INTRODUCTION

Effective community policing requires that the community become involved in problem identification, assessment, and development of solutions. Solutions developed by police and imposed on the community generally fail. Citizens must be encouraged to network within their communities and to assume ownership of problem solving strategies. Police officers should act as catalysts for this process.
—*Edmonton Police Service (1996)*

In the philosophy and practices of community policing, the **community** is paramount. The general public is viewed as a partner in the effort to create and maintain safe and secure communities. The model of community policing provides community residents with increased opportunities for involvement in crime prevention programs, community police stations, and consultative committees. In Ontario, both the *Police Services Act* and the Adequacy Standards include specific directives to involve the community in the design and delivery of policing services.

THE COMMUNITY IN COMMUNITY POLICING

Most discussions and research studies on community policing focus on only one part of the police–community equation: the police. Very little attention has been given to the role and responsibilities of community citizens in the development and implementation of community policing. In fact, at first glance, it would seem that soliciting the participation of the community in the police effort would not be difficult. Public opinion surveys and field research studies have found that:

- most adults and youth have a positive perception of the police;
- in general, community residents prefer proactive policing to reactive policing;
- community residents desire more, not less, contact with police officers;
- there is strong support for increased visibility and accessibility of the police;
- foot patrols are favoured by community residents;
- community police stations are viewed positively by the general public; and
- there are resources in all communities that, if properly mobilized and channelled, can play a significant role in addressing problems of crime and disorder.

The "how to's" of getting the community interested and involved as a partner in policing, however, have proven to be a challenge for police services. In short, there are a number of important issues surrounding the "community" portion of the police–community equation. These are considered below.

Issue 1. Whose Responsibility Is It to Get the Community Involved?

It is one thing to declare that communities are actively responsible for policing their own neighbourhoods as a key principle of community policing and another to achieve this involvement. Among the questions that must be addressed are the following:

- Whose responsibility is it to ensure that communities become involved? The police? The community? The local or provincial government?
- Where will the resources come from to encourage and sustain community involvement? The police? The community?

Issue 2. Who and What Is the Community?

Although the term community appears often, the "who" and "what" remain unspecified. Two sociological definitions of community are widely recognized: (1) community as a locality, and (2) community as "networks of human interactions and social ties" (Gusfield 1975:xvi). It is often assumed that all of a community's people have a common interest and live in the same neighbourhood. Little consideration is given to the opportunities and obstacles presented by culturally, economically, and socially diverse communities composed of many different neighbourhoods. Box 10.1 highlights how a community of interest can assist the police service to solve crime.

Traditionally, the geographic boundaries of policing zones or districts have been established by the police alone, rather than in consultation with community residents. Most often, these boundaries are arbitrary and are set to meet organizational needs, rather than community ones. Needless to say, community residents may define the boundaries of their neighbourhoods differently from the police organization, whose boundaries are generally meaningless to citizens. For example, a police zone or boundary may have a river as one border. Residents on one side of the river may be policed by different groups of officers than residents on the other side, even though residents on both sides of the river view the river collectively and would be considered a community.

It is also important to recognize that a neighbourhood may be only a portion of a community, or may comprise an entire community, particularly in urban centres populated by cultural and ethnic minorities. In Edmonton, for example, the Edmonton Federation of Community Leagues has identified 155 communities (EFCL 2012).

In the City of Vancouver, the issue of community includes large populations of individuals that are diverse in their sexual orientation. This includes gay, lesbian, transgender, and bisexual individuals that together reflect the unique makeup of the

BOX 10.1

ENLISTING COMMUNITIES OF INTEREST TO SOLVE CRIME: THE CASE OF THE STOLEN NISSAN SKYLINE

On March 26, 2008 two men visited a specialty car dealership in Calgary, Alberta. They asked to test-drive a 1991 Nissan Skyline GT-R, a rare performance car made primarily for the Japanese market and rarely seen in North America. They left with the car and did not return with it. A police report was filed. The owner of the car also posted the theft on www.beyond.ca, a website for Canadian auto enthusiasts, to spread the word.

Car enthusiasts connected on the Internet and began actively looking for it. Sightings were posted to the website almost immediately. One person, who had seen the Skyline on the website, pulled up alongside it at a light and gave the driver a "rock out" sign. When the driver looked at him he was able to snap a photo using his cell phone and post it onto Google and Facebook. Within 15 minutes, a forum member added a link to a Google map with directions to the suspect's house. Other members scrambled to narrow their Facebook searches for the suspect to the closest high school. At about 11 p.m., a link to the Facebook profile of the thief appeared online.

In a little more than 24 hours from the time of the first post, members of the forum had spotted the car and assembled a name, photo, home address, and Facebook profile for the person seen behind the wheel of the Skyline. The police were called and the individual arrested. Had the police established an operation to collect the evidence, which the Beyond.ca community was able to achieve, investigative costs would have been several thousand dollars. The arrest has been profiled on a number of social media websites including YouTube.com and was also featured in the *New York Times* and in *Wired*.

This example illustrates how a mobilized community can assist the police in crime detection, investigation, and apprehension. It remains to be seen what deterrent effect social media websites may play in the future. The Beyond.ca site has also played a role in earlier cases of what might be called "open-source crime solving," including a hit and run collision from 2002. Already, many police agencies are turning to websites like YouTube to assist with identifying suspects in unsolved crimes.

For additional information related to this case, use the search term "stolen Calgary Skyline GTR" at www.youtube.com. You can also read about it at www.beyond.ca.

community. Earlier in our discussion, we pointed out that police officers carry out their duties in a wide range of policing environments—from urban neighbourhoods to remote Aboriginal communities—and that many of these communities reflect the cultural diversity that is a defining feature of Canadian society. This requires that the philosophy and practices of community policing be adapted to the specific needs and concerns of individual communities; this, in turn, makes it imperative that police officers have knowledge of the people and communities they are policing.

Issue 3. What Is the Level and Distribution of Community Participation?

It is important to consider both the level of participation in a community and the distribution of that participation (Skogan 1995:15). There may be an "unrepresentativeness" among the community representatives involved in any community policing initiative: people representing certain community interest groups, such as businesspeople, may be more active than people with lower socioeconomic and income levels. Little is understood about the conditions that facilitate or hinder substantial community involvement in community policing initiatives. Ironically, the community residents who are most likely to be "policed" are those who are the least likely to have access to the police, to influence police policy and practices, and to participate in police–community initiatives. This is often the case in communities where there are low levels of home ownership and where the residents are working hard to get out of the community.

There is also the question of what the community is supposed to do. Community residents may not clearly understand the principles of community policing and, like police officers, may equate it with crime prevention. Where community committees do exist, their roles and responsibilities may not be clearly defined or may be focused on a single issue. Traditionally, the hierarchical structure of police services has hindered community input into and involvement with police services. Community policing provides the opportunity for community residents to become involved in a partnership with the police.

Issue 4. Who Trains the Community?

Although police services have taken steps to ensure that community policing is a cornerstone of both recruit and in-service training, little attention has been given to training community residents to assume a role as equal partners in preventing and responding to crime and social disorder. This is referred to in the police literature as "community empowerment"—that is, giving to communities the necessary tools and knowledge to respond effectively to crime and social disorder at the local level. Generally speaking, citizen education initiatives are limited to ride-alongs, citizen academies, neighbourhood watch programs, and citizen foot patrol, all of which will be discussed later in this chapter. Such programs are often presented as "Get to Know Your Local Police" programs. These programs do provide citizens with some insights into police work but they are insufficient, on their own, to prepare citizens for a significant role in dealing with problems.

Training community residents requires the development of workshops and forums on leadership, community building, and problem solving, as well as on strategies for identifying and mobilizing community resources. These programs can be offered under the auspices of the police, municipal or provincial governments, or community organizations. The objective is to build a solid foundation for substantive citizen involvement in police–community partnerships. One such initiative is featured in Box 10.2, which focuses on the Community Mobilization Units in the Toronto Police Service.

BOX 10.2

COMMUNITY POLICING IN BRITISH COLUMBIA: "E" DIVISION RCMP

Prevention and community engagement are integral to the philosophy of Community Policing. RCMP "E" Division's vision is: "to be recognized leaders in Crime Prevention, a core responsibility of effective policing in British Columbia. We support the development, implementation and evaluation of sustainable strategies and initiatives that prevent crime and victimization."

Strategies and initiatives in 2010/11 include:

Creating and implementing the *Youth Officer Training Course* in recognition of the importance of a cooperative partnership between schools and detachments, and the growing demand for the RCMP to provide effective service delivery to schools throughout the country. Creating an effective and balanced approach to engaging youth required that the course content includes topics relating to prevention, intervention, and enforcement. During the three-day trainings, subject-matter experts and resources cover topics ranging from legal issues within school environments to on-line sexual predators targeting school aged children. "E" Division Crime Prevention & Program Support Services (CP&PSS) facilitated five training sessions across the province with over 150 Regular Members, representing more than half of the detachments in "E" Division.

Connecting with the community — RCMP members and staff are actively engaged in the communities they serve outside of their regular police duties. In 67% of detachments, staff are now, or recently were, coaching youth in a total of 19 different sports activities including aikido, basketball, football, hockey and skating. Police officers mentor youth as Big Brothers and Big Sisters in 31% of detachments. They are also contributing to their communities as leaders in Scouting and the Canadian Cadet Program in 26% of detachments, and as active partners in the Vocational Venturer Program, currently operating in Prince George, which provides co-ed youth RCMP training opportunities in addition to traditional scouting outdoor activities.

Reserve Program — As Reservists, retired RCMP members pass on corporate knowledge and mentor younger members while continuing to contribute to their communities. "E" Division has 75 active Reservists who contributed 43,090 hours of work in 2010. Reservist deployments included the 2010 Vancouver Winter Olympic Games, the G8/G20 Summits in Toronto as well as summer policing duties at Christina Lake (Kootenay Boundary Regional Detachment) and Wreck Beach (University Detachment).

© 2011. HER MAJESTY THE QUEEN IN THE RIGHT OF CANADA as represented by The Royal Canadian Mounted Police (RCMP). Reproduced with Permission of the RCMP.

(continues)

Auxiliary Constable Program — There are currently 975 Auxiliary Constables in "E" Division, 108 of whom graduated in 2010 from Basic Auxiliary Constable Training. Throughout the calendar year, these dedicated volunteers contributed approximately 120,000 hours to community policing activities relating to public safety and crime prevention.

Victim Services — Together, over 170 Victim Service staff and over 260 Victim Service volunteers provided thousands of victims, witnesses, family members and others affected by crime and traumatic events across BC with services including: crisis intervention at scene, practical assistance, follow up support, police file updates, court file updates and referral to other services.

Citizens on Patrol — These programs engage community-minded volunteers as "eyes and ears" for the RCMP in their community. They are trained to accurately observe and report suspicious or criminal activity. Results of a province-wide survey undertaken in November 2010 (85.6% response):

- 61 programs currently operate in RCMP jurisdictions in British Columbia;
- Over 1800 volunteers are active with the program; and
- In partnership with the Insurance Corporation of BC, Citizen Patrol volunteers operate both the Stolen Auto Recovery and Lock Out Auto Crime programs.

Source: © 2011. HER MAJESTY THE QUEEN IN THE RIGHT OF CANADA as represented by The Royal Canadian Mounted Police (RCMP). Reproduced with Permission of the RCMP.

Issue 5. The Potential and Limits of Community Involvement

A key question that has generally remained unaddressed in discussions of community policing is whether the community *wants* to become involved in police–community partnerships. There are a variety of reasons why community residents may not become involved in community policing initiatives, including fear of retaliation from the criminal element, apathy, lack of time, hostility to and distrust of the police, a lack of understanding on the part of community residents as to their role, and the diversity of needs among community residents (Grinc 1994). In addition, neighbourhoods are becoming increasingly fluid as residents move regularly in pursuit of educational and employment opportunities and for other personal and professional reasons. Furthermore, research studies have found the following:

- Many citizens understand little about the role and activities of community policing initiatives such as community police stations.
- Community residents rarely access the services offered by community police stations.
- Police services have experienced considerable difficulties in generating and sustaining community interest and involvement in community policing initiatives (Hornick, Borrows, Tjowvold, and Phillips 1990; Liou and Savage 1996; Polowek 1995).

There is also a flip side to this issue: What about segments of the community that may want to become *too* involved in partnerships with the police?

In recent years, police services have been relying increasingly on the private sector and community groups to fund certain police activities and initiatives. Called **P3s**, for "public–private partnerships," the goal is to offset high costs of policing through partnerships with the private sector. The Winnipeg Police Service, for example is constructing new police stations using P3s to support the high costs of facilities. The Ottawa Police Service has also received assistance from the private sector for a number of initiatives. The companies involved include:

- Brinks, an armoured car company that pays for the police to investigate armoured car and other robberies;
- Corel, a computer company that finances "cop cards"—baseball-like cards with pictures of police officers on them—as part of a police program for youth; and

- local car dealers that donate money for the police to combat auto theft (*Ottawa Citizen* 1996:A6).

In some jurisdictions, local car dealerships have provided the vehicles used for patrol.

Critics of the practice of private funding for police programs contend that a dangerous precedent is being set—that is, only special interest groups with financial resources will be provided with police service. Supporters of private funding reply that the increasing involvement of the private sector in funding police services is not only a consequence of reducing operating budgets, but also an important component of the police–community partnership within the framework of community policing. You will have an opportunity to wrestle with this issue in Exercise 1 later in the chapter.

THE ONTARIO MOBILIZATION AND ENGAGEMENT MODEL OF COMMUNITY POLICING

In 2010, the Ontario Association of Chiefs of Police introduced a new community policing model called **Ontario's Mobilization and Engagement Model of Community Policing** (see the illustration on the next page). This model incorporates the key ideas we have discussed throughout the text. For example, the idea that community policing is tailored to the individual needs of communities is clearly reflected by the degree to which a community requires police assistance. For this reason, the model serves as a diagnostic tool in which both the police and community leaders assess how much support is required to achieve a safer community.

The model is broken down into four key areas:

- Enforcement and crime suppression,
- Community mobilization and crime prevention,
- Community safety and consultation, and
- Community engagement and liaison.

Police officers meet with community leaders and determine how a community rates across these four dimensions. For example, in communities having high repeat calls for police service, there is typically a requirement for a high level of attention from police to establish order through frequent high-visibility policing and enforcement.

The model also assists in the identification of strategies which help to maintain or improve overall community safety. For example, in communities requiring a high level of police support, police-led and -initiated strategies such as "hot spot" policing or targeting prolific offenders are necessary to reduce crime and disorder. These strategies place significant demands on the police. The strategy in this stage of community development is to stabilize neighbourhood problems and begin developing community capacity (ability) to take ownership for many problems that lead to feelings of insecurity. The police must apply principles of problem-oriented policing in this stage to ensure positive outcomes are sustained.

The goal for both the police and the community is to move away from a community requiring a high need for police assistance to a low need. While the process may be initiated by the police initially, the police identify community leaders who are able to sustain and build on positive accomplishments and continually engage the community to address many of its crime and disorder problems.

Over time, through the application of community-based policing strategies, intelligence-led policing efforts (see Chapter 3), situational crime prevention efforts (e.g., target hardening), CPTED, and crime prevention through social development, the community is better equipped to manage its own problems and consequently lessen its reliance on the police.

Ontario's Mobilization and Engagement Model of Community Policing

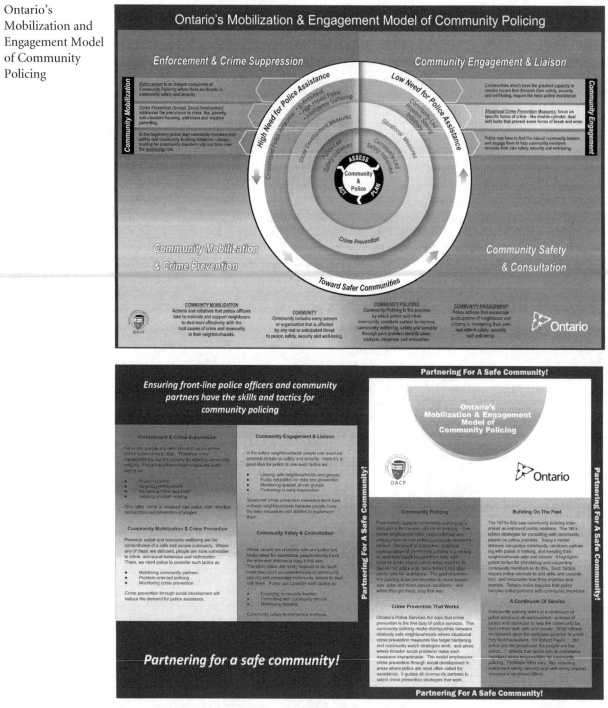

Source: Courtesy of Ontario Association of Chiefs of Police

As you review the model, try to relate key ideas you have learned from each chapter. This will help you to understand how community policing has become much more strategic in its approach.

CULTURAL AND VISIBLE MINORITY COMMUNITIES AND COMMUNITY POLICING

The cultural diversity of rural and urban Canada presents major challenges to police services. They must increase the number of police recruits from cultural and ethnic minorities, ensure that officers receive training that makes them culturally sensitive and aware, and implement strategies that will facilitate the development of police–community partnerships.

Increased immigration and the movement of Aboriginal peoples have fuelled rapid population growth in a number of urban centres such as Vancouver, Montreal, and Toronto. Police agencies in cities (notably the Greater Toronto Area, which is the fastest growing region in the country) are faced with the challenge of developing police–community partnerships with a variety of "communities" within the area.

In recent years, there have been several highly publicized incidents involving police officers and members of racial and ethnic minorities. This has led to increasing pressure on the police from community groups and politicians and to a number of commissions of inquiry into police actions. In 1995, the Commission on Systemic Racism in the Ontario Criminal Justice System issued its report on racism in the provincial justice system. Among the findings of that commission were that both Anglo and non-Anglo residents of Toronto believe that the police do not treat all groups of citizens the same and that Blacks were more likely to feel they had been treated unfairly the last time they had been stopped by the police (Gittens and Cole 1995).

Distrust of the police on the part of community residents may undermine community policing initiatives. In 1996, for example, the RCMP opened a community policing office in the Black Cultural Centre in North Preston, Nova Scotia. This is a community near Halifax with a history of tension and conflict between residents and the police. Despite support from many community residents, subsequent melees and standoffs between the police and angry mobs have challenged both the community and the police to bridge the gap between the RCMP and the community.

This example illustrates that it may take many years to address and overcome the deep-seated suspicions of the police that are held by some community residents, and that the resolve of the police and the community to develop a true partnership will be severely tested along the way.

Police agencies require community support, so they often have specialized units dedicated to responding to issues related to diversity and cultural conflict. In Calgary, for example, the Diversity Resources Unit maintains a number of portfolios that respond to cultural and interest-based diversity (e.g., the gay community). It is important to maintain these units, and at times when cultural tensions are high, these units can be highly effective in defusing racial or interest-based tensions. Calgary's Diversity Resources Unit has been used to address community concerns when citizens have been killed by police, in high-profile use-of-force incidents, in allegations of racial profiling, and in a high-profile police raid on a gay bathhouse.

ABORIGINAL COMMUNITIES AND THE POLICE

Relations between Aboriginal peoples and the police, historically and in contemporary times, have often been characterized by a high degree of mutual suspicion and hostility. Numerous task forces and commissions of inquiry conducted over the past two decades have documented instances in which police officers acted in a discriminatory fashion against Aboriginal peoples. (See Box 10.3 for an example.) This has led to initiatives on the part of the RCMP and provincial and municipal police forces to improve the training and cultural sensitivity of police officers, to establish better lines of communication with First Nations communities, and to support the First Nations police forces that have been created.

In recent years, Aboriginal bands have developed community-based criminal justice services and programs. These initiatives have been designed to address the overrepresentation of Aboriginal peoples at all stages of the criminal justice system—from arrest to incarceration—in most regions of the country. This trend has provided the opportunity for First Nations peoples not only to create autonomous police services,

BOX 10.3

THE IPPERWASH INQUIRY

Anthony O'Brien George, known as Dudley George, was an Aboriginal man who, along with his descendants, grew up on the Stony Point Reserve. He was 38 years old at the time of his death. He and other First Nations men, women, and children occupied Ipperwash Provincial Park on Labour Day, September 4, 1995, to protest the federal government's refusal to return the ownership of the Stony Point Reserve. The federal government had appropriated this reserve in 1942 to use as a military training site pursuant to the *War Measures Act,* and promised to return it after World War II. Numerous requests had been made by First Nations people to have the land returned to them, but after 50 years it remained in the possession of the federal government. Frustration had increased over the five decades.

Two days after the First Nations occupation of Ipperwash Provincial Park an altercation occurred between protestors and the Ontario Provincial Police, and Dudley George was shot and killed by police. The incident prompted a comprehensive inquiry, which was established by the Government of Ontario on November 12, 2003, under the *Public Inquiries Act.* Its mandate was to inquire and report on events surrounding the death of Dudley George. The inquiry was also asked to make recommendations that would avoid violence in similar circumstances in the future. On May 31, 2007, the Honourable Justice Sidney Linden released the Commission of Inquiry's final report containing its findings, conclusions, and recommendations. He ruled that the OPP, the former Ontario government led by Mike Harris, and the federal government all bear responsibility for events that led to George's death.

Among the main findings were the following:

- The disputed land should be returned immediately to the Stony Point First Nation, which should also receive compensation.

- Ontario should establish a permanent, independent, and impartial agency to facilitate and oversee the settling of land and treaty claims.

- Ontario should improve public education about its land claim policies, as well as Aboriginal burial and heritage sites.

- Access to the Ontario land claims process should depend on whether the documentation filed by the First Nations provides clear evidence that there has been a breach of the legal obligations of the Crown.

- The OPP should establish a formal consultation committee with major Aboriginal organizations in Ontario.

- Provincial police should establish an internal process to ensure racist and culturally insensitive behaviour by police is dealt with publicly.

- The province should establish and fund an Ontario Aboriginal Reconciliation Fund.

For more detailed information, or to read the entire Ipperwash Inquiry Report, go to the Attorney General's website at: www.attorneygeneral.jus.gov.on.ca/inquiries/ipperwash/report/vol_1/index.html.

but also to establish partnerships between Aboriginal and non-Aboriginal police services. Box 10.4 summarizes the approach the Government of Ontario is taking to strengthen its relationship with Aboriginal communities.

COMMUNITY POLICING AND SOCIAL DEVELOPMENT

Police agencies such as the Waterloo Regional Police and the Calgary Police Service are adopting a new and different approach to community policing, centred on the concept of social development. The strategy involves focusing not on the problems within a community, but rather on building capacity within a specific area of the community. The police agency and the community work together in a partnership, drawing on existing strengths for the purpose of benefiting the overall health of the municipality.

BOX 10.4

ABORIGINAL JUSTICE STRATEGY

The Province of Ontario has created an "Aboriginal Justice Strategy" (AJS), in partnership with Aboriginal communities, to address their specialized justice needs in the areas of prevention, intervention, reintegration, and relapse prevention. The AJS places an emphasis on prevention for children and youth, promoting community safety in urban and rural Aboriginal communities.

The Ontario Ministry of the Attorney General is attempting to foster the goals of the AJS by working with Aboriginal communities and organizations and other government ministries to design an integrated policy framework related to Aboriginal justice. This is achieved by:

- having Aboriginal communities identify justice priorities within their unique settings;

- establishing better linkages among existing provincial justice programs and the health, education, and social service sectors;

- promoting more effective linkages between relevant Ontario ministries and other levels of government;

- facilitating the effective use of existing resources through strategic coordination, targeted delivery of existing services, and a community development approach.

The Aboriginal Justice Strategy milestones include:

- In 2004, Youth Justice Services held community consultations to explore ways to reduce the overrepresentation of Aboriginal youth in care and find alternatives to custody.

- The Ontario Provincial Police (OPP) continues to work with First Nations that are wishing to administer their own police services. Since 2005, there are 92 First Nations communities policed by eight self-directed services. For communities without self-directed police services, the OPP administers policing for 20 communities under the Ontario First Nations Policing Agreement and provides direct services to 22 other communities.

- A series of working meetings continue with Aboriginal leaders, in partnership with the Ministry of the Attorney General, to develop justice services that respond to the diverse needs of Aboriginal communities across Ontario.

As was noted early in the text, community problems are often complex and deeply rooted, which typically rules out the option of a quick fix. When the unique strengths and resources within the individual community are recognized, the chances of success in resolving the problem are far greater.

One of the key areas for implementing positive change is often within the school setting. Research studies have demonstrated a relationship between school performance and criminal offending in youth. School performance can be a significant predictor of both adolescent and adult criminality. Delinquents tend to be less successful in school than those who are not delinquents, they have lower attendance rates, and they are more likely to leave school early. School dropouts are far more likely to be in trouble with the law and are more likely to be unemployed or underemployed.

These factors underscore the necessity for keeping Canada's youth in school. In its discussion paper "Crime Prevention through Social Development: A Literature Review," the John Howard Society of Alberta notes:

There is growing recognition within both aboriginal and non-Aboriginal communities of the need to stress prevention, rather than remedial strategies, if problems such as literacy and low educational levels are to be banished from our society. Within this prevention strategy, two factors are recognized. The first is that communities and families, not experts and governments, possess the creative energies necessary to find and manage durable community-based prevention initiatives. The second factor is that most human development problems are the result of multiple and intertwined factors or deprivations. Since people are shaped by their total environment, strategies must address this whole environment, not just one specific aspect of it. (CCSD 1991, p. 17; quoted in John Howard Society of Alberta 1995)

A useful way of setting out the particular strengths and capacities of a community is with a community assets map, like the one in Figure 10.1.

DEVELOPING POLICE-COMMUNITY PARTNERSHIPS

In Chapter 7, we discussed the strategies that police services use to implement the philosophy and principles of community policing. These include preparing a business plan, conducting environmental scans, developing partnerships with communities and neighbourhoods, incorporating best practices, and assessing the effectiveness of programs and interventions. Many of these same techniques are also used in problem-oriented policing, discussed in Chapter 5.

Community policing also requires that individual police officers use many of these same approaches in carrying out their duties. The specific demands placed on community police officers (CPOs) will, of course, depend upon the area to which they are assigned. As well, the ability of CPOs to establish community partnerships, to solve problems, and to develop programs will be affected by the level of support provided by the police service. This includes ensuring that officers have the necessary resources to carry out their tasks.

There are a number of steps that police services and CPOs must take to build working relationships with the community.

Step 1. Identify Potential Partners

The first step involves preliminary discussions with community groups, government and non-profit agencies and organizations, and the business community. Potential partners should represent a cross-section of the neighbourhood or community and

Figure 10.1 Community Assets Map

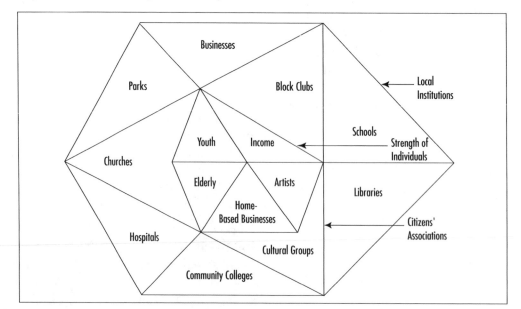

Source: Building a Safer Community-Based Crime Prevention Manual. Reproduced with the permission of the Minister of Public Works and Government Services (2012).

include persons and groups that have traditionally been marginalized, such as low-income residents and youth. CPOs should also make a concerted effort to visit agencies and organizations in the community and introduce themselves. There is no substitute for face-to-face meetings.

Step 2. Develop a Clear Understanding of the Neighbourhood or Community Being Policed

When first assigned to a zone or area, the police officer should review any environmental scans that the police service has conducted, as well as other reports from provincial or municipal ministries and departments relating to current and projected socioeconomic developments; crime patterns; commercial and industrial features; and social, health, and mental health issues and problems. This includes reviewing materials on interventions carried out by officers previously assigned to the area. The officer should not assume that this information will automatically be made available.

It is also recommended that the new CPO meet with officers who have previously policed the area. This will provide the new officer with vital information on current issues and problems, on initiatives that are currently underway in the community, and on interventions that have been attempted in the past. Meeting with these officers enhances the cumulative experience of officers policing the area and provides the incoming officer with information on key community groups and resource persons as well as on troublesome individuals and issues.

Based on this information, the CPO can develop a community profile that will provide useful information for addressing community concerns and problems.

Step 3. Initiate Dialogue

Every opportunity should be taken to interact with community groups and residents in a non–law enforcement capacity. Informal conversations with residents can provide the CPO with important information on community sentiment, the problems and issues faced by the various stakeholder groups in the community, residents' perceptions of previous policing efforts, and past experiences of residents in collaborating with police.

In many communities, youth problems consume a considerable portion of the public's concern and police attention. This includes parties; drag racing; loitering; drinking in public places such as school playgrounds and parks; and vandalism, including "tagging" (graffiti). The CPO should make time to visit places and spaces where youth congregate, be they the local youth centre, the skateboard park, or the 7-Eleven parking lot, to meet youth in a non–law enforcement context.

Experienced police officers make an effort to meet youth, not only to place names to faces, but also to develop a rapport that will be useful in enforcement situations. Youths can be a valuable source of information about their friends and acquaintances, and they can also assist officers in defusing potentially explosive situations at house parties and during parking lot confrontations and drinking incidents. An excellent way to meet young people is to co-sponsor events with the local youth centre or community service organization. This includes police–youth sports events such as softball, basketball, pool events, and volleyball tournaments.

Lower-profile youth offences, such as bullying, intimidation, and exclusion, also require a strategic response by the CPO. The national bullying strategy calls for the early intervention into the lives of young people by addressing issues of antisocial behaviour. In this regard, police personnel, teachers, social workers, parents, and community members require a coordinated effort in dealing with youth violence in the community. For example, in Taber, Alberta, youth care workers, school administrators, and the RCMP have developed a common practice to assess potentially violent behaviour in students before a tragedy occurs.

Finally, CPOs must also be aware of "multi-disciplinary collaborative responses" to threat-making and other forms of violent behaviour in the community environment. There is a need for the CPO to establish a protocol using what is referred to as the four-pronged assessment model. This model encourages the evaluation of potential threats and threat-making behaviour by examining risk factors that include the individual personality of the youth, family dynamics, social dynamics, and school dynamics. Police personnel and other community agencies such as social services professionals and school administration staff serve as agencies within the community that are equipped to strategize and intervene in extreme instances involving violent youth behaviour.

Step 4. Organize Community Meetings

Community meetings provide a forum for citizens to express their concerns about problems in the community. They also enable CPOs to identify citizens who may be interested in serving on a community committee. There are a number of different types of community meetings, including general forums, meetings with specific stakeholder groups, and meetings with community policing committees. We will examine the important issues relating to community meetings in Exercise 1.

Step 5. Identify Issues

CPOs should work with the community to identify the issues that are of greatest concern and of the highest priority. They should try to isolate those issues on which there is consensus and that have the greatest potential to be resolved through police–community collaborative efforts.

Step 6. Formulate a Plan or Develop an Action Plan

The police and the community should formulate a plan that considers all facets of the issues that have been identified and that sets out a clear course of action that has been agreed upon by all parties. Developing an action plan would include:

- determining the level of intervention,
- selecting participants,
- identifying prevention strategy options,
- selecting the best strategies,
- setting goals and objectives, and
- preparing a work plan.

Figure 10.2 provides an outline of the strategies and actions that could be considered.

Step 7. Take Action

Both the police and the community must be involved in implementing the plan of action. The intervention should closely follow that plan. Taking action may require building community support through personal contact. An effective communication strategy is vitally important to ensure that information and ideas are shared among all the interested parties and, as well, to prevent misunderstandings that might undermine the initiative.

Step 8. Maintain the Partnership

One of the greatest challenges facing CPOs is how to sustain community interest and involvement in the partnership. There are a number of strategies that can be used to sustain the police–community partnership, including choosing problems with a high

Figure 10.2 Selecting Strategies and Approaches

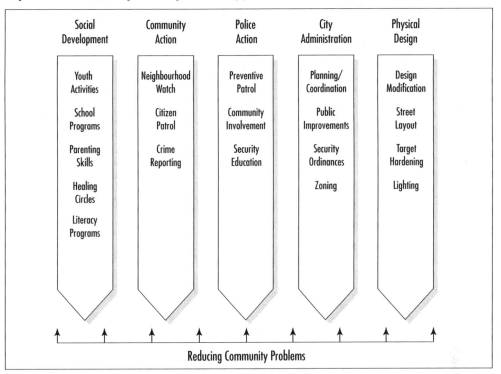

Source: Building a Safer Community-Based Crime Prevention Manual. Reproduced with the permission of the Minister of Public Works and Government Services (2012).

likelihood of success (at least at the outset), publicizing the successes of the partnership, and giving community residents a substantive role to play in addressing the identified issues. Other strategies could include providing ongoing training for all participants to ensure that interest remains high, and creating websites and newsletters to disseminate information, highlight activities, and increase the visibility of the partnership in the community. Rewards and incentives such as public commendations, block parties, and awards dinners can also be offered.

Step 9. Document Activities

The police–community interventions and their outcomes should be recorded. This will create a written record of activities that can be referred to in the future. An evaluation of impacts and outcomes will also suggest whether resources are being used effectively and whether any changes are required in the strategies.

Each CPO should create a personal business plan that outlines the key priorities to be addressed, sets out timelines, and determines the goals and objectives for the year. Among other things, this will provide documentation to supervising officers that can be used for the officer's annual performance assessment.

Figure 10.3 sets out a planning model for community problem solving that can be used to address problems of crime and social disorder.

DETERMINING COMMUNITY PRIORITIES AND CONCERNS: THE COMMUNITY POLICING TOOLBOX

In the past, many police services assumed that the police themselves were in the best position to determine how communities should be policed and resources allocated. Furthermore, there were few if any mechanisms for the community to offer feedback to

Figure 10.3 A Community Problem-Solving Planning Model

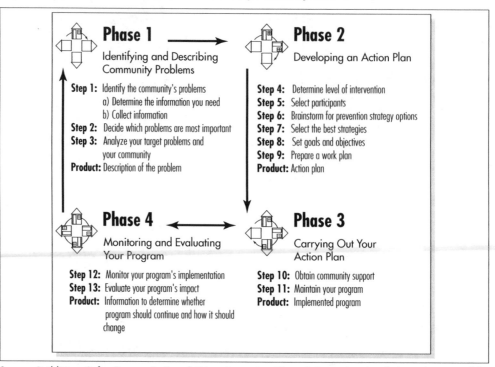

Source: Building a Safer Community-Based Crime Prevention Manual. Reproduced with the permission of the Minister of Public Works and Government Services (2012).

the police on how well the police were doing in addressing the needs and concerns of community residents.

Community policing requires that the police service develop the capacity to determine the priorities and concerns of the community being policed, if such a capacity does not already exist. In addition, it is essential that police services develop ways to solicit continual feedback from the community, so that policies and initiatives can be enhanced, modified, or, if found to be ineffective, discontinued. Police services must also develop mechanisms to communicate with other criminal justice and social service agencies.

Community input is a core component of community policing, which strives to develop true partnerships between the community and the police. The difficulties of fulfilling this mandate should not be underestimated. Community residents often overestimate the abilities of the police to address problems of crime and social disorder; they may also have conflicting expectations of the police or believe that the police should be equally concerned with law enforcement, crime control, crime prevention, community policing, and order maintenance. For most community residents, knowledge of the police is limited to the often-distorted images presented in television shows and the mass media or to encounters with officers during traffic stops.

The Ottawa Police Service has established a program—"Partnership in Action"—designed to nurture and strengthen relationships with the community and to collaboratively work on common problems. For more information, check out the Ottawa Police Service website at www.ottawapolice.ca and then look under the "Community Partnerships" link.

Developing a Community Profile

One of the best ways to determine the needs, concerns, and perceptions of community residents is to construct a **community profile**. This can include information on the demographic characteristics of the community, crime rates, and community issues and concerns, as well as residents' perceptions of crime and of the effectiveness of the police and criminal justice system. Figure 10.4 depicts the possible information sources for a community profile.

There are a number of techniques that can be used to gather information for a community profile. These include community surveys, focus groups, public forums, and community consultative committees.

Community Surveys

Community surveys provide a cost-effective way to gather information from community residents in order to improve service delivery. These surveys are most often conducted by telephone, but can also be carried out by mail or by visiting individual households in the community. The Policing for Results Survey, created by the Ontario Provincial Police and discussed in Box 6.7, illustrates a technique used by one police service to gather information from the community in order to enhance policing effectiveness. Community policing teams in any neighbourhood can use this same technique.

Focus Groups

Focus groups are a widely used, cost-effective technique for obtaining information from various groups of citizens within the community. Focus group discussions bring together individuals who share a common attribute, be it age (adult or youth), gender, or

Figure 10.4 Possible Information Sources for a Community Profile

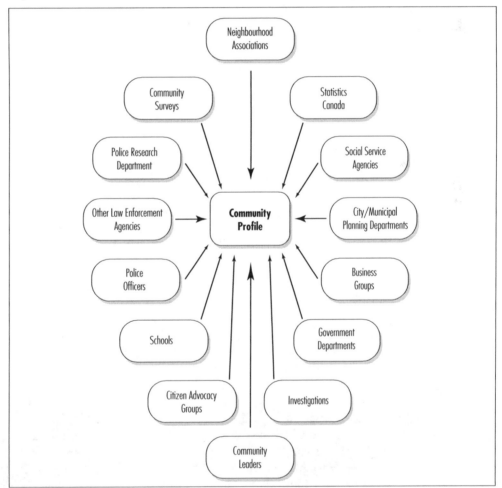

Source: "Developing a Community Profile. A Manual for the Development and Implementation of Community Profiling for Police Planners and Managers", in *Community Policing: Shaping the Future*, published by the Ministry of Solicitor General and Correctional Services in 1991.

experience (victim or offender). A facilitator, preferably a person from outside the community, runs the session and leads a discussion related to the topic at hand. Generally, the intent is to gather information on the perceptions, experiences, and observations of the group; the focus is not to provide a forum for individual residents to relate specific details of their personal situation. A focus group discussion may last several hours. A research assistant, who also attends the session, takes down participants' comments. Through the discussions, the facilitator can draw out the experiences and opinions of the group members and identify the major issues relating to the specific topic.

Focus groups are also valuable in securing the involvement of community residents in the dialogue about how policing services are organized and delivered in the municipality. They make it possible to include a diversity of groups. One cannot assume that everyone has the same view of the police, so it is important to include groups that may be more likely to have contact and potential conflict with the police. Among the different groups in a community are:

- high school students,
- high school-aged youth who are not in school,
- the elderly,
- members of the business community,
- members of visible/cultural minority communities, and
- general community residents.

The topics that might be addressed in a focus group discussion include:

- general perceptions of community life,
- identification of the key issues confronting the community,
- perceptions of crime and social disorder in the community,
- the role of the police in the community,
- citizens' experiences with and expectations of the police,
- suggestions on how to improve the delivery of policing services,
- the nature and extent of involvement in community activities generally and crime prevention initiatives specifically, and
- the potential for increased community involvement in preventing and responding to crime and social disorder.

Focus groups are not designed to solicit the personal experiences of community residents with the police, but rather to gather more general information on a variety of community and policing-related topics. As such, focus groups are not oriented toward documenting specific case incidents.

Public Forums

Public forums (also known as town hall meetings) can raise the profile of community concerns and provide police with a venue where they can explain their goals and objectives. In staging or participating in public forums, the police make themselves available to hear the concerns and priorities of community residents. There is the potential for establishing ongoing lines of communication.

Public forums, however, can be counterproductive. If the forum is dominated by one specific community interest group, or by specific individuals, little progress will be made. Individual citizens may attend public forums with a specific agenda, such as criticizing police actions, relating personal stories and experiences with the police, or preventing other groups from the community from expressing their concerns and needs.

For public forums to be successful and not sidetracked or hijacked by personal agendas, the focus of the forum should be clearly defined and communicated to the community. All parties with a vested interest in the topic at hand should be invited, and a neutral third party—that is, someone not connected to the police—should moderate the proceedings. Other obstacles to establishing partnerships with the community are identified and discussed below.

Multi-Agency Meetings and Liaison Groups

Developing police–community partnerships involves breaking down the barriers that have traditionally separated justice agencies and organizations. There is a recognition that problem solving requires more than a focus on law enforcement and that many of the difficulties experienced by individuals, families, neighbourhoods, and communities are the result of poverty; mental disabilities; health problems such as fetal alcohol syndrome (FAS); and other environmental, psychological, or physical problems.

Increasingly, police services and their officers are collaborating with other agencies and organizations. This includes developing **integrated service teams** made up of representatives from the police, social and mental health services, health agencies, and community organizations. Many police services have Children At Risk Response Teams (CARRTs) composed of a social services worker and a police officer working together in a patrol car to respond to any call where the health, safety, and welfare of a child is deemed to be at risk. Integration is a key feature of the developing model of community based strategic policing.

EDUCATING THE COMMUNITY

One of the biggest challenges facing police services is to develop strategies to educate the community about community policing and the potential for police–community partnerships. Research has found that community residents, even those who have been the victims of crime, tend not to become involved in community policing initiatives, and generally have little knowledge of police activities.

Police services have developed a number of initiatives to address the problems of citizen apathy and disinterest. Larger Canadian police services offer "citizen police academies" to educate citizens about policing, its limitations, and its possibilities. Smaller police services such as the Cornwall Community Police Service actively engage community groups by way of police presentations, displays, and "Fact Sheets" that serve to inform members of the public (see Box 10.5). The Toronto Police Service, through

---

BOX 10.5

CORNWALL COMMUNITY POLICE SERVICE CRIME REDUCTION AND COMMUNITY PARTNERSHIPS: TAKING CRIME DOWN

Taking crime down and crime reduction are high on the list of priorities with the members of the Cornwall Community Police Service. The Crime Reduction and Community Partnerships Division (CRCPD) is actively engaged in presentations and displays to many community groups in order to educate community members in taking crime down.

The officers within the CRCPD also serve as a liaison to many community oriented programs including Halloween safety patrol with Laidlaw Transit Ltd., Neighbourhood Watch, Operation Lookout, V.I.P. (Values, Influences And Peer pressure) Program, and the Adopt-A-School Program.

The officers also present lectures in local schools, community groups, and businesses on such topics as bicycle safety, school bus safety, drinking and driving, drug abuse, traveling alone, robbery prevention, theft prevention, personal safety, and home security, to mention a few.

The Cornwall Community Police Service also offers "fact sheets" on a variety of topics in order to educate and assist the community with crime prevention. The fact sheets are comprised of crime prevention advice that will assist you in lessening your chances of becoming a victim of a crime.

Source: © 2012 Cornwall Community Police Service

its Community Mobilization Units, offers a one-day workshop designed to strengthen community problem-solving and crime prevention (refer to Box 10.2). There are also observer programs in which community residents accompany a police officer for a shift. These programs provide the public with a glimpse into operational front-line policing. In Calgary, for example, citizens are able to ride in HAWC1 or HAWC2, the Calgary Police Service patrol helicopters.

Another important aspect of educating the public is through the strategic use of the media. Police services require a proactive and strategic communication plan if they are to educate the public and, importantly, provide a balanced response to hostile or anti-police media stories. Key individuals such as front-line supervisors and senior police administrators must practise effective communication skills when addressing the media. Communications must also be a strategic part of the planning process, ensuring that new programs and changes to departmental policies are clearly announced and articulated to the public in a timely manner. Within this framework, many police services will delegate a full-time officer who is trained in media relations, acting as the spokesperson for the police service. By keeping an open dialogue and using a strategic communications approach, the police service can avoid many of the pitfalls associated with distorted, negative, or absent media attention.

POTENTIAL OBSTACLES TO ESTABLISHING PARTNERSHIPS WITH THE COMMUNITY

It is important to reiterate that even where a police service is committed to a community policing model and to establishing partnerships with the community, obstacles may be encountered. Many have been noted earlier, such as citizen apathy and disinterest and domination of the police–community dialogue by special interest groups.

In addition, government policies or initiatives that are beyond the control of the police agency may also serve to challenge partnerships with the community. For example, Bill C-58 and federal legislation requiring a national gun registry had been fraught with controversy and criticism. Over $2 billion had been spent on this program, which has placed police agencies in the centre of a heated debate concerning the registration of firearms by typical law-abiding individuals such as farmers, ranchers, and hunters. Bill C-19, *Ending the Long-Gun Registry Act*, came into effect on April 5, 2012.

Some other barriers to effective police–community partnerships are:

* antagonistic feelings toward the police on the part of some groups in the community,
* antagonistic feelings toward some groups in the community on the part of police officers,
* officers who feel ill equipped in terms of training and resources to establish relationships with the community, and
* officers burdened by heavy workloads who do not have the time to plan or implement community policing strategies (Ministry of the Solicitor General and A.R.A. Consultants 1991b:7).

ROLES AND ACTIVITIES FOR COMMUNITY RESIDENTS

In community policing, community residents can play a variety of roles. The most common way for citizens to contribute to the police effort is as volunteers—for example, by serving as police auxiliaries. The business sector may also provide support for police activities. In addition, community residents may be members of service clubs, businesses, and other agencies that enter into partnerships with the police.

Serving as Volunteers

In Chapter 2, we identified the increasing involvement of volunteers in police services as a major trend in Canadian policing. The framework of community policing calls specifically for the participation of the community in a wide range of activities. **Volunteers** assist the police in developing partnerships with the community, provide an opportunity for the community to take ownership of problems, are a continual source of new energy and fresh ideas, and help reduce the workload on patrol officers.

Volunteers can be classified into two groups: internal volunteers, who work directly with a police service supporting police-sponsored programs, and external volunteers, who assist with various groups in the community that have the support of the police. For example, an internal volunteer would be involved in assisting with a police-run activity such as seating guests at a police graduation or fundraiser, while an external volunteer would staff neighbourhood projects such as Neighbourhood Watch or Block Parents.

Citizen volunteers serve in a wide range of capacities, including staffing victim services units and storefronts, serving on community policing committees, participating in special police–community projects, conducting citizen patrols, serving as extra "eyes and ears" for the police, and serving as police auxiliary constables. For example, volunteers of the Durham Regional Police Service are involved in Block Parents, Crime Stoppers, the Police Toy Drive, and Safety Village, a miniature village that is used to teach safety and awareness to elementary schoolchildren.

Another example of volunteer involvement was the 1988 Winter Olympics, when the Calgary Police Service recruited hundreds of volunteers to assist in the operation of events and activities. After the Olympics, nearly 400 volunteers remained with the police service; they now constitute the Special Projects Team. These volunteers assist with many police activities, including police graduations, mock crime scenes, fundraisers, traffic control, and warrant and subpoena programs. Many of the volunteers are seniors who donate many hours of their time to ensure that programs are successful.

There is considerable variation across Ontario in the numbers and activities of volunteers (for one example, see Box 10.6). The guidelines governing the involvement of volunteers in police work are generally developed and enforced by individual police services, although in certain sensitive cases provincial governments may intercede. Another resource in regard to police agency volunteers is available at Volunteer Canada's website at www.volunteer.ca.

BOX 10.6

VOLUNTEER OPPORTUNITIES IN THE OTTAWA POLICE SERVICE

You can help keep our community safe. Become an important part of a unique organization: become a police volunteer. **An experience you'll never forget!**

The Ottawa Police Service believes in Community Policing—solving community problems with the assistance of members of the community. Community Police Centres rely heavily on trained volunteers. Most volunteers assist at Centres in their neighbourhoods. They answer questions about the police service and crime statistics for their area. They may also run crime prevention programs depending on a community's needs. Individuals are selected on the basis of their ability to perform assignment requirements.

Individuals between the ages of 14 and 18, may be interested in participating in the Venturers program. Established in 1984, the Police Venturers program educates and involves youth in police operations to build a mutual understanding between youth and police and interest youth in a possible law enforcement career.

The Ottawa Police Service also seeks men and women that are at least 18 years of age, have no police records and are available for task training. A thorough screening process includes background and reference checks and an interview. Interested persons can get involved as a prospective volunteer with the Ottawa Police Service by applying online for specific vacant volunteer opportunities. The Ottawa Police Service prefers volunteers that can make a commitment for a minimum of one year and can provide four hours a week of their valuable time.

Source: Courtesy of Ottawa Police Services. http://careers-carrieres.ottawapolice.ca/volunteer/index.cfm?lang=en

The Goals of Volunteer Programs

Most police services operate volunteer programs with goals that include:

- focusing on community participation and the use of civilian volunteers to assist police in meeting the needs of the community;
- enhancing public safety through civilian volunteers working together with police throughout the community in the areas of crime prevention, education, special projects, short-term assignments, and other tasks;
- providing assistance to police in delivering complete and efficient service to the community; and
- developing creative programs with and for the community within the economic and budgetary constraints that police face.

In addition to these general types of goals, a police service may develop specific goals and objectives for particular programs that are staffed by volunteers. These are generally set out in a volunteer management manual developed by the police service. The goals of the Winnipeg Police Service Volunteer Program are set out in Box 10.7.

Recruiting and Screening Volunteers

Police services recruit volunteers in a variety of ways, including contacting schools and community service organizations and placing advertisements in newspapers, on radio and television stations, and on the Internet. Current and former volunteers may also be a good source of names of potential candidates. Strategies are often designed to attract Aboriginal volunteers, as well as volunteers from visible and cultural minorities. Every effort should be made to ensure that volunteers reflect the diversity of the community being policed. In addition, volunteers should be recruited from all segments of the community, including youth and senior citizens.

Candidates for volunteer positions complete an application form that includes personal information; education and training; employment history; qualifications and special skills, such as languages spoken other than English; availability; a list of family members including full name, date of birth, and place of birth; and personal references. Applicants may also be required to indicate why they wish to volunteer with the police service and what they expect from the experience.

Applicants generally undergo a security check and a criminal records check, and sign a number of documents including a disclaimer for liability. A volunteer coordinator or a patrol officer responsible for the volunteer program then interviews the applicant.

Training and Retaining Volunteers

Once appointed, volunteers generally undergo an orientation where they receive background information about the police service. They also receive additional training related to the specific positions and activities they will be involved in, such as victim services. Volunteers who will work in storefronts or community policing offices receive training in the proper procedures for taking citizen complaints and completing occurrence reports. Most police services have developed print materials and brochures that provide volunteers with information on police procedures and resources.

A major challenge for police services is retaining volunteers, particularly in view of the competing demands on the time of community residents. Police services use various strategies to reduce turnover and maintain a stable cadre of volunteers, including:

- providing initial and in-service training;
- providing organizational support and resources;
- setting a clear agenda and specific lines of authority and communication;

BOX 10.7

VOLUNTEER POSITIONS WITH THE WINNIPEG POLICE SERVICE

The Winnipeg Police Service has two separate and distinct volunteer programs, the Victim Service Volunteer Program and the Community Volunteer Program. Each program provides volunteers with an opportunity to contribute to the community.

The benefits of volunteering include:

- Gaining insight into the criminal justice system and various aspects of police procedures;
- Becoming aware of issues that are of a concern to specific communities;
- Improving communication and job skills;
- Demonstrating your commitment to your community and your support of the Police Service;
- Receiving training that may not be offered elsewhere or otherwise accessible; and
- Becoming acquainted with other community resources.

The role of the volunteer is to staff the front counter of a police station with an assigned police officer, directly assisting fellow citizens with general information, referrals and police reports.

Victim Services Volunteers

Volunteers team with other volunteers and Police Service personnel to assist victims of crime. This is conducted through outgoing and incoming telephone contact, and by offering support, suggestions, and social and judicial information.

- Answer phones and provide short-term emotional support to victims of crime and tragedy.
- Provide referrals to appropriate community resources.
- Provide crime prevention information.
- Provide information to victims regarding their occurrences by accessing police database.
- Obtain and provide court information to victims of crime.
- Provide Criminal Justice information regarding Victim Bill of Rights, Victim Impact Statements, and Compensation for Victims of Crime.
- Conduct personal home visits for "qualified victims."
- Complete home security checks.
- Volunteer at various police-related events.

Source: Courtesy of the Winnipeg Police Service. http://winnipeg.ca/policerecruiting/volunteer/index.aspx

- ensuring that volunteers are treated as co-workers, not just as free help;
- organizing workshops and conferences for continuing education;
- giving volunteers responsibility and discretion to carry out tasks;
- providing volunteers with the opportunity to assist in goal setting and program development;
- formally recognizing volunteer contributions through awards banquets, press releases, community newsletters, and interdepartmental memos; and
- informally recognizing volunteer contributions through one-on-one meetings, informal lunches, letters of recognition, and telephone calls.

Volunteer Canada has developed a handbook on screening volunteers. For additional information you can contact Volunteer Canada by telephone at 1-800-670-0401, or you can visit their website at www.volunteer.ca.

Auxiliaries

Auxiliaries, also known as **"reserve" police officers**, have been a feature of Canadian police services for many years. Citizen volunteers are provided with training, a uniform, and "sworn" peace officer status while accompanied by a full-time police officer. The application process to become an auxiliary is competitive, and candidates must undergo a background and security check. Often, people involved in auxiliaries are interested in a career in policing and view the position as an opportunity to learn about the role and activities of the police. Others are motivated by a desire to contribute to the overall well-being of the community.

In addition to on-the-job experience, auxiliaries receive basic police training and are often allowed to participate in more advanced in-service training courses. The OPP provides ongoing conferences and workshops for the auxiliary police officers attached to the service.

The Ontario Provincial Police Provincial Auxiliary Program had 868 members in 2008. Auxiliary members are expected to provide 120 hours per year, which amounted to 220,000 volunteered hours in 2007. The Provincial Auxiliary Program has also partnered with a post-secondary institution (Georgian College), and auxiliary constables accepted through this process must complete 1,000 hours of service over the course of four years to obtain their degree. The use of unpaid staff to perform a variety of police-related duties must be managed carefully to avoid inviting criticism or labour challenges from Associations. In the case of the OPP, both the Ontario Provincial Police Association and the Commissioned Officers Association support the role of auxiliaries.

In the field, the tasks performed by auxiliaries may include accompanying a regular member on patrol and assisting with traffic duties at sporting events, parades, and other community events, and in emergency situations where additional personnel are required. Auxiliaries generally do not have access to firearms while on duty. Rather, the primary role of the auxiliary is to serve as an additional pair of "eyes and ears" for regular police members. (In 1999, the Attorney General in British Columbia determined that auxiliary members of the RCMP in that province could no longer wear sidearms—a practice that had been allowed under earlier RCMP guidelines.)

Many police auxiliaries have years of experience and an intimate knowledge of the community, especially in more rural settings. These auxiliary members are a particularly important source of information and assistance for police in regional and provincial services, and for RCMP officers who have recently been transferred into the community.

An informative American website discussing police volunteers belong to the Volunteers in Police Service and is located at www.policevolunteers.org. It provides useful information about managing volunteer programs.

Corporate Sponsorship

Although the private sector is an enthusiastic supporter of police services, its involvement has been controversial. Supporters of private funding argue that the increasing involvement of the private sector is a consequence of reduced operating budgets, and an important component of the police–community partnership. Critics argue that a very dangerous precedent is being set by providing police services only to special-interest groups with financial resources, and that accepting donated vehicles and other resources compromises the independent role of the police.

For these reasons, corporate funding is often provided through privately operated organizations such as Crime Stoppers. The creation of police foundations is one idea under consideration by police services across the country. Donations would be made to the foundation, which would then disburse money through a board. This would assist in maintaining the arm's-length relationship between the police service, which must remain independent, and private-sector donors.

Community policing committees are one of the best ways to establish and sustain a working partnership with the community. The composition and role of a particular committee depends on a number of factors, including the needs and interests of the community.

Types of Community Committees

There are three general types of committees:

- The **consultative community policing committee**. As the name implies, this type of committee advises the police, who assume primary responsibility for responding to the specific issue at hand. Consultative committees focus on gathering information, which they then pass along to the police. They require minimal structure, and meetings can be scheduled on a regular basis or as needed.
- The **multi-functional community policing committee**. The activities of this type of committee extend beyond providing advice and recommendations to the police. Multi-functional committees partner with the police to identify areas of concern and to develop problem-solving responses. Committee members represent a broad cross-section of the community. These committees usually have an executive consisting of a chair, vice-chair, secretary, and treasurer. As well, there may be one or more standing subcommittees responsible for finances, media relations, production of a newsletter, and other areas as required. These committees meet regularly, and as their scope and activities expand, they may consider incorporation as a non-profit or charitable organization. This status will assist the committee in fundraising and raise its profile in the community, and also limit liability for insurance purposes.
- The **interagency community policing committee**. These committees are composed of the police and other agencies and organizations in the community and have a mandate that includes a broad range of community and social issues. These committees formulate plans of action that maximize the expertise and efforts of the participating agencies and organizations. Interagency committees are the most complex type of police–community committee and require a formal operating structure, including an executive, standing committees, and subcommittees. They are often incorporated as non-profit or charitable organizations to assist in fundraising and increase their profile in the community, and for liability insurance purposes (OPP 1997a:3; 1997b: 4-2–4-3).

Other types of committees can be established to address community issues and concerns, such as short-term problem-solving groups that address a specific issue in the community (e.g., graffiti or traffic). Within the framework of community policing, the possibilities for police–community partnerships are limited only by the imagination of the police officers and community residents.

Committee Membership and Member Responsibilities

It is a challenge for patrol officers to create a committee composed of residents and officers who are willing to spend the time and energy to find solutions to community problems. It requires identifying individuals in the community who have a special expertise or skill that can be used by the committee, including someone from the legal profession, someone with access to and knowledge of computer technology, someone with a background in training or education, someone with analytical or evaluation skills, and someone who is familiar with community clubs, businesses, and organizations (OPP 1997b:4–5).

Once members for the community policing committee have been selected, the responsibilities associated with committee membership must be set out. These include, but are certainly not limited to:

- maintaining the confidentiality of sensitive materials,
- attending meetings regularly and being on time,
- understanding committee procedures,
- being willing to volunteer for committee projects,
- controlling the "yap factor" (not engaging in spreading rumours), and
- not engaging in promoting hidden agendas (OPP 1997b:4–7).

Operating Effective Committees

Community policing committees can be an integral component of the police–community partnership only if they operate effectively. The requirements for effective community policing committees are described below.

Running Effective Meetings

For an example of how to run an effective meeting, see Case Study 1.

Defining the Role of Community Policing Committees

Community interest and involvement can be sustained only if the role of the community policing committee is clearly established and community members can be substantively involved in addressing problems and concerns that have been identified as priorities. In the absence of such an arrangement, patrol officers will likely have difficulty recruiting residents to sit on committees and, over time, community involvement will dissipate.

Generating Officer Support and Participation

Community residents must feel that members of the police service are available through the community consultative committees. Every effort should be made to ensure that there is good police presence at the committee meetings and that officers do not leave meetings abruptly to answer outside calls for service, which can be irritating to community attendees. As well, it is important that there be good community representation at the meetings.

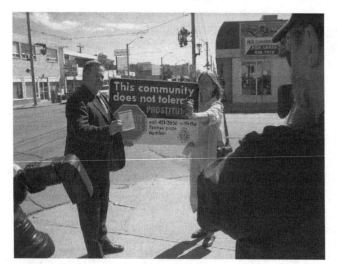

The Edmonton Police Service joined with community partners including the Prostitution Action and Awareness Foundation of Edmonton (PAAFE) and the City of Edmonton in an attempt to ward off prostitution in Edmonton's known problem areas. This highlights community involvement in addressing chronic neighbourhood problems.

Source: Edmonton Police Service

CHAPTER SUMMARY

This chapter has focused on the community portion of community policing, an area that has historically received very little attention. A number of key issues were identified that provided the backdrop for the materials presented in this chapter, including defining who and what is the community, the level and distribution of community involvement in policing, and the potential and limitations of community involvement. Ontario's Mobilization and Engagement Model of Community Policing, developed in 2010, attempts to address many of these issues, particularly in framing the roles for both the police and community. The chapter also discussed the particular difficulties that have been encountered in soliciting the participation of people from Aboriginal communities and from visible and cultural minorities.

There are a number of specific steps that patrol officers must follow to build working relationships with the community, from identifying potential community partners to organizing meetings to developing strategies to sustain community involvement. Community police officers have a number of techniques at their disposal that can be used to determine community priorities and concerns, including community profiles, surveys, focus groups, public forums, and integrated service teams. Officers must also address the potential obstacles to establishing effective partnerships.

Citizens can play a variety of roles in community policing, including serving on community policing committees, volunteering for a wide range of activities, and serving as auxiliary police officers. Police services have developed procedures for screening, recruiting, training, and retaining volunteers.

The discussion concluded with an examination of community policing committees. The various types of committees were identified, the issues surrounding committee membership and member responsibilities were examined, and the strategies for operating effective committees were noted.

CHAPTER REVIEW

Key Terms

- auxiliaries or "reserve" police officers, p. 326
- community, p. 304
- community profile, p. 318
- community surveys, p. 319
- consultative community policing committee, p. 327
- focus groups, p. 319
- integrated service teams, p. 321
- interagency community policing committee, p. 327
- multi-functional community policing committee, p. 327
- Ontario's Mobilization and Engagement Model of Community Policing, p. 309
- P3s (public–private partnerships), p. 308
- public forums, p. 320
- volunteers, p. 323

Key Points

- There are a number of critical issues relating to the community portion of community policing.
- Ontario's Mobilization and Engagement Model of Community Policing serves as an important tool for both the police and community to assess the degree of police support necessary create safe communities.
- Specific strategies are required to engage members of Aboriginal and of visible and cultural minority communities in partnerships with the police.
- Patrol officers must take several key steps to develop partnerships with the community.
- Community profiles, community surveys, focus groups, public forums, and interagency collaboration are tools that can be used to determine community priorities and address community concerns.
- Integrated service teams and collaboration with other agencies and organizations are effective approaches for developing partnerships.
- There are a number of potential obstacles to establishing effective police–community partnerships.

- The most common way that citizens become involved in partnerships with the police is by volunteering.
- Police services have developed procedures for recruiting, screening, training, and retaining community volunteers.
- There are several types of community committees that can be created to identify and address community concerns and problems.

Self-Evaluation

QUESTIONS

1. What are the key issues surrounding the **community** portion of the community policing equation?
2. Discuss the concept behind **community empowerment**.
3. What is a **community profile**, how are community profiles developed, and what role do they play in community policing?
4. Describe the use of **community surveys** in the development of police–community partnerships.
5. What are **focus groups**, and what role do they play in identifying the priorities and concerns of a community?
6. What are the benefits and limitations of **public forums** as a way to gather information from the community?
7. Describe Ontario's Mobilization and Engagement Model of Community Policing and explain how it serves as a diagnostic tool.
8. Describe the role of **integrated service teams** within the framework of community policing.
9. Describe the role of **volunteers** in Ontario policing, noting the key issues surrounding recruitment, screening, training, and retention.
10. Describe the role of **auxiliaries** in Canadian police services.
11. Compare the three types of community policing committees: **consultative community policing committees**, **multi-functional community policing committees**, and **interagency community policing committees**.

KEY IDEAS

1. Which of the following statements describes Ontario's *Police Services Act* and the Adequacy Standards?
   a. They make no mention of the role of the community in policing.
   b. They specifically limit the policing activities that citizens can become involved in.
   c. They direct police services to involve the community in the design and delivery of policing services.
   d. They specify how police services are to involve members of Aboriginal and cultural and visible minority communities.

2. Which of the following is true of community involvement in community policing?
   a. The role of the community is typically well defined.
   b. Representation from all segments of the community may not exist.
   c. Residents who are most likely to be "policed" are often the same individuals who are likely to become involved in police–community relationships.
   d. The vast majority of individuals within a community desire to be involved with their police agency and community policing initiatives.

3. Which of the following is indicated by public opinion surveys and field research studies?
   a. Most adults and youth are skeptical of their police agency.
   b. Community residents would like to have more opportunities to volunteer their services with a police agency.

    c. The public is largely unaware of local community police stations.

    d. There are resources in communities that can be mobilized to address problems of crime and social disorder.

4. What has been revealed by research on Aboriginal and visible- and cultural-minority communities?

    a. These communities typically embrace police–community partnerships.

    b. Many people in these communities share the view that the police do not treat all groups of citizens equally.

    c. Establishing police–community partnerships with these communities is relatively simple and straightforward.

    d. These communities may require initial federal funding as a result of the requirement for translation services.

5. One information-gathering technique brings together individuals in the community who share a common attribute, such as age or gender, in order to provide an opportunity for them to relate their perceptions, experiences, and observations. What is this technique called?

    a. community profile

    b. focus group

    c. community survey

    d. public forum

6. Which of the following is a potential barrier to the development of effective police–community partnerships?

    a. citizen apathy and disinterest

    b. a lack of police resources

    c. legislation limiting the types of police–community relationships that can be developed

    d. opposition by police unions

7. Integrated service teams comprise representatives from which of the following?

    a. minority groups within the community

    b. various crime prevention programs existing in the area

    c. various police agencies existing in a geographic area

    d. the police, health services/health agencies, and community organizations

8. Which of the following statements is true about volunteers in police services?

    a. they are typically limited by departmental policy to a small number of activities

    b. they are engaged in a wide variety of activities

    c. they need not have a background or security check

    d. they must have a college or university degree

9. Which of the following is NOT one of the three general types of community policing committees?

    a. the consultative community policing committee

    b. the multi-functional community policing committee

    c. the legislated community policing committee

    d. the interagency community policing committee

10. Which statement is true about the membership of community policing committees?

    a. Persons from the legal profession should be excluded.

    b. Membership should be given only to those persons with previous volunteer experience.

    c. Membership on the committees should be limited to a one-year term.

    d. Membership selections should require a background check.

The Community and Community Policing: Situations and Strategies

The Community and Community Policing Implementation Checklist

Among the key questions that should be asked to determine whether the community is involved as a partner with the police are the following:

- Has the police service identified the neighbourhoods and groups that make up the community it serves?
- Does the police service have an active program for recruiting, screening, training, and supervising volunteers?
- Are community residents generally aware of the activities of the police and of opportunities available to them to participate in crime prevention and response initiatives?
- Are there training programs for community residents in such areas as community building, problem solving, crime prevention and response strategies, and building partnerships between the community and the police?
- Are materials on how to become a member of a community consultative committee widely available in the community?
- Are specific groups within the community, including youth, people who are visible minorities, Aboriginal people, and the elderly, aware of the programs sponsored by the police in partnership with the community?
- Are there mechanisms in place to allow the residents to participate in identifying problems and concerns?
- Are all sectors of the community represented on community policing committees?
- Is the community involved in addressing substantive areas of concern, including issues related to the activities of the police such as the use of force or dealing with people who are mentally disabled?
- Are there identifiable mechanisms for ongoing community input and feedback into police policies and programs?

Case Studies

Case Study 1. How to Run a Community Meeting

Knowing how to run a community policing committee meeting is essential to developing and sustaining partnerships with the community. It is also important for sustaining the interest, motivation, and participation of community volunteers. Effective meetings are those that:

- take place in an appropriate meeting space where privacy and confidentiality of discussions are assured;
- are conducted without interruptions from telephones, cell phones, and pagers;
- begin on time;
- have a clear (as opposed to a hidden) agenda;
- provide an equal opportunity for all committee members to participate;
- deal with substantive issues;
- make the best use of committee members' time by ensuring that the meeting is required and that the topics are substantive;
- do not meet just for the sake of meeting;
- have an established procedure for conducting discussions and making decisions; and
- end on time.

The OPP Community Policing Development Centre has identified the key factors that contribute to effective community meetings. These are discussed below.

The Chairperson

- *Prepare*: develop the agenda; confirm meeting particulars, including location, time, guest speakers, and refreshments; distribute the agenda.
- *Know the committee members*: be familiar with their skills, time availability, and community contacts.
- *Motivate*: offer encouragement as well as constructive criticism.
- *Delegate authority*: ensure that committee members understand their roles and responsibilities.
- *Preside at meetings*: establish clear guidelines for running the meeting; follow the set agenda; involve all members in discussions and decision making; complete the agenda within the declared time frame.
- *Evaluate progress*: solicit feedback from committee members on the quality and effectiveness of meetings; be open to constructive suggestions for how meetings might be improved.

The Agenda

The agenda is the set of items to be covered during the meeting. There should not be too many items to cover during a single session, and the items should not be too different from one another. Meetings are most productive when committee members can focus their attention and discuss one general topic for most of the meeting time. All committee members should have the opportunity to contribute items to the agenda, and the chairperson must not be seen as pursuing a personal agenda by including some items but excluding others.

A typical agenda follows this outline:

- Call the meeting to order.
- Seek approval of the agenda.
- Read the minutes of the last meeting.
- Seek approval of the minutes of the last meeting.
- Present officers' reports (president, treasurer, etc.).
- Present standing committees' reports.
- Present special committees' reports.
- Discuss unfinished or postponed business.
- Discuss any new business.
- Set date for the next meeting, including time and location.
- Adjourn.

Meeting Dynamics

The OPP offers the following advice for improving the effectiveness of meetings:

- Schedule meetings early in the morning, when committee members are likely to be more alert.
- The attention span of committee members usually drops after 15 to 20 minutes; a good strategy is to place an item of general interest at this stage to revive attention.
- Organize the agenda in descending order of importance to ensure that important items are dealt with first.
- Place time limits on the discussion period and decision making for agenda items.
- Guest speakers and special presentations are a good way to maintain interest.
- Schedule breaks in the agenda.

- Ensure that there is continuity from discussions and decisions taken in previous committee meetings.

Group Decision Making

Ideally, the interests, experience, and skills of members enhance the effectiveness of committee meetings. For these talents to be put to good use, however, the meeting environment should encourage the expression of individual views and opinions while at the same time facilitating consensus. Effective group decision making is enhanced when:

- the issues are clearly identified;
- alternative courses of action are discussed;
- the pros and cons of alternative courses of action are discussed;
- a solution is chosen by consensus, show of hands, or secret ballot;
- responsibilities for implementing the solution are assigned to committee members;
- the outcome of the solution is evaluated within a set period; and
- the outcome of the solution is shared.

Committee members are more likely to remain motivated to participate in meetings if the committee makes decisions that result in positive outcomes and if individual members are given the responsibility for implementing the solutions that are formulated.

Physical Set-Up

A comfortable group will likely be a productive group.

—*OPP Community Policing (1997)*

The physical setting in which the meeting takes place can have a significant impact on effectiveness. A meeting site should have the following characteristics:

- a room that seats all members comfortably,
- comfortable seating that allows everyone to see and hear one another,
- adequate lighting,
- proper temperature and ventilation,
- writing materials and space,
- access to washrooms,
- coatrooms,
- audio-visual equipment if necessary,
- refreshments,
- convenient parking or accessibility, and
- few outside distractions.

Patrol officers must make an effort to develop the skills required to create, manage, and sustain community policing committees to ensure the effectiveness of this core component of the police–community partnership.

Case Study 2. "Cop Camp"–A Summer Program for Youth

One of the more innovative community policing programs is Cop Camp, a week-long educational program that provides youth and their parents with the opportunity to learn about policing and police officers. These camps are often offered in conjunction with police school liaison programs, with youth participants recruited from the student body. In British Columbia, versions of Cop Camp have been operated in the greater Vancouver area for several years by the RCMP, and on lower Vancouver Island by police agencies such as the Saanich Police Department. In recent times, Cop Camp has evolved as a strategic means of long-range recruiting, inspiring young people to pursue a career in policing and to remain loyal to the sponsoring police service.

In most instances, the camp is restricted to a specific number of individuals. Youths who are selected for the camp are screened to ensure they will be able to complete the program. The parents or guardians of the youth must also sign a waiver allowing them to participate in the program.

The camp is generally restricted to one or two groups of 24 to 48 youths, depending upon the resources available. Camps may be offered for four different age groups: junior (ages 6, 7, and 8), intermediate (ages 9, 10, and 11), teens (ages 12, 13, and 14), and young adults (ages 15, 16, and 17). Due to the complexities involved in running such a program, as well as the scarce resources that often exist, an agency may only offer teen or young adult camps.

One of the major obstacles to operating a police camp is committing financial resources and personnel to a program that can only be operated during the summer months, when school is not in session. This is typically a time when police services and community groups experience staff shortages due to scheduled holiday leaves. One solution is for summer students or Neighbourhood Watch volunteers to coordinate the camp. The Hamilton-Wentworth Regional Police have operated such a camp since 1994 in collaboration with parents and community organizations.

A Day in the Life of a Cop

The camp is run by police officers who serve as instructors on police-related topics. They describe a typical day in the life of a police officer. Both classroom learning and hands-on experience are involved. Among the topics covered at a typical camp are:

- life-saving skills, such as first aid training and swimming;
- forensic sciences and crime investigation, including methods of photographing a crime scene, detecting evidence by lifting fingerprints, and engaging a crime artist;
- a tour of the communication centre and 911-dispatch centre;
- a traffic squad presentation on the use of a roadside-screening device, how a breathalyzer works, and how serious motor vehicle accidents are investigated, as well as the all-time favourite—the use of radar and road screening devices;
- general duty patrol, including attending calls for service and patrolling the community;
- bike squad, including the methods employed by bike officers and the advantages of being out of a patrol car;
- emergency response team, including the equipment used and an overview of the strategies employed when dealing with critical incidents;
- a use-of-force presentation on the compliance tools and physical force options used by police officers;
- drug squad, including marijuana-growing operations;
- dog squad;
- victim services; and
- community police stations.

Cop camps may also include field trips to various government agencies and facilities. For example, an organized tour may include a brief visit to the local police training academy, a crime lab, or the local courthouse where evidence is being given in a court case. It may also include visiting the emergency ward of the local hospital. In addition to providing youth with the opportunity to become familiar with organizations and resources in the community, cop camp serves as an outreach program for youth in the community, providing valuable life skills and positive role modelling.

Case Study 3. How Not to Do It: Community Policing Horror Stories

The following stories illustrate community policing gone wrong (Woods 2000).

Horror Story 1. Collaboration Requires Community Input

New community policing officers (CPOs) are often a little anxious and intimidated before their first community meeting. One CPO, George, had a full agenda and was eager to get started. His community policing training had taught him about the difficulty in developing effective community resource groups. Often, initial meetings are encumbered by miscellaneous complaints and bickering until individuals learn to function as a group. George hoped to avoid unnecessary complications by beginning his meeting by declaring, "I have a lot to cover, so I won't listen to any complaints. We are going to stick to the issues. If I hear any complaints, I'm leaving."

- **Community's Perception:** The police are not interested in community input.
- **Discussion:** It will come as no surprise that George's project was unsuccessful. He took control of the meeting and determined the agenda. The participants were not given the opportunity to be equal or active partners.
- **Moral of the Story:** Although it may be difficult for officers to relinquish control, the committee members must feel that their input is valued. This will ensure the success of the collaborative effort.

Horror Story 2. Collaboration Requires Community Involvement

Shortly after proclaiming a community policing philosophy, the Thomasville Police Department declared it had a problem with unregistered bicycles. Two officers were assigned to confiscate any unlicensed bikes. To carry out the assignment, the officers needed to work with dirty, oily bikes, so they were given permission to work in civilian clothes. The department did not have a marked vehicle large enough to hold the bicycles, so an unmarked van was used to transport the seized bikes. When the officers found an unlicensed bike, it was confiscated and placed in the van.

Several children had their bicycles confiscated and were told to walk home. The police department was flooded with calls from angry parents complaining of thugs who were stealing their children's bicycles.

- **Community's Perception:** Community policing is merely rhetoric. The police department does not actually consult the public before they respond.
- **Discussion:** Aside from the obvious flaws in this problem-solving strategy, this example points out the importance of community participation in problem identification. Clearly, the police department would have benefited from community input before carrying out this initiative. Community involvement might have refocused police concerns, foreseen the shortcomings of this particular strategy, and helped to formulate a more appropriate response to the problem.
- **Moral of the Story:** Involve the community in the identification of and response to problems of crime and social disorder in the community.

Horror Story 3. Collaboration Requires Developing Appropriate Instruments for Acquiring Community Input

In an effort to canvass public opinion, the Forest Township Police Department assigned officers to distribute and collect questionnaires. About 1,500 surveys (4 percent of the population) were completed and returned to the department. The surveys were then placed in a file cabinet and forgotten, and no changes were made to police policies or activities.

- **Community's Perception:** Although community policing involves public relations, there is no substantive change in police behaviour.
- **Discussion:** Every individual wants to think that his or her opinion is important. The goodwill achieved by soliciting public opinion dissipates when citizens realize that their input does not matter. In this example, the public's concerns were dismissed without consideration. The survey process wasted the time and efforts of citizens and officers alike.
- **Moral of the Story:** A department contemplating a public survey should ask itself the following questions:
    - What are we trying to learn?
    - Do we have the expertise to develop, conduct, and analyze a useful survey? If not, who does?
    - Is a survey the best means of obtaining the information we seek?
    - Are we prepared to act on the results?

EXERCISES: KNOWLEDGE INTO PRACTICE

Exercise 1. The Limits of Community Involvement: The Issue of Corporate Sponsorship

Newspaper Editorial

"Buddy, can you spare a sponsorship?" It hasn't quite come to that. But it's a shock that community police stations in some Vancouver suburbs are all but panhandling local businesses for vehicles, bicycles, and cell phones that they can't afford in exchange for discreet advertising. It's a disturbing sign of the times.

What happens if a patrol cruiser festooned with Acme Pewter Fork's logo pulls over a speeding car that happens to be driven by Acme's president? Where will it end? Could we trust the RCMP (Royal Canadian Manufacturers' Police) to track down international commercial frauds, in co-operation with the FBI (Federal Bureau of Investments)?

Source: *Vancouver Sun*, 1998. Editorial. March 28, A22.

List what you consider to be the positive features of corporate sponsorship of police services.

What limits, if any, would you place on corporate sponsorship of police services?

Do you think the police should accept donations of patrol vehicles from a private business?

           Yes   No

Why?

_____

_____

_____

_____

_____

From a private citizen?

           Yes   No

Why?

_____

_____

_____

_____

_____

Exercise 2. Community Surveys

Many police services, including the Ontario Provincial Police, the Calgary Police Service, the RCMP, and the Peel Regional Police, use community surveys to determine community levels of satisfaction with police services (see Chapter 6). Design a survey to be administered to a sample of community residents in order to assess police performance. Consider the following.

List the major categories of information that should be included on the survey.

1. _____

2. _____

3. _____

4. _____

5. _____

6. _____

7. _____

8. _____

9. _____

10. _____

List ten questions that you would include on the survey, and provide a rationale for why each question was included.

	Question	Rationale
1.		
2.		
3.		
4.		
5.		
6.		
7.		
8.		
9.		
10.		

How would the specific questions you include on the survey be affected by the following:

A. The socio-demographic makeup of the community, such as age groups, economic levels, ethnicity, etc.?

_____

_____

_____

_____

_____

B. The location of the community; that is, is it an urban, suburban, regional, city, rural, or remote community?

_____

_____

_____

_____

_____

Note the strengths and limitations of the various ways of administering the survey:

A. By telephone—calling households in the community

_____

_____

_____

_____

B. In person—visiting households and having an occupant complete the survey

_____

_____

_____

_____

_____

C. Through various groups in the community—visiting schools, seniors' retirement homes, service clubs such as the Lions Club, etc.

_____

_____

_____

_____

_____

Final Exercise

The following exercise challenges you to apply the main ideas and concepts you have been studying throughout all nine chapters of this book. Good luck.

Creating the Ideal City Police Service

As an expert in community policing, you have been hired by a municipality to create a municipal police service in Ideal City. Residents of Ideal City are unhappy with their current police service. A number of high-profile cases (a murder and a large drug conspiracy) have recently been thrown out of court because of serious *Charter* breaches that the police could have easily avoided. In addition, many residents feel they have no voice in terms of deciding the police service's priorities.

Accessing the police has proven problematic. The police take considerable time to arrive at complaints and then seem disinterested while at the scene. Officers are commonly quoted as saying there is little they can do. Recent press releases advise that minor thefts, marijuana-growing operations, stolen cars, and all cheque frauds must be reported in person at police stations, yet police stations are not always open. Case numbers will be assigned, but no investigation will occur. In the last community survey, many citizens stated they wanted improved access to the police service, including the online ability to report crime.

Residents of Ideal City perceive that the quality of life has dropped in their community. There is more graffiti on buildings, and scary-looking people loiter in public areas and ride public transit. Transit stations have developed a reputation for being unsafe, with considerable drug-dealing taking place. Seniors, many of whom depend on public transit, are too afraid to ride.

Ideal City has a population of 350,000 people and a current policing budget of $35 million. The average cost per police officer in the municipality is $100,000, including salary and benefits. People under 19 make up 25 percent of the population, and 18 percent are over 60. The city is experiencing significant growth of approximately 23,000 people per year, due primarily to immigration, although a significant number of people are moving into the city from adjoining municipalities.

Crime rates have generally been decreasing although in the last few years there seems to be greater coverage of violent crime in the media and a number of high profile crimes (shootings, car-jackings) are linked to gang 'turf wars'. A number of criminal organizations are suspected of having infiltrated the municipal infrastructure. Some of these groups are highly visible, such as outlaw motorcycle gangs. Other groups are believed to be at work, including the Mafia and Eastern European criminals. White-collar crime is seldom reported, but business analysts agree that economic losses due to white-collar offenders outstrip costs related to property crimes and crimes of violence.

Ideal City is experiencing significant demands on its social services. Many people have difficulty accessing available social services and are seeking alternative ways of coping with problems. The roads have become congested due to increasing urban density, and the local media are reporting numerous examples of road rage. In addition, there has been a considerable rise in the number of motor vehicle accidents.

The Task: Your company, Public Safety Consulting, has been hired to propose improved policing services for Ideal City. What steps would you recommend to the local government to improve policing in Ideal City? What should the Ideal City police service look like in terms of (a) organizational structure, (b) mission and value statements, (c) recruitment and training, (d) administrative features, (e) operational strategies, and (f) performance assessment?

Parting Thoughts: Creating the Community Policing Police Service

The materials presented in this text have highlighted the key requirements for creating a police service based on the principles and practices of community policing, which are listed below. These criteria can be used to evaluate police services and to make recommendations for how the service can adopt and implement community policing.

1. Continued reliance on random, preventative patrol should be minimized. Random, preventive patrol should be used only when police visibility is an issue.
2. Citizens will accept a range of response times for different types of calls.
3. Differential police response strategies should be implemented to improve the effective management of the dispatch function.
4. Effective management of the patrol function depends on intelligent management of the dispatch function.
5. Effective management of criminal investigations depends indirectly on intelligent management of the dispatch function and relates directly to management of the patrol function.
6. Case management systems must be developed and implemented to fit the needs of various investigative functions.
7. Work demand and resource allocation studies are necessary to ensure equitable deployment of personnel.
8. Crime and operational analysis procedures are vital in managing patrol and investigative functions.
9. The use of directed and self-directed patrol activities for officers should increase when and where appropriate.
10. Officers assigned to the patrol function must be actively involved in criminal investigations (e.g., conducting follow-up investigations, recommending early case closures).
11. Patrol officers need enhanced status and enriched job responsibilities.
12. Attention must be devoted to reassessing the purpose and function of existing beat configurations.
13. The police must take steps to identify citizen service expectations and work with citizens in addressing and resolving neighbourhood crime and disorder problems.
14. To facilitate the development of stronger ties with the community, policies requiring frequent rotation of officers across shifts must be seriously considered.

15. Regular public forums should take place so the police and the public (preferably patrol officers and neighbourhood residents) frequently exchange information.
16. Performance measurement systems should serve as a management tool that guides personnel development and facilitates organizational change.
17. More meaningful performance evaluation criteria must be developed to reflect the changes in officers' roles and responsibilities.
18. Training curricula must be designed so that they are more relevant and supportive of patrol and investigative operations.
19. Disciplinary processes must become part of a system that incorporates education, training, and counselling as strategies designed to assist officers experiencing behavioural problems.
20. Management styles must adapt to varying situations and personalities.
21. Managers must begin directing their attention toward the qualitative aspects of service delivery processes and outcomes.
22. Police agencies must cultivate leaders who are comfortable and effective working in an environment characterized by constant demands for change (Oettmeier and Wycoff 1997).

REFERENCES

Edmonton Police Service. 1996. *Community Policing in Edmonton, 1996*. Edmonton: Community and Organizational Support Section, Edmonton Police Service.

EFCL (Edmonton Federation of Community Leagues). 2012. Online (http://www.efcl .org/Home/tabid/348/Default.aspx).

EPS (Empowered Student Partnerships). 2012. Online (http://www.esponline.ca).

Gittens, M. and D. Cole. 1995. *Report of the Commission on Systemic Racism in the Ontario Criminal Justice System. A Community Summary*. Toronto: Queen's Printer for Ontario.

Grinc, R.M. 1994. "'Angels in Marble': Problems in Stimulating Community Involvement in Community Policing." *Crime and Delinquency* 40(3):437–68.

Gusfield, J. 1975. *The Community: A Critical Response*. New York: HarperCollins.

Hornick, J.P., B.A. Borrows, I. Tjowvold, and D.M. Phillips. 1990. *An Evaluation of the Neighbourhood Foot Patrol Program of the Edmonton Police Service*. Ottawa: Solicitor General of Canada.

John Howard Society of Alberta. 1995. *Crime Prevention through Social Development: A Literature Review*. Calgary: Wild Rose Foundation.

Liou, K.T. and E.G. Savage. 1996. "Citizen Perceptions of Community Policing Impact." *Public Administration Quarterly* 20(2):163–79.

Ministry of Aboriginal Affairs. 2005. "Ontario's New Approach to Aboriginal Affairs." Online (http://www.aboriginalaffairs.gov.on.ca/english/policy/newapproach/ newapproach03.asp#justice).

Ministry of Aboriginal Affairs. 2007. "Ontario's Support for First Nations Policing." Online (http://www.aboriginalaffairs.gov.on.ca/english/news/2007/may31bg3_07.asp).

Ministry of the Solicitor General and A.R.A. Consultants. 1991a. "Developing a Community Profile: A Manual for the Development and Implementation of Community Profiling for Police Planners and Managers." In *Ontario Provincial Police: Shaping Our Future*. Toronto: Ministry of the Solicitor General, Province of Ontario.

Ministry of the Solicitor General and A.R.A. Consultants. 1991b. "Working with the Community. A Manual for Building Police-Community Partnerships." In *Ontario Provincial Police: Shaping Our Future*. Toronto: Ministry of the Solicitor General, Province of Ontario.

Oettmeier, T. and M.A. Wycoff. 1997. *Personal Performance Evaluations in the Community Policing Context*. Washington, DC: Community Policing Consortium.

Ontario Provincial Police. 1997a. "Community Partnerships." *CPDC News* 2 (August): p. 5.

Ontario Provincial Police. 1997b. *Community Policing "How Do We Do It" Manual*. Oakville: Community Policing Development Centre.

Ontario Provincial Police. 2000. *Annual Report, 1999*. Oakville, ON.

Ottawa Police Service. 2012. Online (http://careers-carrieres.ottawapolice.ca/volunteer/index.cfm?lang=en).

Polowek, K. 1995. *Community Policing: Is It Working and How Do We Know? An Introductory Guide for Police Managers and Police Boards*. Victoria: Ministry of Attorney General.

Prairie Research Associates Inc. 1996. *Building a Safer Canada: A Community-Based Crime Prevention Manual*. Ottawa: Department of Justice.

Skogan, W.G. 1995. *Community Participation and Community Policing*. Chicago: Center for Urban Affairs and Policy Research, University of Chicago.

Toronto Police Service. 1999. *Partners in Community Safety*. Toronto: Toronto Police Service.

Toronto Police Service. 2008. Community Mobilization. Online (http://www.torontopolice.on.ca/communitymobilization).

Vancouver Sun. 1998. Editorial. March 28, A22.

Woods, D.J. 2000. *Community Policing Pages*. Online (http://www.concentric.net/~dwoods).

Index